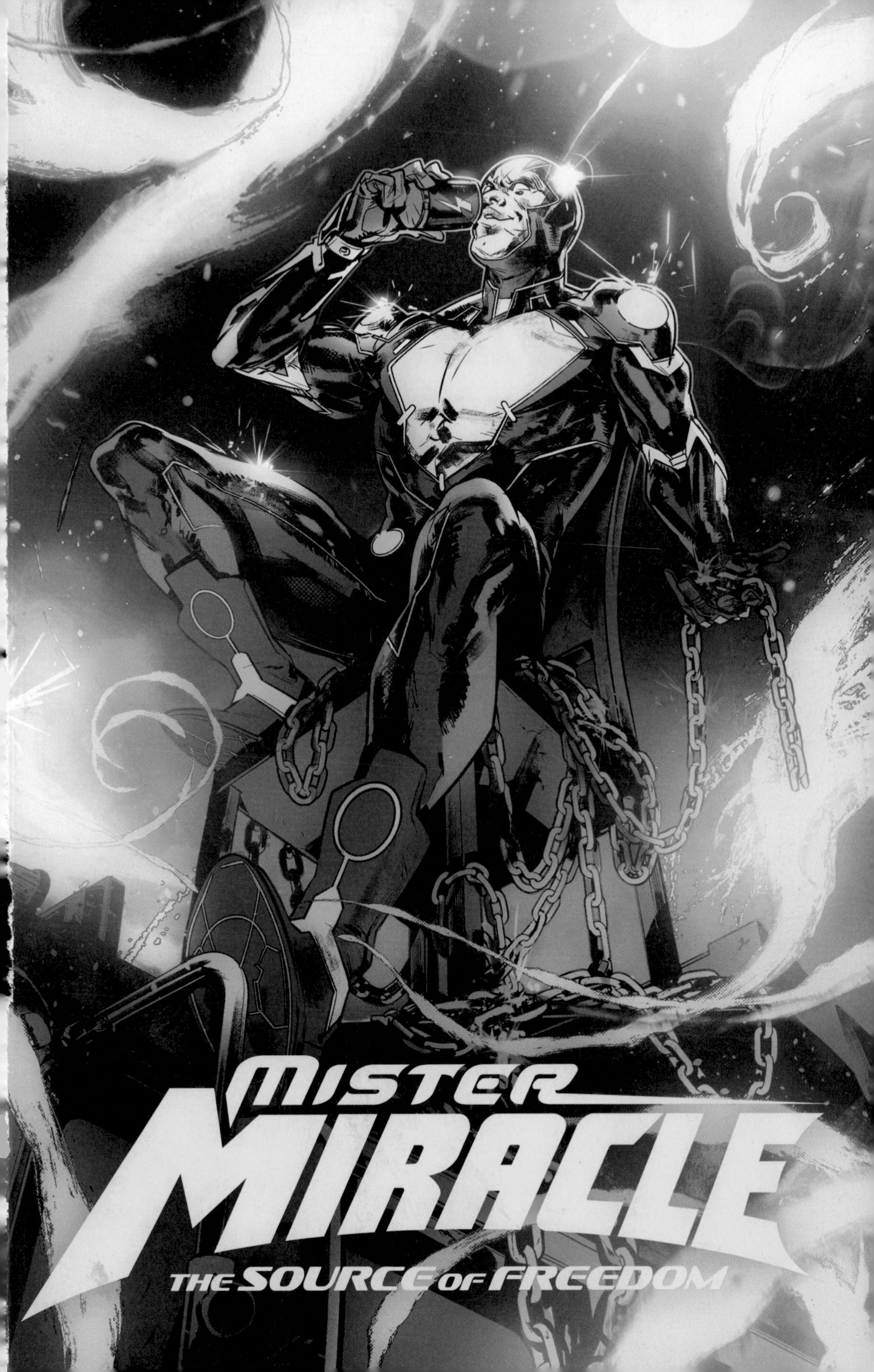
MISTER
MIRACLE
THE SOURCE OF FREEDOM

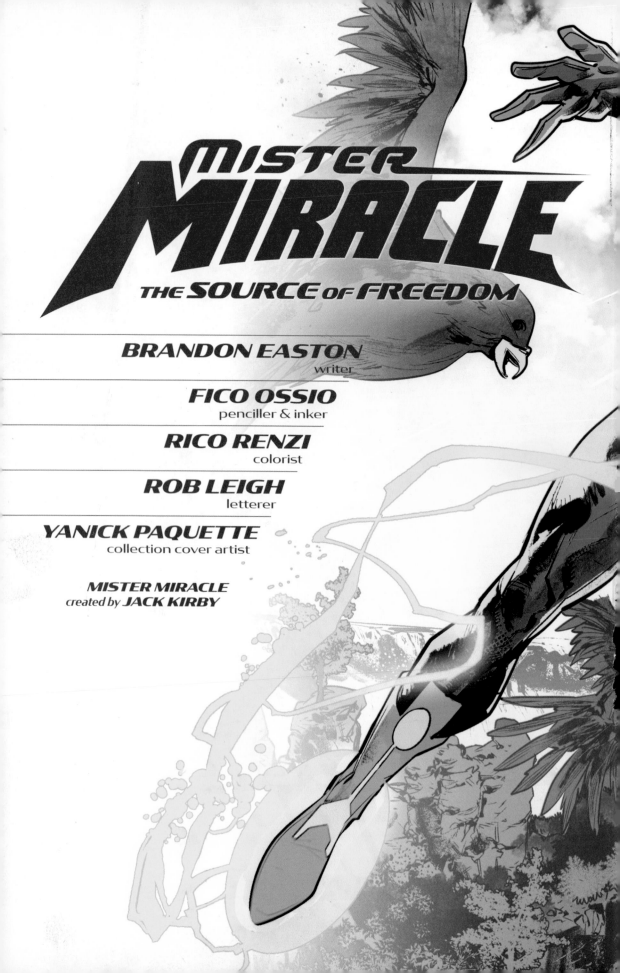

MISTER MIRACLE

THE SOURCE of FREEDOM

BRANDON EASTON
writer

FICO OSSIO
penciller & inker

RICO RENZI
colorist

ROB LEIGH
letterer

YANICK PAQUETTE
collection cover artist

MISTER MIRACLE
created by **JACK KIRBY**

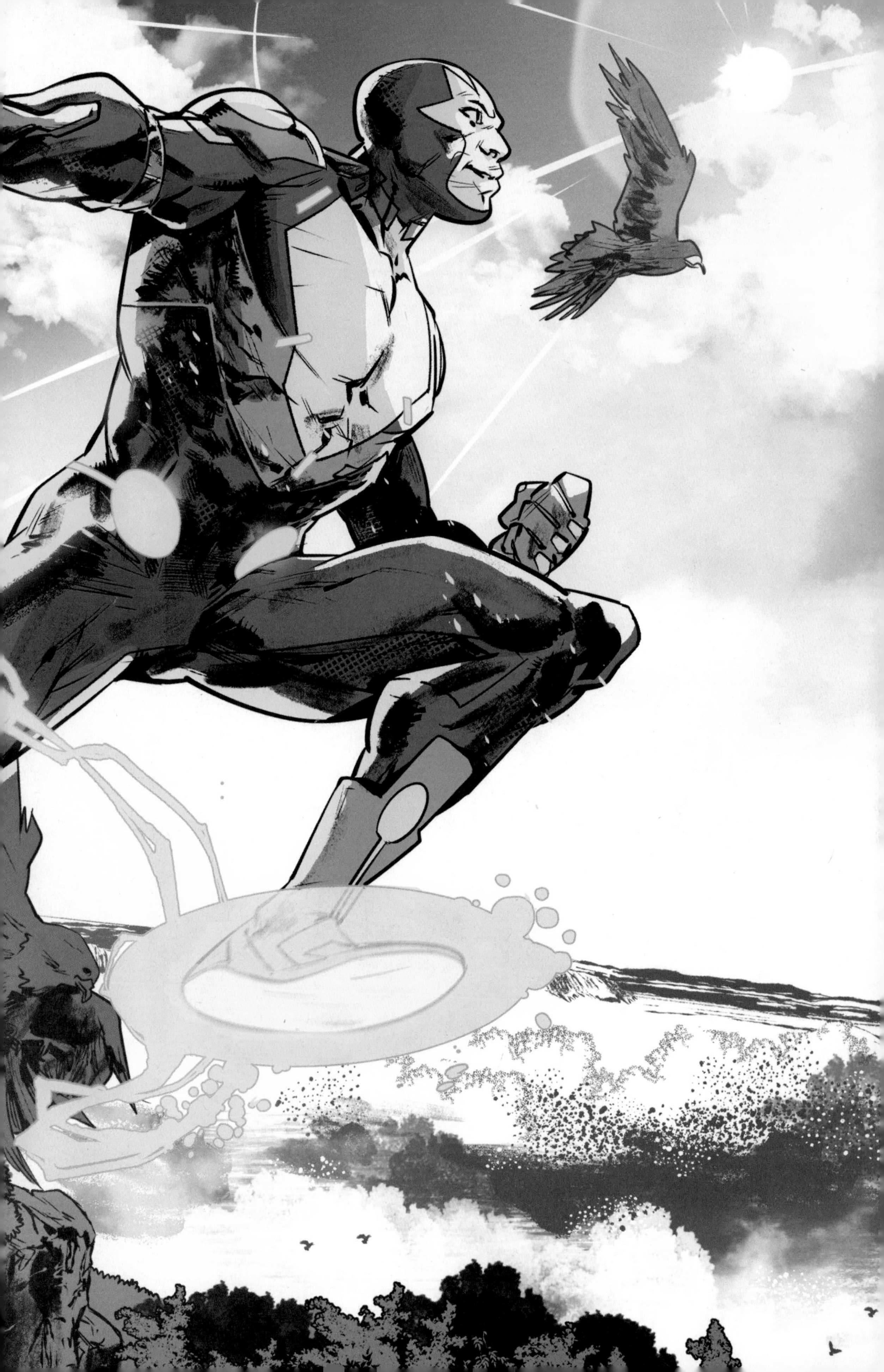

MICHAEL McCALISTER
Editor – Original Series & Collected Edition

DIEGO LOPEZ
Editor – Original Series

STEVE COOK
Design Director – Books

CURTIS KING JR.
Publication Design

CHRISTY SAWYER
Publication Production

MARIE JAVINS
Editor-in-Chief, DC Comics

DANIEL CHERRY III
Senior VP – General Manager

JIM LEE
Publisher & Chief Creative Officer

DON FALLETTI
VP – Manufacturing Operations & Workflow Management

LAWRENCE GANEM
VP – Talent Services

ALISON GILL
Senior VP – Manufacturing & Operations

JEFFREY KAUFMAN
VP – Editorial Strategy & Programming

NICK J. NAPOLITANO
VP – Manufacturing Administration & Design

NANCY SPEARS
VP – Revenue

MISTER MIRACLE: THE SOURCE OF FREEDOM

DC Comics, 2900 West Alameda Ave., Burbank, CA 91505
Printed by Transcontinental Interglobe,
Beauceville, QC, Canada. 2/25/22. First Printing.
ISBN: 978-1-77951-435-6

Library of Congress Cataloging-in-Publication Data is available.

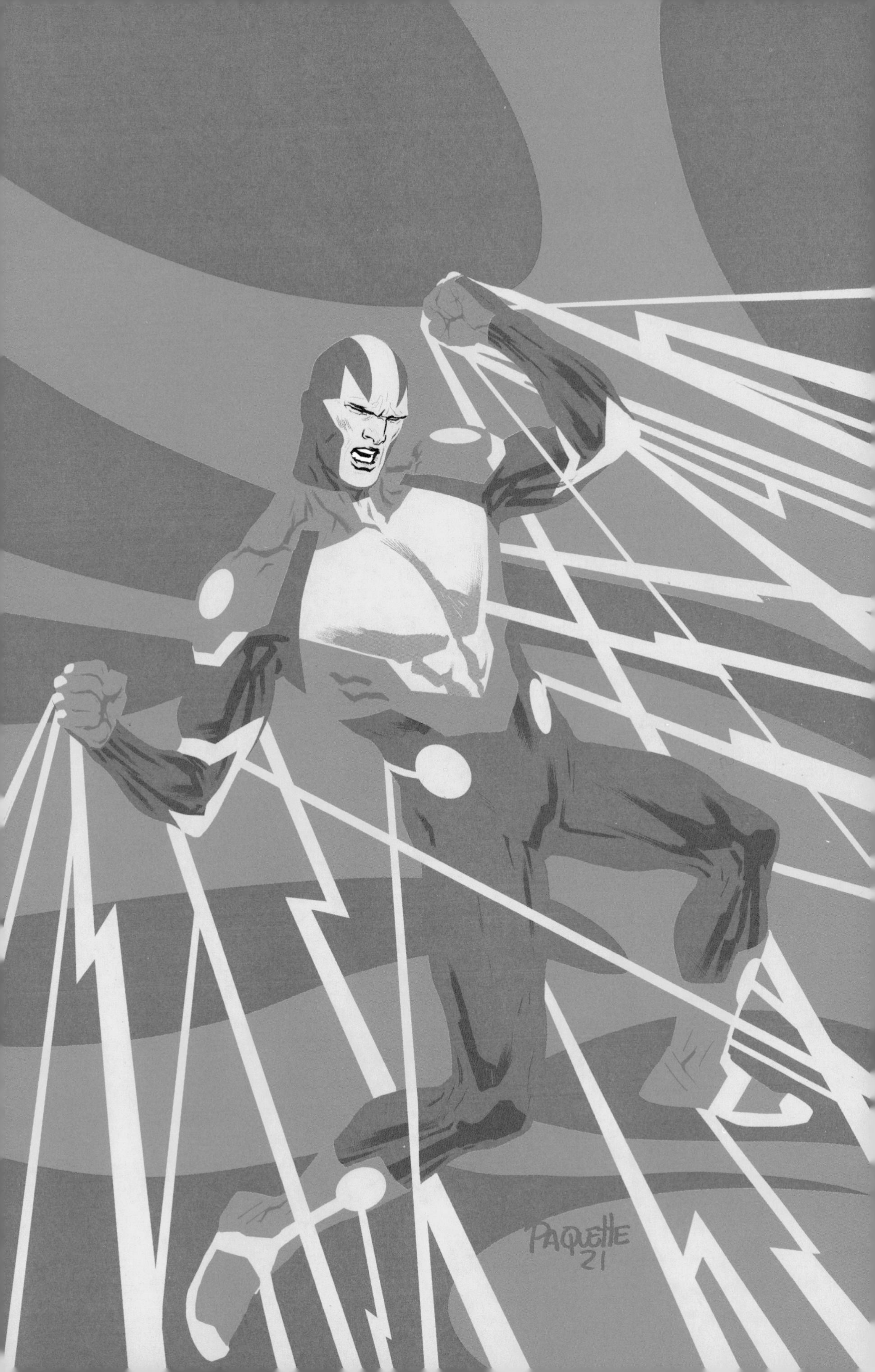
PAQUETTE
21

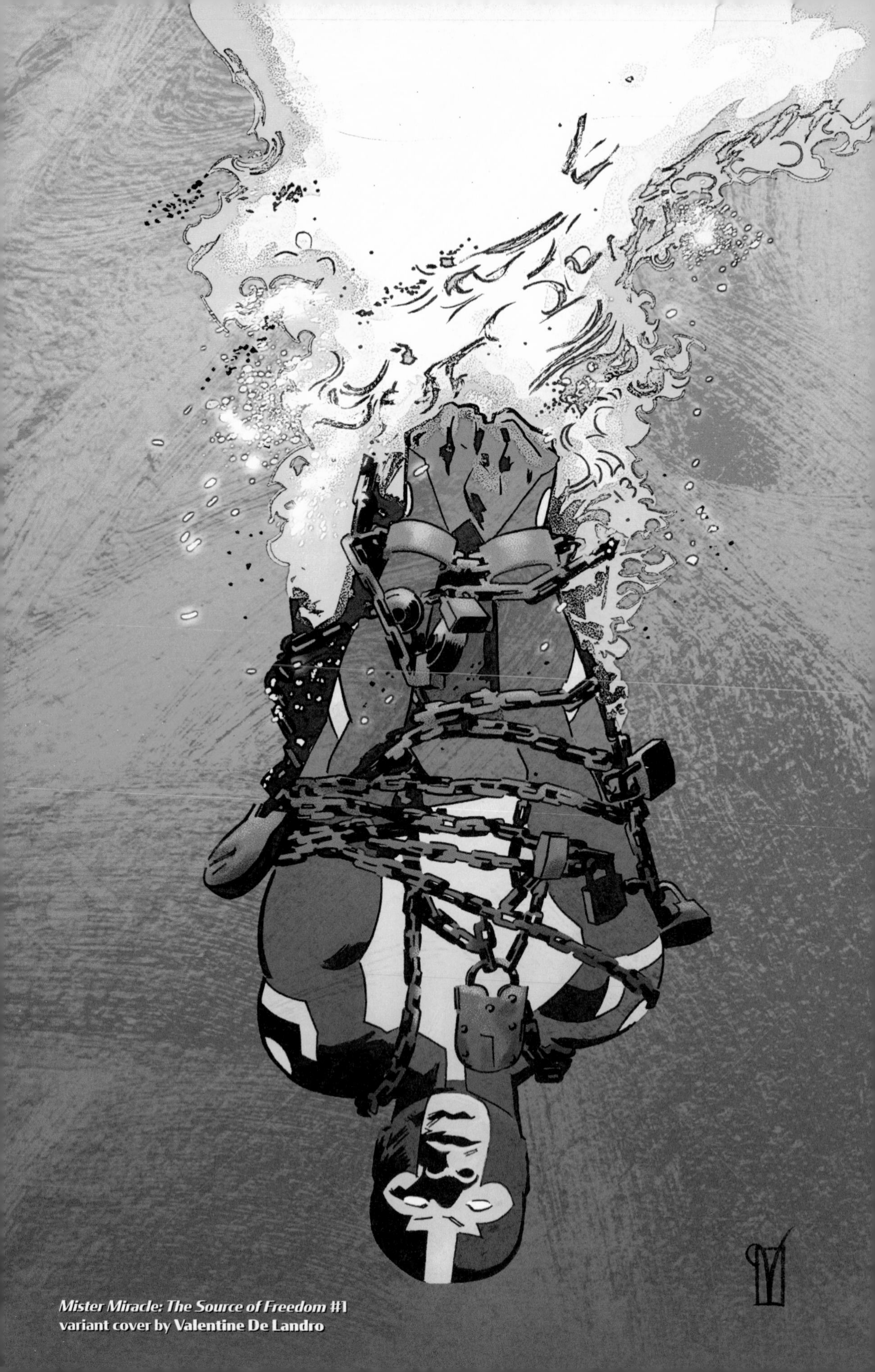

Mister Miracle: The Source of Freedom #1
variant cover by Valentine De Landro

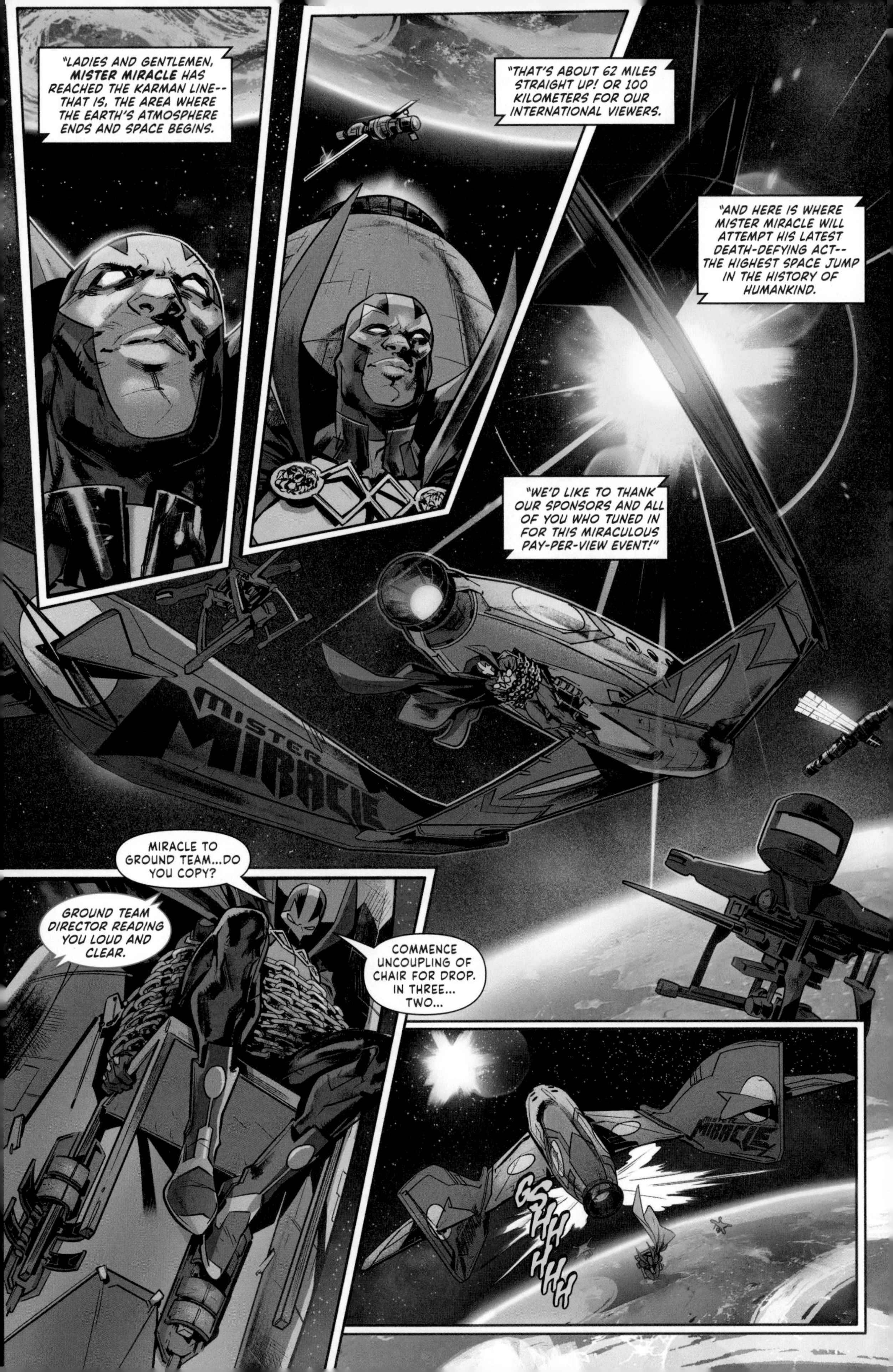
"LADIES AND GENTLEMEN, **MISTER MIRACLE** HAS REACHED THE KARMAN LINE-- THAT IS, THE AREA WHERE THE EARTH'S ATMOSPHERE ENDS AND SPACE BEGINS.
"THAT'S ABOUT 62 MILES STRAIGHT UP! OR 100 KILOMETERS FOR OUR INTERNATIONAL VIEWERS.
"AND HERE IS WHERE MISTER MIRACLE WILL ATTEMPT HIS LATEST DEATH-DEFYING ACT-- THE HIGHEST SPACE JUMP IN THE HISTORY OF HUMANKIND.
"WE'D LIKE TO THANK OUR SPONSORS AND ALL OF YOU WHO TUNED IN FOR THIS MIRACULOUS PAY-PER-VIEW EVENT!"
MISTER MIRACLE
MIRACLE TO GROUND TEAM...DO YOU COPY?
GROUND TEAM DIRECTOR READING YOU LOUD AND CLEAR.
COMMENCE UNCOUPLING OF CHAIR FOR DROP. IN THREE... TWO...
GSHHHHH

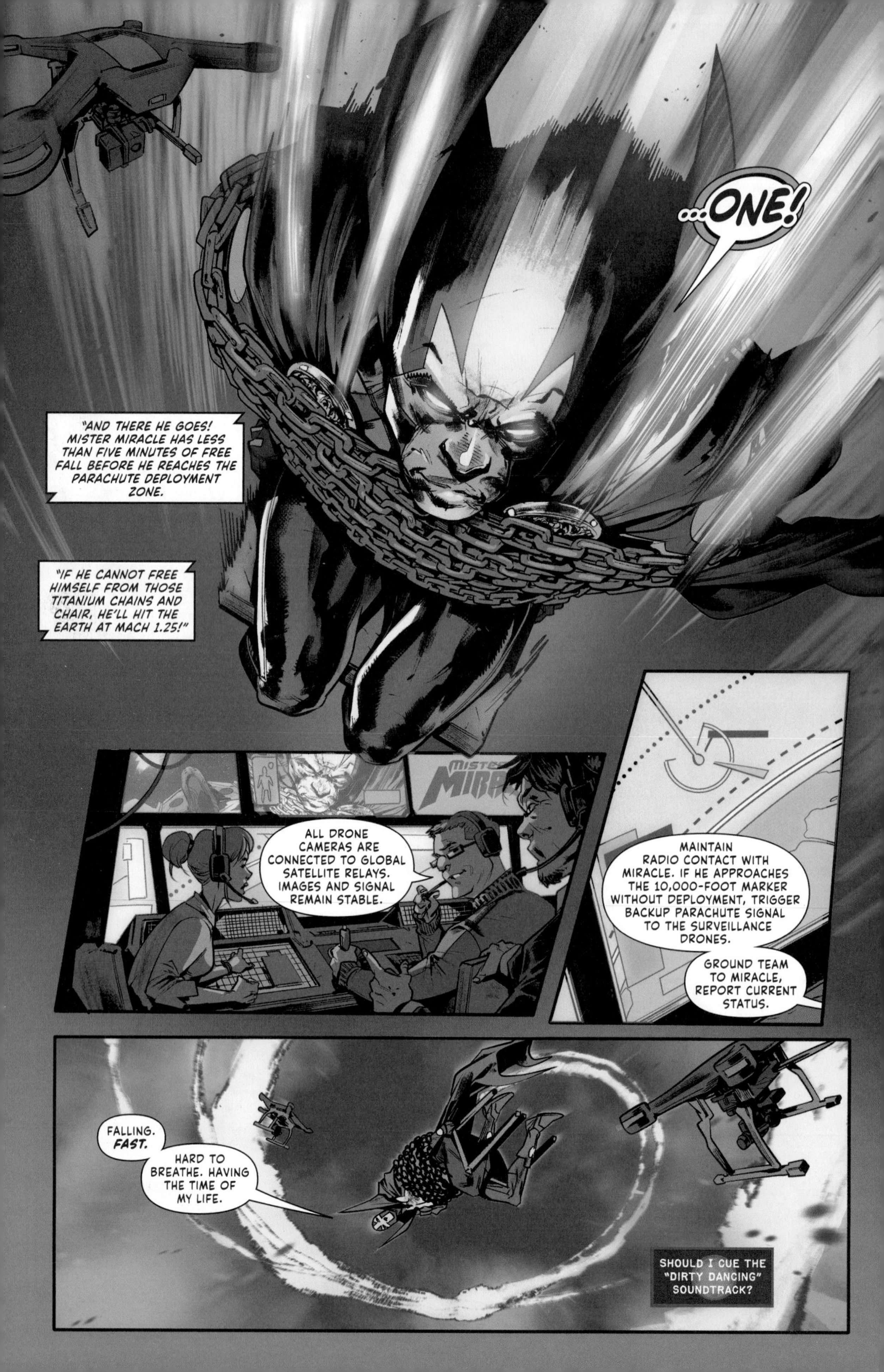
...ONE!
"AND THERE HE GOES! MISTER MIRACLE HAS LESS THAN FIVE MINUTES OF FREE FALL BEFORE HE REACHES THE PARACHUTE DEPLOYMENT ZONE.
"IF HE CANNOT FREE HIMSELF FROM THOSE TITANIUM CHAINS AND CHAIR, HE'LL HIT THE EARTH AT MACH 1.25!"
ALL DRONE CAMERAS ARE CONNECTED TO GLOBAL SATELLITE RELAYS. IMAGES AND SIGNAL REMAIN STABLE.
MAINTAIN RADIO CONTACT WITH MIRACLE. IF HE APPROACHES THE 10,000-FOOT MARKER WITHOUT DEPLOYMENT, TRIGGER BACKUP PARACHUTE SIGNAL TO THE SURVEILLANCE DRONES.
GROUND TEAM TO MIRACLE, REPORT CURRENT STATUS.
FALLING. FAST.
HARD TO BREATHE. HAVING THE TIME OF MY LIFE.
SHOULD I CUE THE "DIRTY DANCING" SOUNDTRACK?

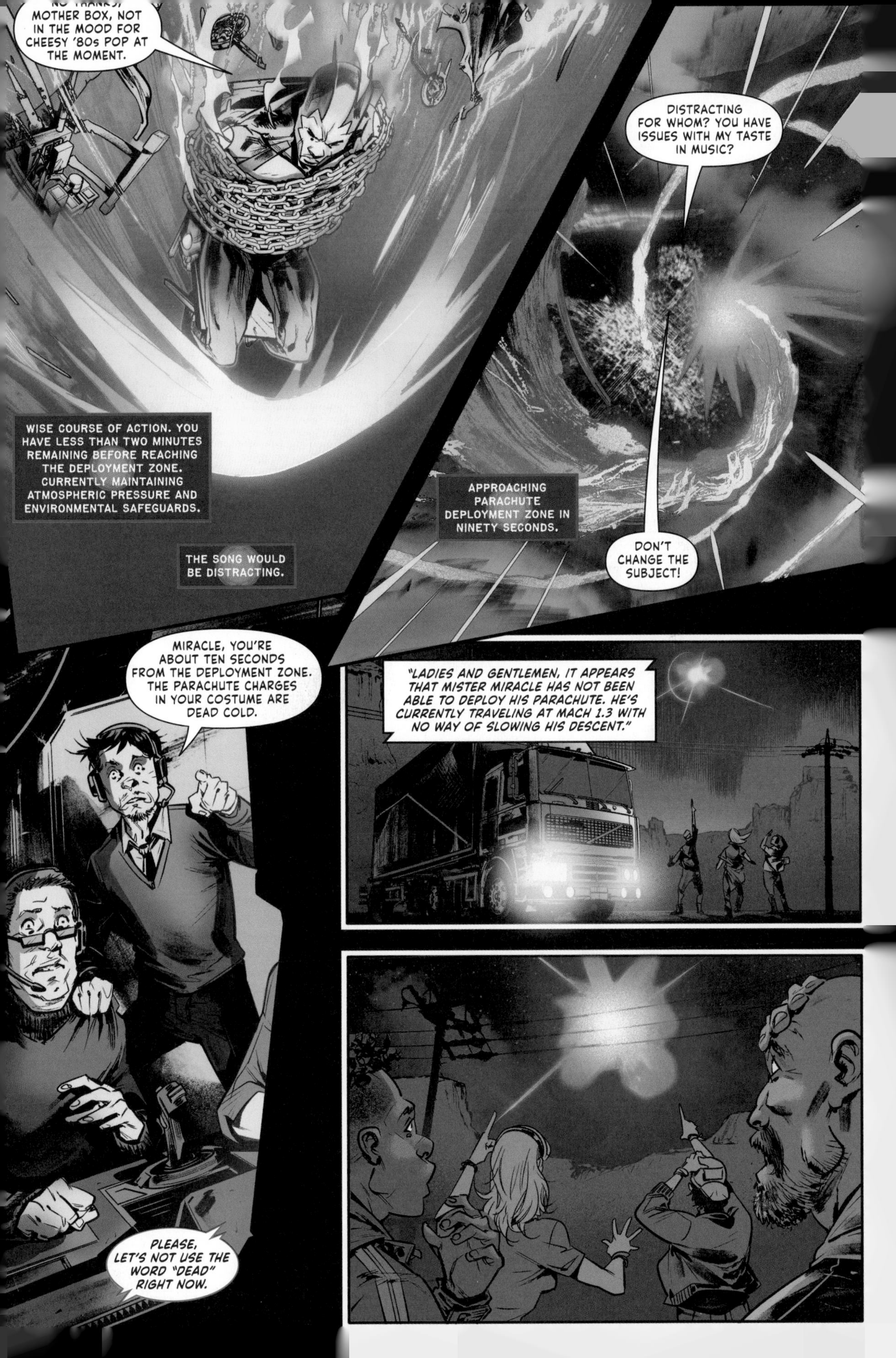
MOTHER BOX, NOT IN THE MOOD FOR CHEESY '80s POP AT THE MOMENT.
WISE COURSE OF ACTION. YOU HAVE LESS THAN TWO MINUTES REMAINING BEFORE REACHING THE DEPLOYMENT ZONE. CURRENTLY MAINTAINING ATMOSPHERIC PRESSURE AND ENVIRONMENTAL SAFEGUARDS.
THE SONG WOULD BE DISTRACTING.
DISTRACTING FOR WHOM? YOU HAVE ISSUES WITH MY TASTE IN MUSIC?
APPROACHING PARACHUTE DEPLOYMENT ZONE IN NINETY SECONDS.
DON'T CHANGE THE SUBJECT!
MIRACLE, YOU'RE ABOUT TEN SECONDS FROM THE DEPLOYMENT ZONE. THE PARACHUTE CHARGES IN YOUR COSTUME ARE DEAD COLD.
PLEASE, LET'S NOT USE THE WORD "DEAD" RIGHT NOW.
"LADIES AND GENTLEMEN, IT APPEARS THAT MISTER MIRACLE HAS NOT BEEN ABLE TO DEPLOY HIS PARACHUTE. HE'S CURRENTLY TRAVELING AT MACH 1.3 WITH NO WAY OF SLOWING HIS DESCENT."

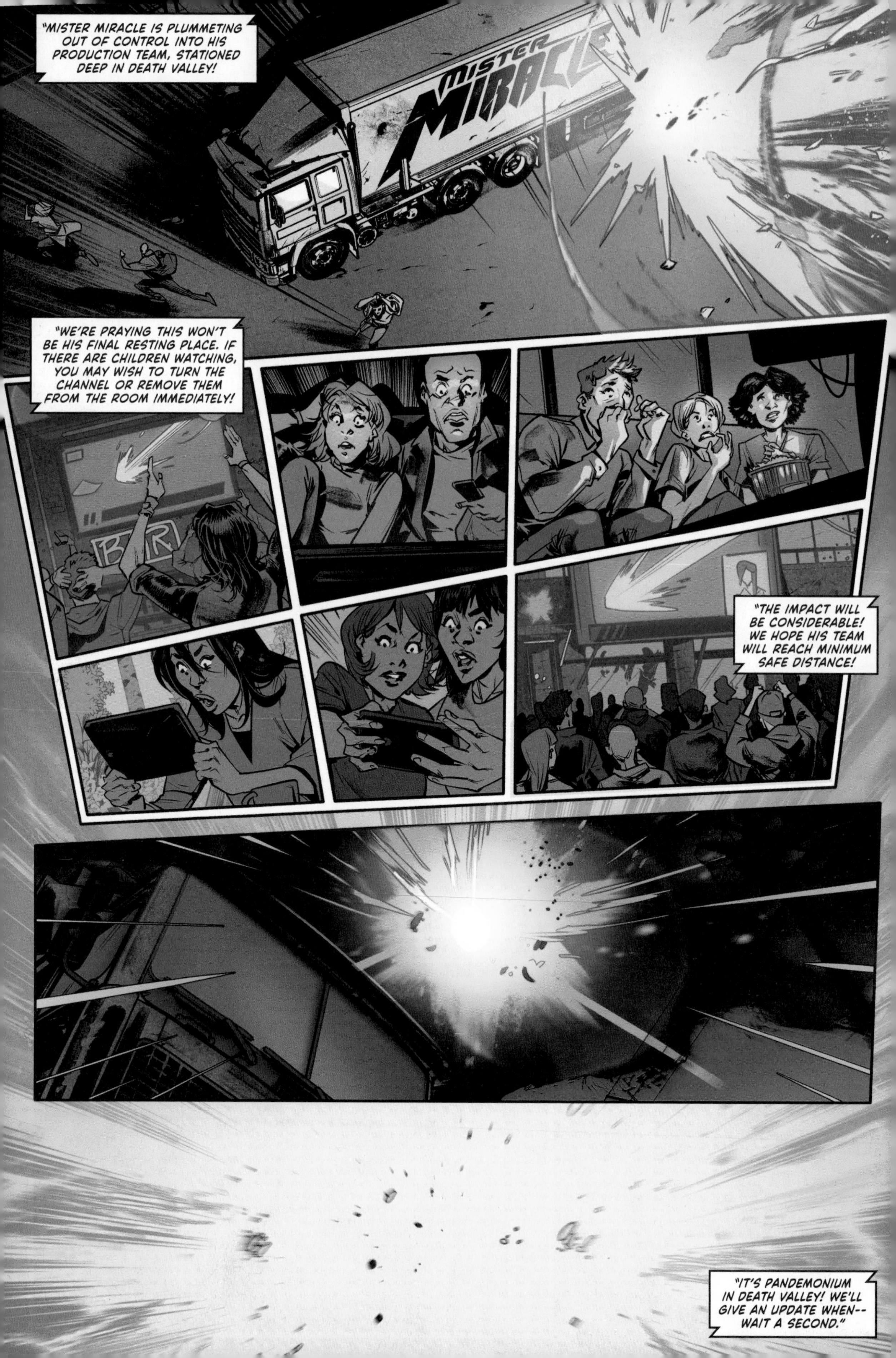
"MISTER MIRACLE IS PLUMMETING OUT OF CONTROL INTO HIS PRODUCTION TEAM, STATIONED DEEP IN DEATH VALLEY!
MISTER MIRACLE
"WE'RE PRAYING THIS WON'T BE HIS FINAL RESTING PLACE. IF THERE ARE CHILDREN WATCHING, YOU MAY WISH TO TURN THE CHANNEL OR REMOVE THEM FROM THE ROOM IMMEDIATELY!
"THE IMPACT WILL BE CONSIDERABLE! WE HOPE HIS TEAM WILL REACH MINIMUM SAFE DISTANCE!
"IT'S PANDEMONIUM IN DEATH VALLEY! WE'LL GIVE AN UPDATE WHEN-- WAIT A SECOND."

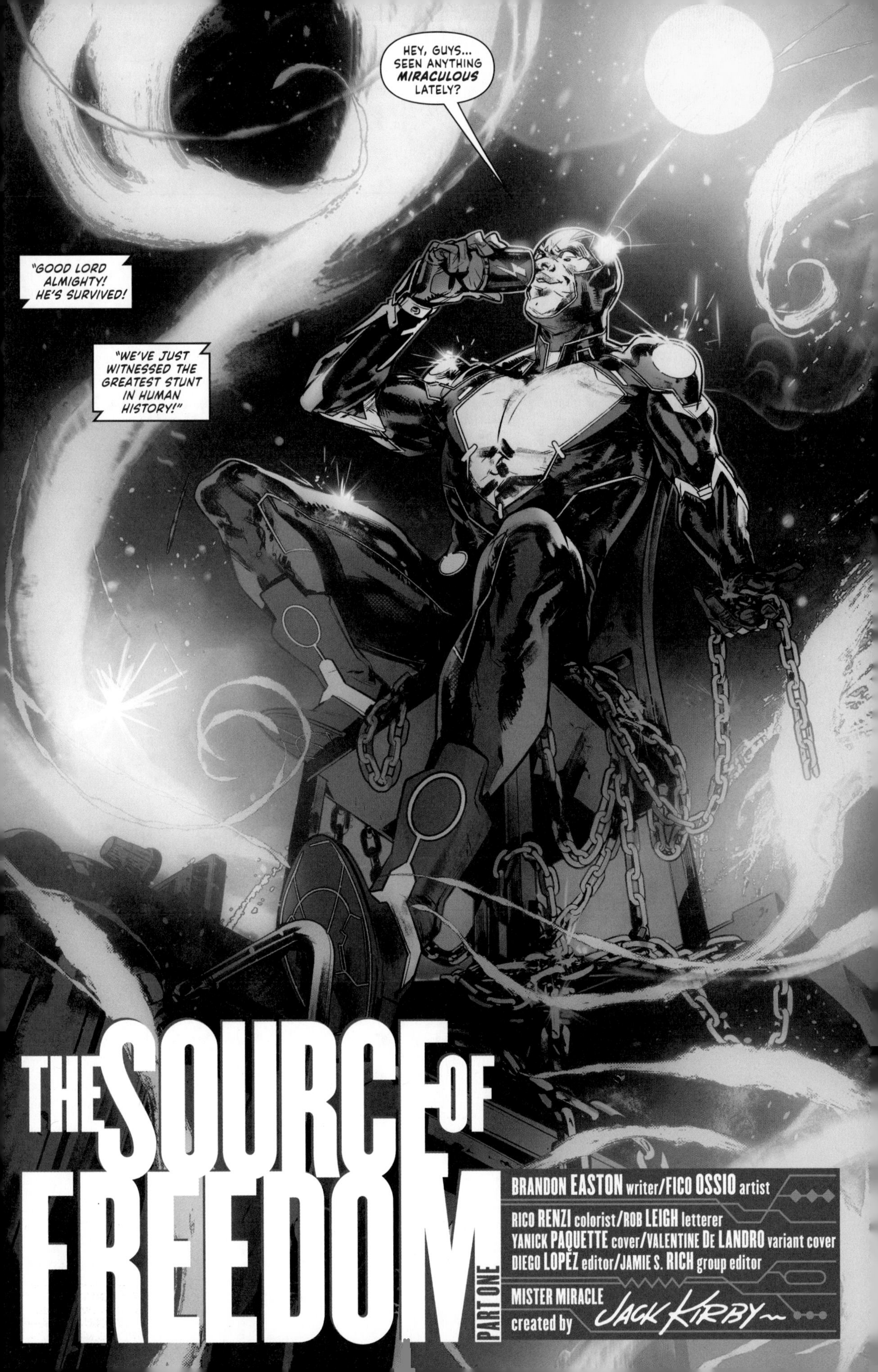
HEY, GUYS... SEEN ANYTHING MIRACULOUS LATELY?
"GOOD LORD ALMIGHTY! HE'S SURVIVED!
"WE'VE JUST WITNESSED THE GREATEST STUNT IN HUMAN HISTORY!"
THE SOURCE OF FREEDOM
PART ONE
BRANDON EASTON writer/FICO OSSIO artist
RICO RENZI colorist/ROB LEIGH letterer
YANICK PAQUETTE cover/VALENTINE DE LANDRO variant cover
DIEGO LOPEZ editor/JAMIE S. RICH group editor
MISTER MIRACLE created by JACK KIRBY

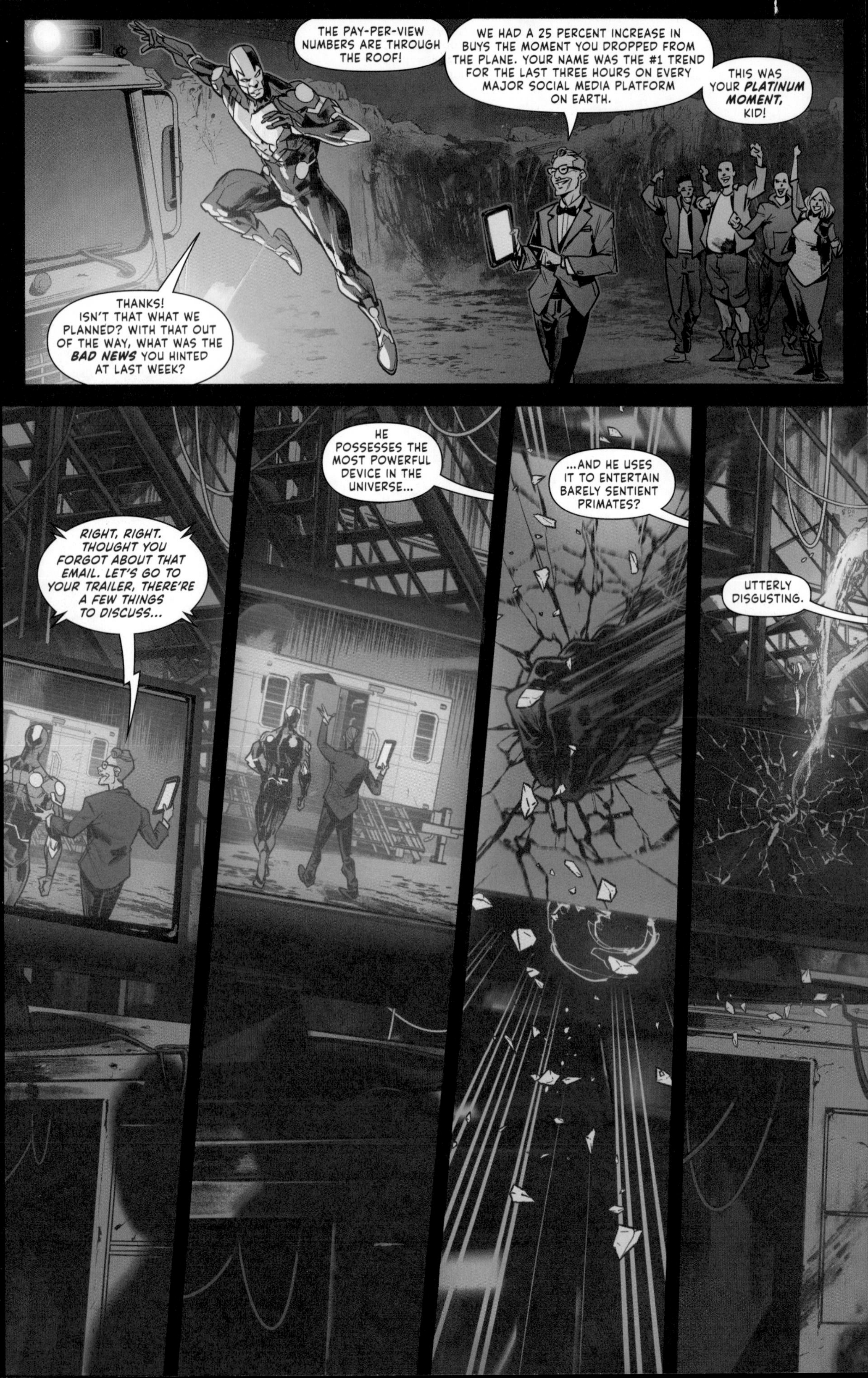
THE PAY-PER-VIEW NUMBERS ARE THROUGH THE ROOF!
WE HAD A 25 PERCENT INCREASE IN BUYS THE MOMENT YOU DROPPED FROM THE PLANE. YOUR NAME WAS THE #1 TREND FOR THE LAST THREE HOURS ON EVERY MAJOR SOCIAL MEDIA PLATFORM ON EARTH.
THIS WAS YOUR **PLATINUM MOMENT,** KID!
THANKS! ISN'T THAT WHAT WE PLANNED? WITH THAT OUT OF THE WAY, WHAT WAS THE **BAD NEWS** YOU HINTED AT LAST WEEK?
RIGHT, RIGHT. THOUGHT YOU FORGOT ABOUT THAT EMAIL. LET'S GO TO YOUR TRAILER, THERE'RE A FEW THINGS TO DISCUSS...
HE POSSESSES THE MOST POWERFUL DEVICE IN THE UNIVERSE...
...AND HE USES IT TO ENTERTAIN BARELY SENTIENT PRIMATES?
UTTERLY DISGUSTING.

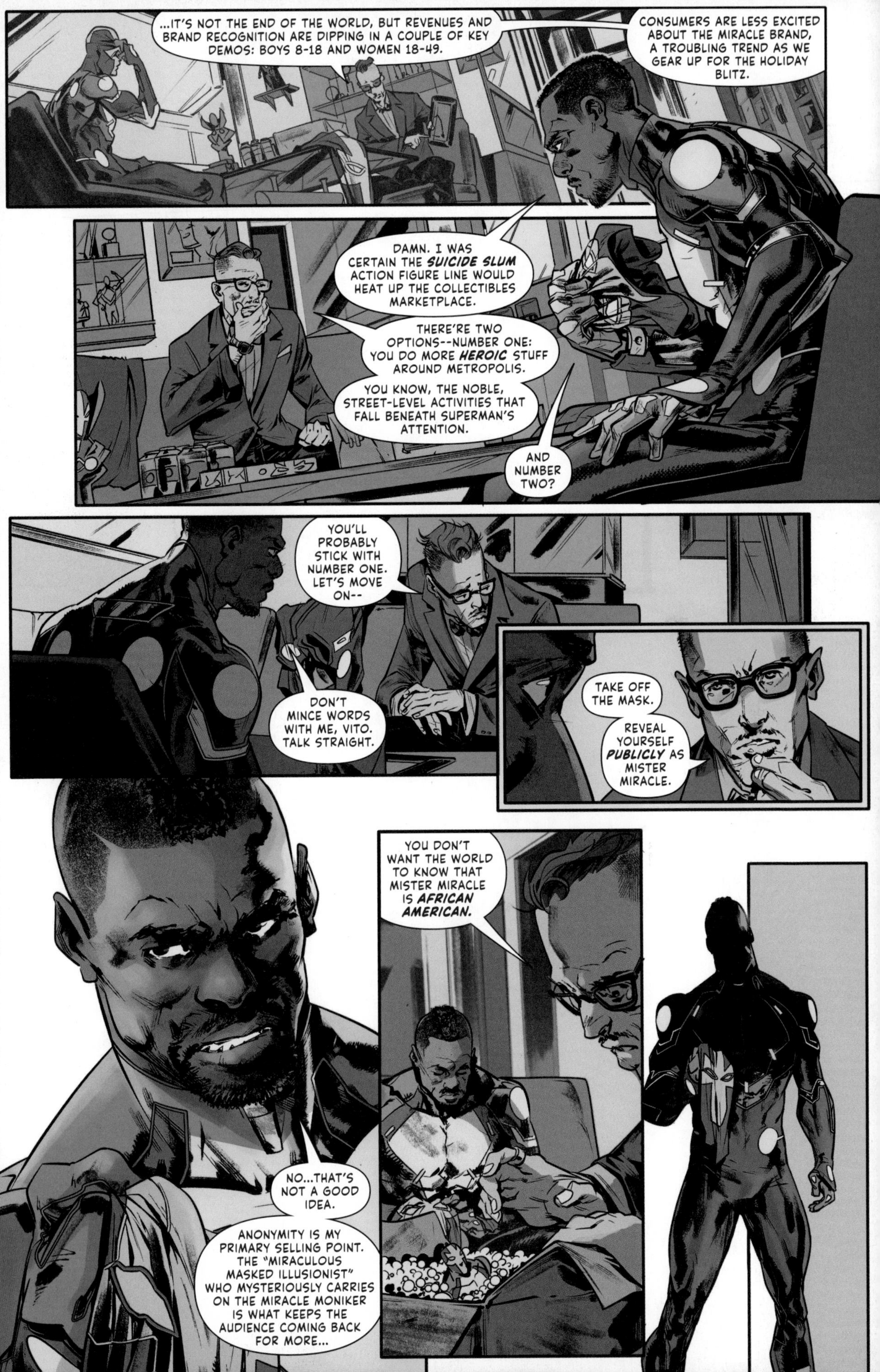
...IT'S NOT THE END OF THE WORLD, BUT REVENUES AND BRAND RECOGNITION ARE DIPPING IN A COUPLE OF KEY DEMOS: BOYS 8-18 AND WOMEN 18-49.
CONSUMERS ARE LESS EXCITED ABOUT THE MIRACLE BRAND, A TROUBLING TREND AS WE GEAR UP FOR THE HOLIDAY BLITZ.
DAMN. I WAS CERTAIN THE SUICIDE SLUM ACTION FIGURE LINE WOULD HEAT UP THE COLLECTIBLES MARKETPLACE.
THERE'RE TWO OPTIONS--NUMBER ONE: YOU DO MORE HEROIC STUFF AROUND METROPOLIS.
YOU KNOW, THE NOBLE, STREET-LEVEL ACTIVITIES THAT FALL BENEATH SUPERMAN'S ATTENTION.
AND NUMBER TWO?
YOU'LL PROBABLY STICK WITH NUMBER ONE. LET'S MOVE ON--
DON'T MINCE WORDS WITH ME, VITO. TALK STRAIGHT.
TAKE OFF THE MASK.
REVEAL YOURSELF PUBLICLY AS MISTER MIRACLE.
YOU DON'T WANT THE WORLD TO KNOW THAT MISTER MIRACLE IS AFRICAN AMERICAN.
NO...THAT'S NOT A GOOD IDEA.
ANONYMITY IS MY PRIMARY SELLING POINT. THE "MIRACULOUS MASKED ILLUSIONIST" WHO MYSTERIOUSLY CARRIES ON THE MIRACLE MONIKER IS WHAT KEEPS THE AUDIENCE COMING BACK FOR MORE...

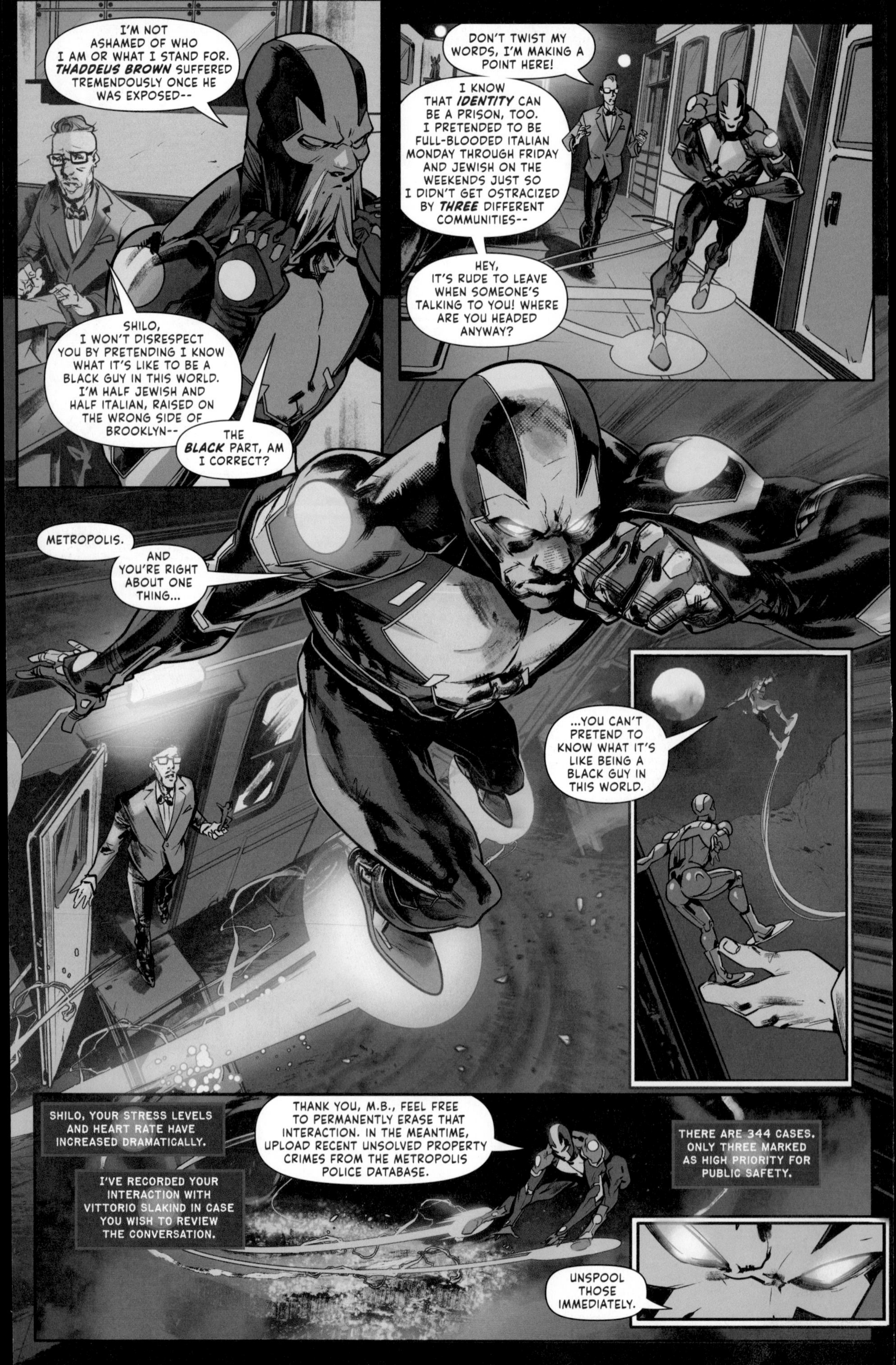
I'M NOT ASHAMED OF WHO I AM OR WHAT I STAND FOR. THADDEUS BROWN SUFFERED TREMENDOUSLY ONCE HE WAS EXPOSED--
SHILO, I WON'T DISRESPECT YOU BY PRETENDING I KNOW WHAT IT'S LIKE TO BE A BLACK GUY IN THIS WORLD. I'M HALF JEWISH AND HALF ITALIAN, RAISED ON THE WRONG SIDE OF BROOKLYN--
THE BLACK PART, AM I CORRECT?
DON'T TWIST MY WORDS, I'M MAKING A POINT HERE!
I KNOW THAT IDENTITY CAN BE A PRISON, TOO. I PRETENDED TO BE FULL-BLOODED ITALIAN MONDAY THROUGH FRIDAY AND JEWISH ON THE WEEKENDS JUST SO I DIDN'T GET OSTRACIZED BY THREE DIFFERENT COMMUNITIES--
HEY, IT'S RUDE TO LEAVE WHEN SOMEONE'S TALKING TO YOU! WHERE ARE YOU HEADED ANYWAY?
METROPOLIS.
AND YOU'RE RIGHT ABOUT ONE THING...
...YOU CAN'T PRETEND TO KNOW WHAT IT'S LIKE BEING A BLACK GUY IN THIS WORLD.
SHILO, YOUR STRESS LEVELS AND HEART RATE HAVE INCREASED DRAMATICALLY.
I'VE RECORDED YOUR INTERACTION WITH VITTORIO SLAKIND IN CASE YOU WISH TO REVIEW THE CONVERSATION.
THANK YOU, M.B., FEEL FREE TO PERMANENTLY ERASE THAT INTERACTION. IN THE MEANTIME, UPLOAD RECENT UNSOLVED PROPERTY CRIMES FROM THE METROPOLIS POLICE DATABASE.
THERE ARE 344 CASES. ONLY THREE MARKED AS HIGH PRIORITY FOR PUBLIC SAFETY.
UNSPOOL THOSE IMMEDIATELY.

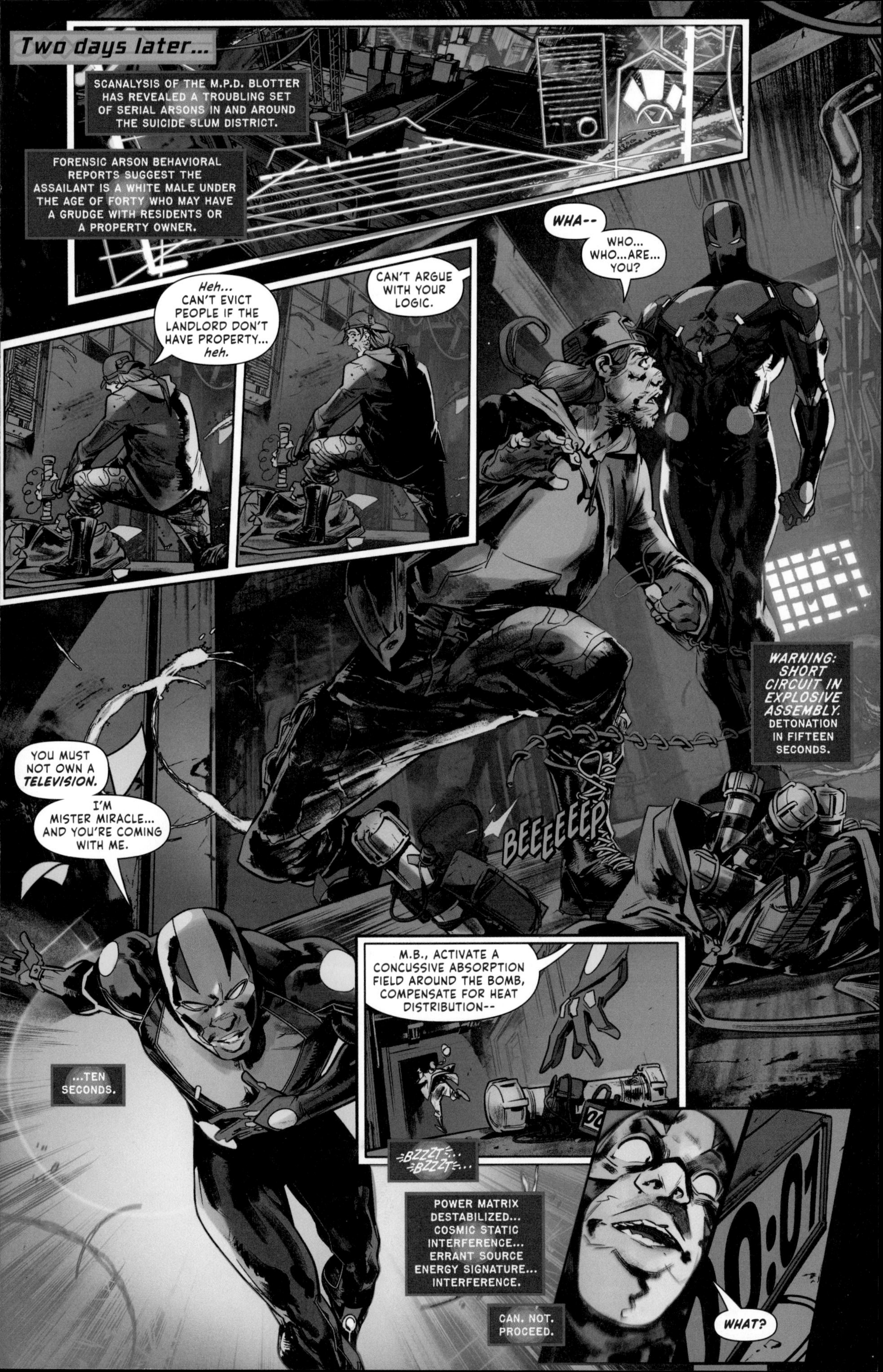

Two days later...
SCANALYSIS OF THE M.P.D. BLOTTER HAS REVEALED A TROUBLING SET OF SERIAL ARSONS IN AND AROUND THE SUICIDE SLUM DISTRICT.
FORENSIC ARSON BEHAVIORAL REPORTS SUGGEST THE ASSAILANT IS A WHITE MALE UNDER THE AGE OF FORTY WHO MAY HAVE A GRUDGE WITH RESIDENTS OR A PROPERTY OWNER.
Heh... CAN'T EVICT PEOPLE IF THE LANDLORD DON'T HAVE PROPERTY... heh.
CAN'T ARGUE WITH YOUR LOGIC.
WHA--
WHO... WHO...ARE... YOU?
YOU MUST NOT OWN A TELEVISION.
I'M MISTER MIRACLE... AND YOU'RE COMING WITH ME.
WARNING: SHORT CIRCUIT IN EXPLOSIVE ASSEMBLY. DETONATION IN FIFTEEN SECONDS.
BEEEEEEP
...TEN SECONDS.
M.B., ACTIVATE A CONCUSSIVE ABSORPTION FIELD AROUND THE BOMB, COMPENSATE FOR HEAT DISTRIBUTION--
BZZZT BZZZT
POWER MATRIX DESTABILIZED... COSMIC STATIC INTERFERENCE... ERRANT SOURCE ENERGY SIGNATURE... INTERFERENCE.
CAN. NOT. PROCEED.
0:01
WHAT?

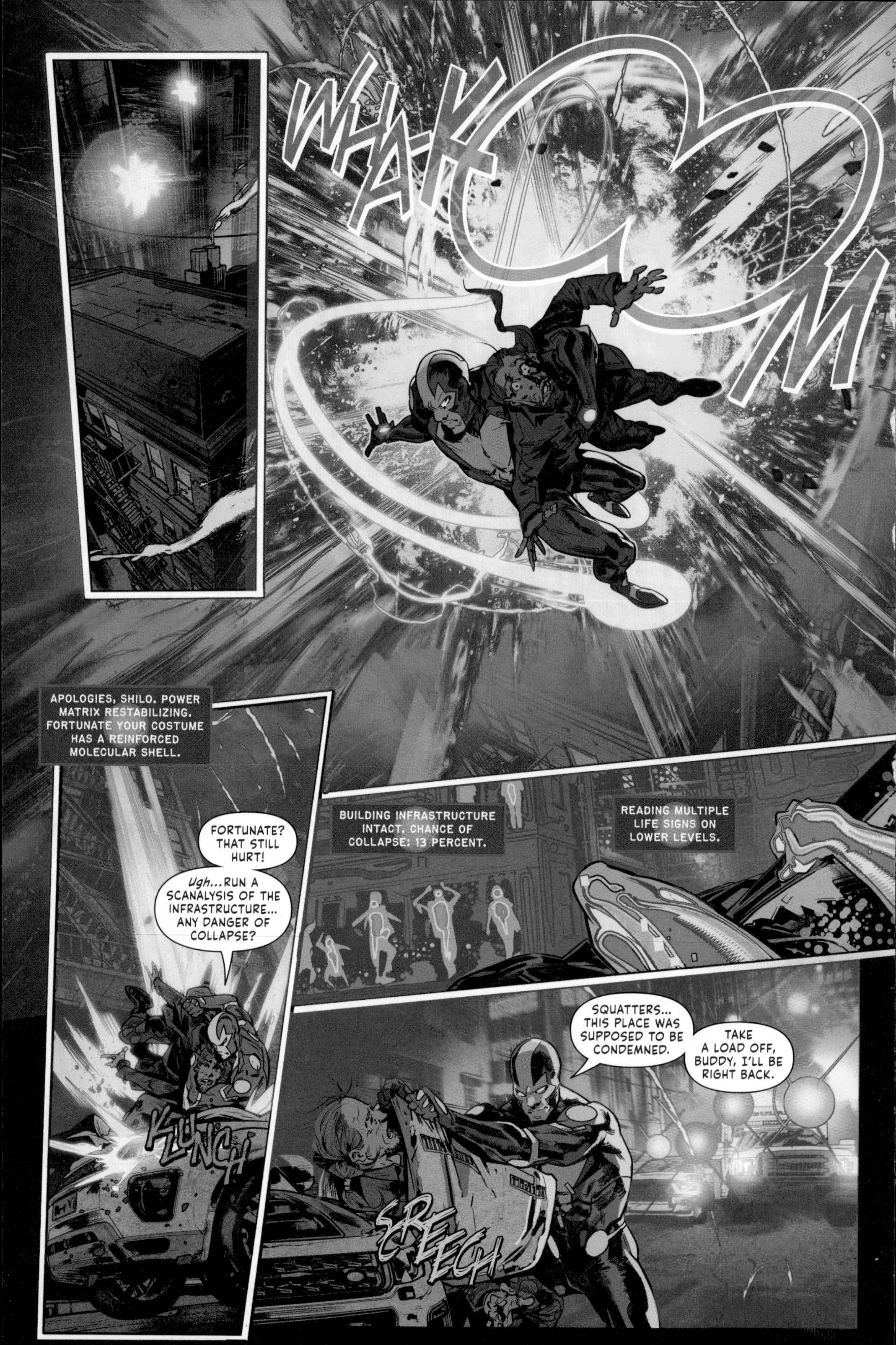

WHAKOOM
APOLOGIES, SHILO. POWER MATRIX RESTABILIZING. FORTUNATE YOUR COSTUME HAS A REINFORCED MOLECULAR SHELL.
FORTUNATE? THAT STILL HURT!
Ugh...RUN A SCANALYSIS OF THE INFRASTRUCTURE... ANY DANGER OF COLLAPSE?
KLUNCH
BUILDING INFRASTRUCTURE INTACT. CHANCE OF COLLAPSE: 13 PERCENT.
READING MULTIPLE LIFE SIGNS ON LOWER LEVELS.
SQUATTERS... THIS PLACE WAS SUPPOSED TO BE CONDEMNED.
TAKE A LOAD OFF, BUDDY, I'LL BE RIGHT BACK.
SCREEECH

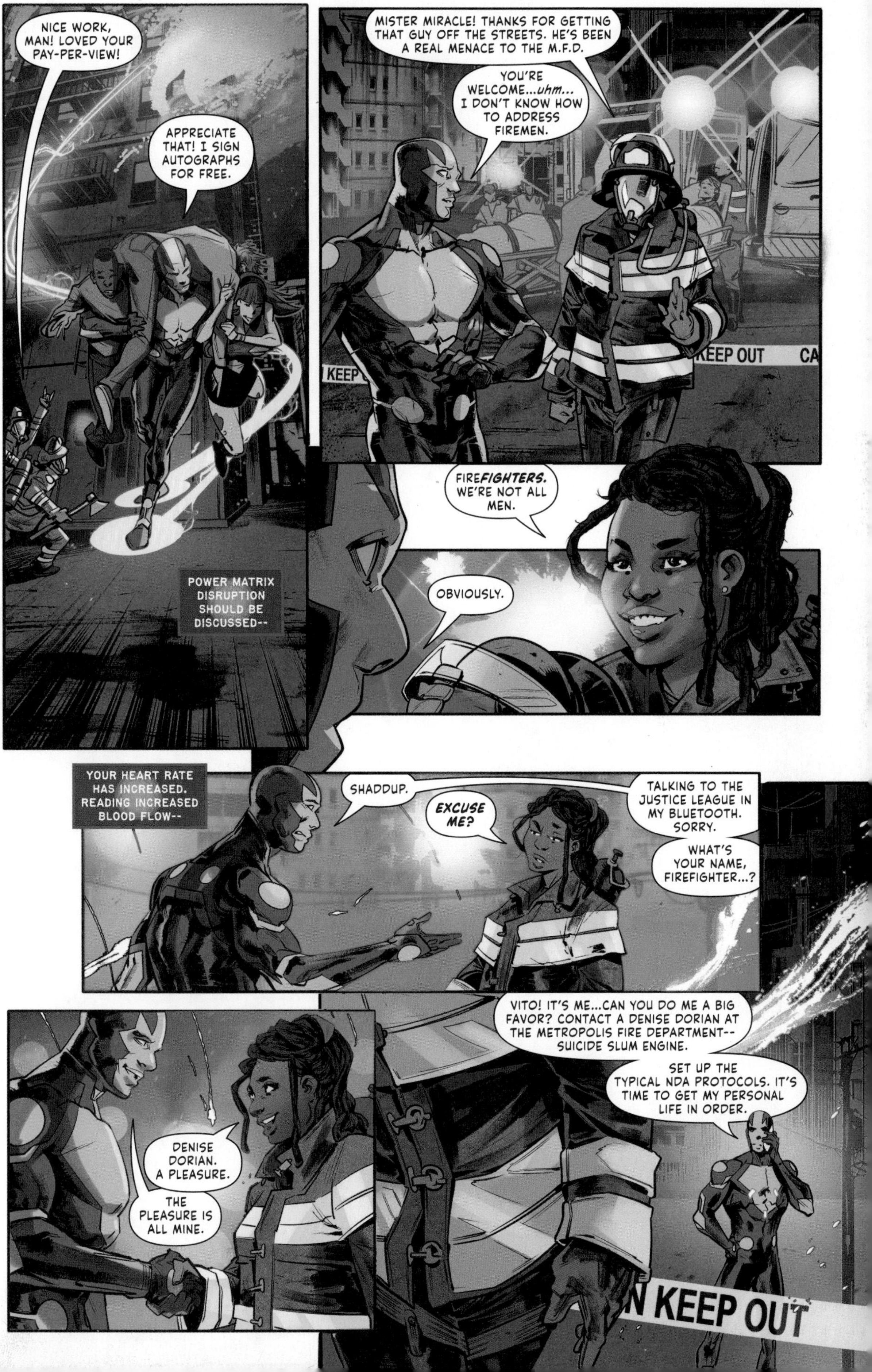
NICE WORK, MAN! LOVED YOUR PAY-PER-VIEW!
APPRECIATE THAT! I SIGN AUTOGRAPHS FOR FREE.
POWER MATRIX DISRUPTION SHOULD BE DISCUSSED--
MISTER MIRACLE! THANKS FOR GETTING THAT GUY OFF THE STREETS. HE'S BEEN A REAL MENACE TO THE M.F.D.
YOU'RE WELCOME...*uhm*... I DON'T KNOW HOW TO ADDRESS FIREMEN.
KEEP OUT
CA
KEEP
FIRE***FIGHTERS.*** WE'RE NOT ALL MEN.
OBVIOUSLY.
YOUR HEART RATE HAS INCREASED. READING INCREASED BLOOD FLOW--
SHADDUP.
EXCUSE ME?
TALKING TO THE JUSTICE LEAGUE IN MY BLUETOOTH. SORRY.
WHAT'S YOUR NAME, FIREFIGHTER...?
DENISE DORIAN. A PLEASURE.
THE PLEASURE IS ALL MINE.
VITO! IT'S ME...CAN YOU DO ME A BIG FAVOR? CONTACT A DENISE DORIAN AT THE METROPOLIS FIRE DEPARTMENT-- SUICIDE SLUM ENGINE.
SET UP THE TYPICAL NDA PROTOCOLS. IT'S TIME TO GET MY PERSONAL LIFE IN ORDER.
N KEEP OUT

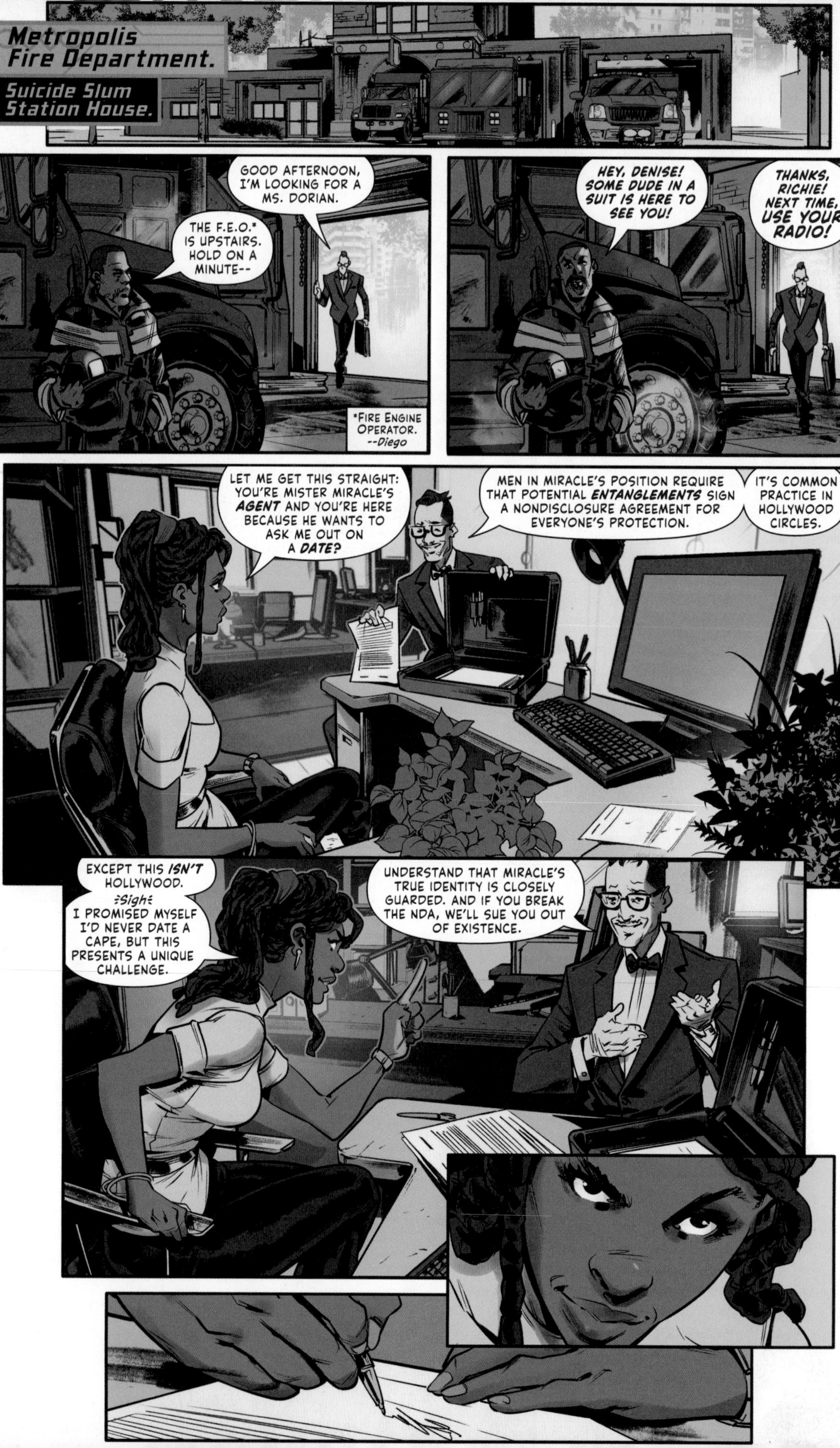
Metropolis Fire Department.
Suicide Slum Station House.
GOOD AFTERNOON, I'M LOOKING FOR A MS. DORIAN.
THE F.E.O.* IS UPSTAIRS. HOLD ON A MINUTE--
*FIRE ENGINE OPERATOR. --Diego
HEY, DENISE! SOME DUDE IN A SUIT IS HERE TO SEE YOU!
THANKS, RICHIE! NEXT TIME, USE YOUR RADIO!
LET ME GET THIS STRAIGHT: YOU'RE MISTER MIRACLE'S AGENT AND YOU'RE HERE BECAUSE HE WANTS TO ASK ME OUT ON A DATE?
MEN IN MIRACLE'S POSITION REQUIRE THAT POTENTIAL ENTANGLEMENTS SIGN A NONDISCLOSURE AGREEMENT FOR EVERYONE'S PROTECTION.
IT'S COMMON PRACTICE IN HOLLYWOOD CIRCLES.
EXCEPT THIS ISN'T HOLLYWOOD.
Sigh
I PROMISED MYSELF I'D NEVER DATE A CAPE, BUT THIS PRESENTS A UNIQUE CHALLENGE.
UNDERSTAND THAT MIRACLE'S TRUE IDENTITY IS CLOSELY GUARDED. AND IF YOU BREAK THE NDA, WE'LL SUE YOU OUT OF EXISTENCE.

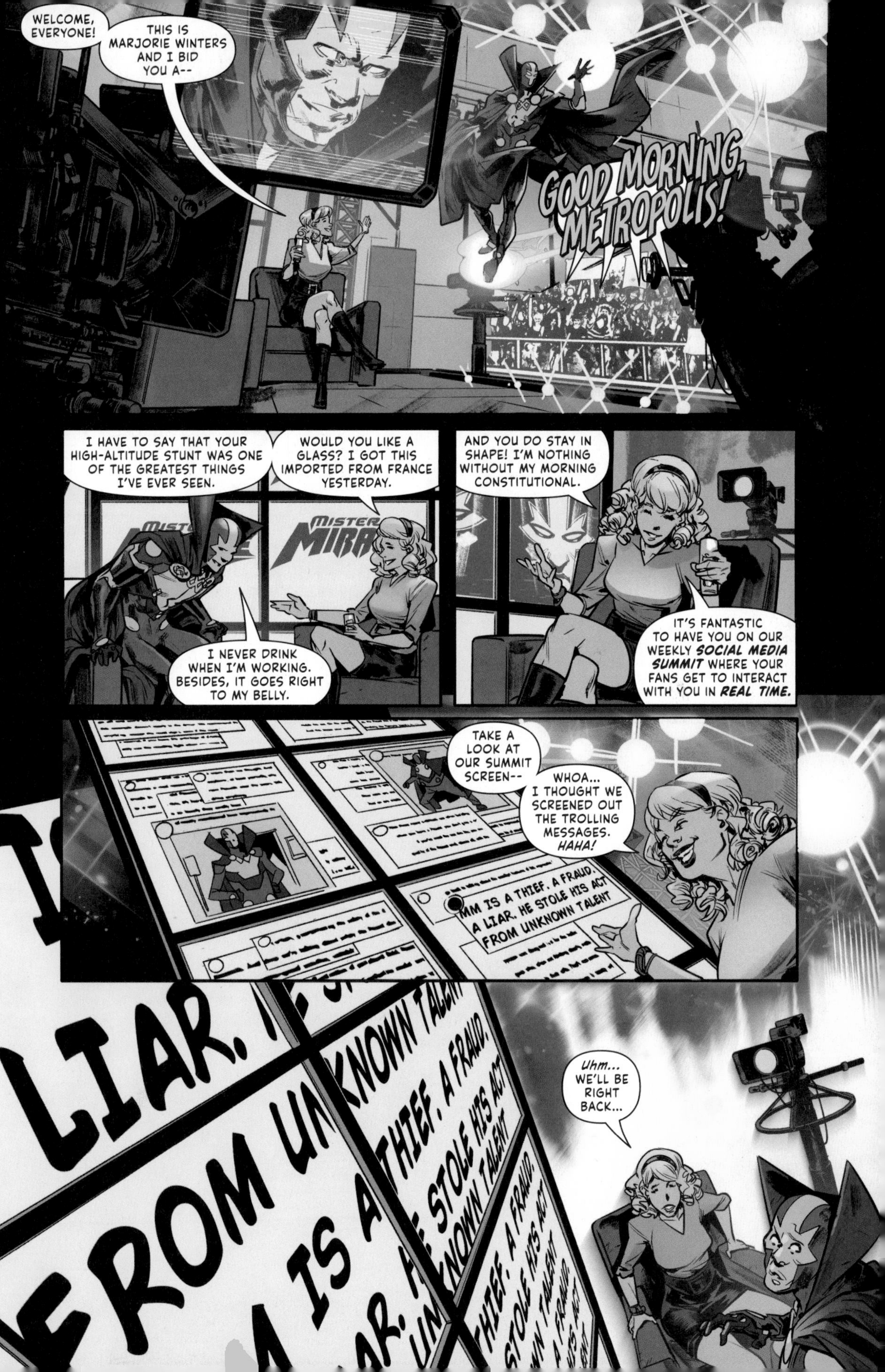

WELCOME, EVERYONE!
THIS IS MARJORIE WINTERS AND I BID YOU A--
GOOD MORNING, METROPOLIS!
I HAVE TO SAY THAT YOUR HIGH-ALTITUDE STUNT WAS ONE OF THE GREATEST THINGS I'VE EVER SEEN.
WOULD YOU LIKE A GLASS? I GOT THIS IMPORTED FROM FRANCE YESTERDAY.
I NEVER DRINK WHEN I'M WORKING. BESIDES, IT GOES RIGHT TO MY BELLY.
AND YOU DO STAY IN SHAPE! I'M NOTHING WITHOUT MY MORNING CONSTITUTIONAL.
IT'S FANTASTIC TO HAVE YOU ON OUR WEEKLY ***SOCIAL MEDIA SUMMIT*** WHERE YOUR FANS GET TO INTERACT WITH YOU IN ***REAL TIME.***
TAKE A LOOK AT OUR SUMMIT SCREEN--
WHOA... I THOUGHT WE SCREENED OUT THE TROLLING MESSAGES. *HAHA!*
MM IS A THIEF. A FRAUD. A LIAR. HE STOLE HIS ACT FROM UNKNOWN TALENT
LIAR.
FROM UN
A IS A
THIEF. A FRAUD.
HE STOLE HIS ACT
UNKNOWN TALENT
Uhm... WE'LL BE RIGHT BACK...

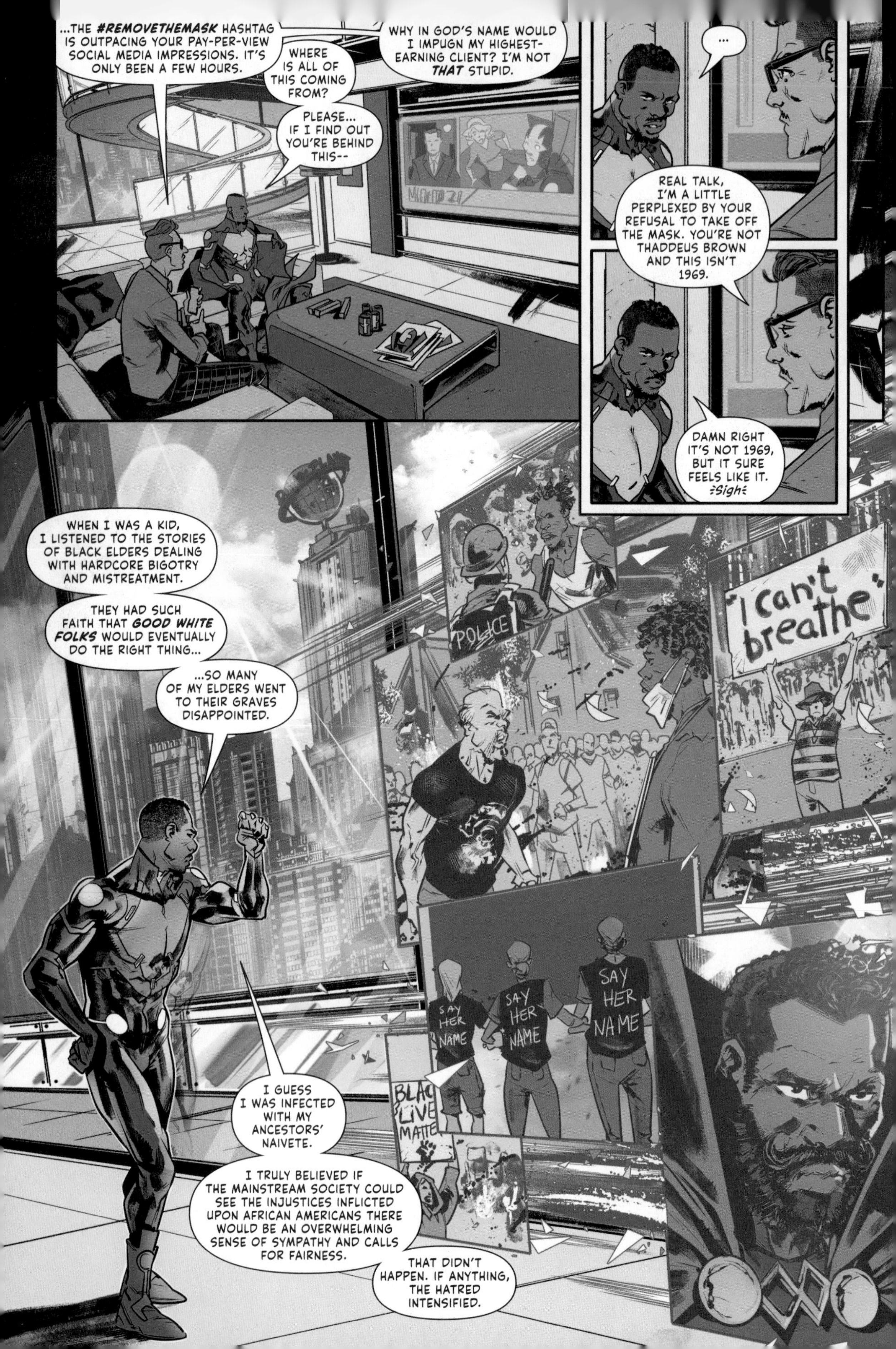
...THE #REMOVETHEMASK HASHTAG IS OUTPACING YOUR PAY-PER-VIEW SOCIAL MEDIA IMPRESSIONS. IT'S ONLY BEEN A FEW HOURS.
WHERE IS ALL OF THIS COMING FROM?
WHY IN GOD'S NAME WOULD I IMPUGN MY HIGHEST-EARNING CLIENT? I'M NOT THAT STUPID.
PLEASE... IF I FIND OUT YOU'RE BEHIND THIS--
...
REAL TALK, I'M A LITTLE PERPLEXED BY YOUR REFUSAL TO TAKE OFF THE MASK. YOU'RE NOT THADDEUS BROWN AND THIS ISN'T 1969.
DAMN RIGHT IT'S NOT 1969, BUT IT SURE FEELS LIKE IT. Sigh
WHEN I WAS A KID, I LISTENED TO THE STORIES OF BLACK ELDERS DEALING WITH HARDCORE BIGOTRY AND MISTREATMENT.
THEY HAD SUCH FAITH THAT GOOD WHITE FOLKS WOULD EVENTUALLY DO THE RIGHT THING...
...SO MANY OF MY ELDERS WENT TO THEIR GRAVES DISAPPOINTED.
POLICE
"I can't breathe"
SAY HER NAME
SAY HER NAME
SAY HER NAME
I GUESS I WAS INFECTED WITH MY ANCESTORS' NAIVETE.
I TRULY BELIEVED IF THE MAINSTREAM SOCIETY COULD SEE THE INJUSTICES INFLICTED UPON AFRICAN AMERICANS THERE WOULD BE AN OVERWHELMING SENSE OF SYMPATHY AND CALLS FOR FAIRNESS.
THAT DIDN'T HAPPEN. IF ANYTHING, THE HATRED INTENSIFIED.

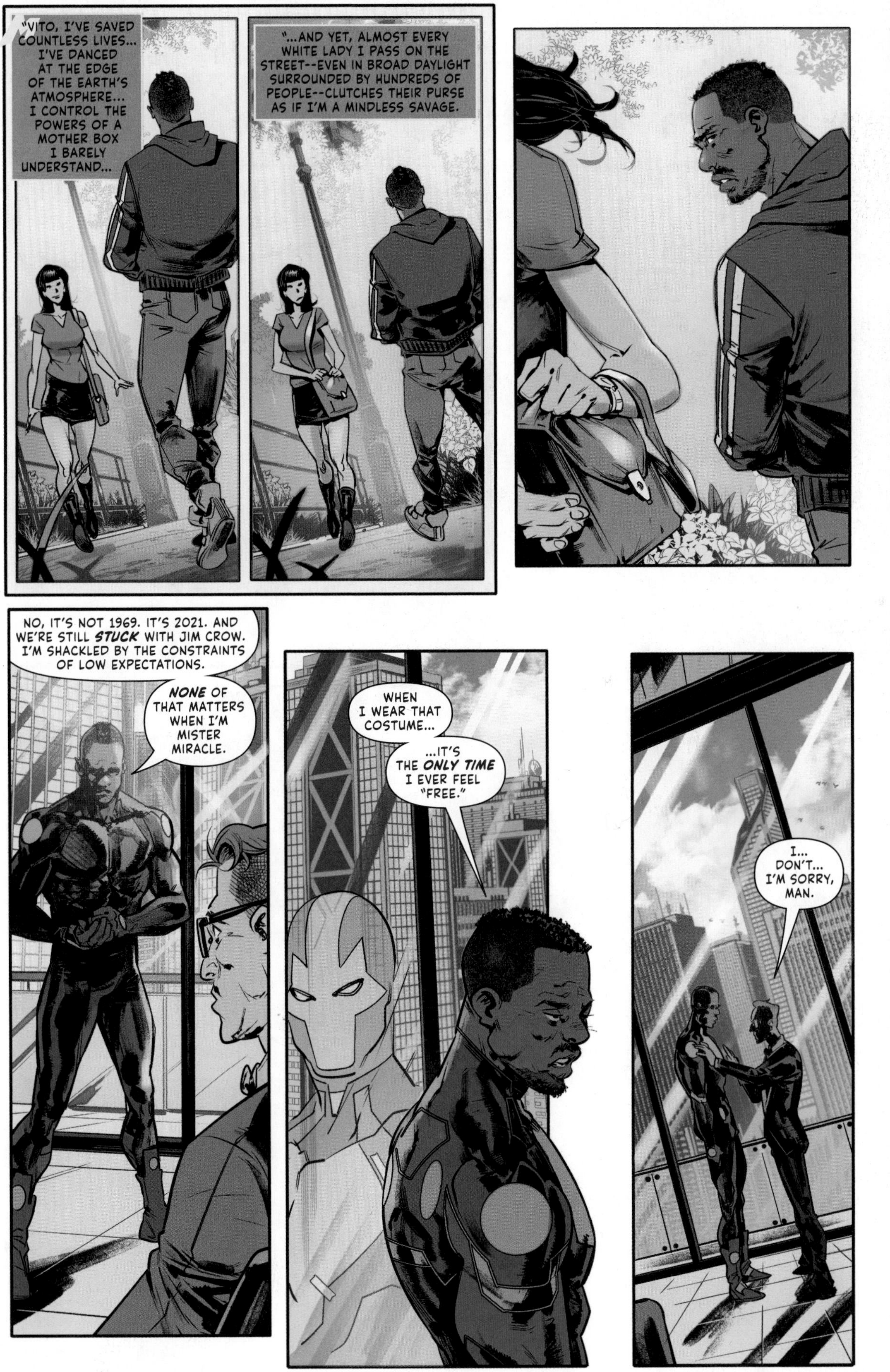
"VITO, I'VE SAVED COUNTLESS LIVES... I'VE DANCED AT THE EDGE OF THE EARTH'S ATMOSPHERE... I CONTROL THE POWERS OF A MOTHER BOX I BARELY UNDERSTAND...
"...AND YET, ALMOST EVERY WHITE LADY I PASS ON THE STREET--EVEN IN BROAD DAYLIGHT SURROUNDED BY HUNDREDS OF PEOPLE--CLUTCHES THEIR PURSE AS IF I'M A MINDLESS SAVAGE.
NO, IT'S NOT 1969. IT'S 2021. AND WE'RE STILL STUCK WITH JIM CROW. I'M SHACKLED BY THE CONSTRAINTS OF LOW EXPECTATIONS.
NONE OF THAT MATTERS WHEN I'M MISTER MIRACLE.
WHEN I WEAR THAT COSTUME...
...IT'S THE ONLY TIME I EVER FEEL "FREE."
I... DON'T... I'M SORRY, MAN.

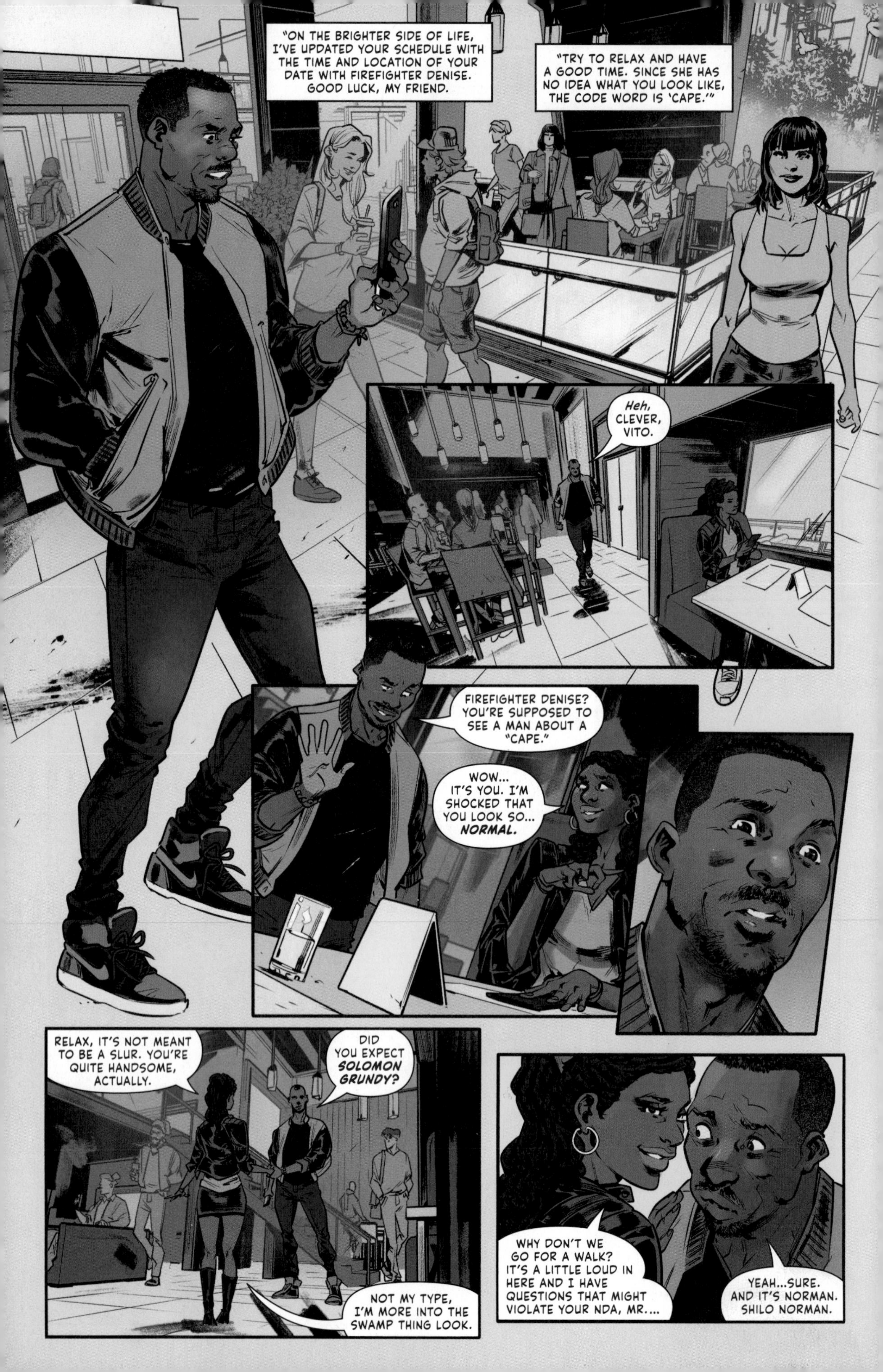
"ON THE BRIGHTER SIDE OF LIFE, I'VE UPDATED YOUR SCHEDULE WITH THE TIME AND LOCATION OF YOUR DATE WITH FIREFIGHTER DENISE. GOOD LUCK, MY FRIEND.
"TRY TO RELAX AND HAVE A GOOD TIME. SINCE SHE HAS NO IDEA WHAT YOU LOOK LIKE, THE CODE WORD IS 'CAPE.'"
Heh, CLEVER, VITO.
FIREFIGHTER DENISE? YOU'RE SUPPOSED TO SEE A MAN ABOUT A "CAPE."
WOW... IT'S YOU. I'M SHOCKED THAT YOU LOOK SO... **NORMAL.**
RELAX, IT'S NOT MEANT TO BE A SLUR. YOU'RE QUITE HANDSOME, ACTUALLY.
DID YOU EXPECT ***SOLOMON GRUNDY?***
NOT MY TYPE, I'M MORE INTO THE SWAMP THING LOOK.
WHY DON'T WE GO FOR A WALK? IT'S A LITTLE LOUD IN HERE AND I HAVE QUESTIONS THAT MIGHT VIOLATE YOUR NDA, MR....
YEAH...SURE. AND IT'S NORMAN. SHILO NORMAN.

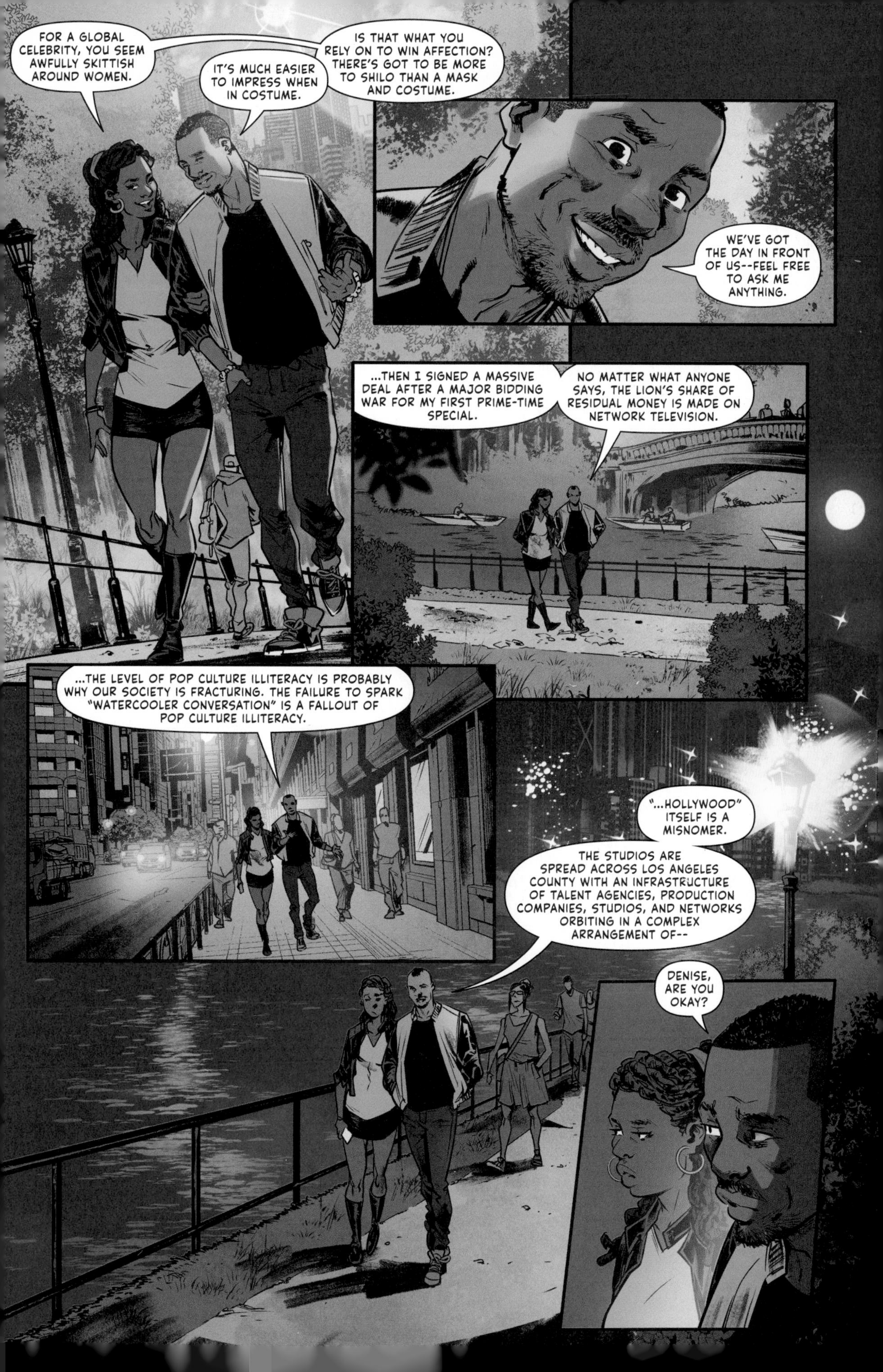
FOR A GLOBAL CELEBRITY, YOU SEEM AWFULLY SKITTISH AROUND WOMEN.
IT'S MUCH EASIER TO IMPRESS WHEN IN COSTUME.
IS THAT WHAT YOU RELY ON TO WIN AFFECTION? THERE'S GOT TO BE MORE TO SHILO THAN A MASK AND COSTUME.
WE'VE GOT THE DAY IN FRONT OF US--FEEL FREE TO ASK ME ANYTHING.
...THEN I SIGNED A MASSIVE DEAL AFTER A MAJOR BIDDING WAR FOR MY FIRST PRIME-TIME SPECIAL.
NO MATTER WHAT ANYONE SAYS, THE LION'S SHARE OF RESIDUAL MONEY IS MADE ON NETWORK TELEVISION.
...THE LEVEL OF POP CULTURE ILLITERACY IS PROBABLY WHY OUR SOCIETY IS FRACTURING. THE FAILURE TO SPARK "WATERCOOLER CONVERSATION" IS A FALLOUT OF POP CULTURE ILLITERACY.
"...HOLLYWOOD" ITSELF IS A MISNOMER.
THE STUDIOS ARE SPREAD ACROSS LOS ANGELES COUNTY WITH AN INFRASTRUCTURE OF TALENT AGENCIES, PRODUCTION COMPANIES, STUDIOS, AND NETWORKS ORBITING IN A COMPLEX ARRANGEMENT OF--
DENISE, ARE YOU OKAY?

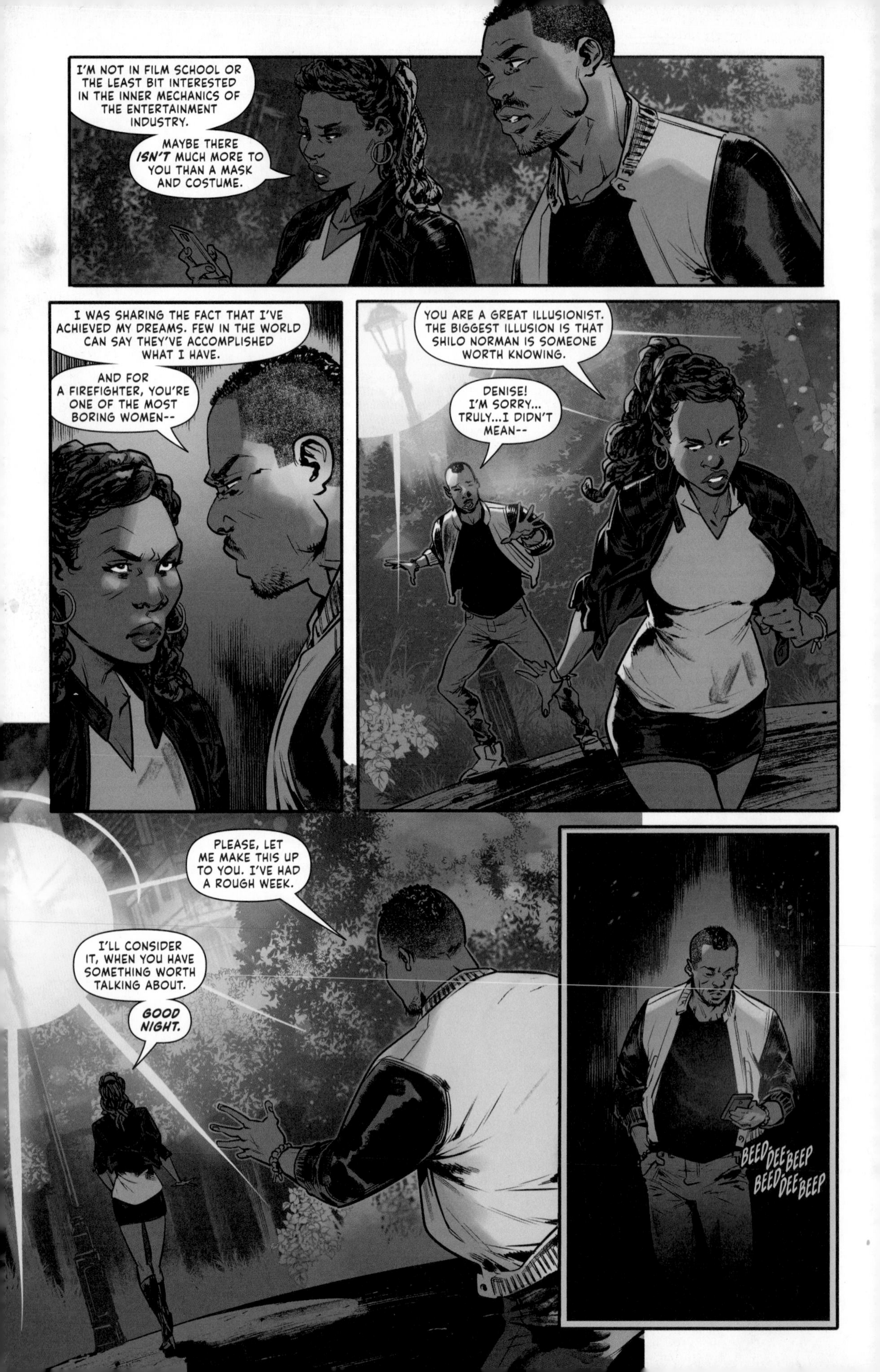
I'M NOT IN FILM SCHOOL OR THE LEAST BIT INTERESTED IN THE INNER MECHANICS OF THE ENTERTAINMENT INDUSTRY.
MAYBE THERE *ISN'T* MUCH MORE TO YOU THAN A MASK AND COSTUME.
I WAS SHARING THE FACT THAT I'VE ACHIEVED MY DREAMS. FEW IN THE WORLD CAN SAY THEY'VE ACCOMPLISHED WHAT I HAVE.
AND FOR A FIREFIGHTER, YOU'RE ONE OF THE MOST BORING WOMEN--
YOU ARE A GREAT ILLUSIONIST. THE BIGGEST ILLUSION IS THAT SHILO NORMAN IS SOMEONE WORTH KNOWING.
DENISE! I'M SORRY... TRULY...I DIDN'T MEAN--
PLEASE, LET ME MAKE THIS UP TO YOU. I'VE HAD A ROUGH WEEK.
I'LL CONSIDER IT, WHEN YOU HAVE SOMETHING WORTH TALKING ABOUT.
GOOD NIGHT.
BEED DEE BEEP
BEED DEE BEEP

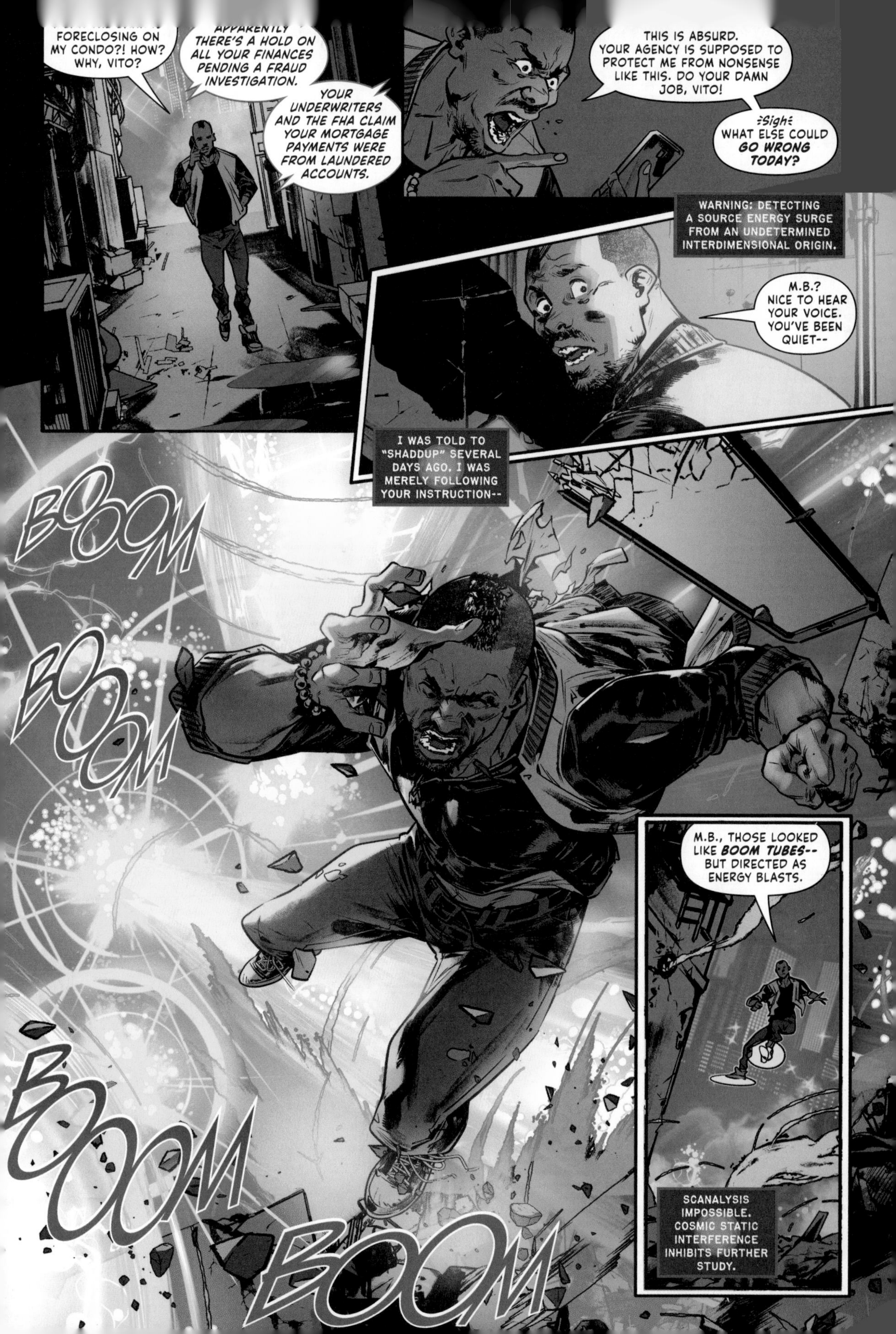
FORECLOSING ON MY CONDO?! HOW? WHY, VITO?
APPARENTLY THERE'S A HOLD ON ALL YOUR FINANCES PENDING A FRAUD INVESTIGATION.
YOUR UNDERWRITERS AND THE FHA CLAIM YOUR MORTGAGE PAYMENTS WERE FROM LAUNDERED ACCOUNTS.
THIS IS ABSURD. YOUR AGENCY IS SUPPOSED TO PROTECT ME FROM NONSENSE LIKE THIS. DO YOUR DAMN JOB, VITO!
Sigh
WHAT ELSE COULD GO WRONG TODAY?
WARNING: DETECTING A SOURCE ENERGY SURGE FROM AN UNDETERMINED INTERDIMENSIONAL ORIGIN.
M.B.? NICE TO HEAR YOUR VOICE. YOU'VE BEEN QUIET--
I WAS TOLD TO "SHADDUP" SEVERAL DAYS AGO. I WAS MERELY FOLLOWING YOUR INSTRUCTION--
BOOOM
BOOOM
BOOOM
BOOM
M.B., THOSE LOOKED LIKE BOOM TUBES--BUT DIRECTED AS ENERGY BLASTS.
SCANALYSIS IMPOSSIBLE. COSMIC STATIC INTERFERENCE INHIBITS FURTHER STUDY.

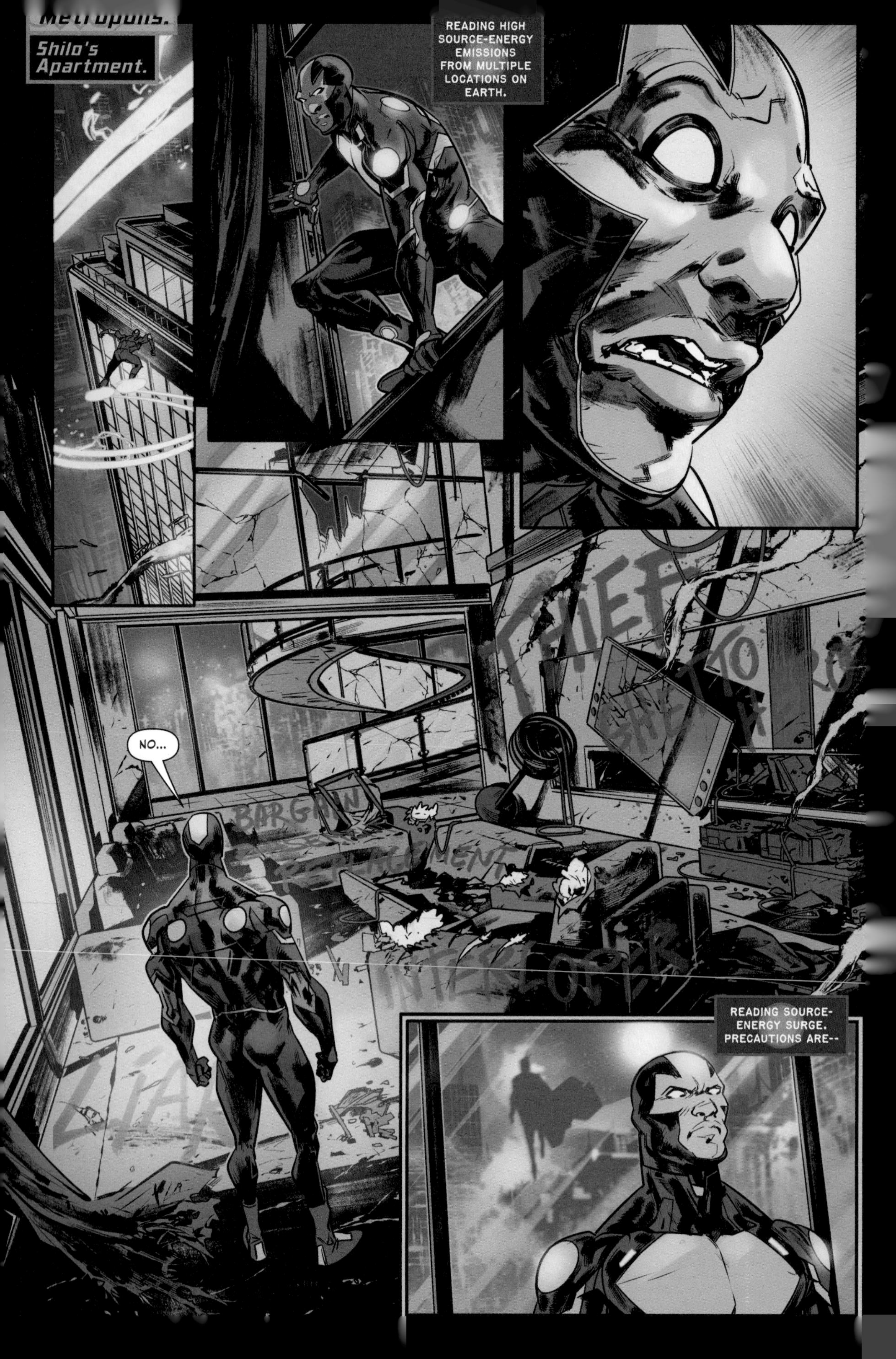
Metropolis.
Shilo's Apartment.
READING HIGH SOURCE-ENERGY EMISSIONS FROM MULTIPLE LOCATIONS ON EARTH.
NO...
READING SOURCE-ENERGY SURGE. PRECAUTIONS ARE--

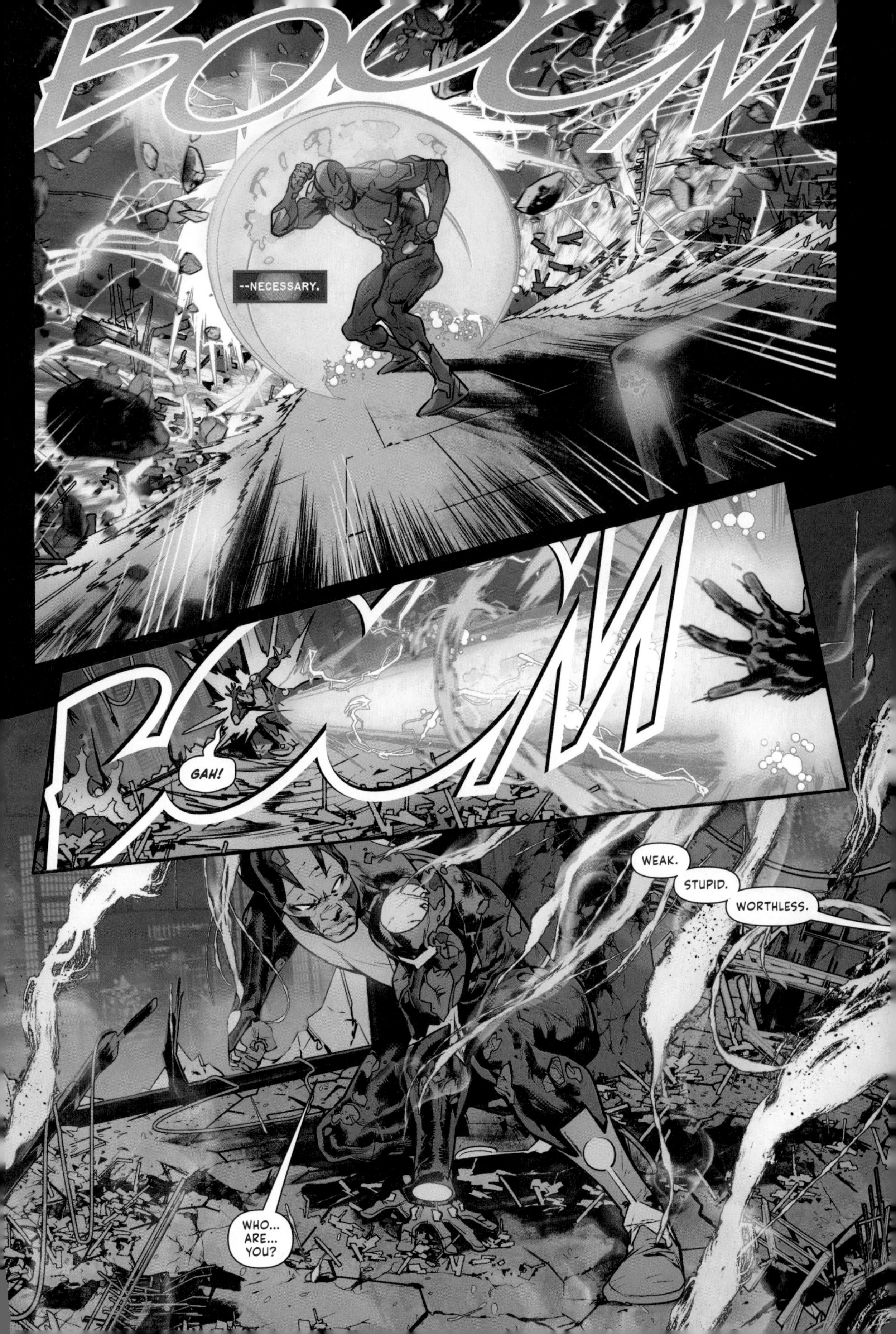
BOOOM
--NECESSARY.
BOOM
GAH!
WEAK.
STUPID.
WORTHLESS.
WHO... ARE... YOU?

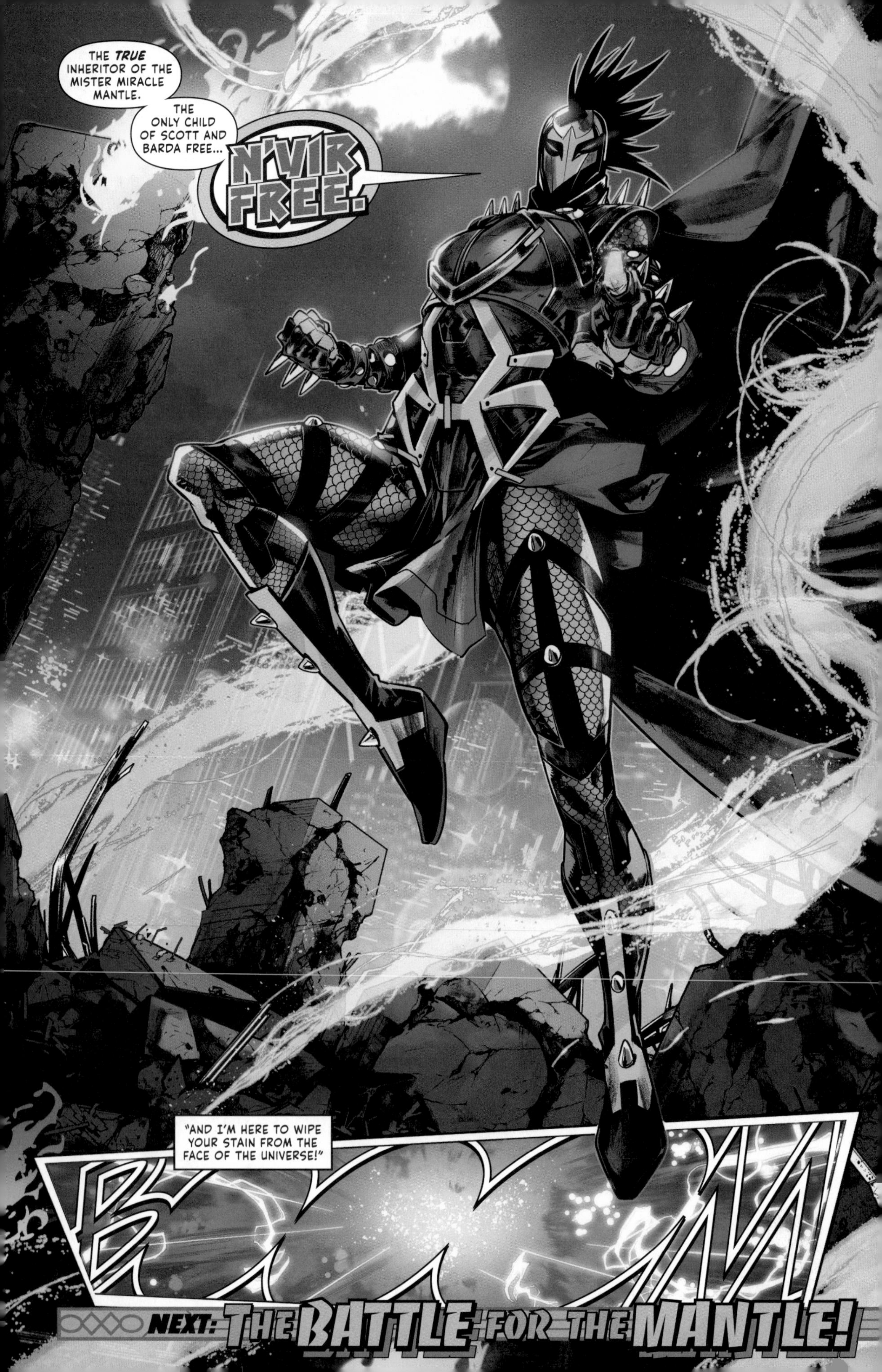
THE *TRUE* INHERITOR OF THE MISTER MIRACLE MANTLE.
THE ONLY CHILD OF SCOTT AND BARDA FREE...
N'VIR FREE.
"AND I'M HERE TO WIPE YOUR STAIN FROM THE FACE OF THE UNIVERSE!"
NEXT: THE BATTLE FOR THE MANTLE!

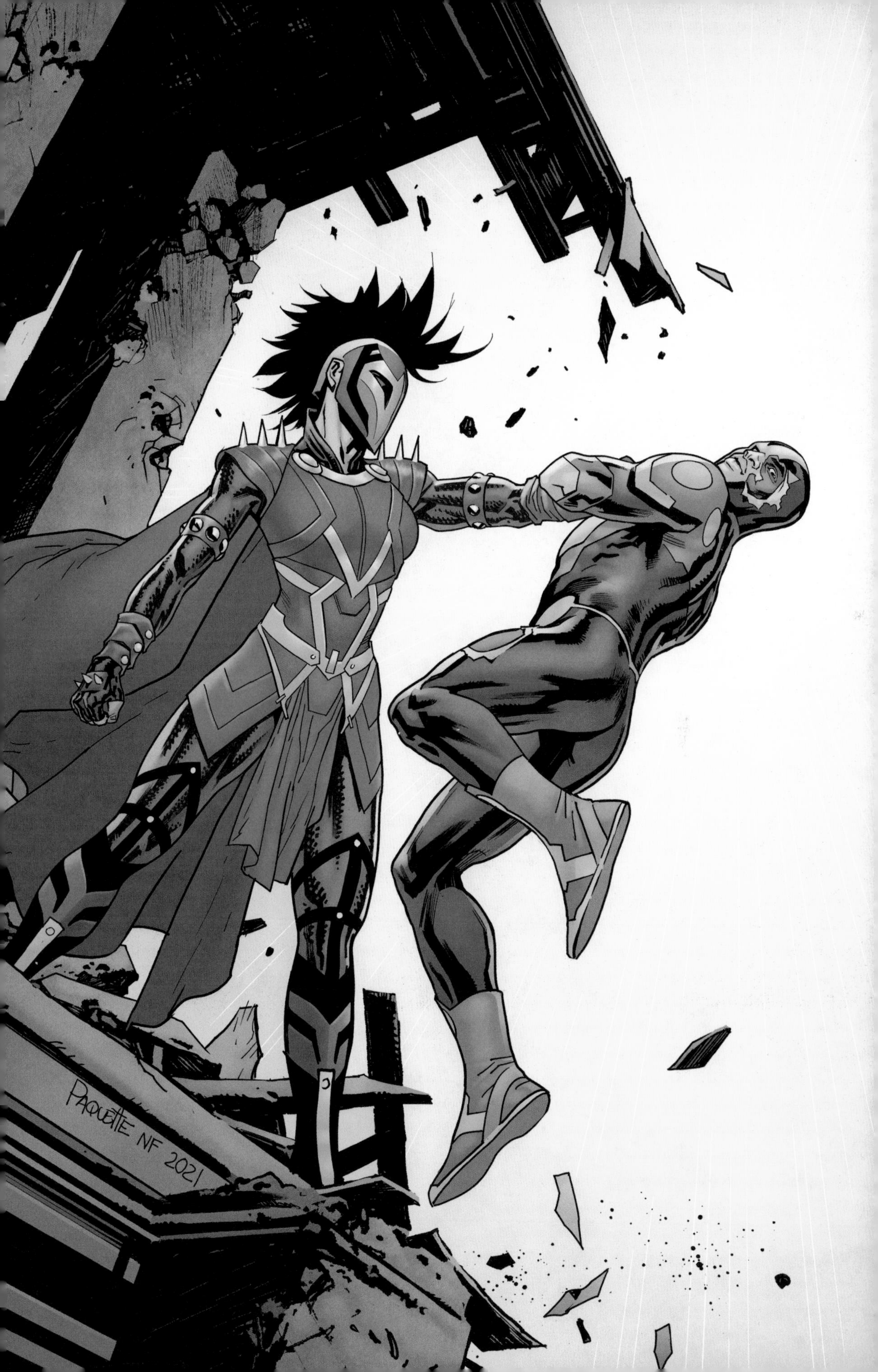
PAQUETTE NF 2021

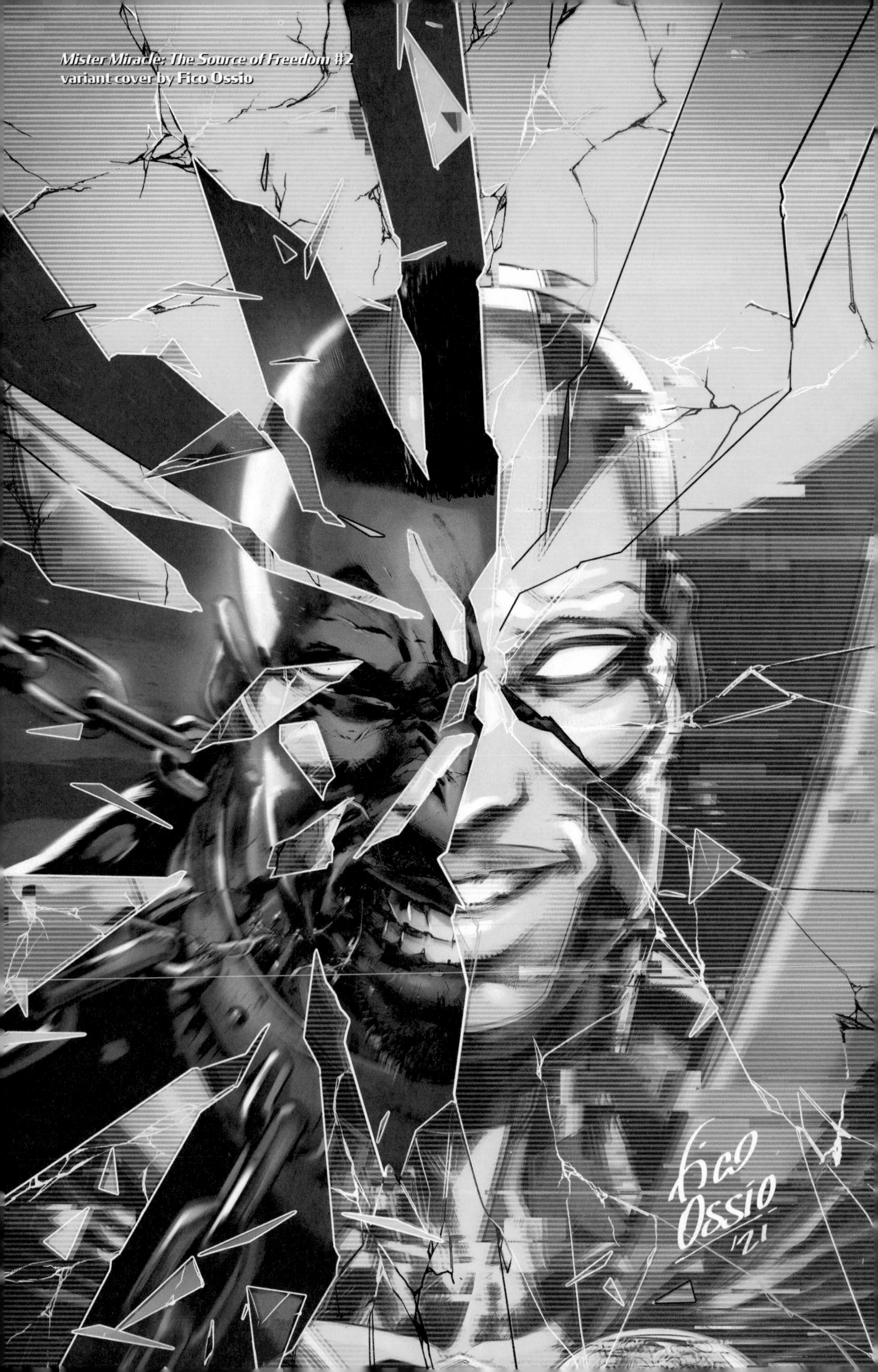

Mister Miracle: The Source of Freedom #2
variant cover by Fico Ossio

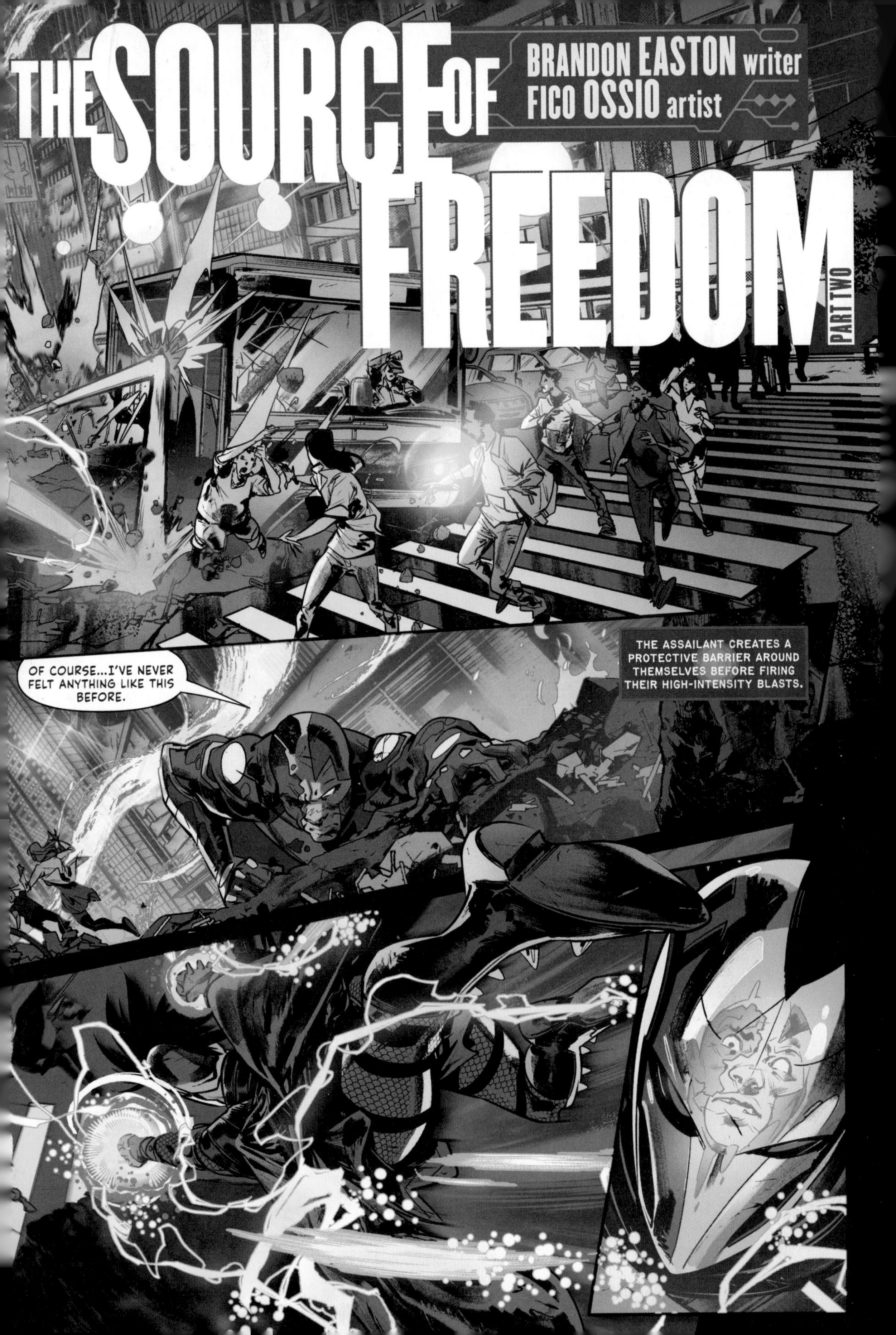
THE SOURCE OF FREEDOM
PART TWO
BRANDON EASTON writer
FICO OSSIO artist
OF COURSE...I'VE NEVER FELT ANYTHING LIKE THIS BEFORE.
THE ASSAILANT CREATES A PROTECTIVE BARRIER AROUND THEMSELVES BEFORE FIRING THEIR HIGH-INTENSITY BLASTS.

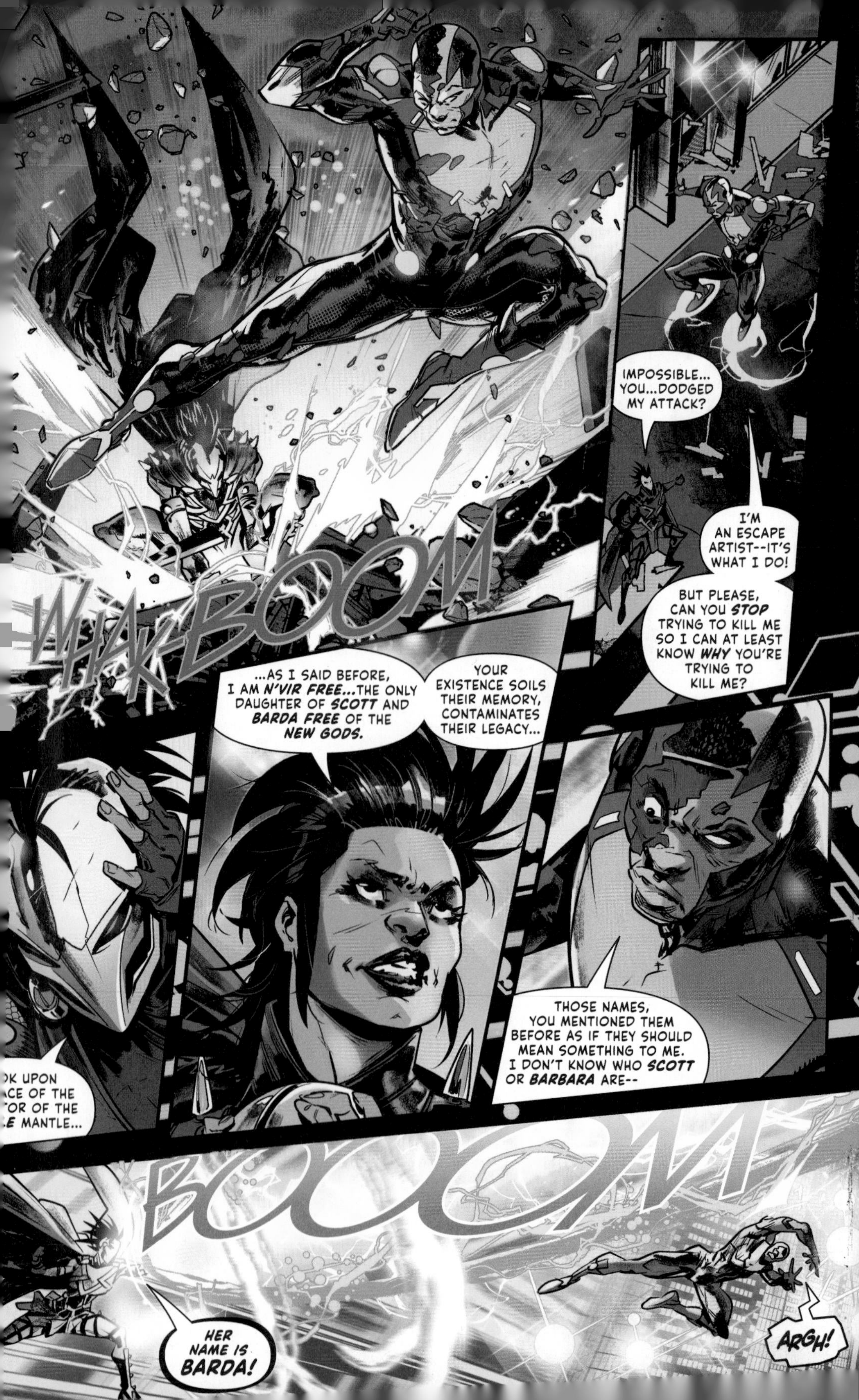
WHAK-BOOM
IMPOSSIBLE... YOU...DODGED MY ATTACK?
I'M AN ESCAPE ARTIST--IT'S WHAT I DO!
BUT PLEASE, CAN YOU STOP TRYING TO KILL ME SO I CAN AT LEAST KNOW WHY YOU'RE TRYING TO KILL ME?
OK UPON
ACE OF THE
TOR OF THE
E MANTLE...
...AS I SAID BEFORE, I AM N'VIR FREE...THE ONLY DAUGHTER OF SCOTT AND BARDA FREE OF THE NEW GODS.
YOUR EXISTENCE SOILS THEIR MEMORY, CONTAMINATES THEIR LEGACY...
THOSE NAMES, YOU MENTIONED THEM BEFORE AS IF THEY SHOULD MEAN SOMETHING TO ME. I DON'T KNOW WHO SCOTT OR BARBARA ARE--
BOOOM
HER NAME IS BARDA!
ARGH!

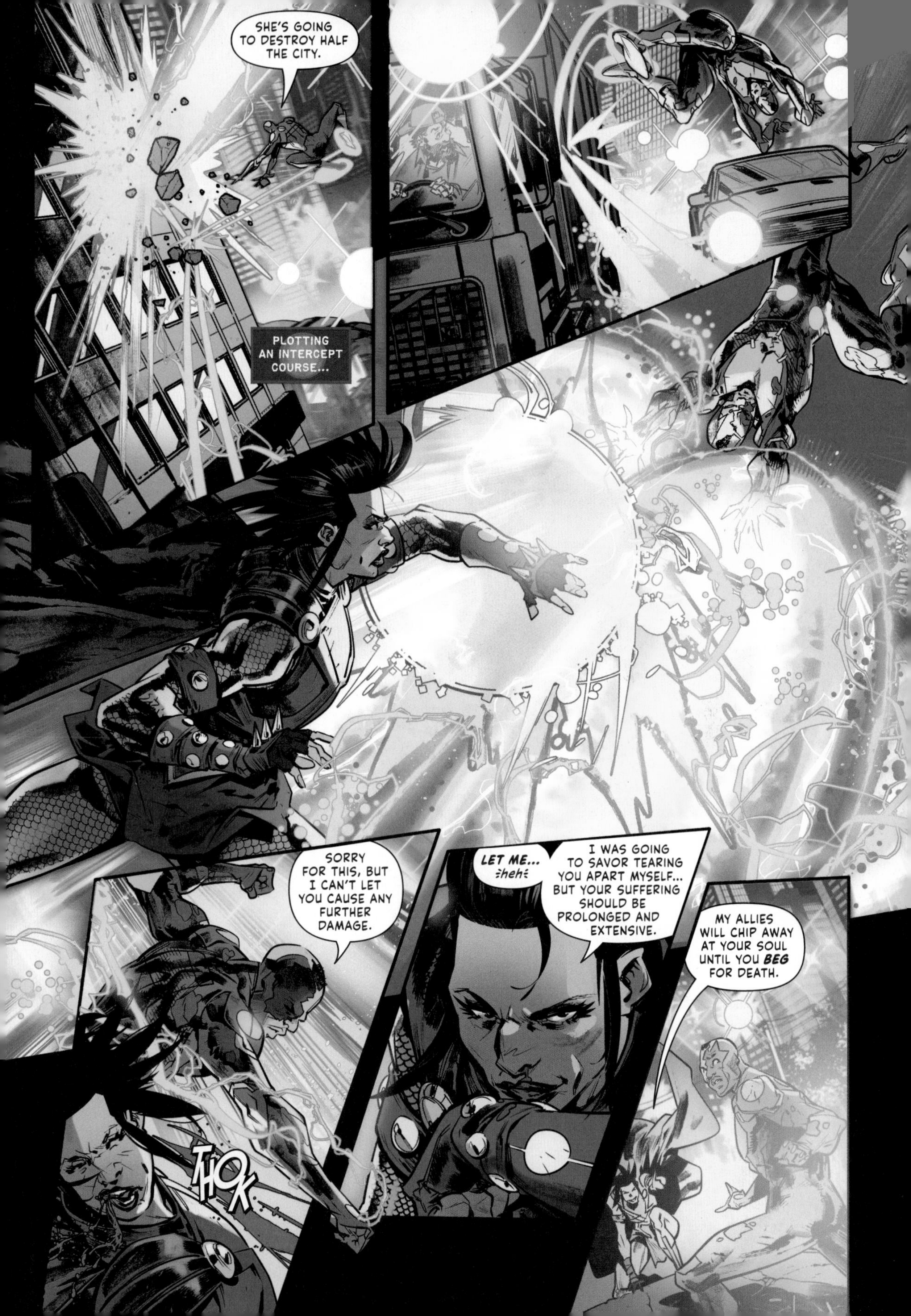

SHE'S GOING TO DESTROY HALF THE CITY.
PLOTTING AN INTERCEPT COURSE...
SORRY FOR THIS, BUT I CAN'T LET YOU CAUSE ANY FURTHER DAMAGE.
THOK
LET ME... *heh*
I WAS GOING TO SAVOR TEARING YOU APART MYSELF... BUT YOUR SUFFERING SHOULD BE PROLONGED AND EXTENSIVE.
MY ALLIES WILL CHIP AWAY AT YOUR SOUL UNTIL YOU *BEG* FOR DEATH.

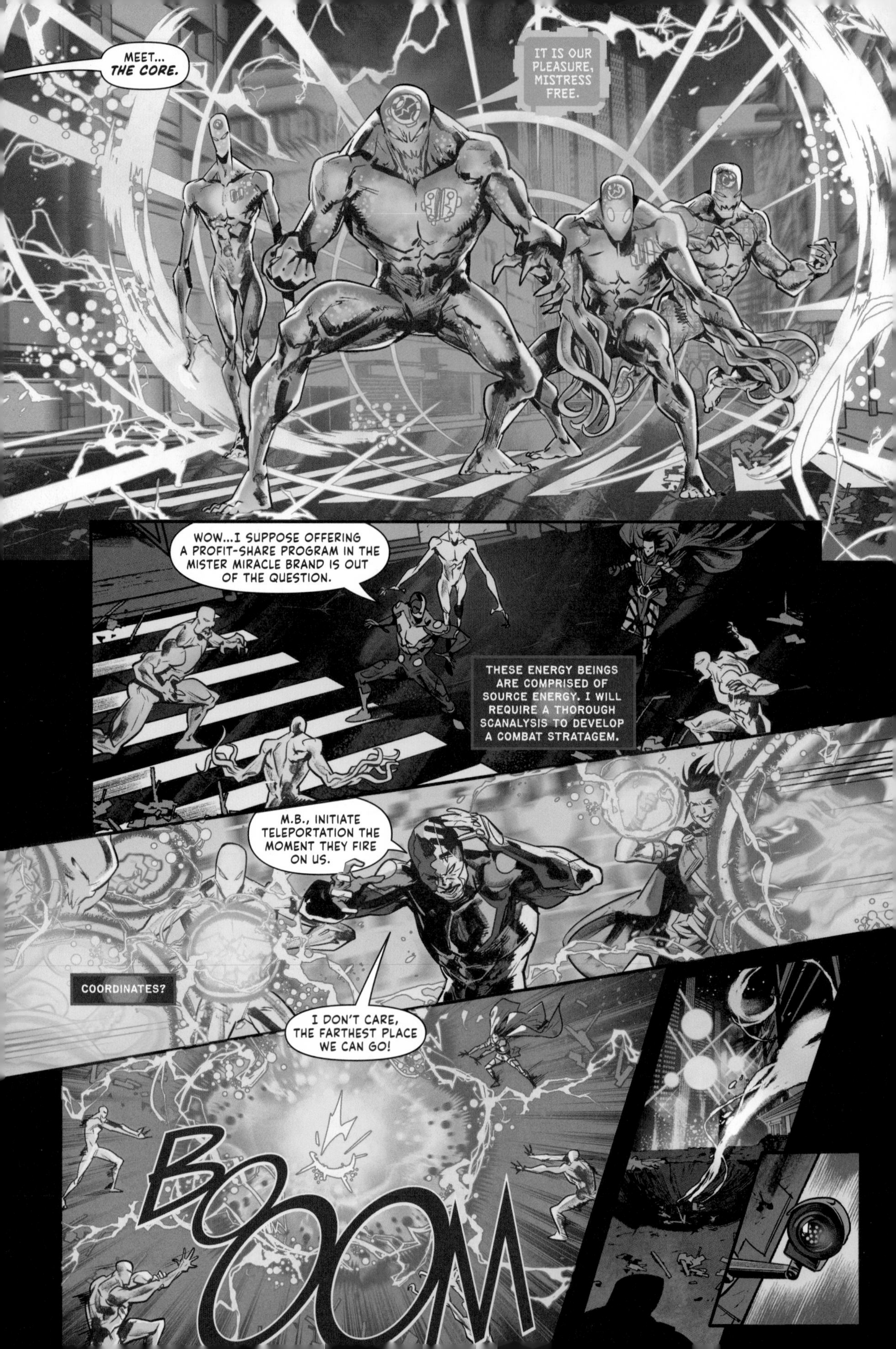
MEET... THE CORE.
IT IS OUR PLEASURE, MISTRESS FREE.
WOW...I SUPPOSE OFFERING A PROFIT-SHARE PROGRAM IN THE MISTER MIRACLE BRAND IS OUT OF THE QUESTION.
THESE ENERGY BEINGS ARE COMPRISED OF SOURCE ENERGY. I WILL REQUIRE A THOROUGH SCANALYSIS TO DEVELOP A COMBAT STRATAGEM.
M.B., INITIATE TELEPORTATION THE MOMENT THEY FIRE ON US.
COORDINATES?
I DON'T CARE, THE FARTHEST PLACE WE CAN GO!
BOOOM

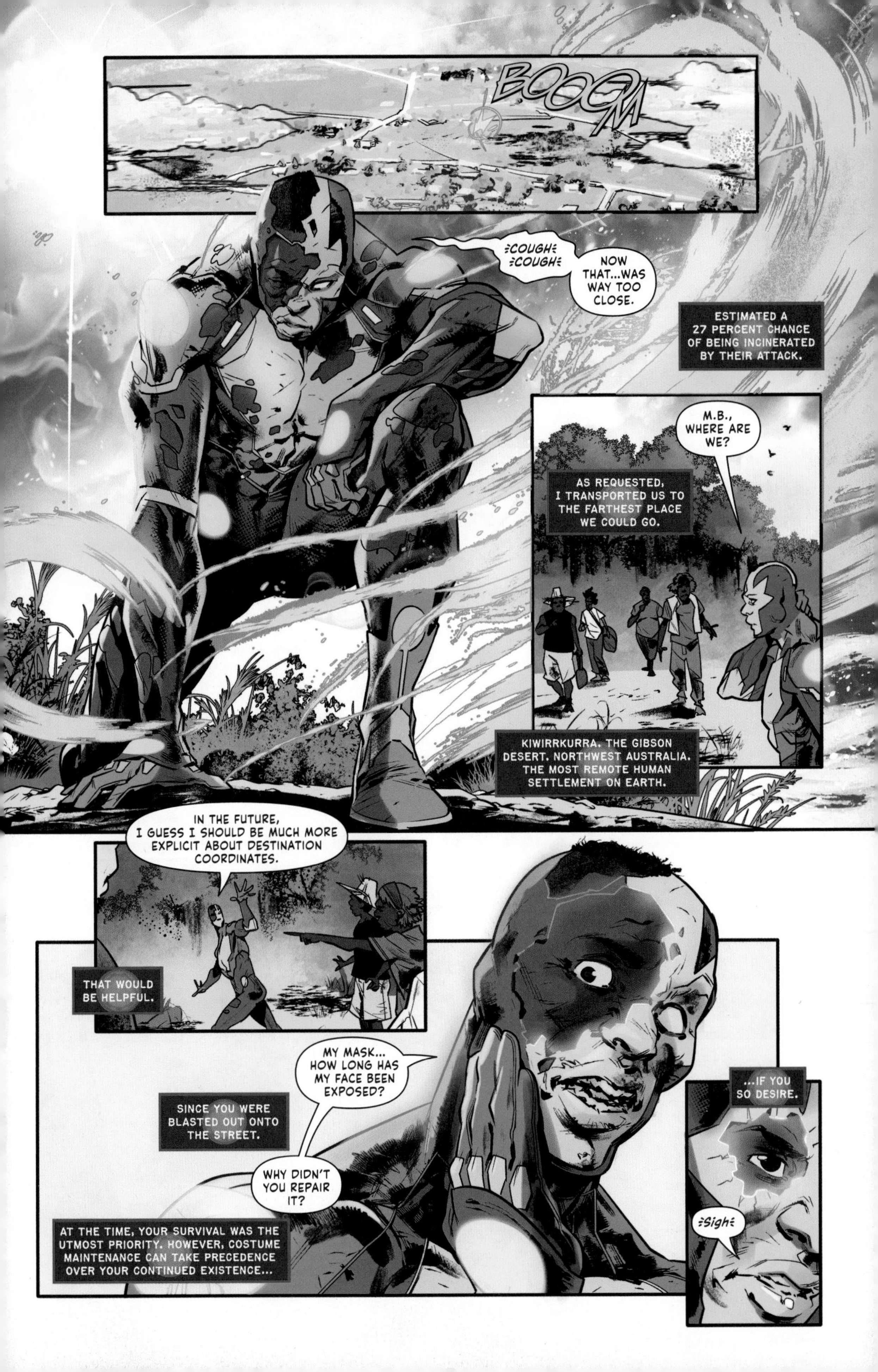
BOOOM
COUGH COUGH
NOW THAT...WAS WAY TOO CLOSE.
ESTIMATED A 27 PERCENT CHANCE OF BEING INCINERATED BY THEIR ATTACK.
M.B., WHERE ARE WE?
AS REQUESTED, I TRANSPORTED US TO THE FARTHEST PLACE WE COULD GO.
KIWIRRKURRA. THE GIBSON DESERT. NORTHWEST AUSTRALIA. THE MOST REMOTE HUMAN SETTLEMENT ON EARTH.
IN THE FUTURE, I GUESS I SHOULD BE MUCH MORE EXPLICIT ABOUT DESTINATION COORDINATES.
THAT WOULD BE HELPFUL.
MY MASK... HOW LONG HAS MY FACE BEEN EXPOSED?
SINCE YOU WERE BLASTED OUT ONTO THE STREET.
WHY DIDN'T YOU REPAIR IT?
AT THE TIME, YOUR SURVIVAL WAS THE UTMOST PRIORITY. HOWEVER, COSTUME MAINTENANCE CAN TAKE PRECEDENCE OVER YOUR CONTINUED EXISTENCE...
...IF YOU SO DESIRE.
Sigh

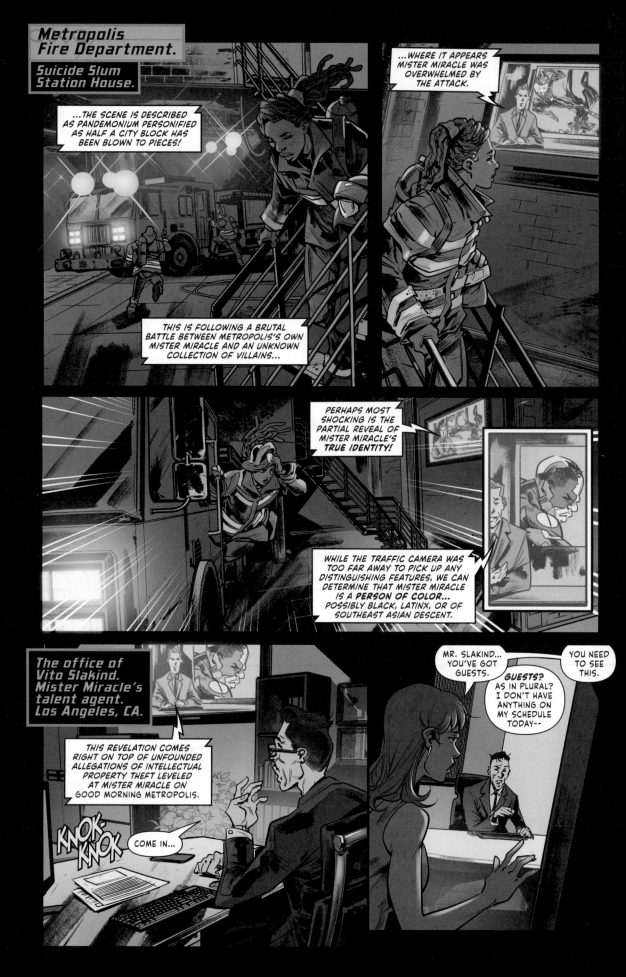

Metropolis Fire Department.

Suicide Slum Station House.

...THE SCENE IS DESCRIBED AS PANDEMONIUM PERSONIFIED AS HALF A CITY BLOCK HAS BEEN BLOWN TO PIECES!

THIS IS FOLLOWING A BRUTAL BATTLE BETWEEN METROPOLIS'S OWN MISTER MIRACLE AND AN UNKNOWN COLLECTION OF VILLAINS...

...WHERE IT APPEARS MISTER MIRACLE WAS OVERWHELMED BY THE ATTACK.

PERHAPS MOST SHOCKING IS THE PARTIAL REVEAL OF MISTER MIRACLE'S TRUE IDENTITY!

WHILE THE TRAFFIC CAMERA WAS TOO FAR AWAY TO PICK UP ANY DISTINGUISHING FEATURES, WE CAN DETERMINE THAT MISTER MIRACLE IS A PERSON OF COLOR... POSSIBLY BLACK, LATINX, OR OF SOUTHEAST ASIAN DESCENT.

The office of Vito Slakind. Mister Miracle's talent agent. Los Angeles, CA.

THIS REVELATION COMES RIGHT ON TOP OF UNFOUNDED ALLEGATIONS OF INTELLECTUAL PROPERTY THEFT LEVELED AT MISTER MIRACLE ON GOOD MORNING METROPOLIS.

KNOK-KNOK

COME IN...

MR. SLAKIND... YOU'VE GOT GUESTS.

YOU NEED TO SEE THIS.

GUESTS? AS IN PLURAL? I DON'T HAVE ANYTHING ON MY SCHEDULE TODAY--

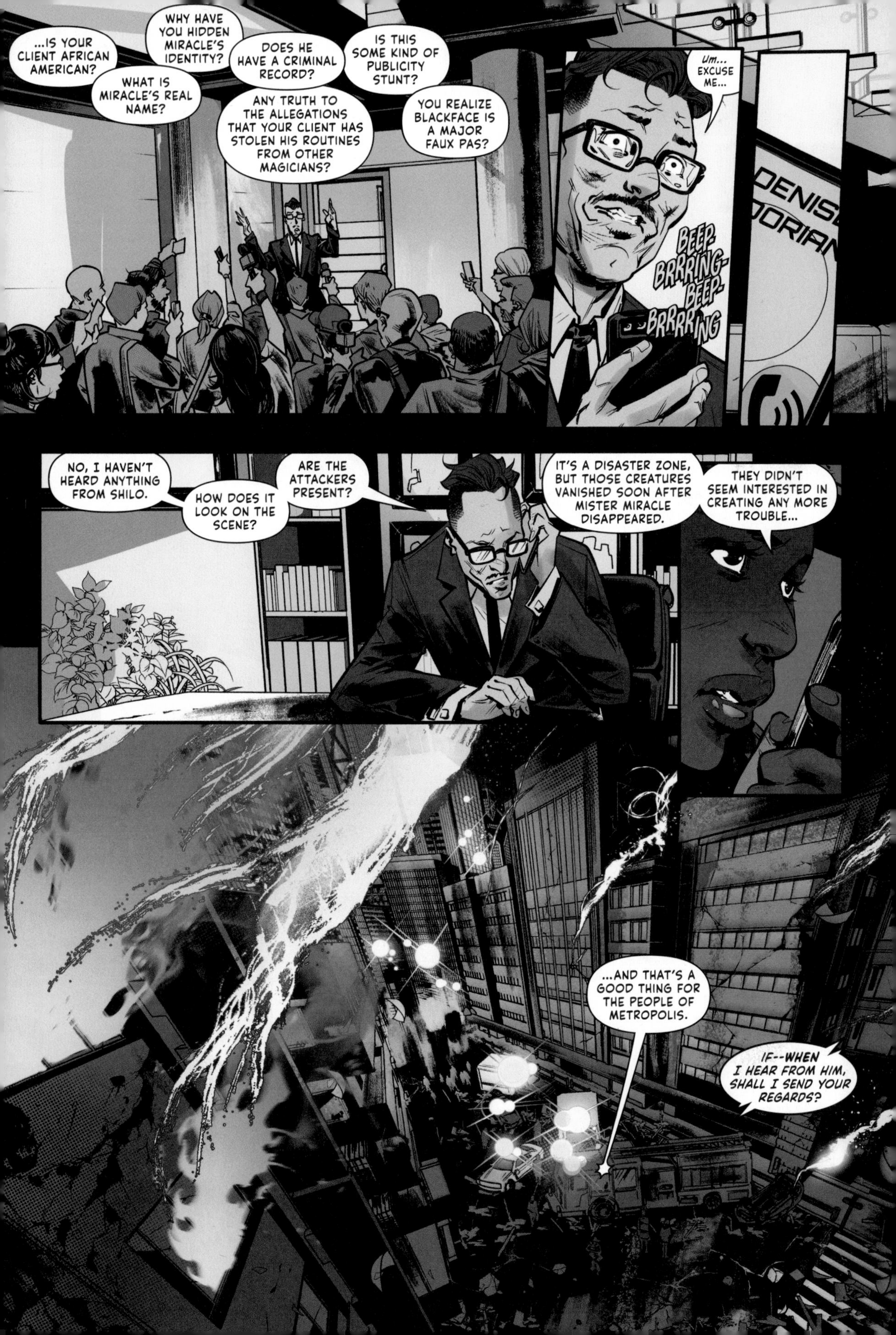
...IS YOUR CLIENT AFRICAN AMERICAN?
WHY HAVE YOU HIDDEN MIRACLE'S IDENTITY?
WHAT IS MIRACLE'S REAL NAME?
DOES HE HAVE A CRIMINAL RECORD?
ANY TRUTH TO THE ALLEGATIONS THAT YOUR CLIENT HAS STOLEN HIS ROUTINES FROM OTHER MAGICIANS?
IS THIS SOME KIND OF PUBLICITY STUNT?
YOU REALIZE BLACKFACE IS A MAJOR FAUX PAS?
Um... EXCUSE ME...
BEEP-BRRRING-BEEP-BRRRRING
DENISE DORIAN
NO, I HAVEN'T HEARD ANYTHING FROM SHILO.
HOW DOES IT LOOK ON THE SCENE?
ARE THE ATTACKERS PRESENT?
IT'S A DISASTER ZONE, BUT THOSE CREATURES VANISHED SOON AFTER MISTER MIRACLE DISAPPEARED.
THEY DIDN'T SEEM INTERESTED IN CREATING ANY MORE TROUBLE...
...AND THAT'S A GOOD THING FOR THE PEOPLE OF METROPOLIS.
IF--WHEN I HEAR FROM HIM, SHALL I SEND YOUR REGARDS?

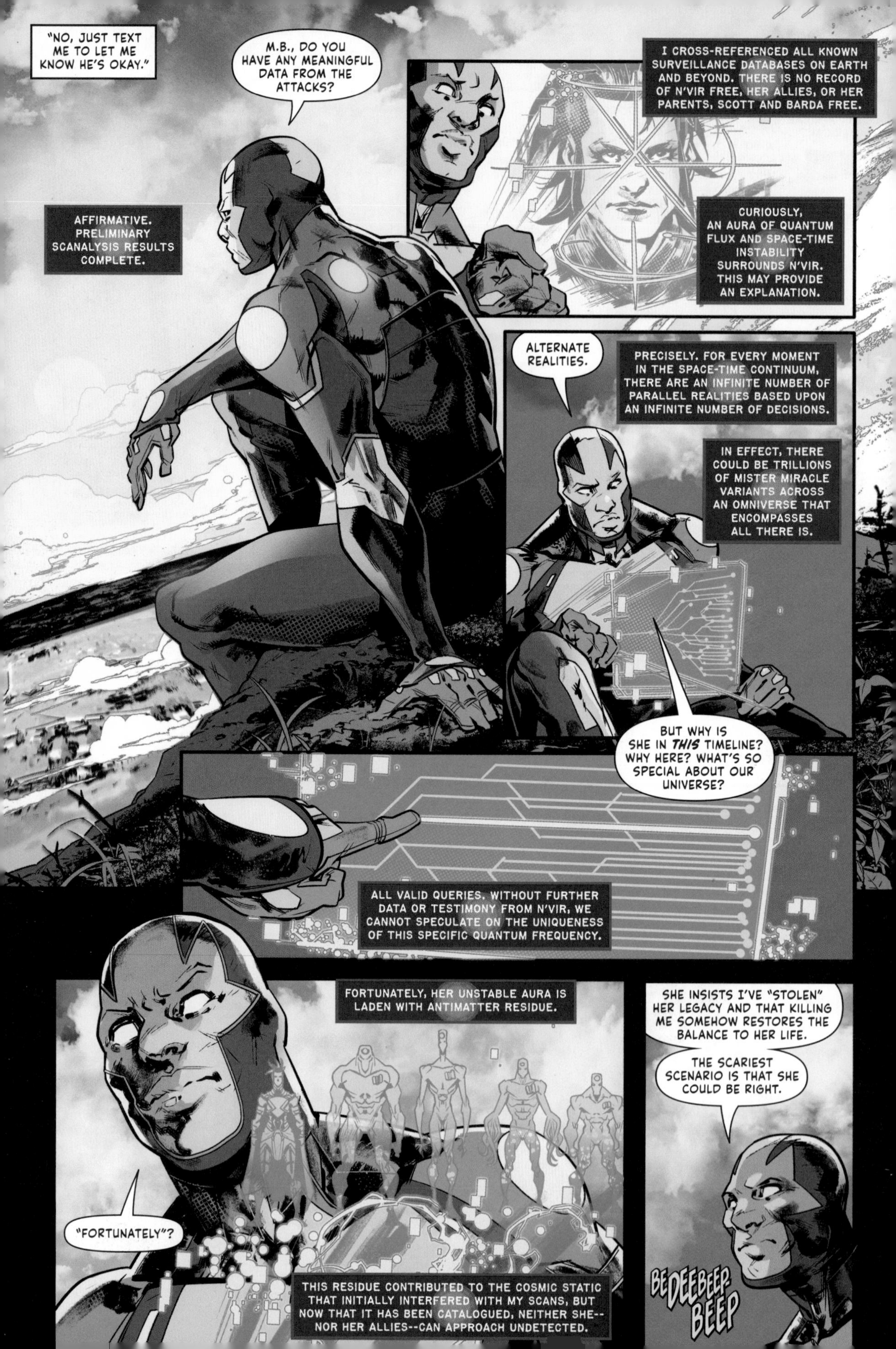
"NO, JUST TEXT ME TO LET ME KNOW HE'S OKAY."
M.B., DO YOU HAVE ANY MEANINGFUL DATA FROM THE ATTACKS?
AFFIRMATIVE. PRELIMINARY SCANALYSIS RESULTS COMPLETE.
I CROSS-REFERENCED ALL KNOWN SURVEILLANCE DATABASES ON EARTH AND BEYOND. THERE IS NO RECORD OF N'VIR FREE, HER ALLIES, OR HER PARENTS, SCOTT AND BARDA FREE.
CURIOUSLY, AN AURA OF QUANTUM FLUX AND SPACE-TIME INSTABILITY SURROUNDS N'VIR. THIS MAY PROVIDE AN EXPLANATION.
ALTERNATE REALITIES.
PRECISELY. FOR EVERY MOMENT IN THE SPACE-TIME CONTINUUM, THERE ARE AN INFINITE NUMBER OF PARALLEL REALITIES BASED UPON AN INFINITE NUMBER OF DECISIONS.
IN EFFECT, THERE COULD BE TRILLIONS OF MISTER MIRACLE VARIANTS ACROSS AN OMNIVERSE THAT ENCOMPASSES ALL THERE IS.
BUT WHY IS SHE IN *THIS* TIMELINE? WHY HERE? WHAT'S SO SPECIAL ABOUT OUR UNIVERSE?
ALL VALID QUERIES. WITHOUT FURTHER DATA OR TESTIMONY FROM N'VIR, WE CANNOT SPECULATE ON THE UNIQUENESS OF THIS SPECIFIC QUANTUM FREQUENCY.
FORTUNATELY, HER UNSTABLE AURA IS LADEN WITH ANTIMATTER RESIDUE.
"FORTUNATELY"?
THIS RESIDUE CONTRIBUTED TO THE COSMIC STATIC THAT INITIALLY INTERFERED WITH MY SCANS, BUT NOW THAT IT HAS BEEN CATALOGUED, NEITHER SHE--NOR HER ALLIES--CAN APPROACH UNDETECTED.
SHE INSISTS I'VE "STOLEN" HER LEGACY AND THAT KILLING ME SOMEHOW RESTORES THE BALANCE TO HER LIFE.
THE SCARIEST SCENARIO IS THAT SHE COULD BE RIGHT.
BEDEEBEEP BEEP

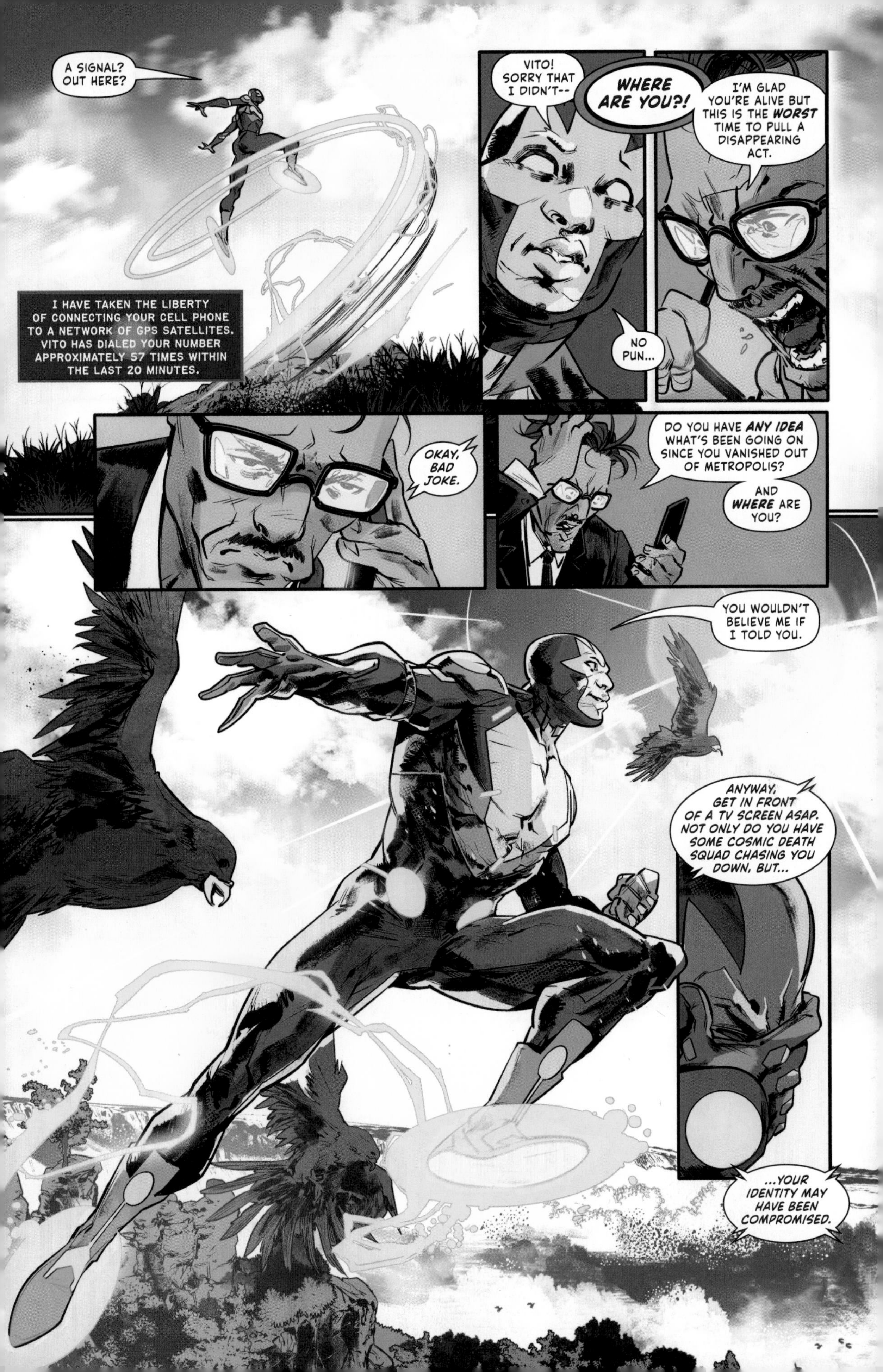
A SIGNAL? OUT HERE?
I HAVE TAKEN THE LIBERTY OF CONNECTING YOUR CELL PHONE TO A NETWORK OF GPS SATELLITES. VITO HAS DIALED YOUR NUMBER APPROXIMATELY 57 TIMES WITHIN THE LAST 20 MINUTES.
VITO! SORRY THAT I DIDN'T--
WHERE ARE YOU?!
I'M GLAD YOU'RE ALIVE BUT THIS IS THE WORST TIME TO PULL A DISAPPEARING ACT.
NO PUN...
OKAY, BAD JOKE.
DO YOU HAVE ANY IDEA WHAT'S BEEN GOING ON SINCE YOU VANISHED OUT OF METROPOLIS?
AND WHERE ARE YOU?
YOU WOULDN'T BELIEVE ME IF I TOLD YOU.
ANYWAY, GET IN FRONT OF A TV SCREEN ASAP. NOT ONLY DO YOU HAVE SOME COSMIC DEATH SQUAD CHASING YOU DOWN, BUT...
...YOUR IDENTITY MAY HAVE BEEN COMPROMISED.

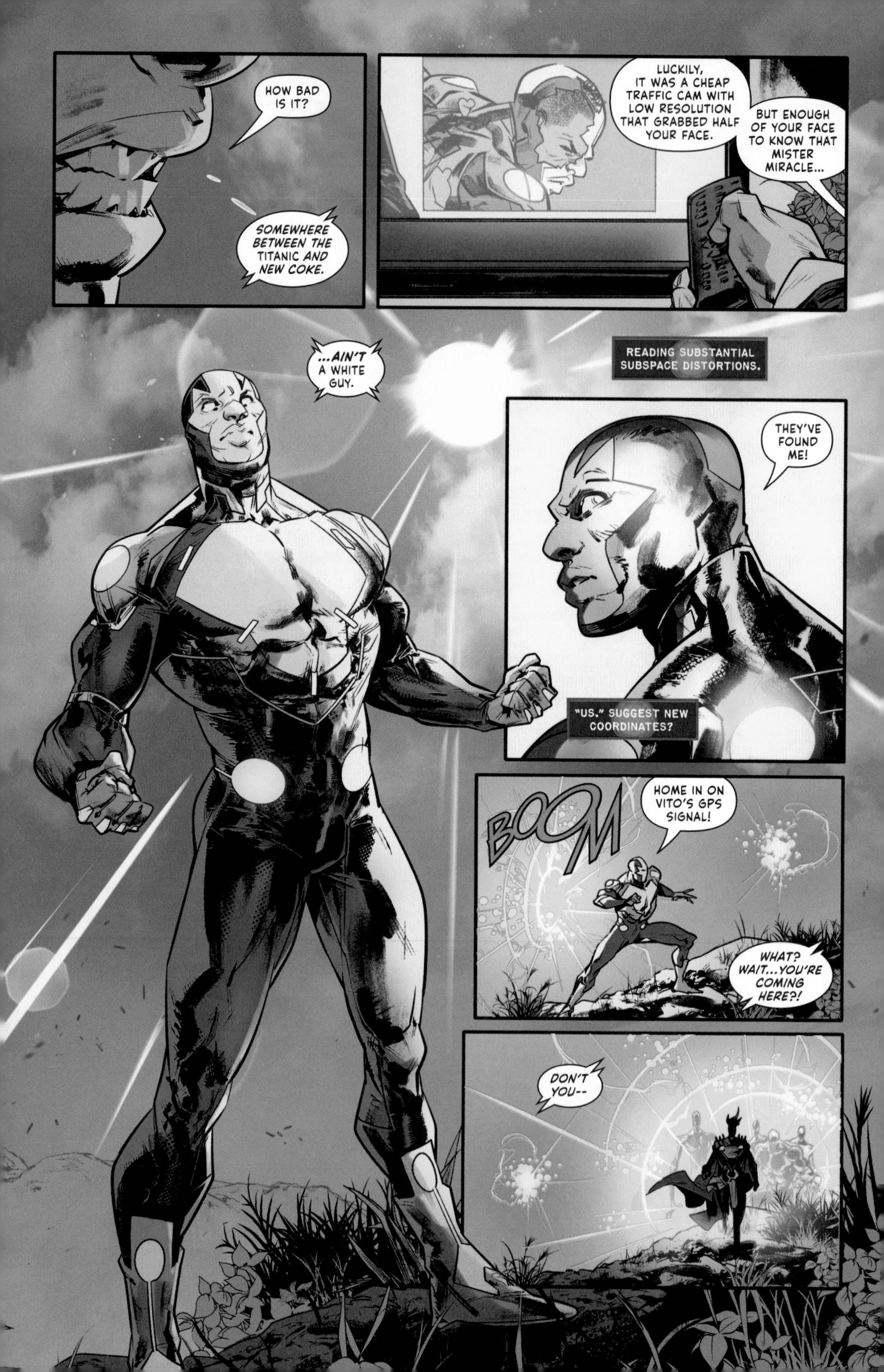
HOW BAD IS IT?
SOMEWHERE BETWEEN THE TITANIC AND NEW COKE.
LUCKILY, IT WAS A CHEAP TRAFFIC CAM WITH LOW RESOLUTION THAT GRABBED HALF YOUR FACE.
BUT ENOUGH OF YOUR FACE TO KNOW THAT MISTER MIRACLE...
...AIN'T A WHITE GUY.
READING SUBSTANTIAL SUBSPACE DISTORTIONS.
THEY'VE FOUND ME!
"US." SUGGEST NEW COORDINATES?
BOOM
HOME IN ON VITO'S GPS SIGNAL!
WHAT? WAIT...YOU'RE COMING HERE?!
DON'T YOU--

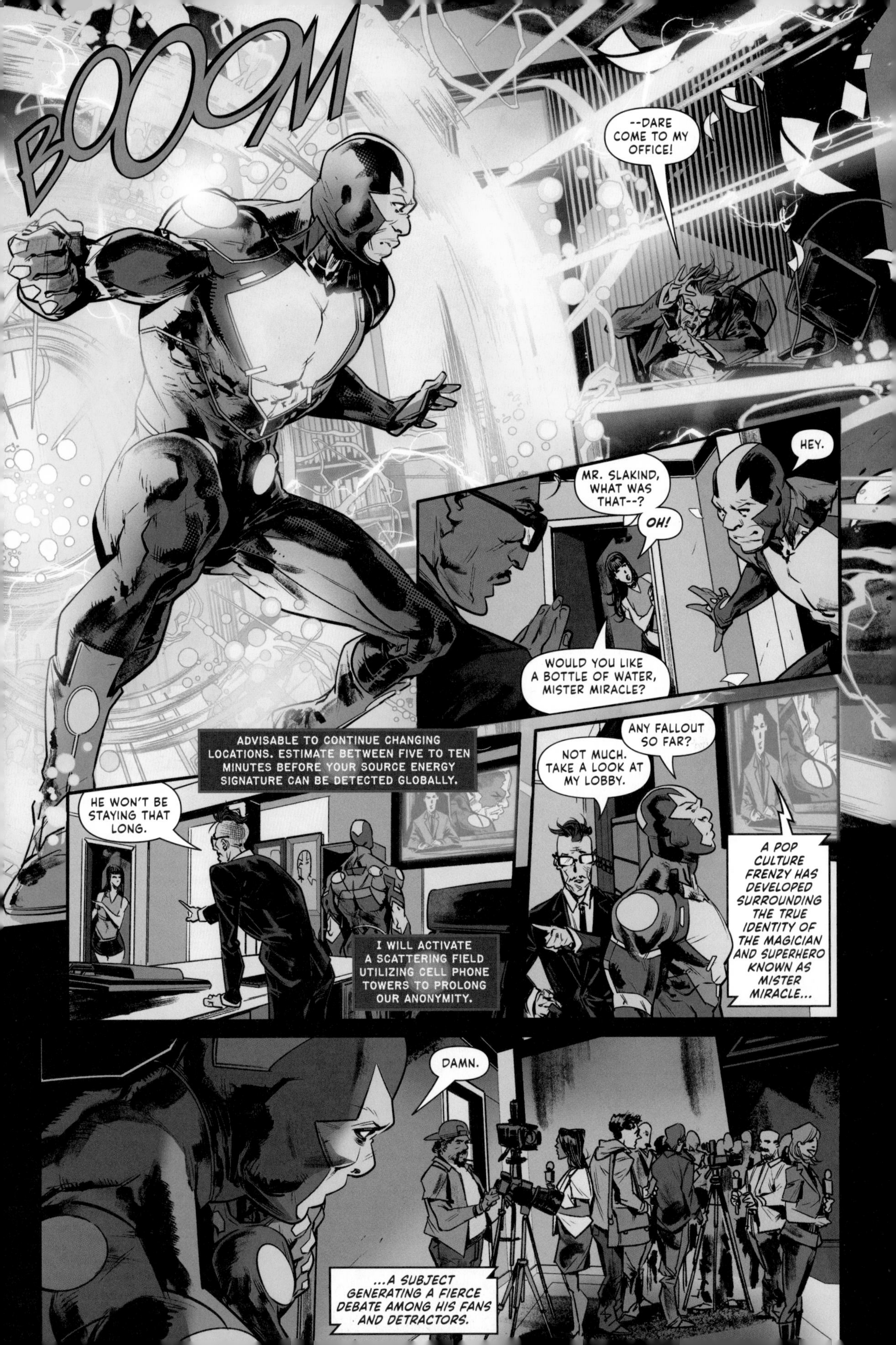
BOOOM
--DARE COME TO MY OFFICE!
MR. SLAKIND, WHAT WAS THAT--?
OH!
HEY.
WOULD YOU LIKE A BOTTLE OF WATER, MISTER MIRACLE?
ADVISABLE TO CONTINUE CHANGING LOCATIONS. ESTIMATE BETWEEN FIVE TO TEN MINUTES BEFORE YOUR SOURCE ENERGY SIGNATURE CAN BE DETECTED GLOBALLY.
HE WON'T BE STAYING THAT LONG.
I WILL ACTIVATE A SCATTERING FIELD UTILIZING CELL PHONE TOWERS TO PROLONG OUR ANONYMITY.
ANY FALLOUT SO FAR?
NOT MUCH. TAKE A LOOK AT MY LOBBY.
A POP CULTURE FRENZY HAS DEVELOPED SURROUNDING THE TRUE IDENTITY OF THE MAGICIAN AND SUPERHERO KNOWN AS MISTER MIRACLE...
DAMN.
...A SUBJECT GENERATING A FIERCE DEBATE AMONG HIS FANS AND DETRACTORS.

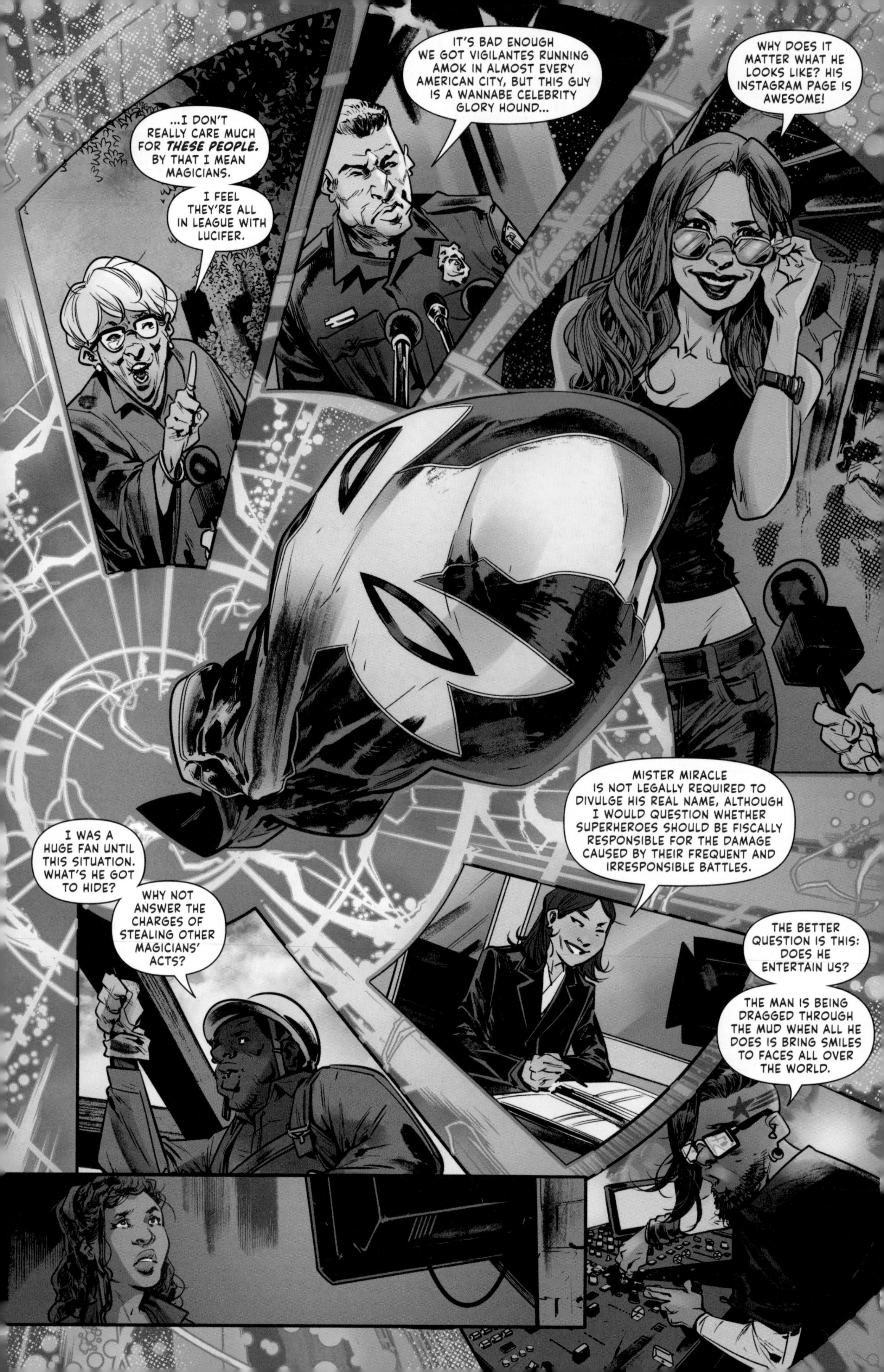
...I DON'T REALLY CARE MUCH FOR *THESE PEOPLE.* BY THAT I MEAN MAGICIANS.
I FEEL THEY'RE ALL IN LEAGUE WITH LUCIFER.
IT'S BAD ENOUGH WE GOT VIGILANTES RUNNING AMOK IN ALMOST EVERY AMERICAN CITY, BUT THIS GUY IS A WANNABE CELEBRITY GLORY HOUND...
WHY DOES IT MATTER WHAT HE LOOKS LIKE? HIS INSTAGRAM PAGE IS AWESOME!
I WAS A HUGE FAN UNTIL THIS SITUATION. WHAT'S HE GOT TO HIDE?
WHY NOT ANSWER THE CHARGES OF STEALING OTHER MAGICIANS' ACTS?
MISTER MIRACLE IS NOT LEGALLY REQUIRED TO DIVULGE HIS REAL NAME, ALTHOUGH I WOULD QUESTION WHETHER SUPERHEROES SHOULD BE FISCALLY RESPONSIBLE FOR THE DAMAGE CAUSED BY THEIR FREQUENT AND IRRESPONSIBLE BATTLES.
THE BETTER QUESTION IS THIS: DOES HE ENTERTAIN US?
THE MAN IS BEING DRAGGED THROUGH THE MUD WHEN ALL HE DOES IS BRING SMILES TO FACES ALL OVER THE WORLD.

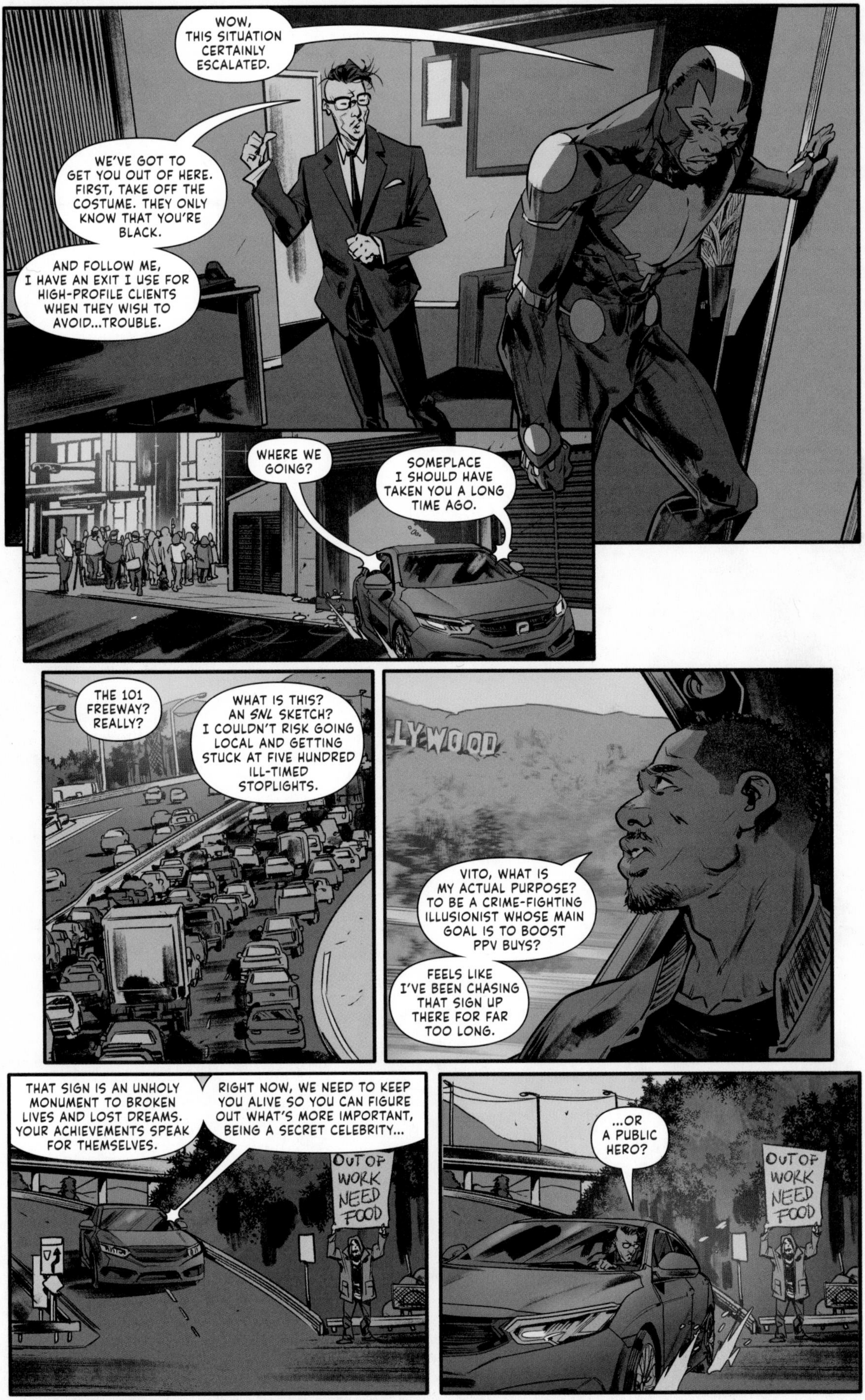
WOW, THIS SITUATION CERTAINLY ESCALATED.
WE'VE GOT TO GET YOU OUT OF HERE. FIRST, TAKE OFF THE COSTUME. THEY ONLY KNOW THAT YOU'RE BLACK.
AND FOLLOW ME, I HAVE AN EXIT I USE FOR HIGH-PROFILE CLIENTS WHEN THEY WISH TO AVOID...TROUBLE.
WHERE WE GOING?
SOMEPLACE I SHOULD HAVE TAKEN YOU A LONG TIME AGO.
THE 101 FREEWAY? REALLY?
WHAT IS THIS? AN *SNL* SKETCH? I COULDN'T RISK GOING LOCAL AND GETTING STUCK AT FIVE HUNDRED ILL-TIMED STOPLIGHTS.
LYWOOD
VITO, WHAT IS MY ACTUAL PURPOSE? TO BE A CRIME-FIGHTING ILLUSIONIST WHOSE MAIN GOAL IS TO BOOST PPV BUYS?
FEELS LIKE I'VE BEEN CHASING THAT SIGN UP THERE FOR FAR TOO LONG.
THAT SIGN IS AN UNHOLY MONUMENT TO BROKEN LIVES AND LOST DREAMS. YOUR ACHIEVEMENTS SPEAK FOR THEMSELVES.
RIGHT NOW, WE NEED TO KEEP YOU ALIVE SO YOU CAN FIGURE OUT WHAT'S MORE IMPORTANT, BEING A SECRET CELEBRITY...
OUT OF WORK NEED FOOD
...OR A PUBLIC HERO?
OUT OF WORK NEED FOOD

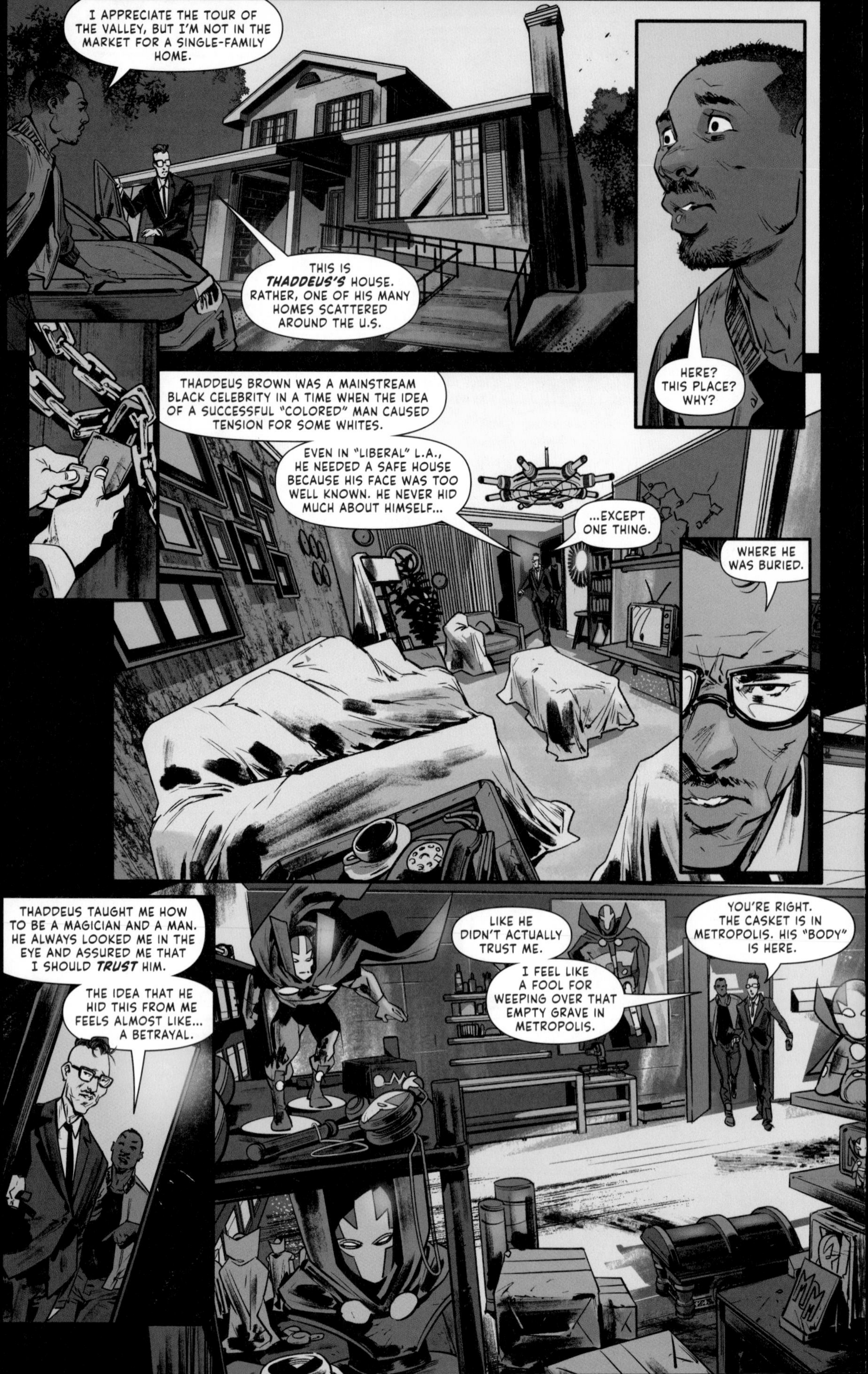
I APPRECIATE THE TOUR OF THE VALLEY, BUT I'M NOT IN THE MARKET FOR A SINGLE-FAMILY HOME.
THIS IS *THADDEUS'S* HOUSE. RATHER, ONE OF HIS MANY HOMES SCATTERED AROUND THE U.S.
HERE? THIS PLACE? WHY?
THADDEUS BROWN WAS A MAINSTREAM BLACK CELEBRITY IN A TIME WHEN THE IDEA OF A SUCCESSFUL "COLORED" MAN CAUSED TENSION FOR SOME WHITES.
EVEN IN "LIBERAL" L.A., HE NEEDED A SAFE HOUSE BECAUSE HIS FACE WAS TOO WELL KNOWN. HE NEVER HID MUCH ABOUT HIMSELF...
...EXCEPT ONE THING.
WHERE HE WAS BURIED.
THADDEUS TAUGHT ME HOW TO BE A MAGICIAN AND A MAN. HE ALWAYS LOOKED ME IN THE EYE AND ASSURED ME THAT I SHOULD *TRUST* HIM.
THE IDEA THAT HE HID THIS FROM ME FEELS ALMOST LIKE... A BETRAYAL.
LIKE HE DIDN'T ACTUALLY TRUST ME.
I FEEL LIKE A FOOL FOR WEEPING OVER THAT EMPTY GRAVE IN METROPOLIS.
YOU'RE RIGHT. THE CASKET IS IN METROPOLIS. HIS "BODY" IS HERE.

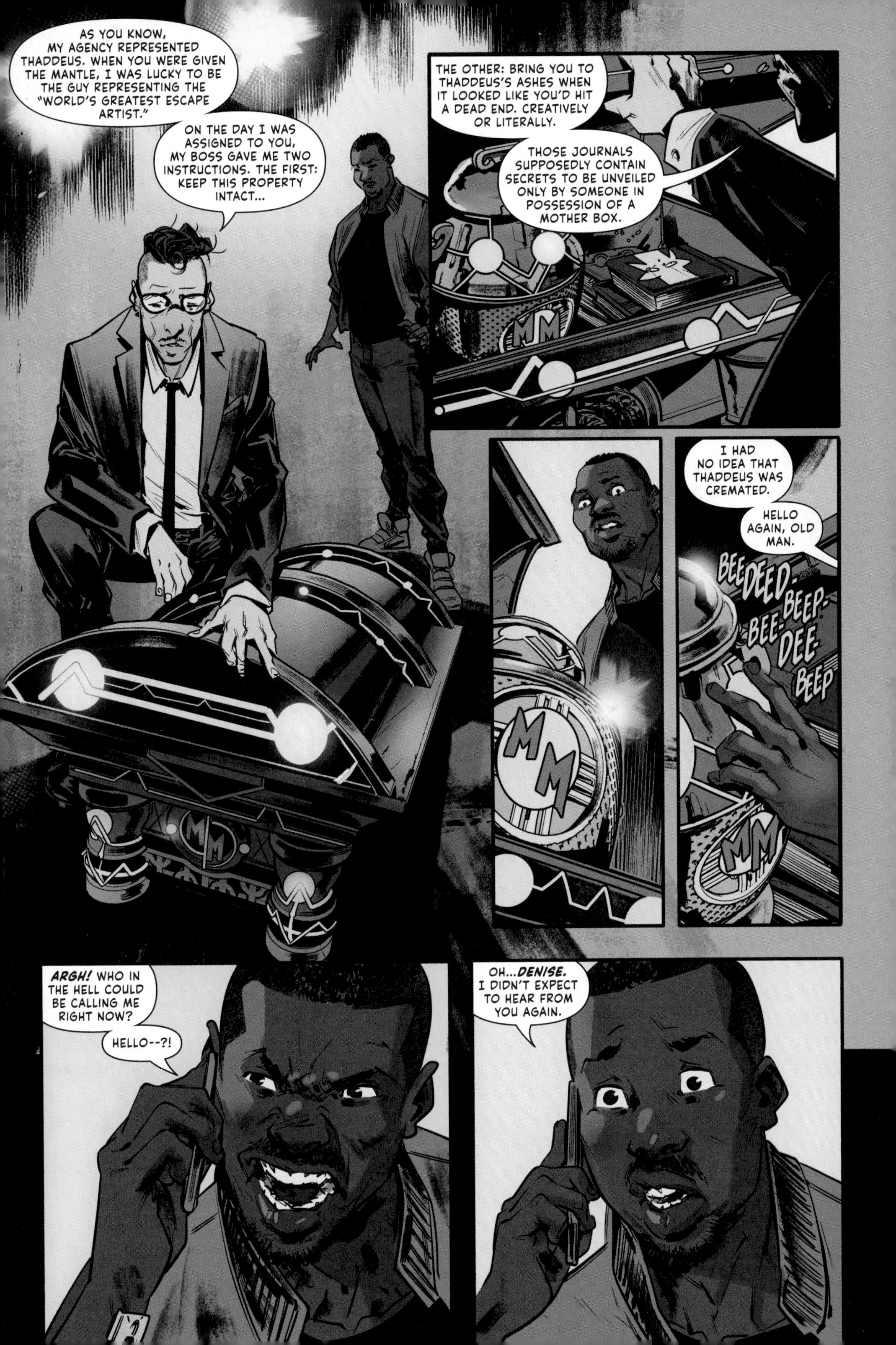
AS YOU KNOW, MY AGENCY REPRESENTED THADDEUS. WHEN YOU WERE GIVEN THE MANTLE, I WAS LUCKY TO BE THE GUY REPRESENTING THE "WORLD'S GREATEST ESCAPE ARTIST."
ON THE DAY I WAS ASSIGNED TO YOU, MY BOSS GAVE ME TWO INSTRUCTIONS. THE FIRST: KEEP THIS PROPERTY INTACT...
THE OTHER: BRING YOU TO THADDEUS'S ASHES WHEN IT LOOKED LIKE YOU'D HIT A DEAD END. CREATIVELY OR LITERALLY.
THOSE JOURNALS SUPPOSEDLY CONTAIN SECRETS TO BE UNVEILED ONLY BY SOMEONE IN POSSESSION OF A MOTHER BOX.
I HAD NO IDEA THAT THADDEUS WAS CREMATED.
HELLO AGAIN, OLD MAN.
BEEDEED-BEE-BEEP-DEE-BEEP
ARGH! WHO IN THE HELL COULD BE CALLING ME RIGHT NOW?
HELLO--?!
OH...DENISE. I DIDN'T EXPECT TO HEAR FROM YOU AGAIN.

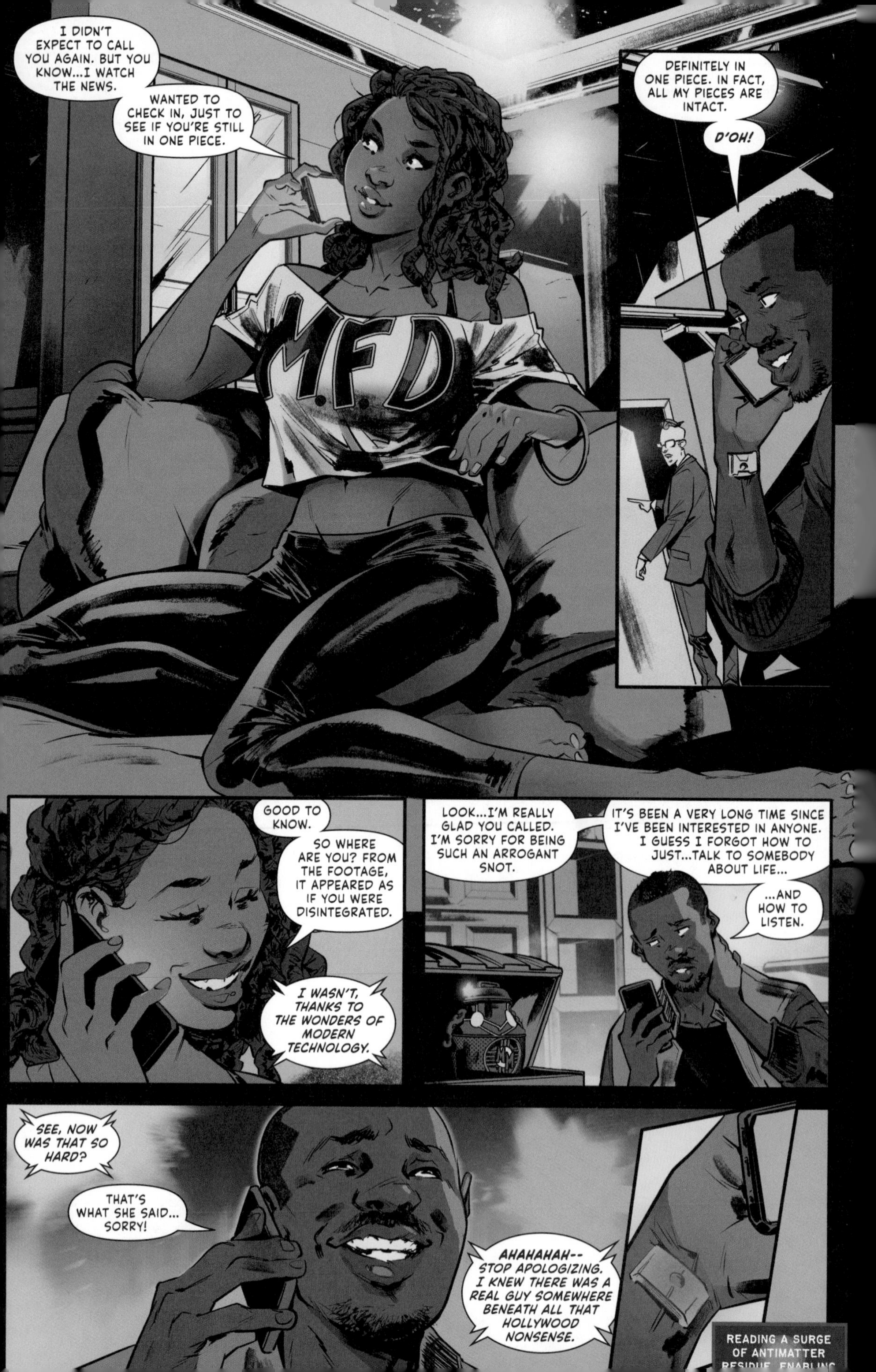
I DIDN'T EXPECT TO CALL YOU AGAIN. BUT YOU KNOW...I WATCH THE NEWS.
WANTED TO CHECK IN, JUST TO SEE IF YOU'RE STILL IN ONE PIECE.
DEFINITELY IN ONE PIECE. IN FACT, ALL MY PIECES ARE INTACT.
D'OH!
GOOD TO KNOW.
SO WHERE ARE YOU? FROM THE FOOTAGE, IT APPEARED AS IF YOU WERE DISINTEGRATED.
I WASN'T, THANKS TO THE WONDERS OF MODERN TECHNOLOGY.
LOOK...I'M REALLY GLAD YOU CALLED. I'M SORRY FOR BEING SUCH AN ARROGANT SNOT.
IT'S BEEN A VERY LONG TIME SINCE I'VE BEEN INTERESTED IN ANYONE. I GUESS I FORGOT HOW TO JUST...TALK TO SOMEBODY ABOUT LIFE...
...AND HOW TO LISTEN.
SEE, NOW WAS THAT SO HARD?
THAT'S WHAT SHE SAID... SORRY!
AHAHAHAH-- STOP APOLOGIZING. I KNEW THERE WAS A REAL GUY SOMEWHERE BENEATH ALL THAT HOLLYWOOD NONSENSE.
READING A SURGE OF ANTIMATTER

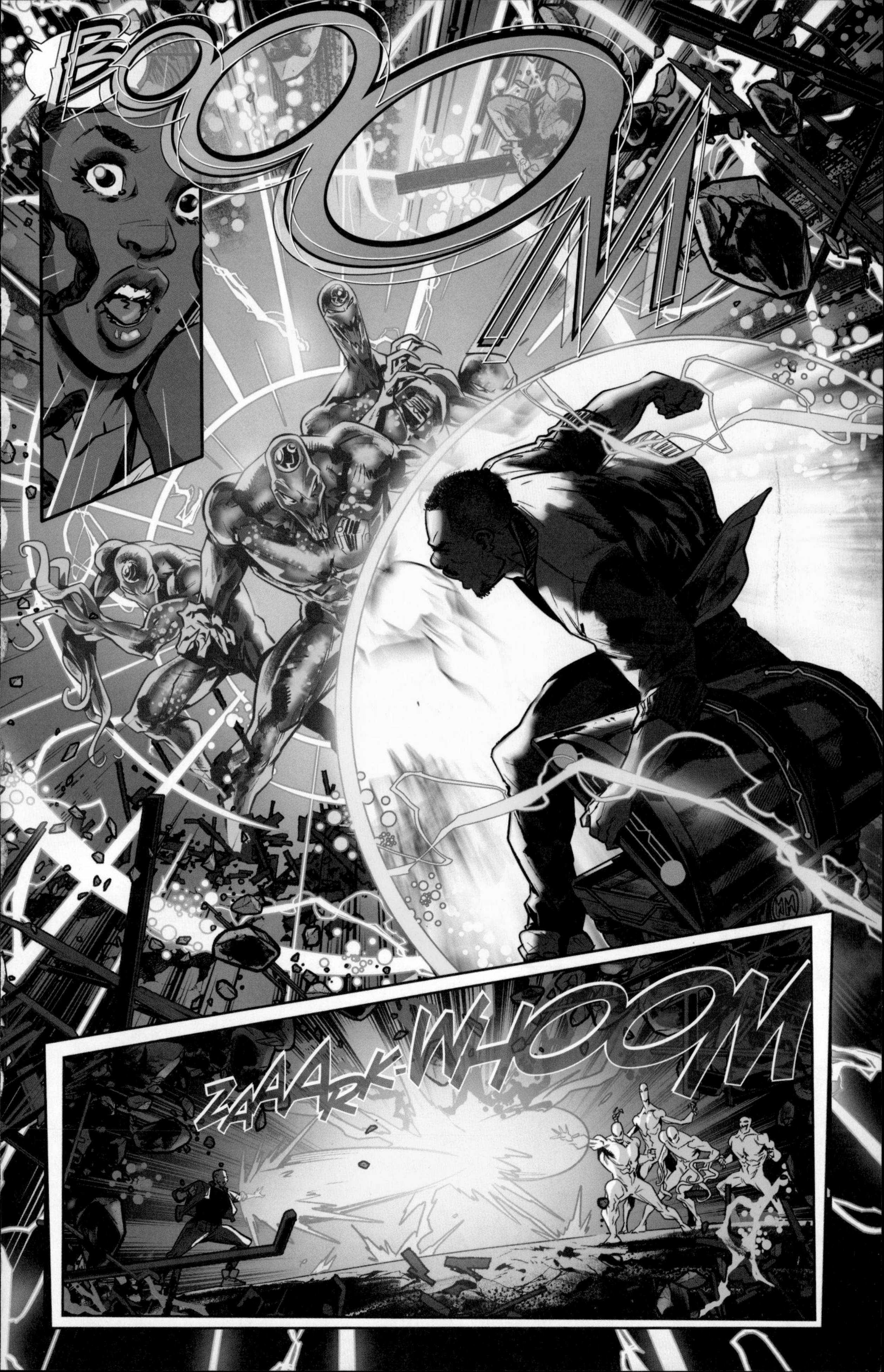
BOOM
ZAAARK-WHOOM

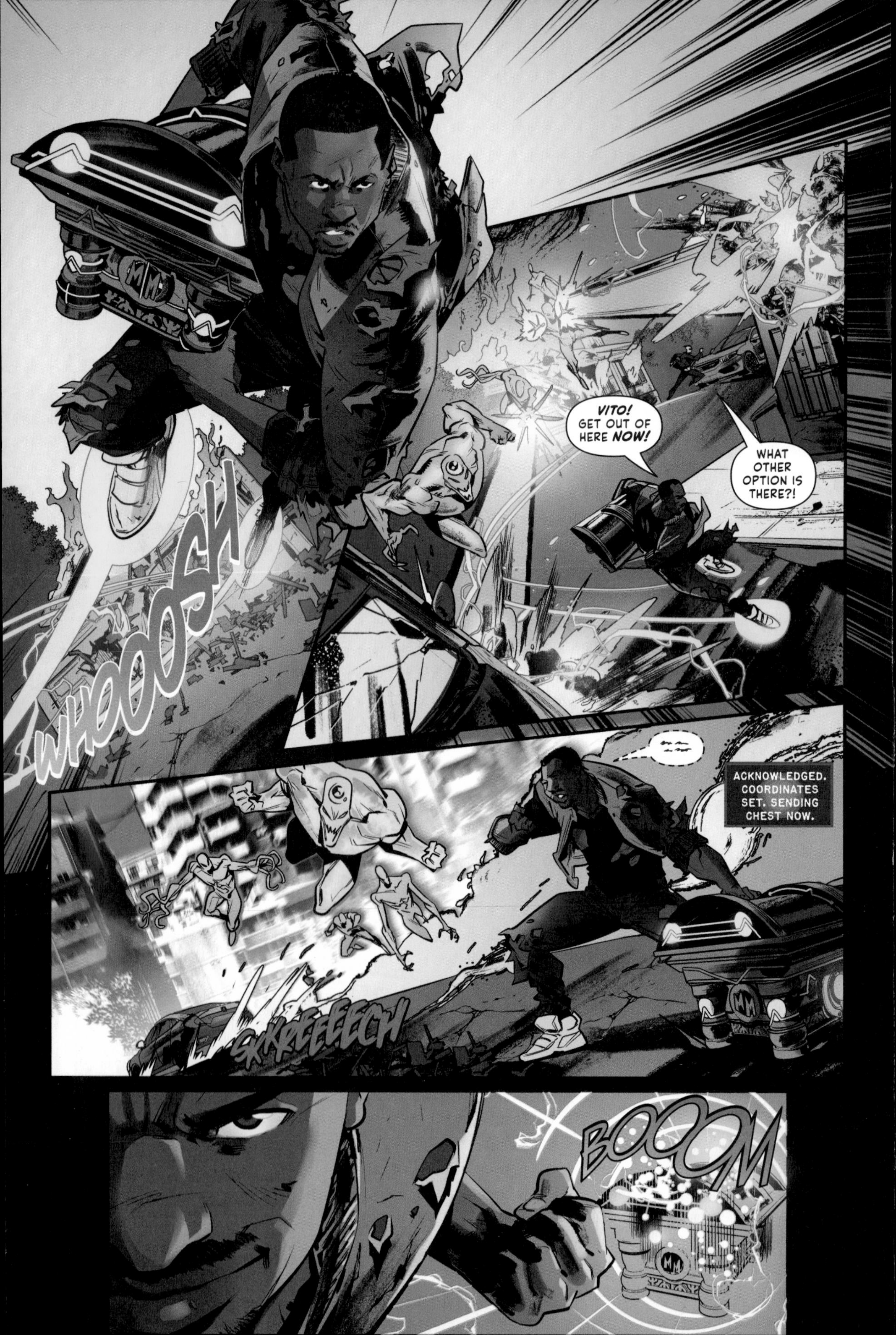
VITO! GET OUT OF HERE NOW!
WHAT OTHER OPTION IS THERE?!
WHOOOSH
ACKNOWLEDGED. COORDINATES SET. SENDING CHEST NOW.
SKREEEEECH
BOOOM

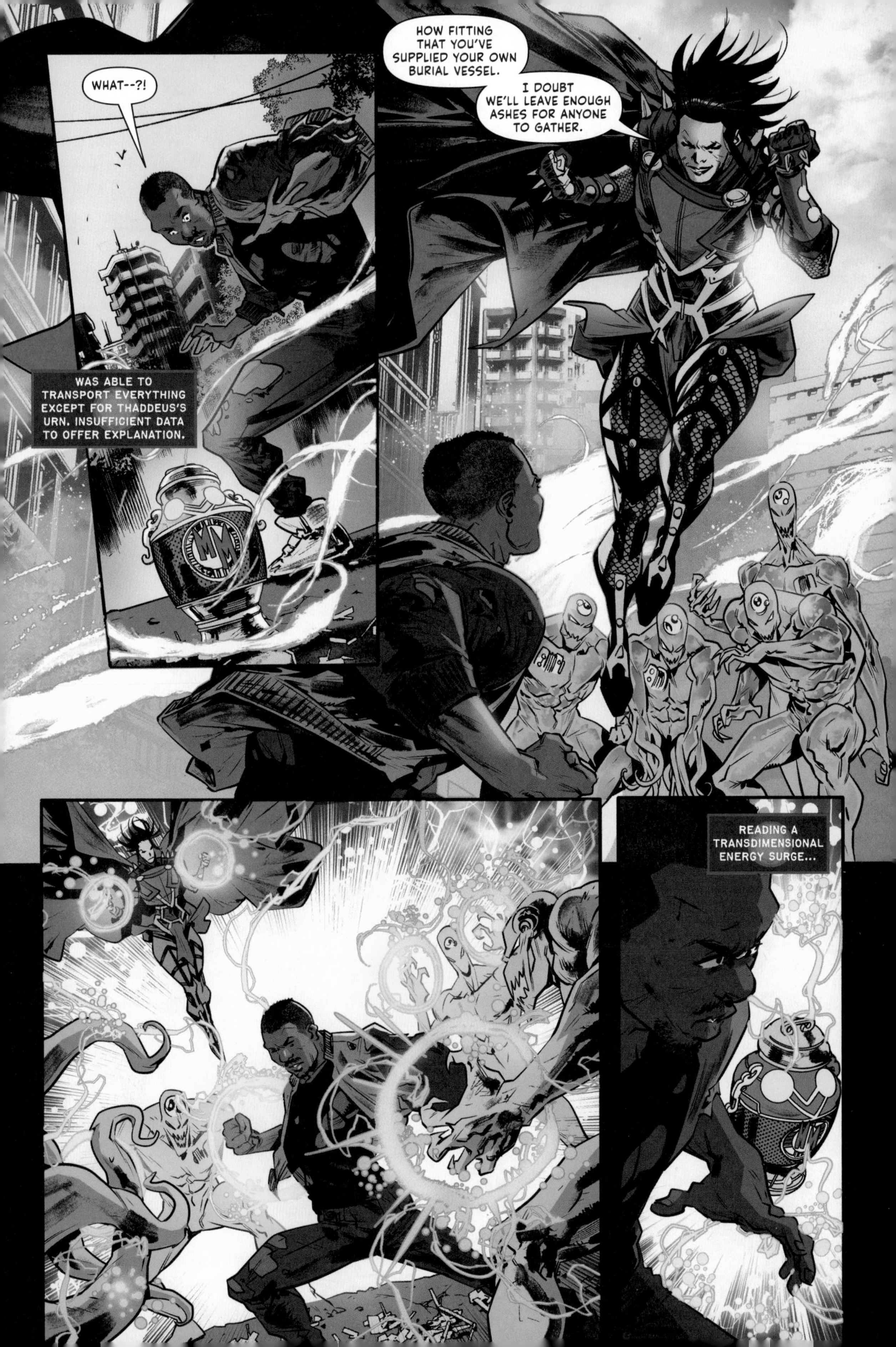
WHAT--?!
HOW FITTING THAT YOU'VE SUPPLIED YOUR OWN BURIAL VESSEL.
I DOUBT WE'LL LEAVE ENOUGH ASHES FOR ANYONE TO GATHER.
WAS ABLE TO TRANSPORT EVERYTHING EXCEPT FOR THADDEUS'S URN. INSUFFICIENT DATA TO OFFER EXPLANATION.
READING A TRANSDIMENSIONAL ENERGY SURGE...

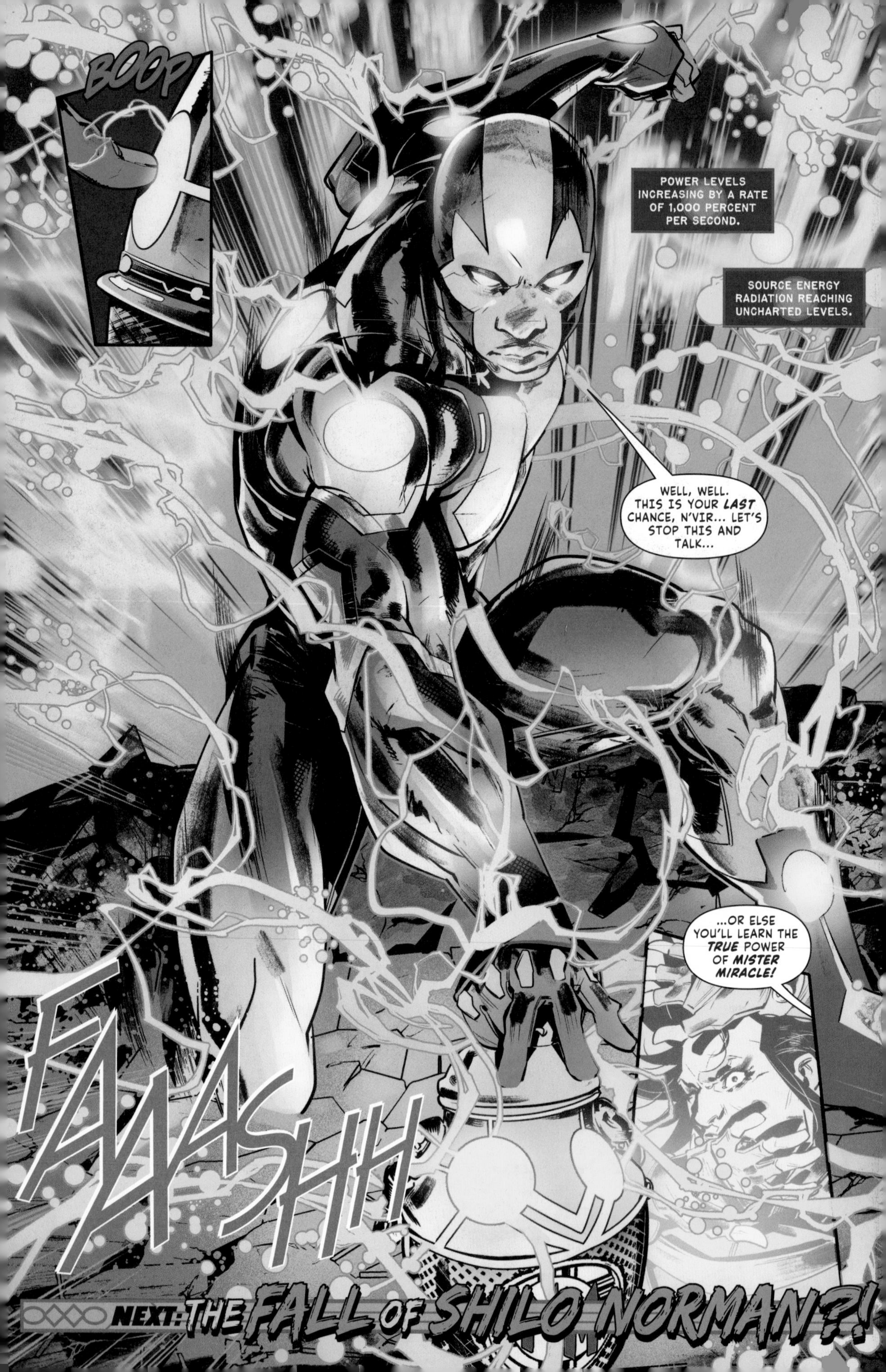
BOOP
POWER LEVELS INCREASING BY A RATE OF 1,000 PERCENT PER SECOND.
SOURCE ENERGY RADIATION REACHING UNCHARTED LEVELS.
WELL, WELL. THIS IS YOUR LAST CHANCE, N'VIR... LET'S STOP THIS AND TALK...
...OR ELSE YOU'LL LEARN THE TRUE POWER OF MISTER MIRACLE!
FZZASHH
NEXT: THE FALL OF SHILO NORMAN?!

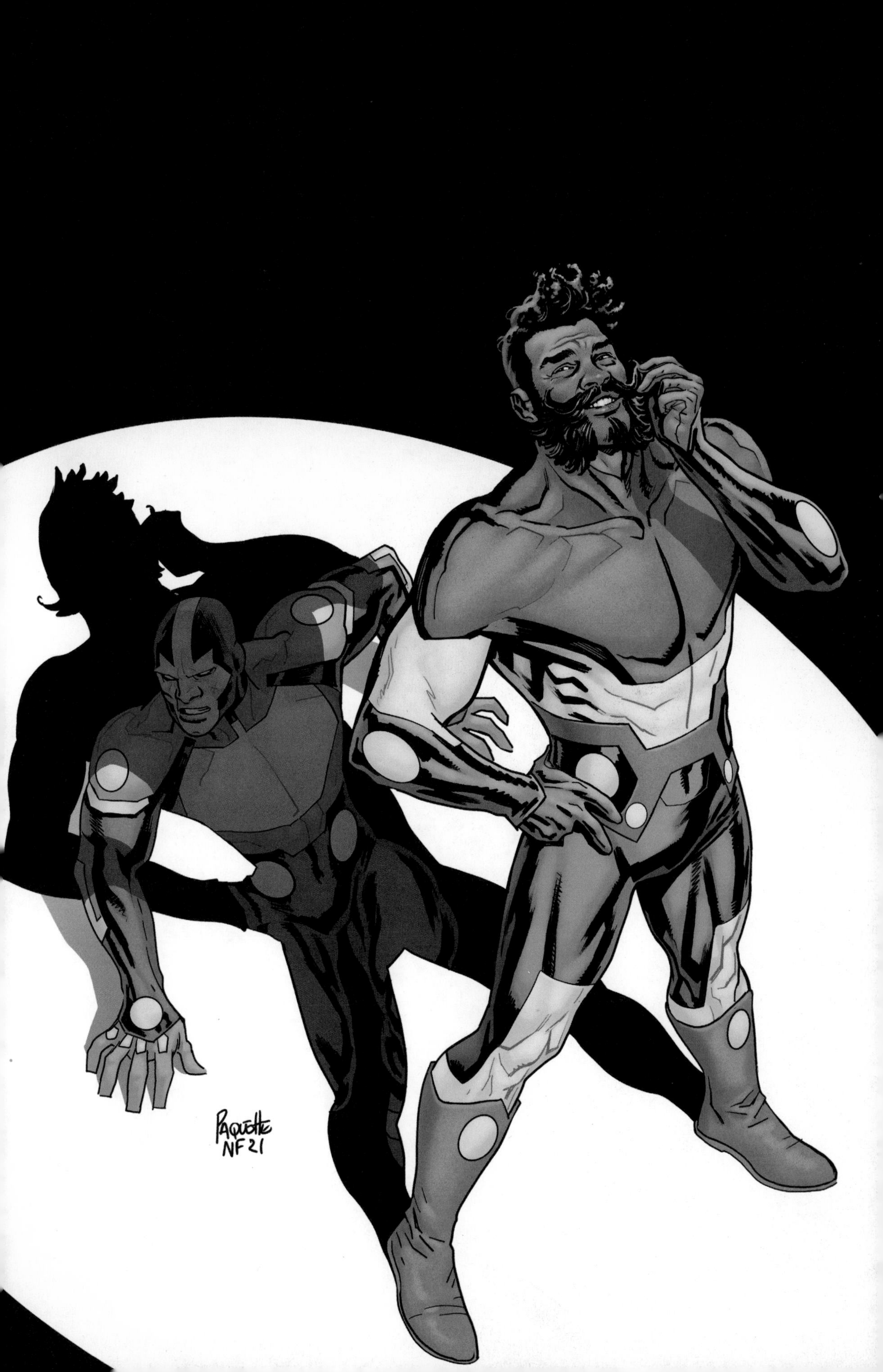
PAQUETTE
NF21

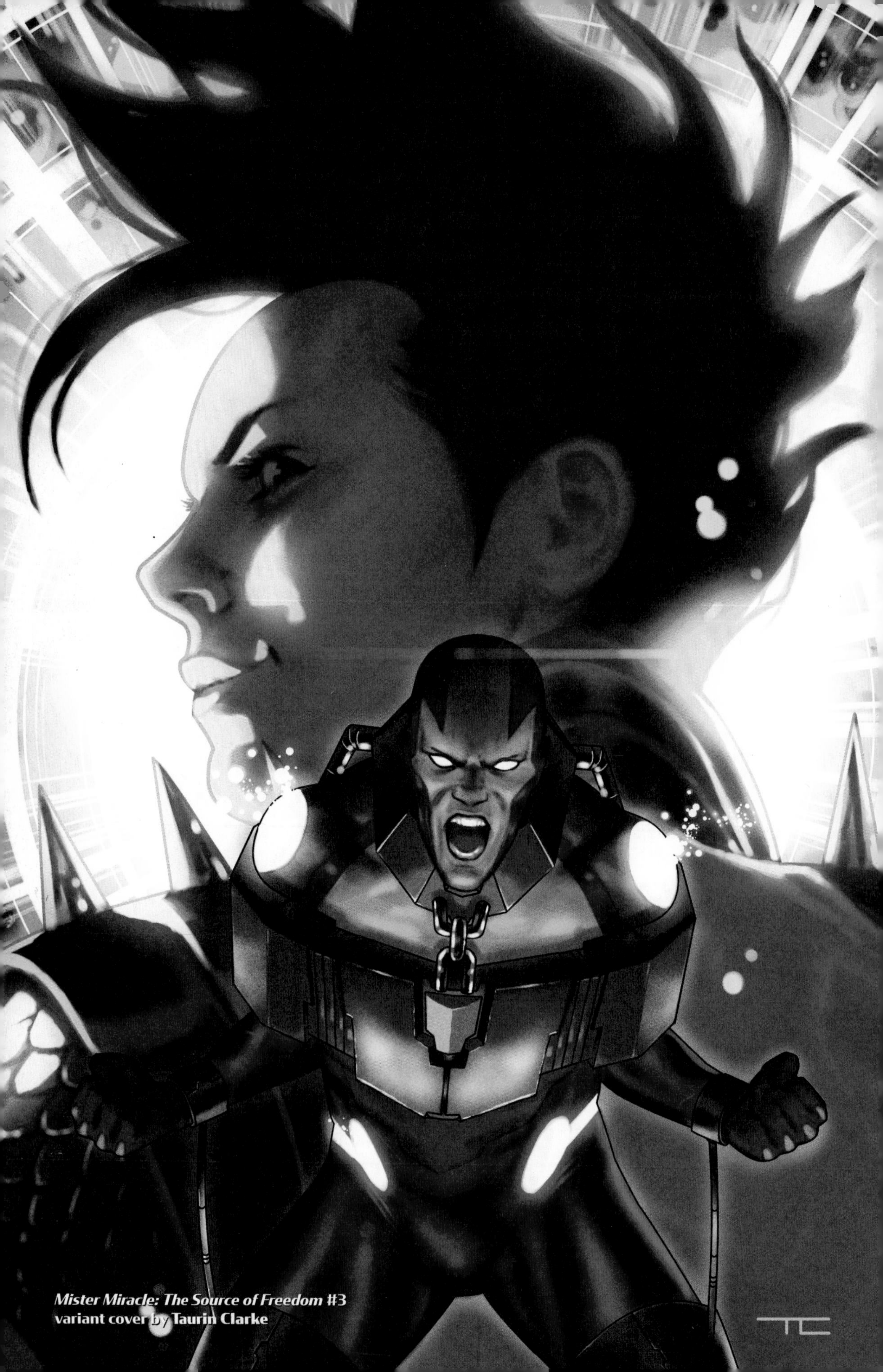
TC

Mister Miracle: The Source of Freedom #3
variant cover by Taurin Clarke

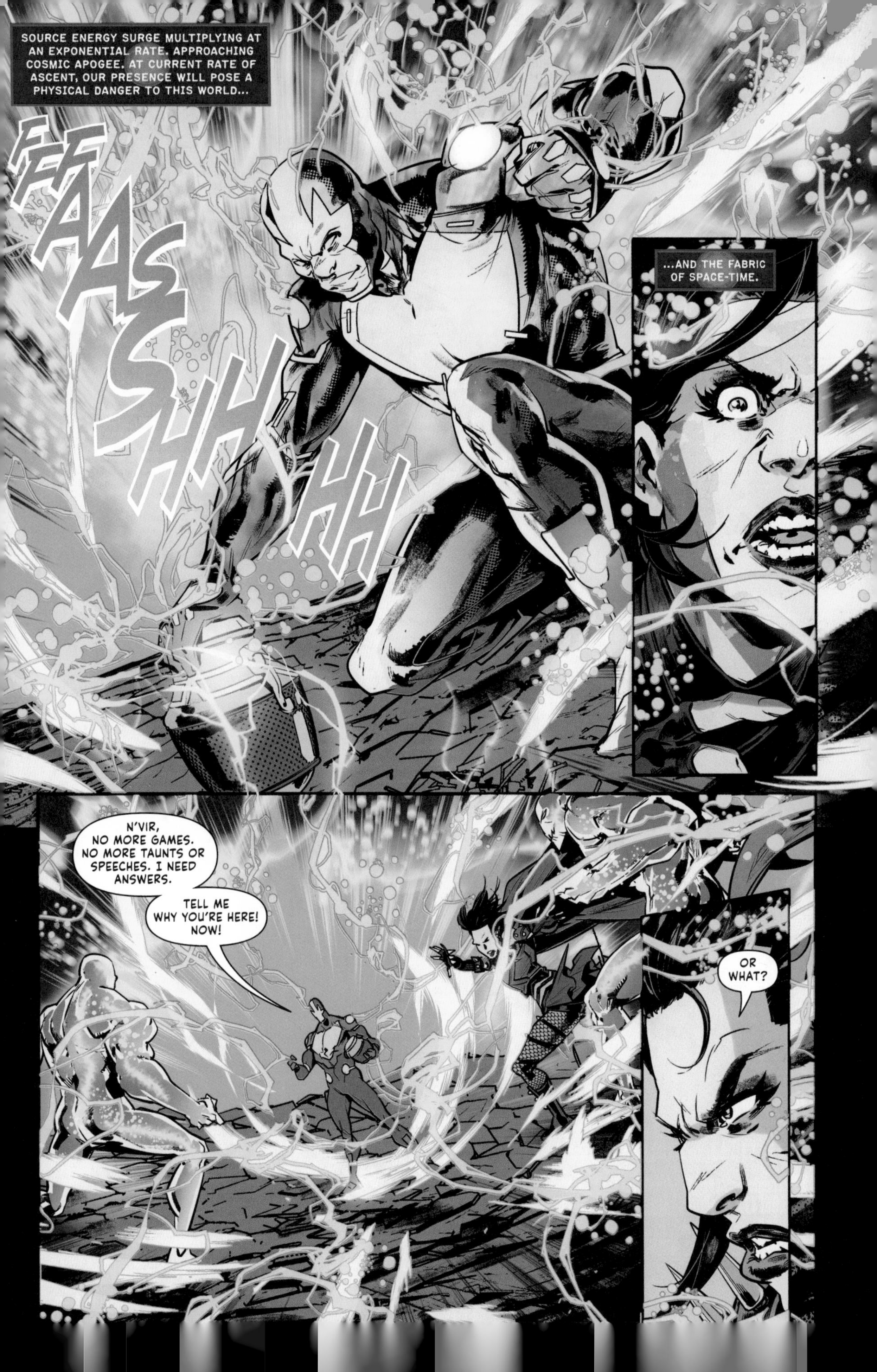
SOURCE ENERGY SURGE MULTIPLYING AT AN EXPONENTIAL RATE. APPROACHING COSMIC APOGEE. AT CURRENT RATE OF ASCENT, OUR PRESENCE WILL POSE A PHYSICAL DANGER TO THIS WORLD...
FFFAASSHHHH
...AND THE FABRIC OF SPACE-TIME.
N'VIR, NO MORE GAMES. NO MORE TAUNTS OR SPEECHES. I NEED ANSWERS.
TELL ME WHY YOU'RE HERE! NOW!
OR WHAT?

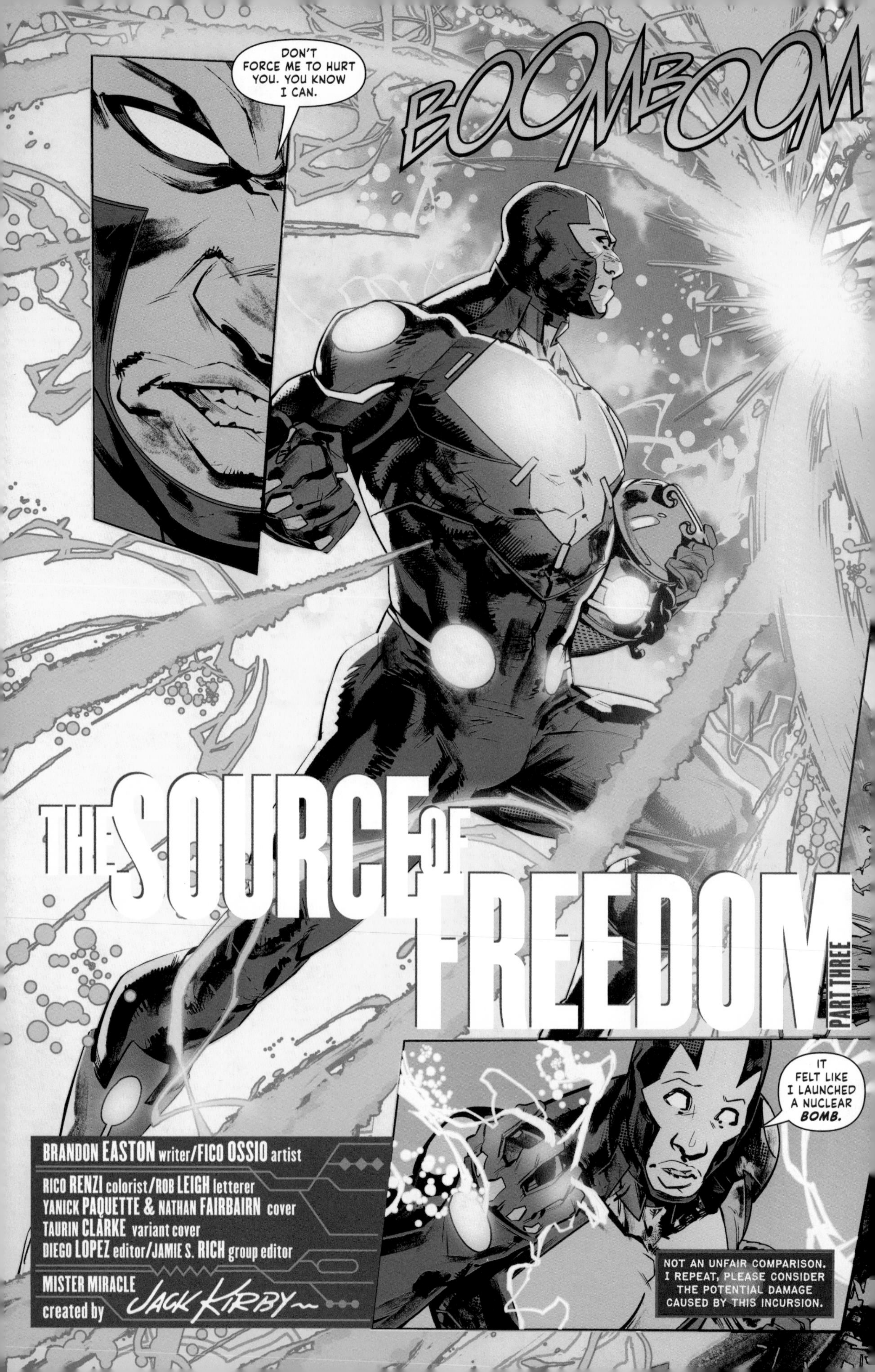

DON'T FORCE ME TO HURT YOU. YOU KNOW I CAN.
BOOMBOOM
THE SOURCE OF FREEDOM
PART THREE
IT FELT LIKE I LAUNCHED A NUCLEAR *BOMB.*
NOT AN UNFAIR COMPARISON. I REPEAT, PLEASE CONSIDER THE POTENTIAL DAMAGE CAUSED BY THIS INCURSION.
BRANDON EASTON writer/FICO OSSIO artist
RICO RENZI colorist/ROB LEIGH letterer
YANICK PAQUETTE & NATHAN FAIRBAIRN cover
TAURIN CLARKE variant cover
DIEGO LOPEZ editor/JAMIE S. RICH group editor
MISTER MIRACLE created by JACK KIRBY

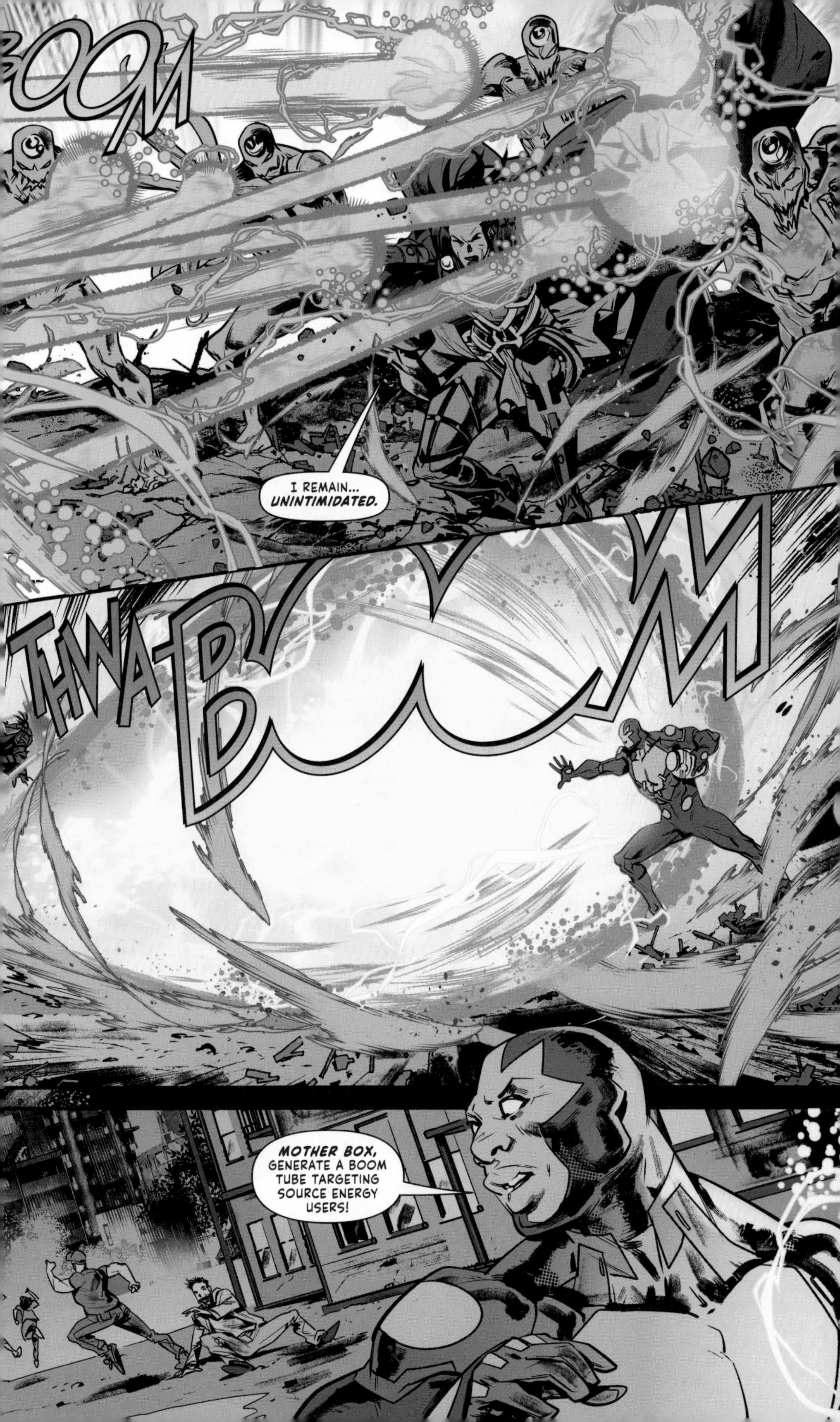
BOOM
I REMAIN... UNINTIMIDATED.
THWA-BOOM
MOTHER BOX, GENERATE A BOOM TUBE TARGETING SOURCE ENERGY USERS!

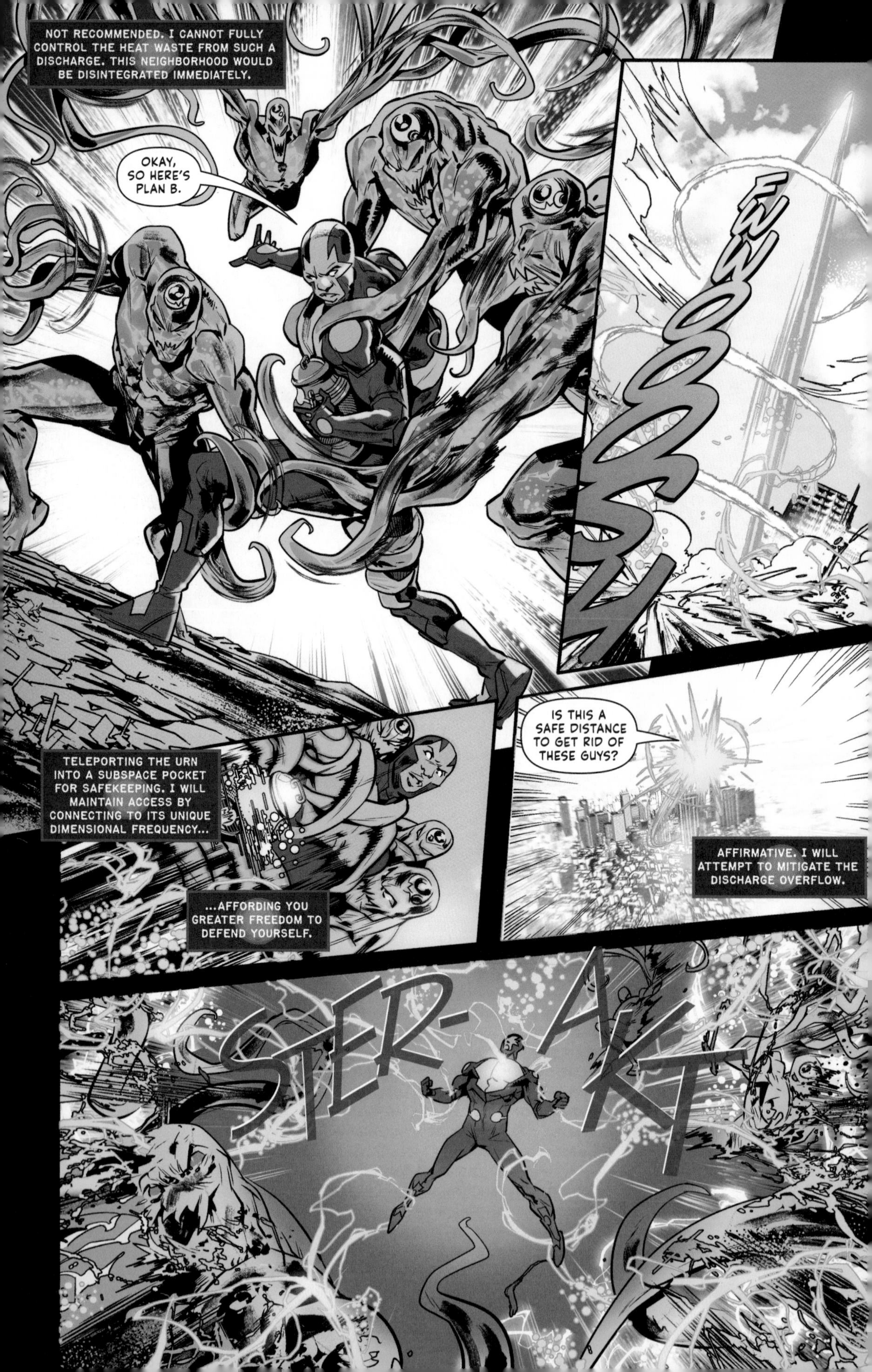
NOT RECOMMENDED. I CANNOT FULLY CONTROL THE HEAT WASTE FROM SUCH A DISCHARGE. THIS NEIGHBORHOOD WOULD BE DISINTEGRATED IMMEDIATELY.
OKAY, SO HERE'S PLAN B.
FWOOOSSSH
TELEPORTING THE URN INTO A SUBSPACE POCKET FOR SAFEKEEPING. I WILL MAINTAIN ACCESS BY CONNECTING TO ITS UNIQUE DIMENSIONAL FREQUENCY...
...AFFORDING YOU GREATER FREEDOM TO DEFEND YOURSELF.
IS THIS A SAFE DISTANCE TO GET RID OF THESE GUYS?
AFFIRMATIVE. I WILL ATTEMPT TO MITIGATE THE DISCHARGE OVERFLOW.
STER-AKT

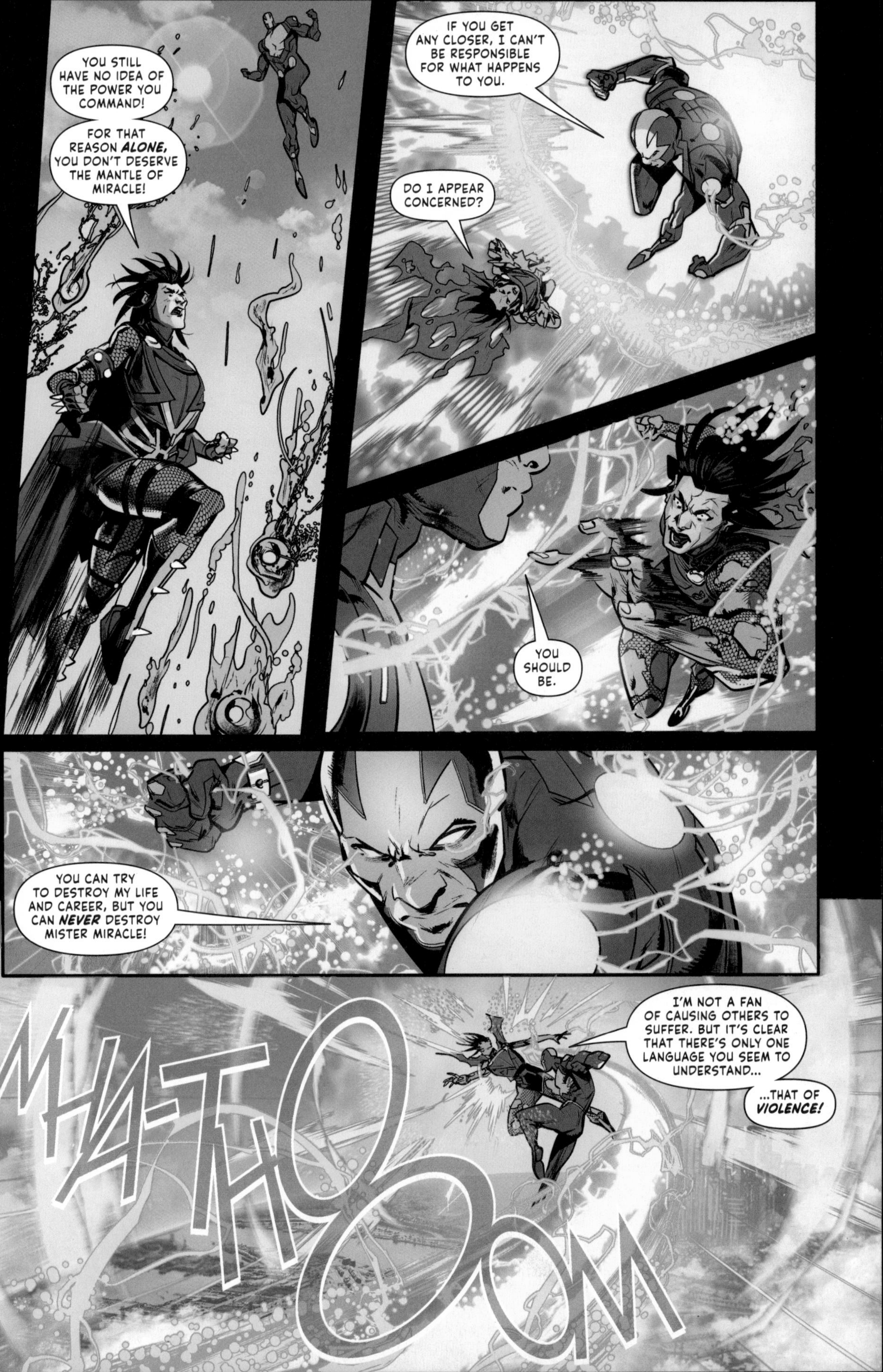

YOU STILL HAVE NO IDEA OF THE POWER YOU COMMAND!
FOR THAT REASON ***ALONE,*** YOU DON'T DESERVE THE MANTLE OF MIRACLE!
IF YOU GET ANY CLOSER, I CAN'T BE RESPONSIBLE FOR WHAT HAPPENS TO YOU.
DO I APPEAR CONCERNED?
YOU SHOULD BE.
YOU CAN TRY TO DESTROY MY LIFE AND CAREER, BUT YOU CAN ***NEVER*** DESTROY MISTER MIRACLE!
WHA-THOOOM
I'M NOT A FAN OF CAUSING OTHERS TO SUFFER. BUT IT'S CLEAR THAT THERE'S ONLY ONE LANGUAGE YOU SEEM TO UNDERSTAND...
...THAT OF ***VIOLENCE!***

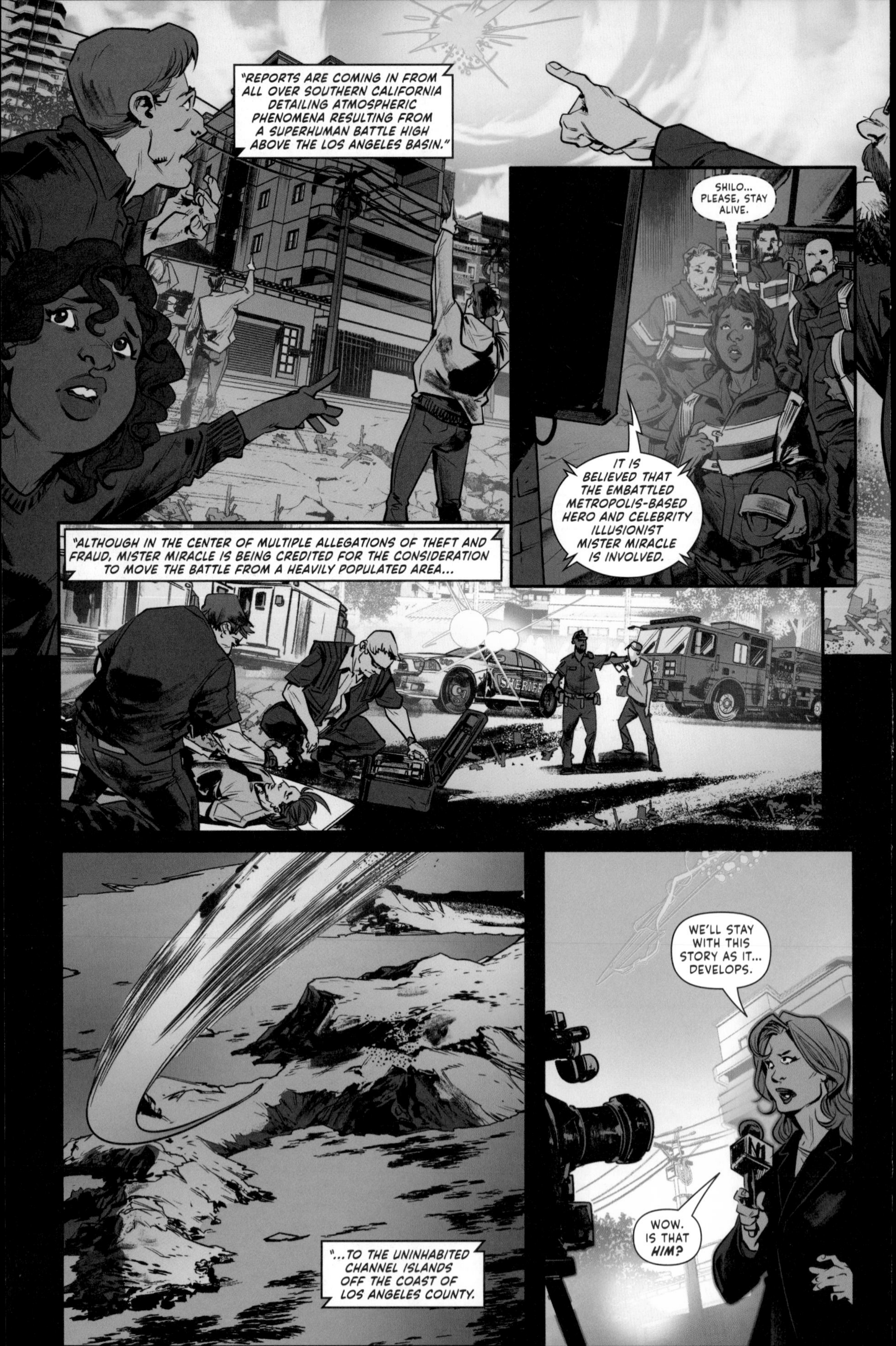
"REPORTS ARE COMING IN FROM ALL OVER SOUTHERN CALIFORNIA DETAILING ATMOSPHERIC PHENOMENA RESULTING FROM A SUPERHUMAN BATTLE HIGH ABOVE THE LOS ANGELES BASIN."
SHILO... PLEASE, STAY ALIVE.
IT IS BELIEVED THAT THE EMBATTLED METROPOLIS-BASED HERO AND CELEBRITY ILLUSIONIST MISTER MIRACLE IS INVOLVED.
"ALTHOUGH IN THE CENTER OF MULTIPLE ALLEGATIONS OF THEFT AND FRAUD, MISTER MIRACLE IS BEING CREDITED FOR THE CONSIDERATION TO MOVE THE BATTLE FROM A HEAVILY POPULATED AREA...
SHERIFF
"...TO THE UNINHABITED CHANNEL ISLANDS OFF THE COAST OF LOS ANGELES COUNTY.
WE'LL STAY WITH THIS STORY AS IT... DEVELOPS.
WOW. IS THAT *HIM?*

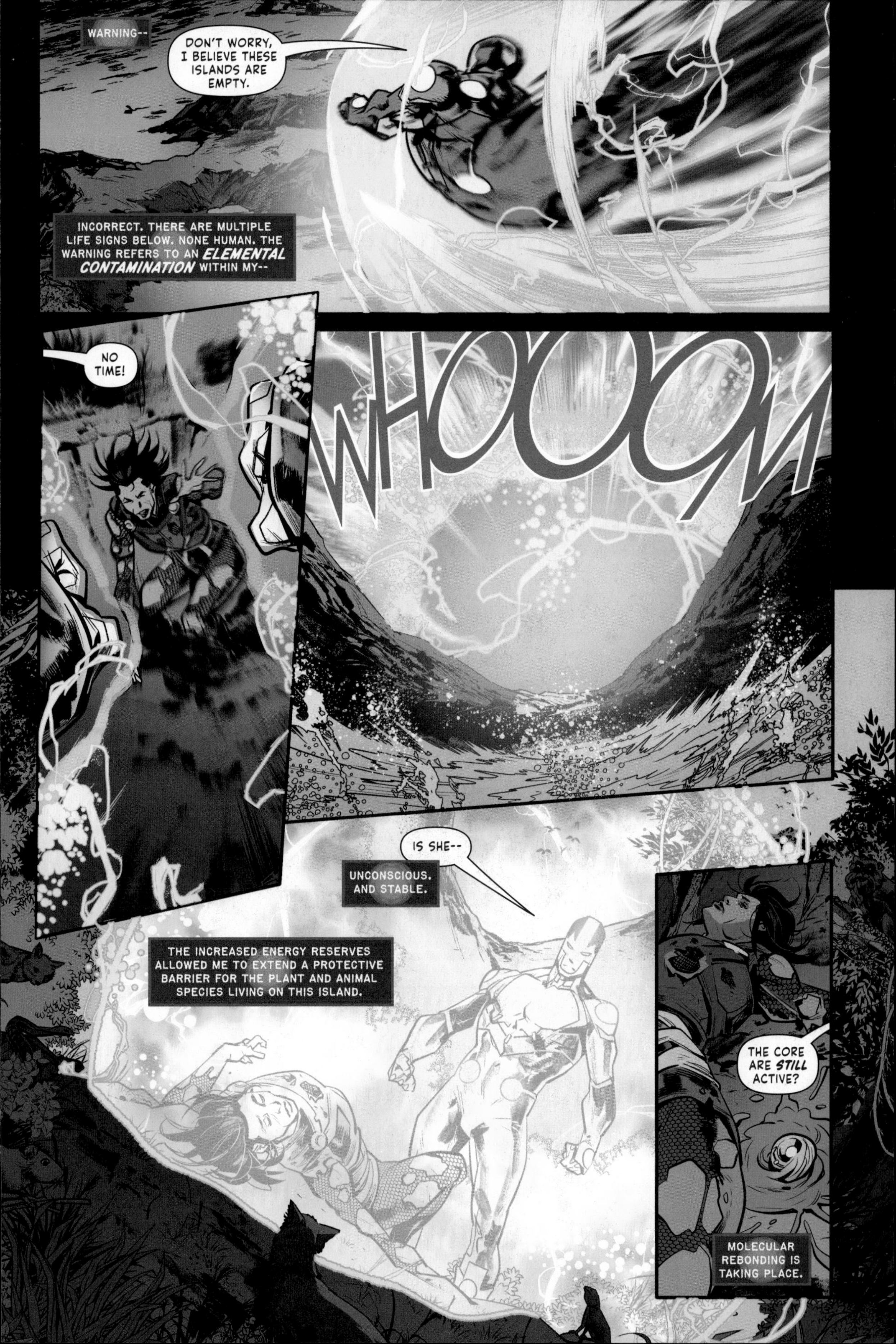
WARNING--
DON'T WORRY, I BELIEVE THESE ISLANDS ARE EMPTY.
INCORRECT. THERE ARE MULTIPLE LIFE SIGNS BELOW. NONE HUMAN. THE WARNING REFERS TO AN ELEMENTAL CONTAMINATION WITHIN MY--
NO TIME!
WHOOOM
IS SHE--
UNCONSCIOUS. AND STABLE.
THE INCREASED ENERGY RESERVES ALLOWED ME TO EXTEND A PROTECTIVE BARRIER FOR THE PLANT AND ANIMAL SPECIES LIVING ON THIS ISLAND.
THE CORE ARE STILL ACTIVE?
MOLECULAR REBONDING IS TAKING PLACE.

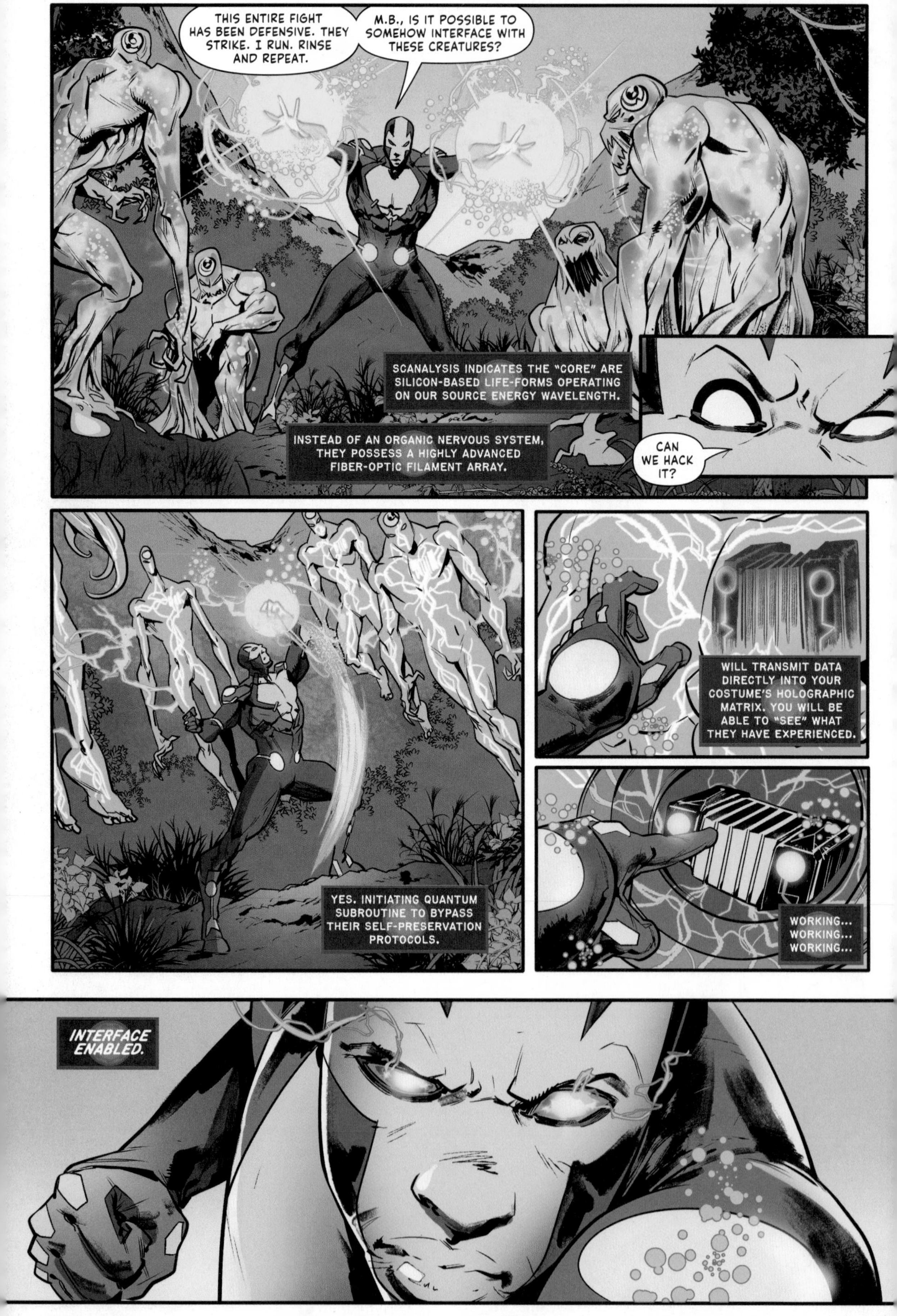

THIS ENTIRE FIGHT HAS BEEN DEFENSIVE. THEY STRIKE. I RUN. RINSE AND REPEAT.
M.B., IS IT POSSIBLE TO SOMEHOW INTERFACE WITH THESE CREATURES?
SCANALYSIS INDICATES THE "CORE" ARE SILICON-BASED LIFE-FORMS OPERATING ON OUR SOURCE ENERGY WAVELENGTH.
INSTEAD OF AN ORGANIC NERVOUS SYSTEM, THEY POSSESS A HIGHLY ADVANCED FIBER-OPTIC FILAMENT ARRAY.
CAN WE HACK IT?
YES. INITIATING QUANTUM SUBROUTINE TO BYPASS THEIR SELF-PRESERVATION PROTOCOLS.
WILL TRANSMIT DATA DIRECTLY INTO YOUR COSTUME'S HOLOGRAPHIC MATRIX. YOU WILL BE ABLE TO "SEE" WHAT THEY HAVE EXPERIENCED.
WORKING... WORKING... WORKING...
INTERFACE ENABLED.

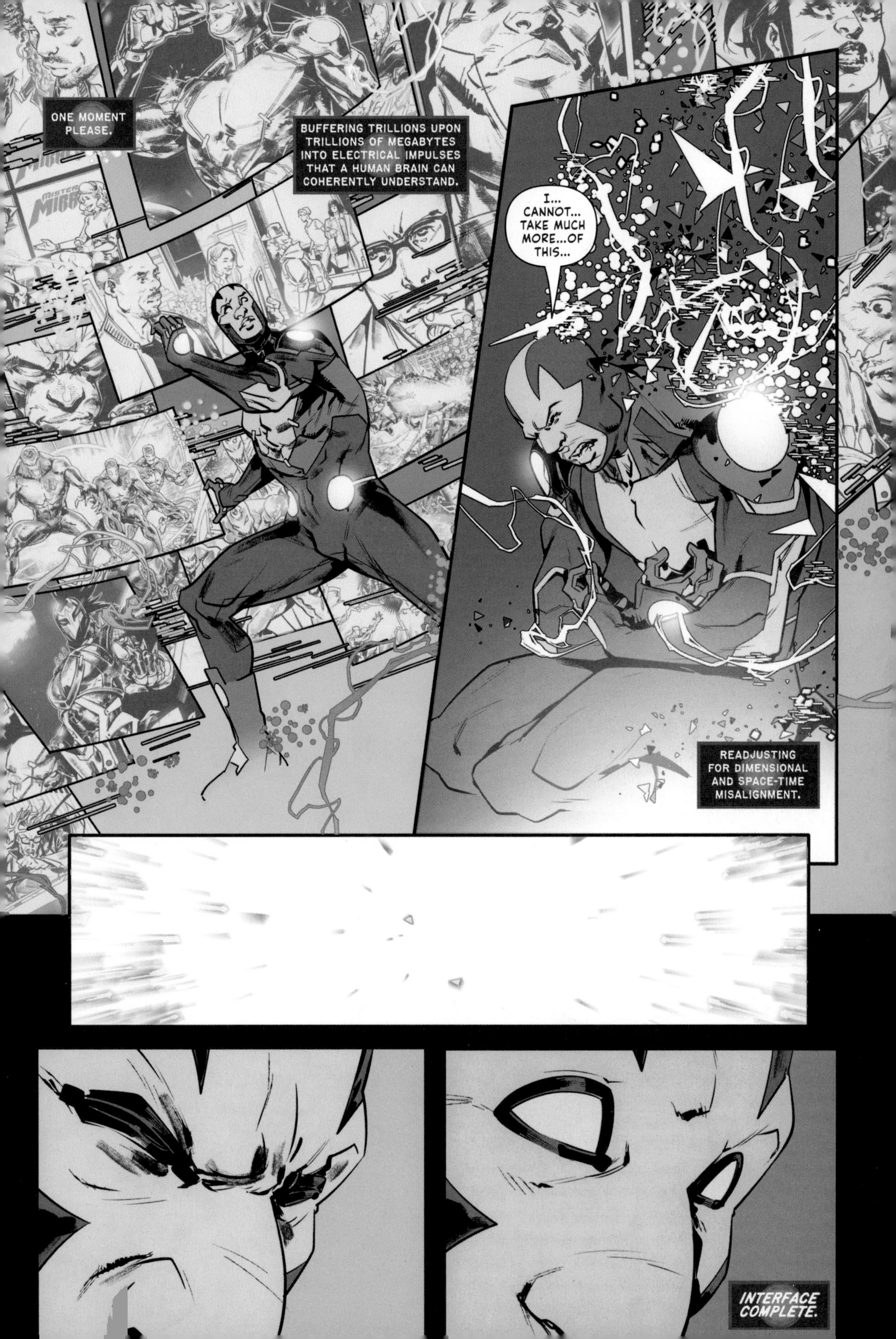
ONE MOMENT PLEASE.
BUFFERING TRILLIONS UPON TRILLIONS OF MEGABYTES INTO ELECTRICAL IMPULSES THAT A HUMAN BRAIN CAN COHERENTLY UNDERSTAND.
I... CANNOT... TAKE MUCH MORE...OF THIS...
READJUSTING FOR DIMENSIONAL AND SPACE-TIME MISALIGNMENT.
INTERFACE COMPLETE.

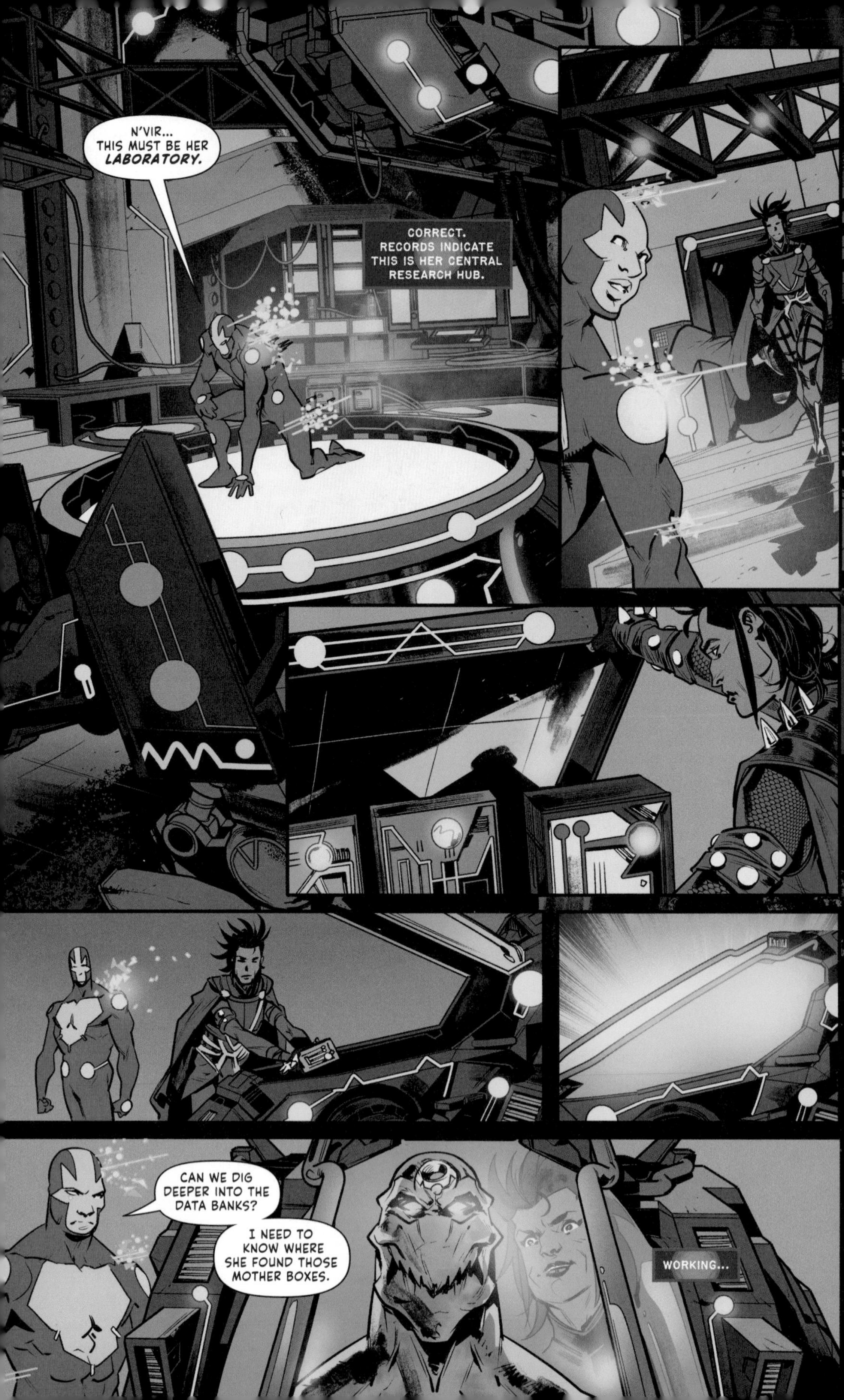

N'VIR... THIS MUST BE HER *LABORATORY.*
CORRECT. RECORDS INDICATE THIS IS HER CENTRAL RESEARCH HUB.
CAN WE DIG DEEPER INTO THE DATA BANKS?
I NEED TO KNOW WHERE SHE FOUND THOSE MOTHER BOXES.
WORKING...

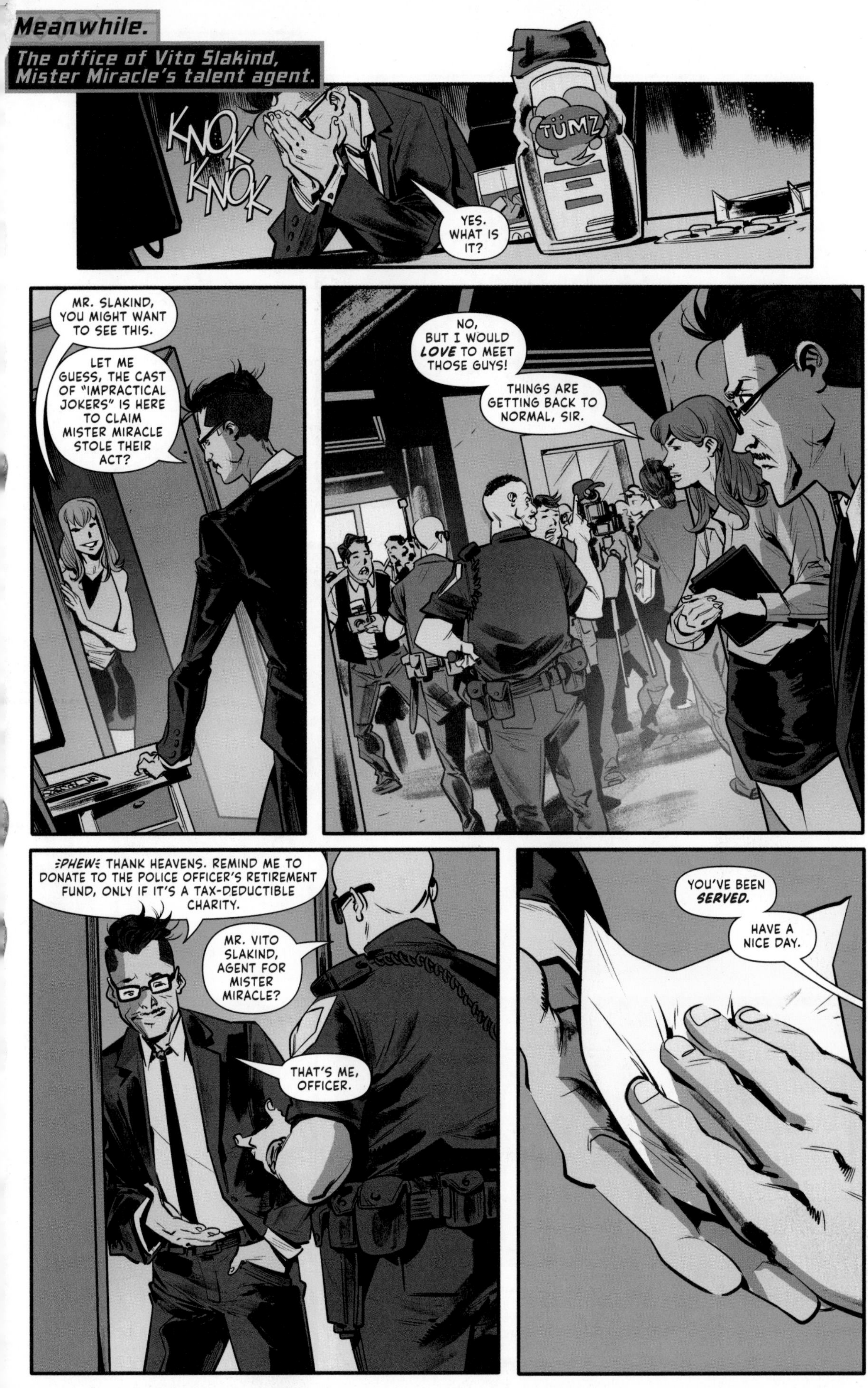
Meanwhile.
The office of Vito Slakind, Mister Miracle's talent agent.
KNOCK KNOCK
TÜMZ
YES. WHAT IS IT?
MR. SLAKIND, YOU MIGHT WANT TO SEE THIS.
LET ME GUESS, THE CAST OF "IMPRACTICAL JOKERS" IS HERE TO CLAIM MISTER MIRACLE STOLE THEIR ACT?
NO, BUT I WOULD LOVE TO MEET THOSE GUYS!
THINGS ARE GETTING BACK TO NORMAL, SIR.
=PHEW= THANK HEAVENS. REMIND ME TO DONATE TO THE POLICE OFFICER'S RETIREMENT FUND, ONLY IF IT'S A TAX-DEDUCTIBLE CHARITY.
MR. VITO SLAKIND, AGENT FOR MISTER MIRACLE?
THAT'S ME, OFFICER.
YOU'VE BEEN SERVED.
HAVE A NICE DAY.

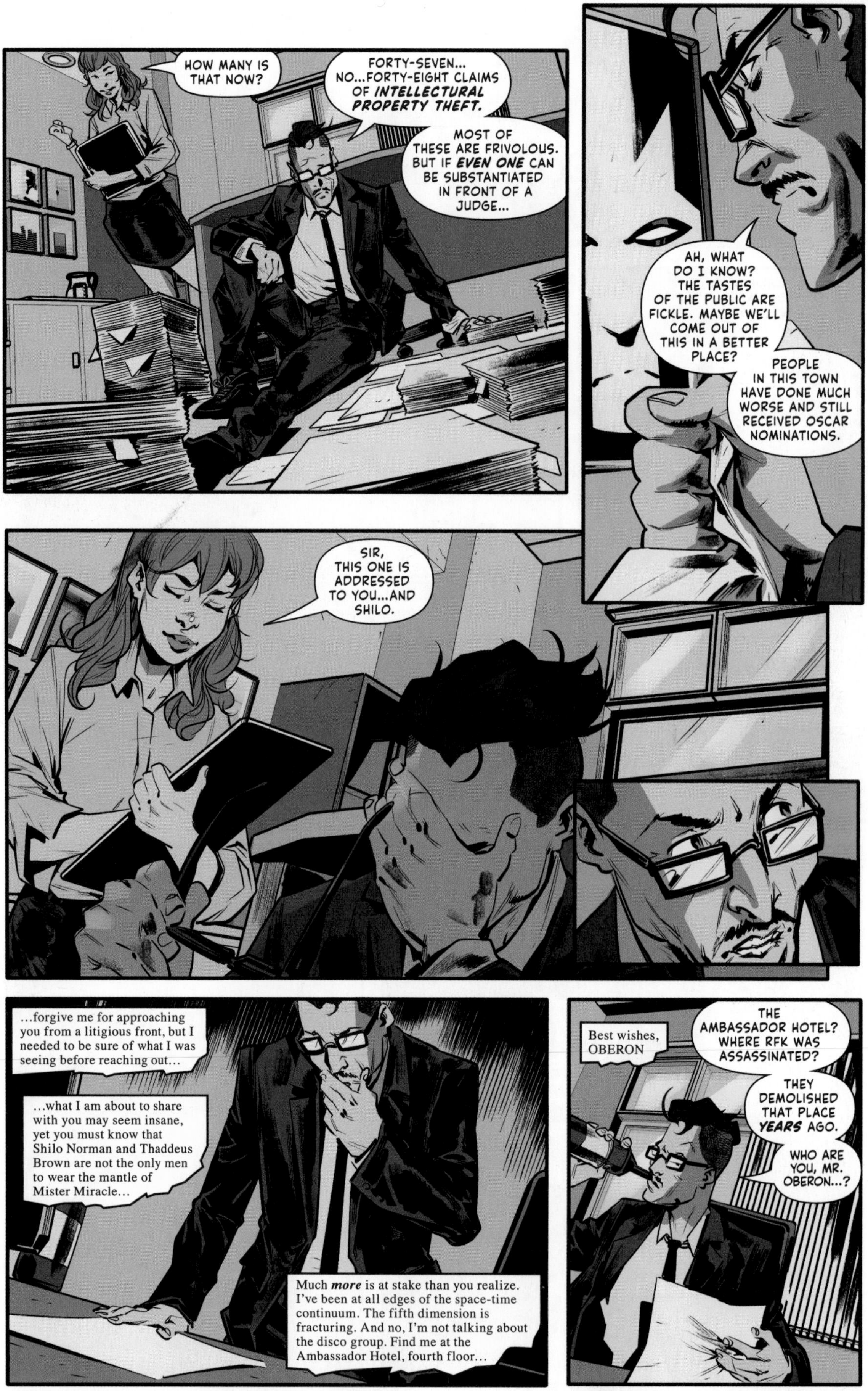
HOW MANY IS THAT NOW?
FORTY-SEVEN... NO...FORTY-EIGHT CLAIMS OF *INTELLECTURAL PROPERTY THEFT.*
MOST OF THESE ARE FRIVOLOUS. BUT IF *EVEN ONE* CAN BE SUBSTANTIATED IN FRONT OF A JUDGE...
AH, WHAT DO I KNOW? THE TASTES OF THE PUBLIC ARE FICKLE. MAYBE WE'LL COME OUT OF THIS IN A BETTER PLACE?
PEOPLE IN THIS TOWN HAVE DONE MUCH WORSE AND STILL RECEIVED OSCAR NOMINATIONS.
SIR, THIS ONE IS ADDRESSED TO YOU...AND SHILO.
...forgive me for approaching you from a litigious front, but I needed to be sure of what I was seeing before reaching out...
...what I am about to share with you may seem insane, yet you must know that Shilo Norman and Thaddeus Brown are not the only men to wear the mantle of Mister Miracle...
Much *more* is at stake than you realize. I've been at all edges of the space-time continuum. The fifth dimension is fracturing. And no, I'm not talking about the disco group. Find me at the Ambassador Hotel, fourth floor...
Best wishes, OBERON
THE AMBASSADOR HOTEL? WHERE RFK WAS ASSASSINATED?
THEY DEMOLISHED THAT PLACE *YEARS* AGO.
WHO ARE YOU, MR. OBERON...?

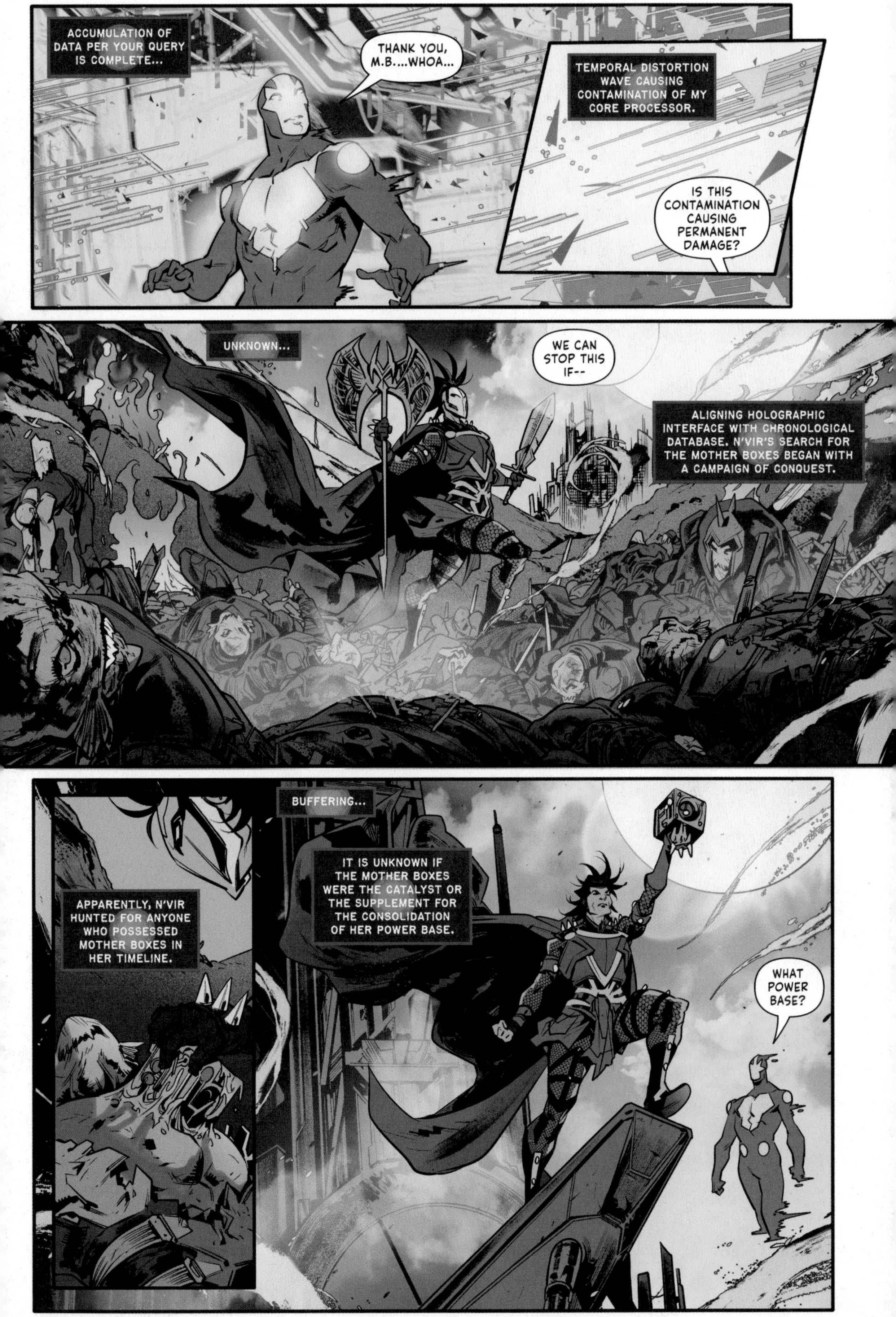
ACCUMULATION OF DATA PER YOUR QUERY IS COMPLETE...
THANK YOU, M.B....WHOA...
TEMPORAL DISTORTION WAVE CAUSING CONTAMINATION OF MY CORE PROCESSOR.
IS THIS CONTAMINATION CAUSING PERMANENT DAMAGE?
UNKNOWN...
WE CAN STOP THIS IF--
ALIGNING HOLOGRAPHIC INTERFACE WITH CHRONOLOGICAL DATABASE. N'VIR'S SEARCH FOR THE MOTHER BOXES BEGAN WITH A CAMPAIGN OF CONQUEST.
APPARENTLY, N'VIR HUNTED FOR ANYONE WHO POSSESSED MOTHER BOXES IN HER TIMELINE.
BUFFERING...
IT IS UNKNOWN IF THE MOTHER BOXES WERE THE CATALYST OR THE SUPPLEMENT FOR THE CONSOLIDATION OF HER POWER BASE.
WHAT POWER BASE?

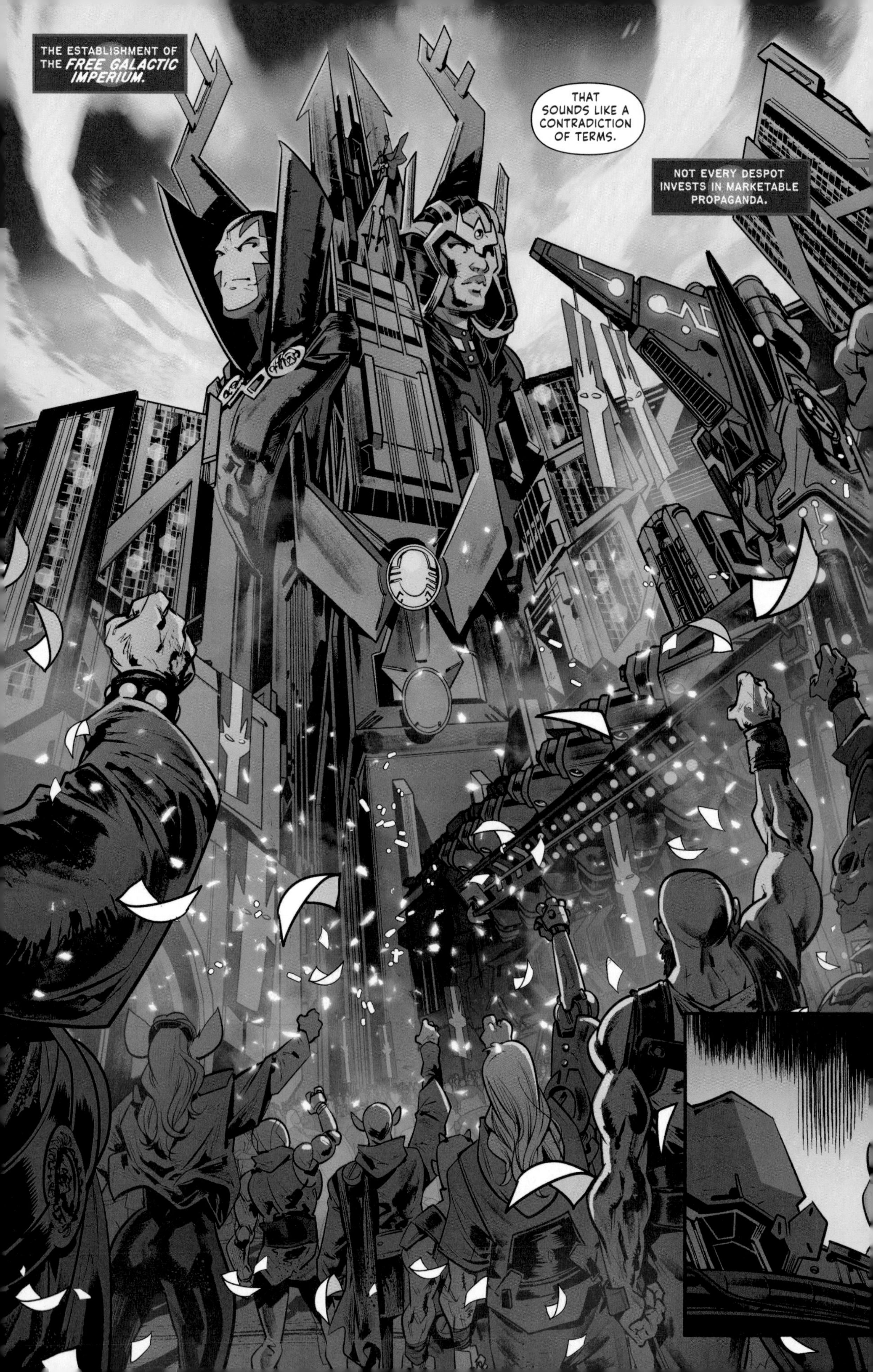
THE ESTABLISHMENT OF THE *FREE GALACTIC IMPERIUM.*
THAT SOUNDS LIKE A CONTRADICTION OF TERMS.
NOT EVERY DESPOT INVESTS IN MARKETABLE PROPAGANDA.

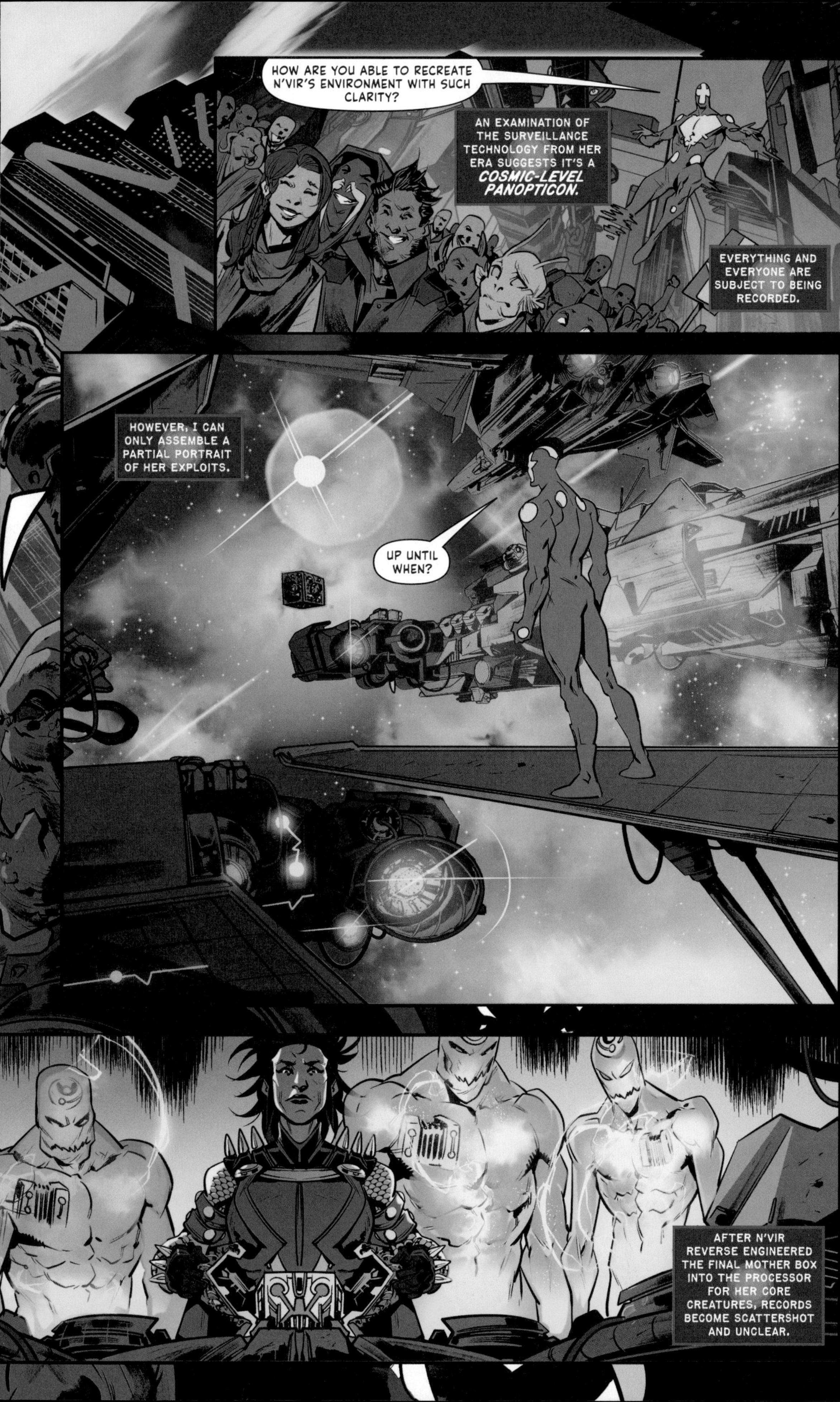
HOW ARE YOU ABLE TO RECREATE N'VIR'S ENVIRONMENT WITH SUCH CLARITY?
AN EXAMINATION OF THE SURVEILLANCE TECHNOLOGY FROM HER ERA SUGGESTS IT'S A COSMIC-LEVEL PANOPTICON.
EVERYTHING AND EVERYONE ARE SUBJECT TO BEING RECORDED.
HOWEVER, I CAN ONLY ASSEMBLE A PARTIAL PORTRAIT OF HER EXPLOITS.
UP UNTIL WHEN?
AFTER N'VIR REVERSE ENGINEERED THE FINAL MOTHER BOX INTO THE PROCESSOR FOR HER CORE CREATURES, RECORDS BECOME SCATTERSHOT AND UNCLEAR.

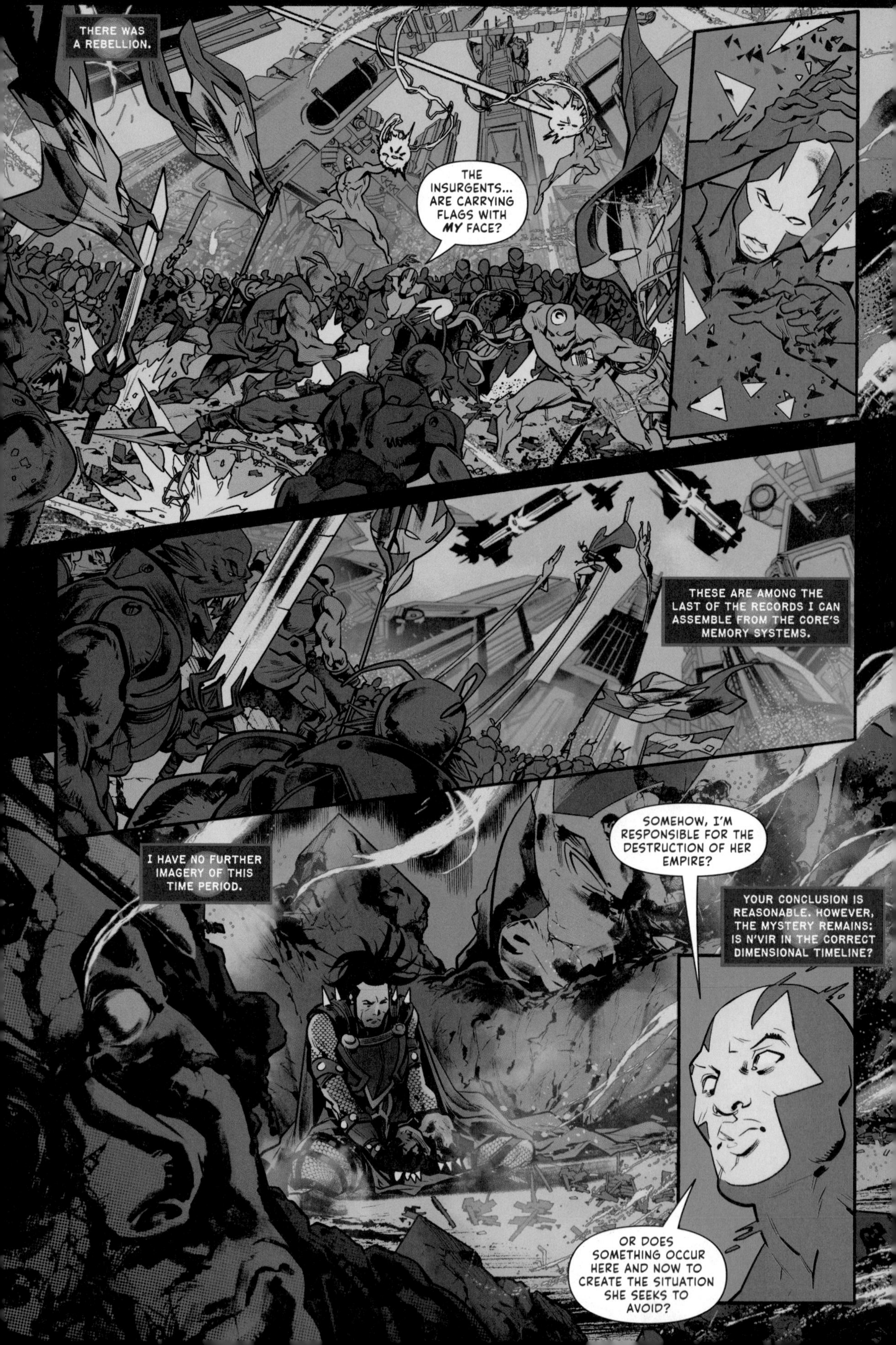
THERE WAS A REBELLION.
THE INSURGENTS... ARE CARRYING FLAGS WITH MY FACE?
THESE ARE AMONG THE LAST OF THE RECORDS I CAN ASSEMBLE FROM THE CORE'S MEMORY SYSTEMS.
I HAVE NO FURTHER IMAGERY OF THIS TIME PERIOD.
SOMEHOW, I'M RESPONSIBLE FOR THE DESTRUCTION OF HER EMPIRE?
YOUR CONCLUSION IS REASONABLE. HOWEVER, THE MYSTERY REMAINS: IS N'VIR IN THE CORRECT DIMENSIONAL TIMELINE?
OR DOES SOMETHING OCCUR HERE AND NOW TO CREATE THE SITUATION SHE SEEKS TO AVOID?

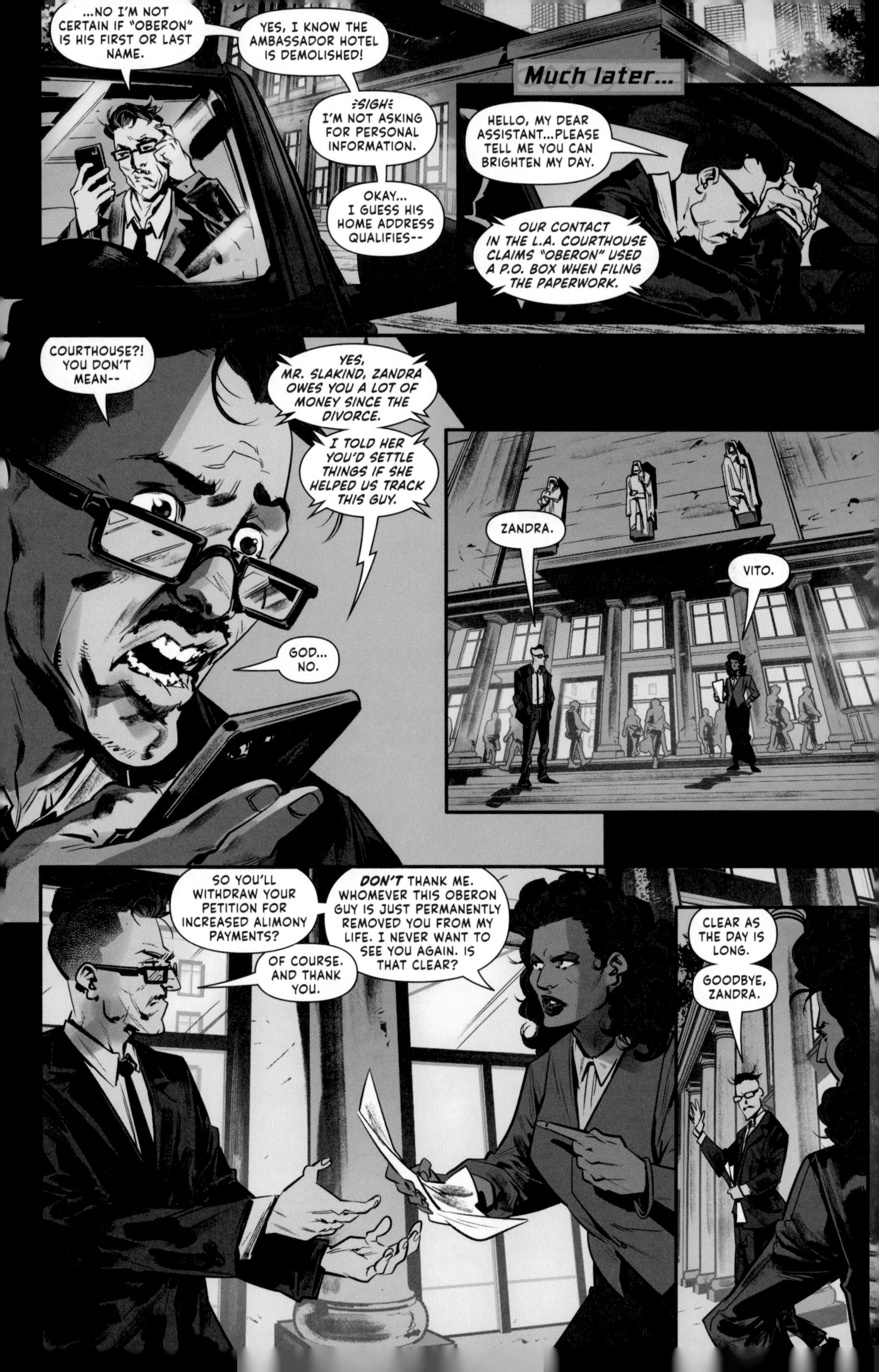
...NO I'M NOT CERTAIN IF "OBERON" IS HIS FIRST OR LAST NAME.
YES, I KNOW THE AMBASSADOR HOTEL IS DEMOLISHED!
SIGH I'M NOT ASKING FOR PERSONAL INFORMATION.
OKAY... I GUESS HIS HOME ADDRESS QUALIFIES--
Much later...
HELLO, MY DEAR ASSISTANT...PLEASE TELL ME YOU CAN BRIGHTEN MY DAY.
OUR CONTACT IN THE L.A. COURTHOUSE CLAIMS "OBERON" USED A P.O. BOX WHEN FILING THE PAPERWORK.
COURTHOUSE?! YOU DON'T MEAN--
YES, MR. SLAKIND, ZANDRA OWES YOU A LOT OF MONEY SINCE THE DIVORCE.
I TOLD HER YOU'D SETTLE THINGS IF SHE HELPED US TRACK THIS GUY.
GOD... NO.
ZANDRA.
VITO.
SO YOU'LL WITHDRAW YOUR PETITION FOR INCREASED ALIMONY PAYMENTS?
OF COURSE. AND THANK YOU.
DON'T THANK ME. WHOMEVER THIS OBERON GUY IS JUST PERMANENTLY REMOVED YOU FROM MY LIFE. I NEVER WANT TO SEE YOU AGAIN. IS THAT CLEAR?
CLEAR AS THE DAY IS LONG.
GOODBYE, ZANDRA.

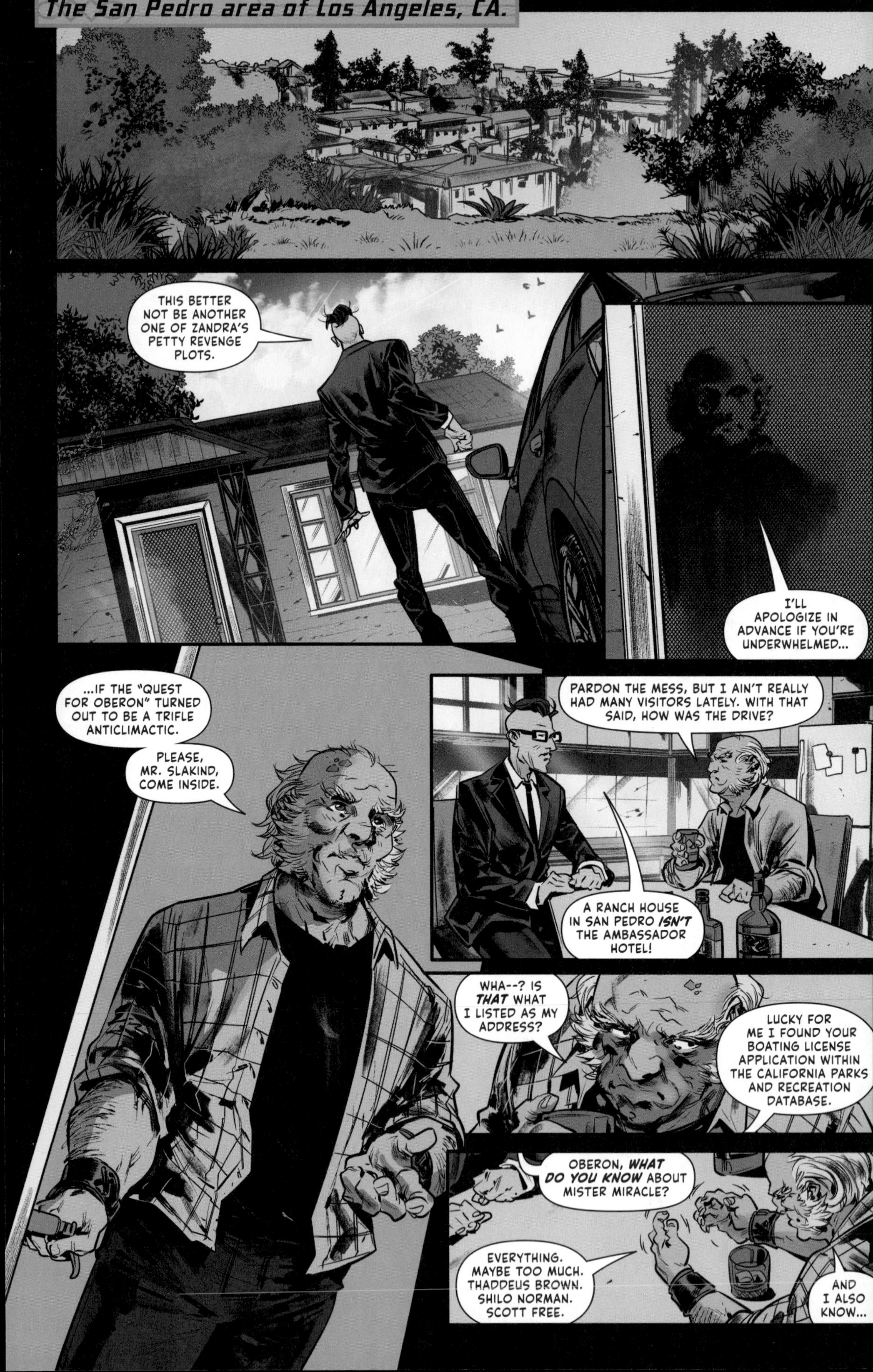
The San Pedro area of Los Angeles, CA.
THIS BETTER NOT BE ANOTHER ONE OF ZANDRA'S PETTY REVENGE PLOTS.
I'LL APOLOGIZE IN ADVANCE IF YOU'RE UNDERWHELMED...
...IF THE "QUEST FOR OBERON" TURNED OUT TO BE A TRIFLE ANTICLIMACTIC.
PLEASE, MR. SLAKIND, COME INSIDE.
PARDON THE MESS, BUT I AIN'T REALLY HAD MANY VISITORS LATELY. WITH THAT SAID, HOW WAS THE DRIVE?
A RANCH HOUSE IN SAN PEDRO ISN'T THE AMBASSADOR HOTEL!
WHA--? IS THAT WHAT I LISTED AS MY ADDRESS?
LUCKY FOR ME I FOUND YOUR BOATING LICENSE APPLICATION WITHIN THE CALIFORNIA PARKS AND RECREATION DATABASE.
OBERON, WHAT DO YOU KNOW ABOUT MISTER MIRACLE?
EVERYTHING. MAYBE TOO MUCH. THADDEUS BROWN. SHILO NORMAN. SCOTT FREE.
AND I ALSO KNOW...

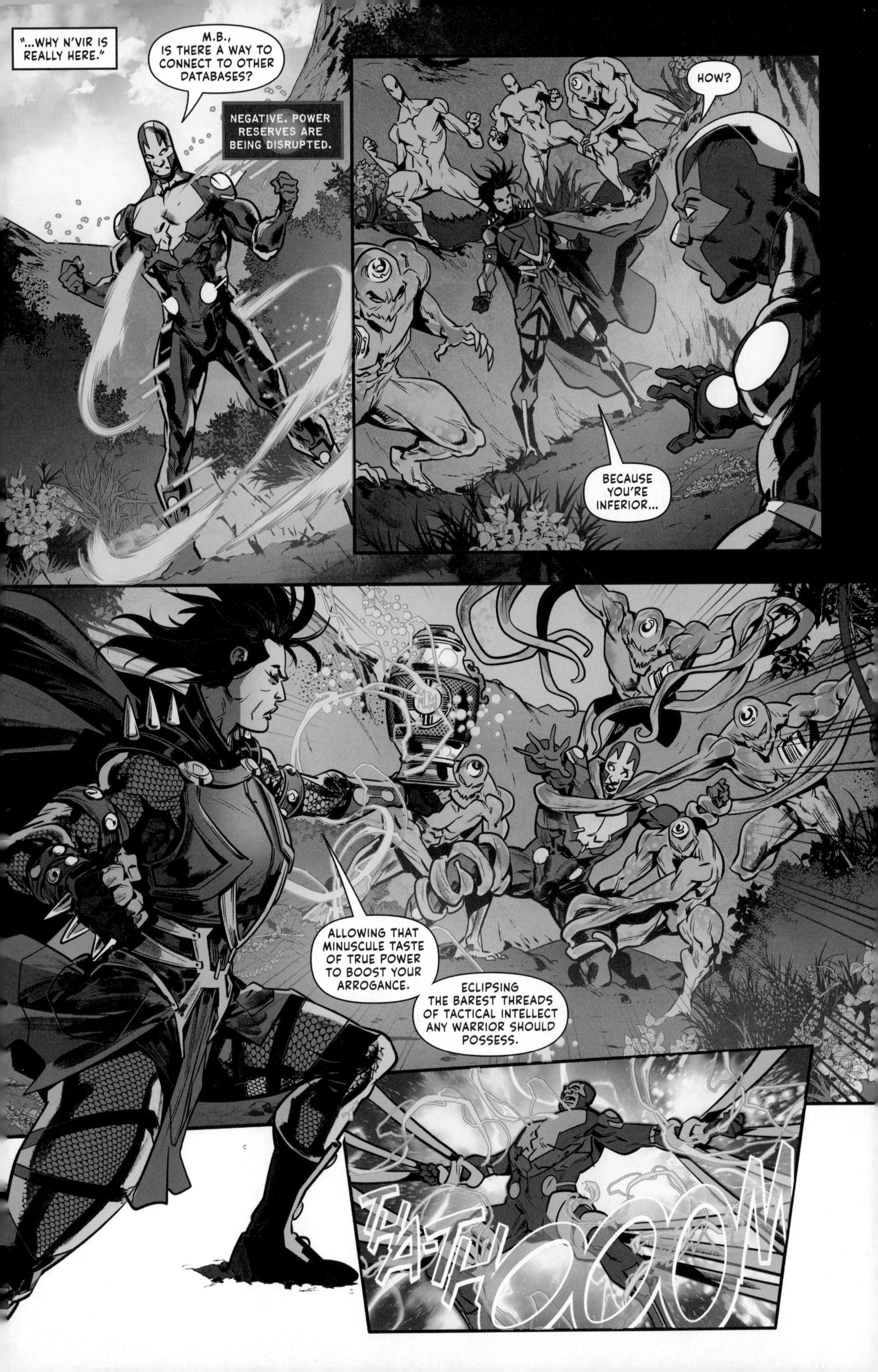
"...WHY N'VIR IS REALLY HERE."
M.B., IS THERE A WAY TO CONNECT TO OTHER DATABASES?
NEGATIVE. POWER RESERVES ARE BEING DISRUPTED.
HOW?
BECAUSE YOU'RE INFERIOR...
ALLOWING THAT MINUSCULE TASTE OF TRUE POWER TO BOOST YOUR ARROGANCE.
ECLIPSING THE BAREST THREADS OF TACTICAL INTELLECT ANY WARRIOR SHOULD POSSESS.
THA-THOOOOM

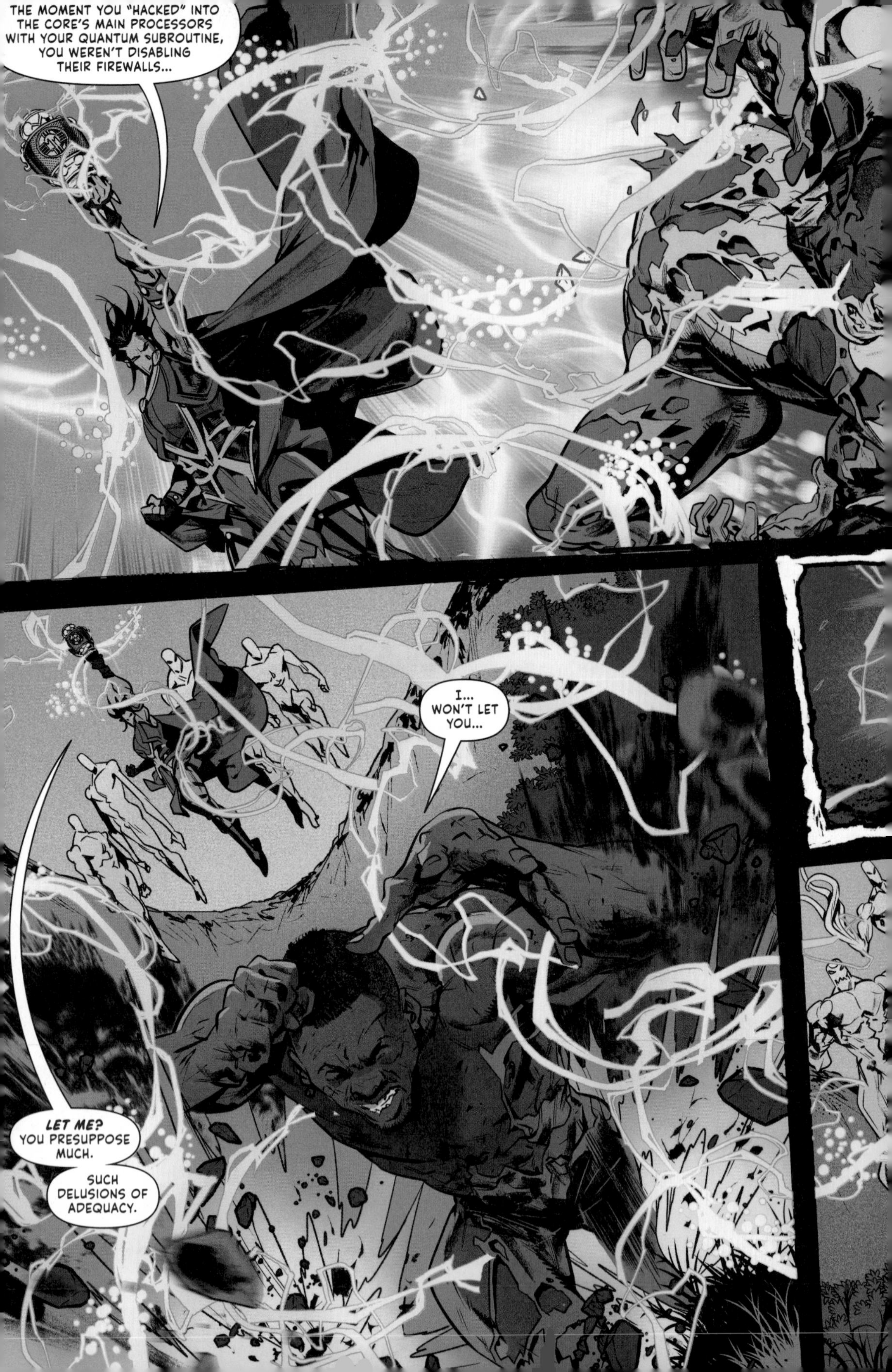
THE MOMENT YOU "HACKED" INTO THE CORE'S MAIN PROCESSORS WITH YOUR QUANTUM SUBROUTINE, YOU WEREN'T DISABLING THEIR FIREWALLS...
I... WON'T LET YOU...
LET ME? YOU PRESUPPOSE MUCH.
SUCH DELUSIONS OF ADEQUACY.

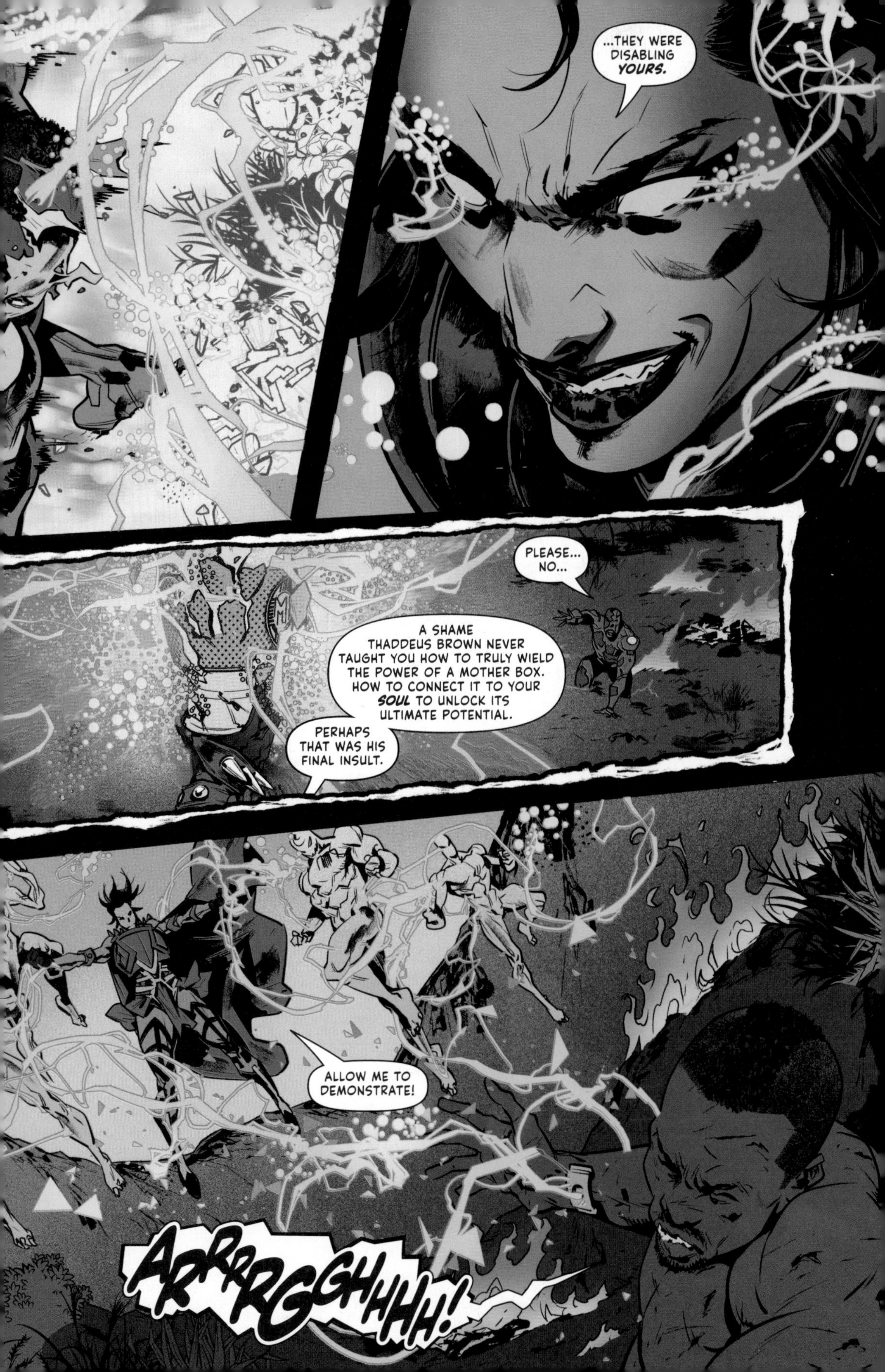
...THEY WERE DISABLING *YOURS.*
PLEASE... NO...
A SHAME THADDEUS BROWN NEVER TAUGHT YOU HOW TO TRULY WIELD THE POWER OF A MOTHER BOX. HOW TO CONNECT IT TO YOUR *SOUL* TO UNLOCK ITS ULTIMATE POTENTIAL.
PERHAPS THAT WAS HIS FINAL INSULT.
ALLOW ME TO DEMONSTRATE!
ARRRRGGHHHHH!

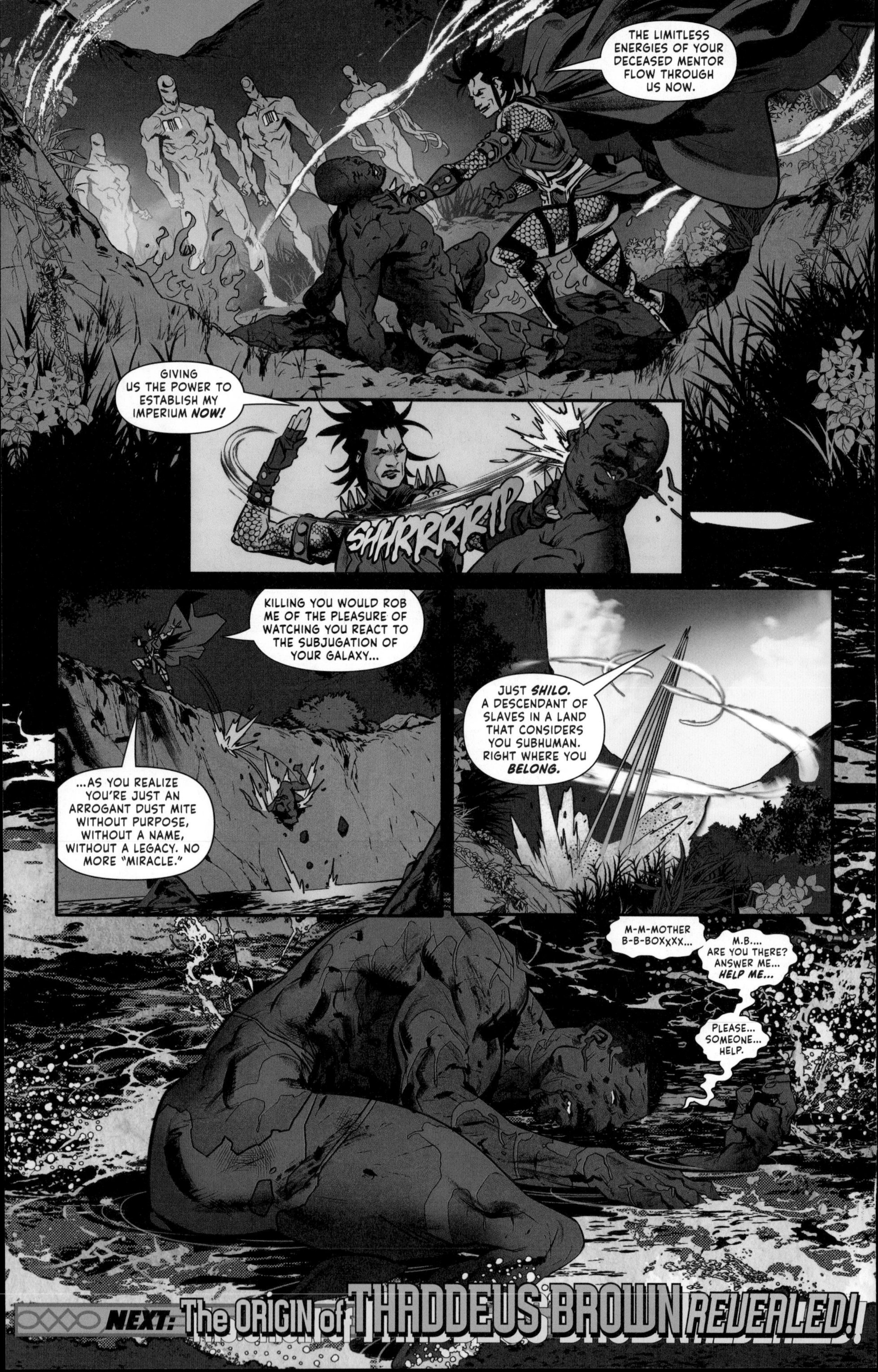
THE LIMITLESS ENERGIES OF YOUR DECEASED MENTOR FLOW THROUGH US NOW.
GIVING US THE POWER TO ESTABLISH MY IMPERIUM *NOW!*
SHHRRRRIP
KILLING YOU WOULD ROB ME OF THE PLEASURE OF WATCHING YOU REACT TO THE SUBJUGATION OF YOUR GALAXY...
...AS YOU REALIZE YOU'RE JUST AN ARROGANT DUST MITE WITHOUT PURPOSE, WITHOUT A NAME, WITHOUT A LEGACY. NO MORE "MIRACLE."
JUST *SHILO.* A DESCENDANT OF SLAVES IN A LAND THAT CONSIDERS YOU SUBHUMAN. RIGHT WHERE YOU *BELONG.*
M-M-MOTHER B-B-BOXxxx...
M.B.... ARE YOU THERE? ANSWER ME... *HELP ME...*
PLEASE... SOMEONE... HELP.
NEXT: The ORIGIN of THADDEUS BROWN REVEALED!

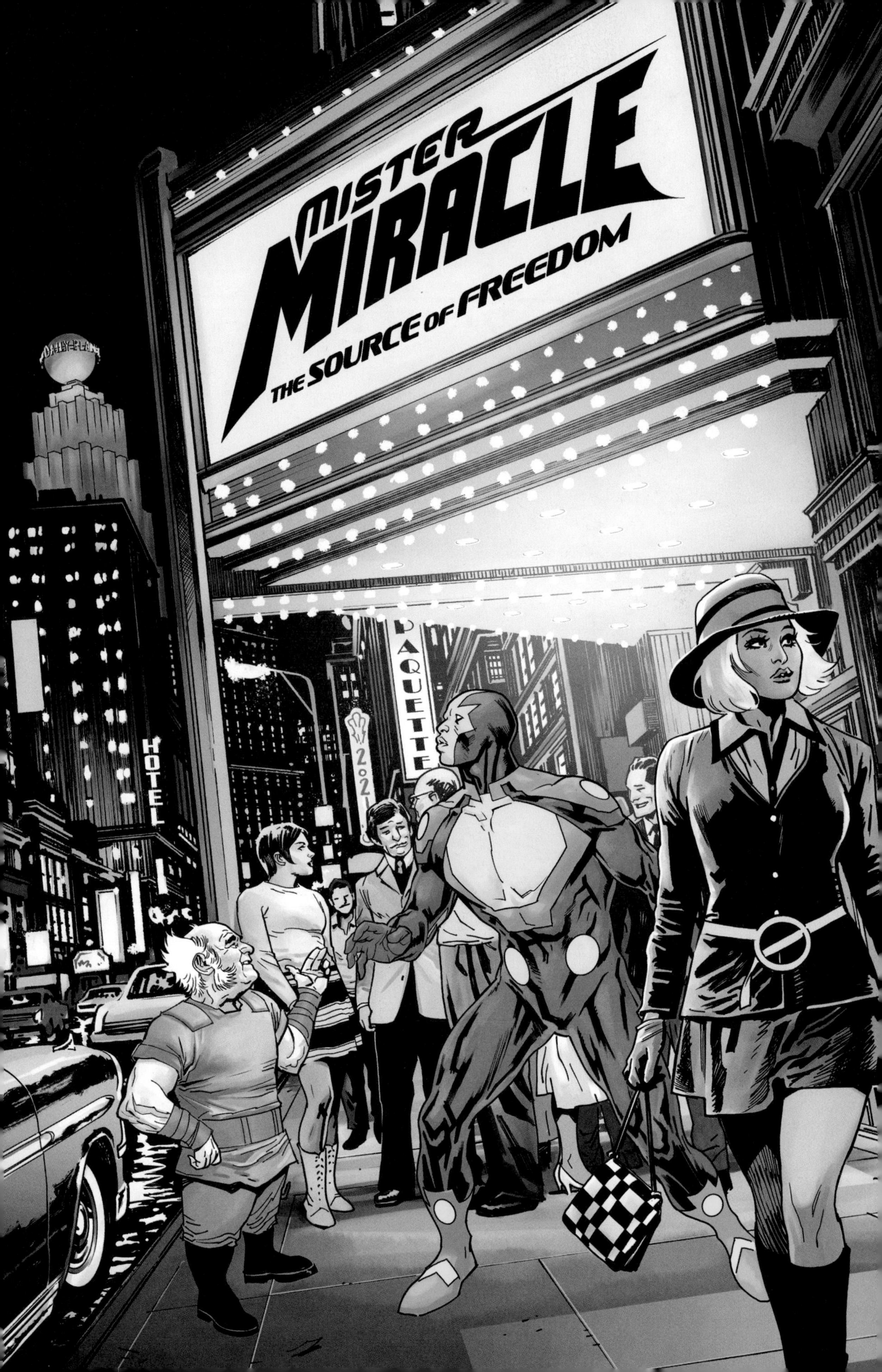
MISTER MIRACLE
THE SOURCE OF FREEDOM
PAQUETTE
HOTEL

Mister Miracle: The Source of Freedom #4
variant cover by **Juni Ba**

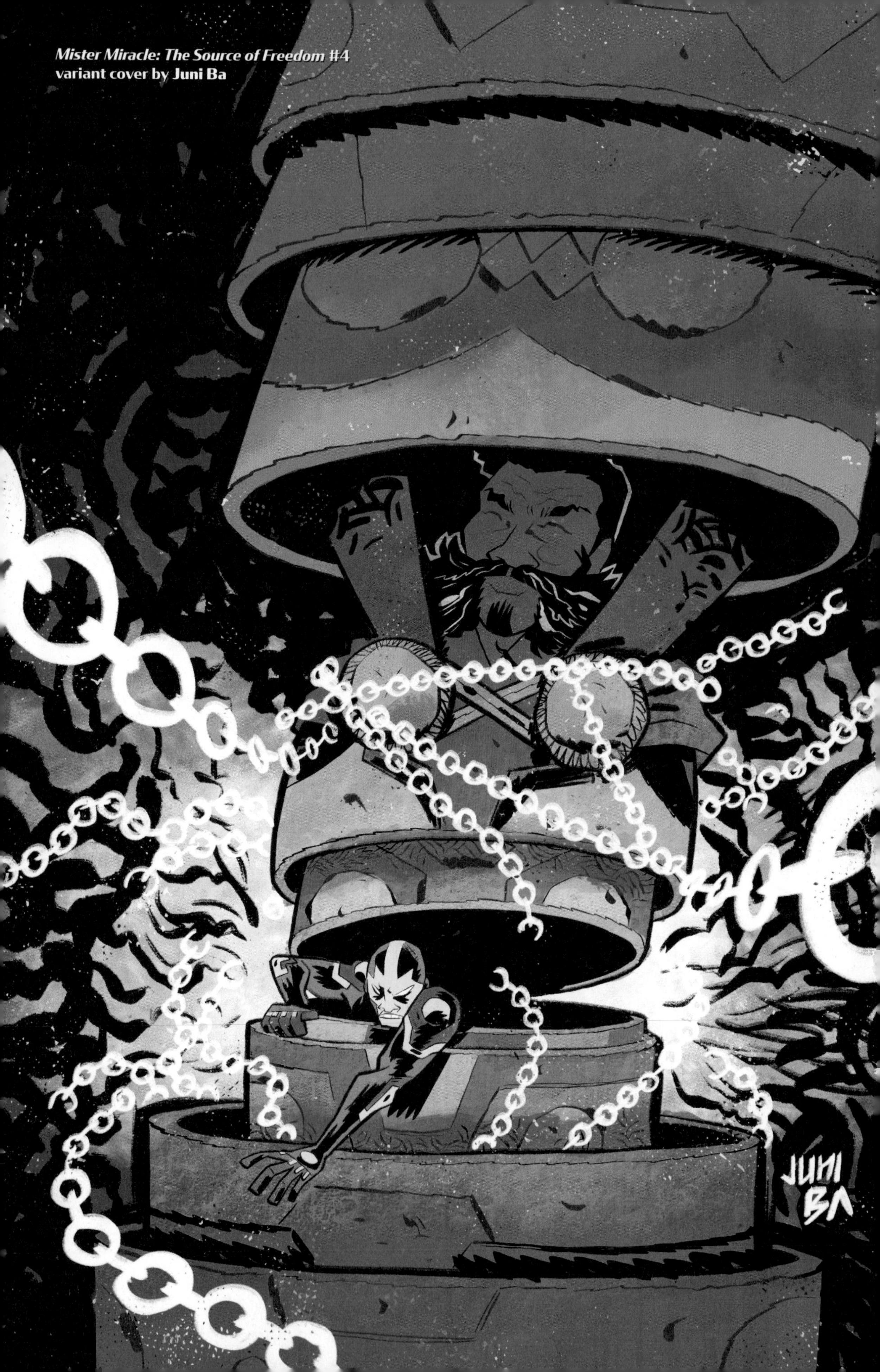

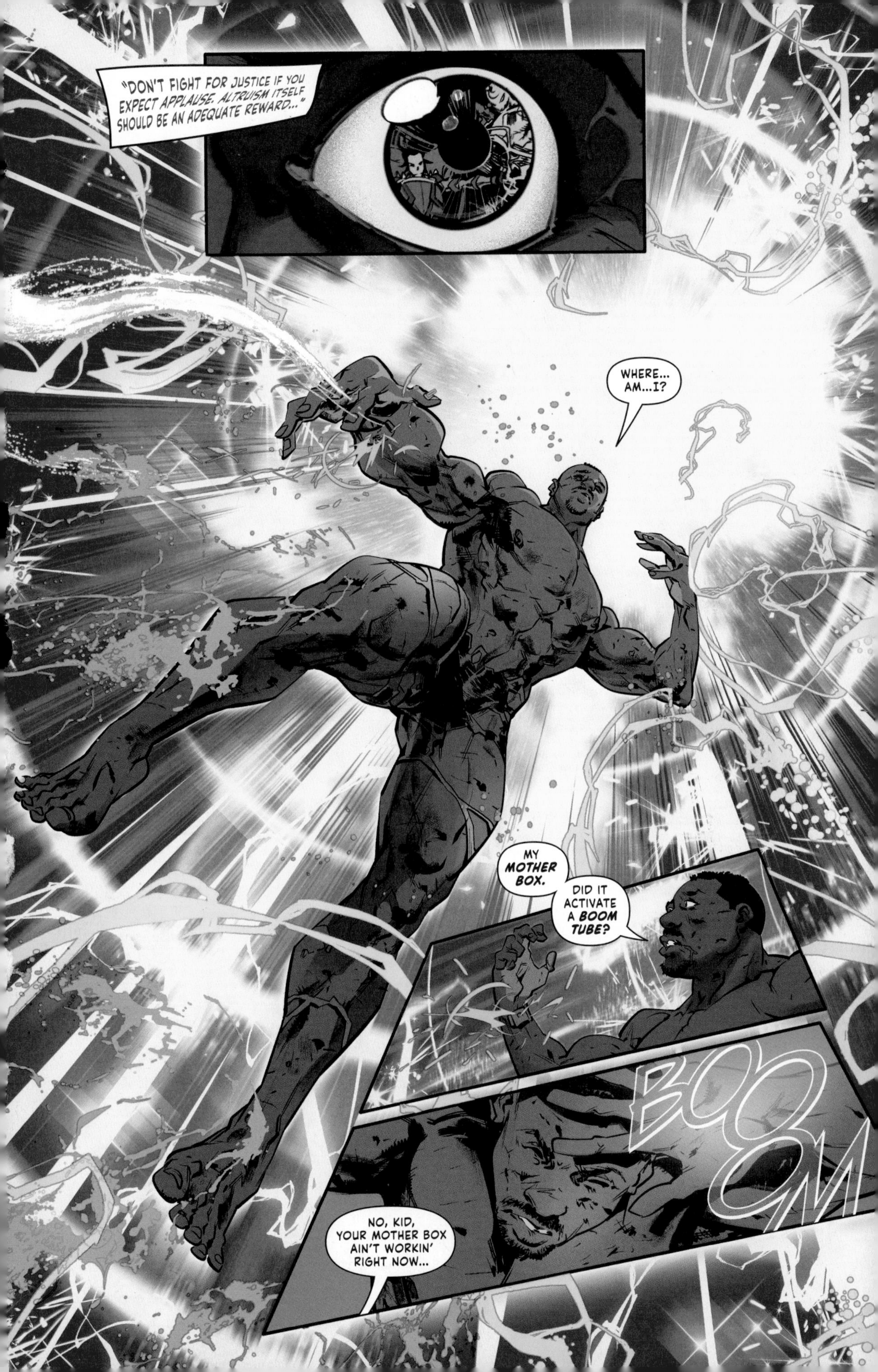
"DON'T FIGHT FOR JUSTICE IF YOU EXPECT APPLAUSE. ALTRUISM ITSELF SHOULD BE AN ADEQUATE REWARD..."
WHERE... AM...I?
MY MOTHER BOX.
DID IT ACTIVATE A BOOM TUBE?
BOOOM
NO, KID, YOUR MOTHER BOX AIN'T WORKIN' RIGHT NOW...

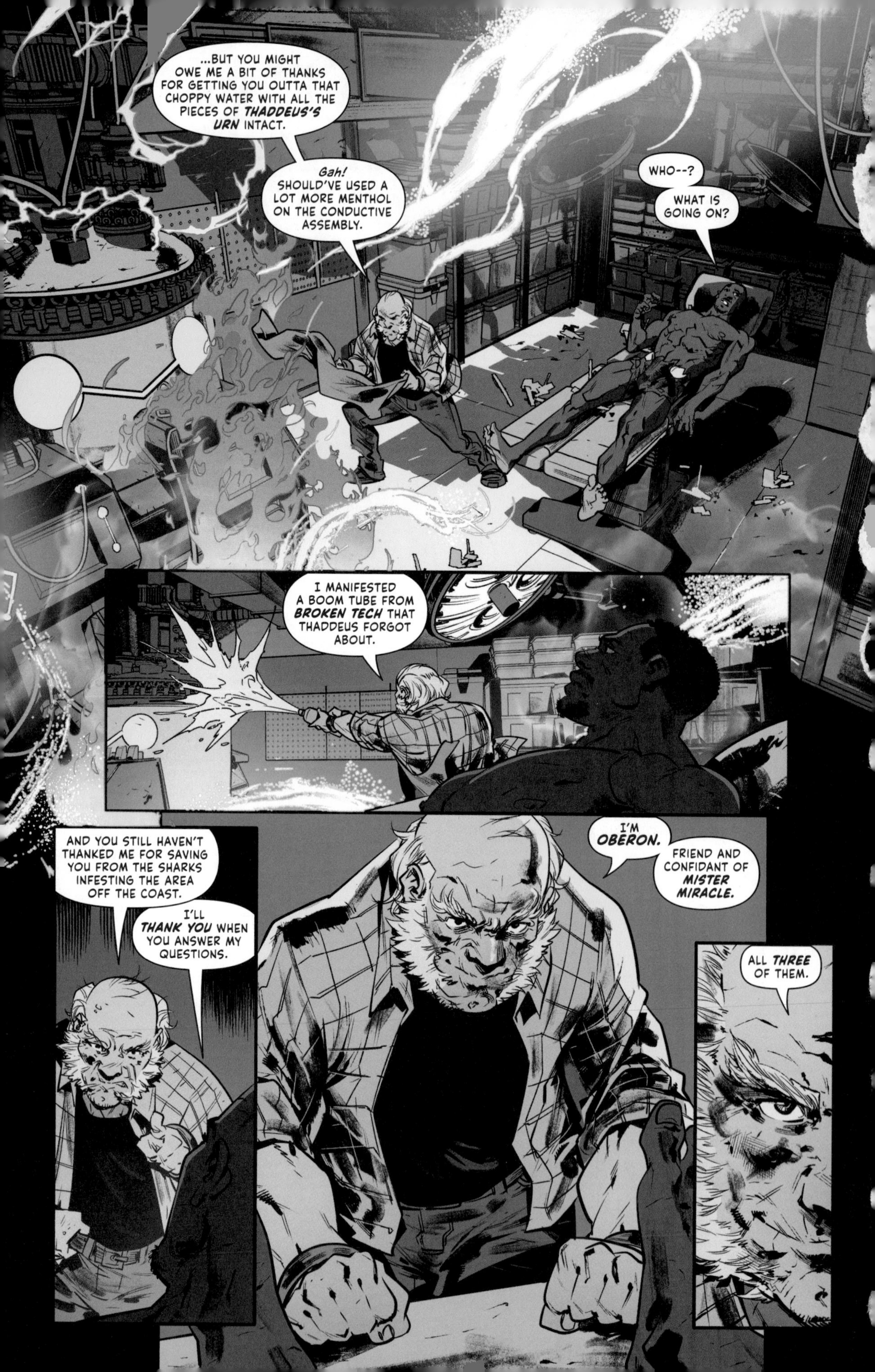
...BUT YOU MIGHT OWE ME A BIT OF THANKS FOR GETTING YOU OUTTA THAT CHOPPY WATER WITH ALL THE PIECES OF THADDEUS'S URN INTACT.
Gah! SHOULD'VE USED A LOT MORE MENTHOL ON THE CONDUCTIVE ASSEMBLY.
WHO--?
WHAT IS GOING ON?
I MANIFESTED A BOOM TUBE FROM BROKEN TECH THAT THADDEUS FORGOT ABOUT.
AND YOU STILL HAVEN'T THANKED ME FOR SAVING YOU FROM THE SHARKS INFESTING THE AREA OFF THE COAST.
I'LL THANK YOU WHEN YOU ANSWER MY QUESTIONS.
I'M OBERON.
FRIEND AND CONFIDANT OF MISTER MIRACLE.
ALL THREE OF THEM.

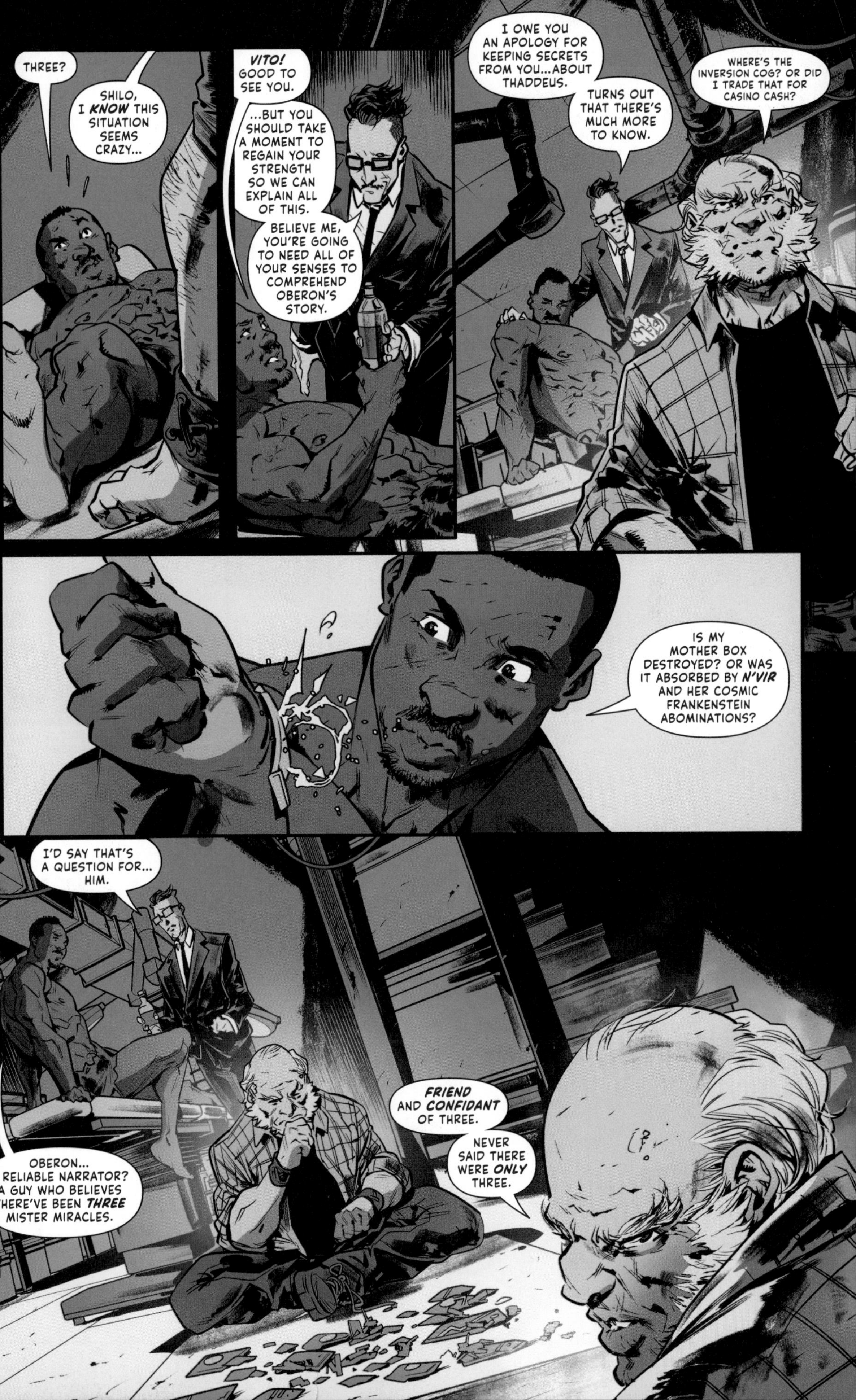
THREE?
SHILO, I KNOW THIS SITUATION SEEMS CRAZY...
VITO! GOOD TO SEE YOU.
...BUT YOU SHOULD TAKE A MOMENT TO REGAIN YOUR STRENGTH SO WE CAN EXPLAIN ALL OF THIS.
BELIEVE ME, YOU'RE GOING TO NEED ALL OF YOUR SENSES TO COMPREHEND OBERON'S STORY.
I OWE YOU AN APOLOGY FOR KEEPING SECRETS FROM YOU...ABOUT THADDEUS.
TURNS OUT THAT THERE'S MUCH MORE TO KNOW.
WHERE'S THE INVERSION COG? OR DID I TRADE THAT FOR CASINO CASH?
IS MY MOTHER BOX DESTROYED? OR WAS IT ABSORBED BY N'VIR AND HER COSMIC FRANKENSTEIN ABOMINATIONS?
I'D SAY THAT'S A QUESTION FOR... HIM.
OBERON... A RELIABLE NARRATOR? A GUY WHO BELIEVES THERE'VE BEEN THREE MISTER MIRACLES.
FRIEND AND CONFIDANT OF THREE.
NEVER SAID THERE WERE ONLY THREE.

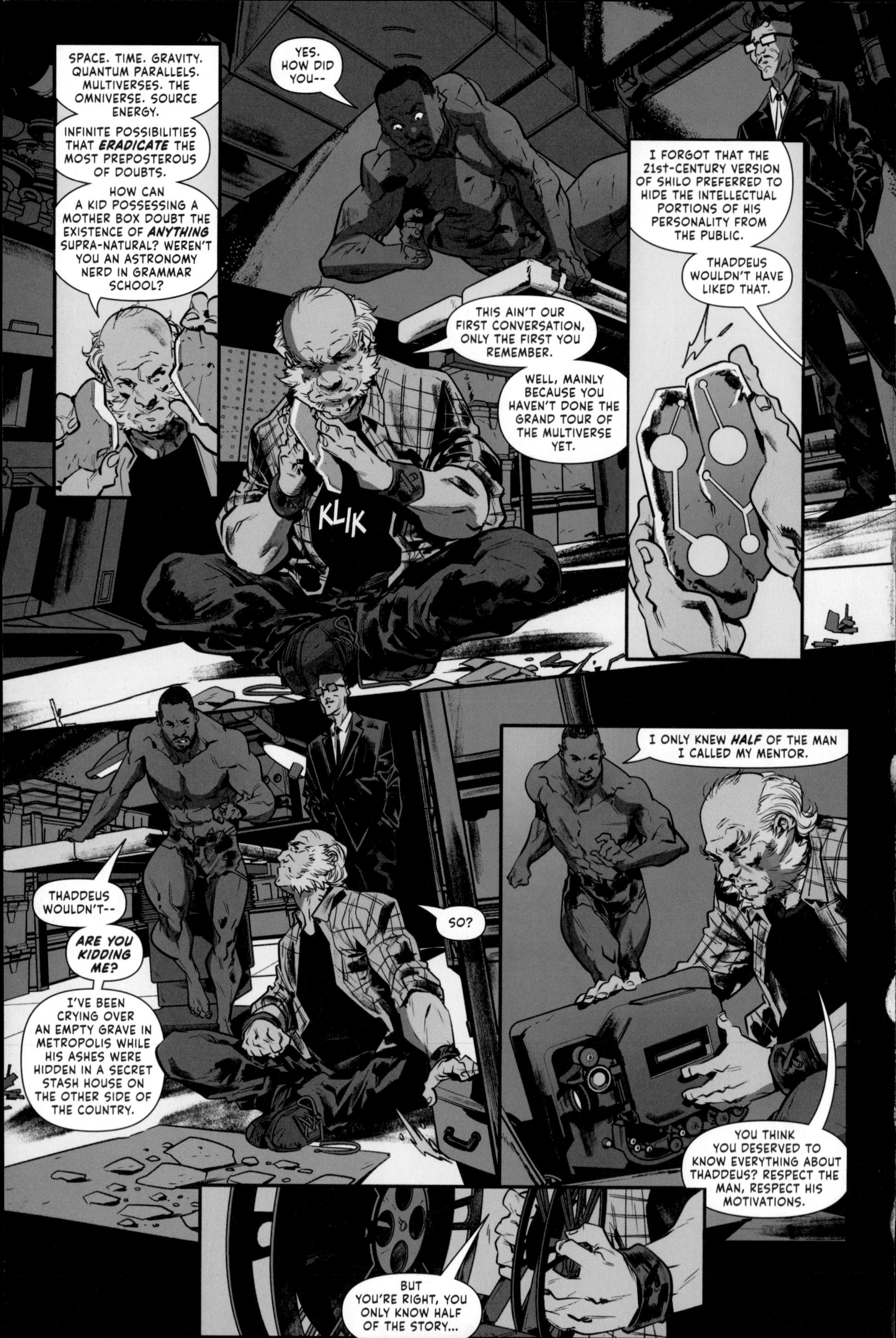
SPACE. TIME. GRAVITY. QUANTUM PARALLELS. MULTIVERSES. THE OMNIVERSE. SOURCE ENERGY.
INFINITE POSSIBILITIES THAT ERADICATE THE MOST PREPOSTEROUS OF DOUBTS.
HOW CAN A KID POSSESSING A MOTHER BOX DOUBT THE EXISTENCE OF ANYTHING SUPRA-NATURAL? WEREN'T YOU AN ASTRONOMY NERD IN GRAMMAR SCHOOL?
YES. HOW DID YOU--
THIS AIN'T OUR FIRST CONVERSATION, ONLY THE FIRST YOU REMEMBER.
WELL, MAINLY BECAUSE YOU HAVEN'T DONE THE GRAND TOUR OF THE MULTIVERSE YET.
KLIK
I FORGOT THAT THE 21st-CENTURY VERSION OF SHILO PREFERRED TO HIDE THE INTELLECTUAL PORTIONS OF HIS PERSONALITY FROM THE PUBLIC.
THADDEUS WOULDN'T HAVE LIKED THAT.
THADDEUS WOULDN'T--
SO?
ARE YOU KIDDING ME?
I'VE BEEN CRYING OVER AN EMPTY GRAVE IN METROPOLIS WHILE HIS ASHES WERE HIDDEN IN A SECRET STASH HOUSE ON THE OTHER SIDE OF THE COUNTRY.
I ONLY KNEW HALF OF THE MAN I CALLED MY MENTOR.
YOU THINK YOU DESERVED TO KNOW EVERYTHING ABOUT THADDEUS? RESPECT THE MAN, RESPECT HIS MOTIVATIONS.
BUT YOU'RE RIGHT, YOU ONLY KNOW HALF OF THE STORY...

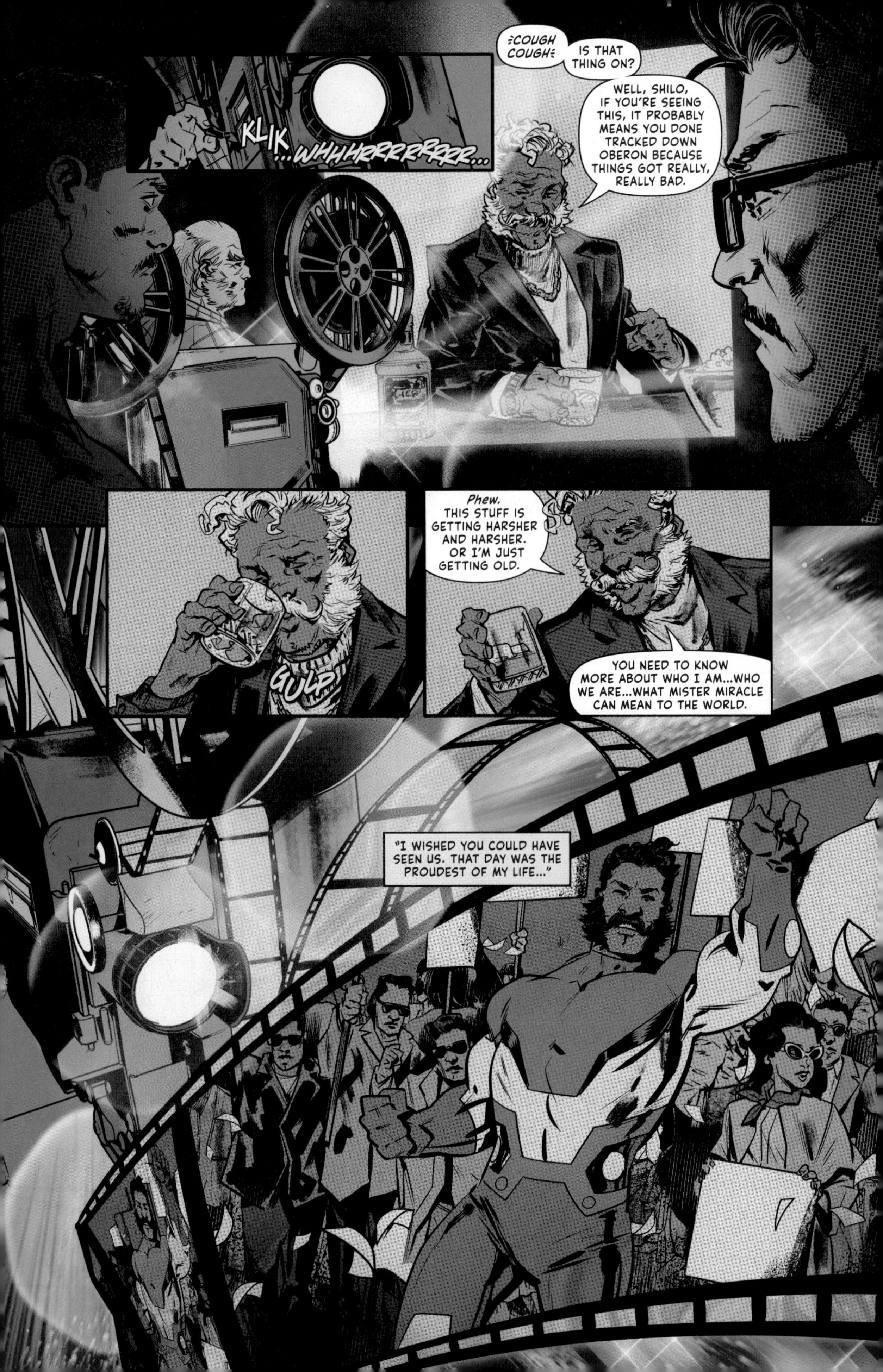
KLIK...WHHHRRRRRRRR...
=COUGH COUGH=
IS THAT THING ON?
WELL, SHILO, IF YOU'RE SEEING THIS, IT PROBABLY MEANS YOU DONE TRACKED DOWN OBERON BECAUSE THINGS GOT REALLY, REALLY BAD.
GULP
Phew. THIS STUFF IS GETTING HARSHER AND HARSHER. OR I'M JUST GETTING OLD.
YOU NEED TO KNOW MORE ABOUT WHO I AM...WHO WE ARE...WHAT MISTER MIRACLE CAN MEAN TO THE WORLD.
"I WISHED YOU COULD HAVE SEEN US. THAT DAY WAS THE PROUDEST OF MY LIFE..."

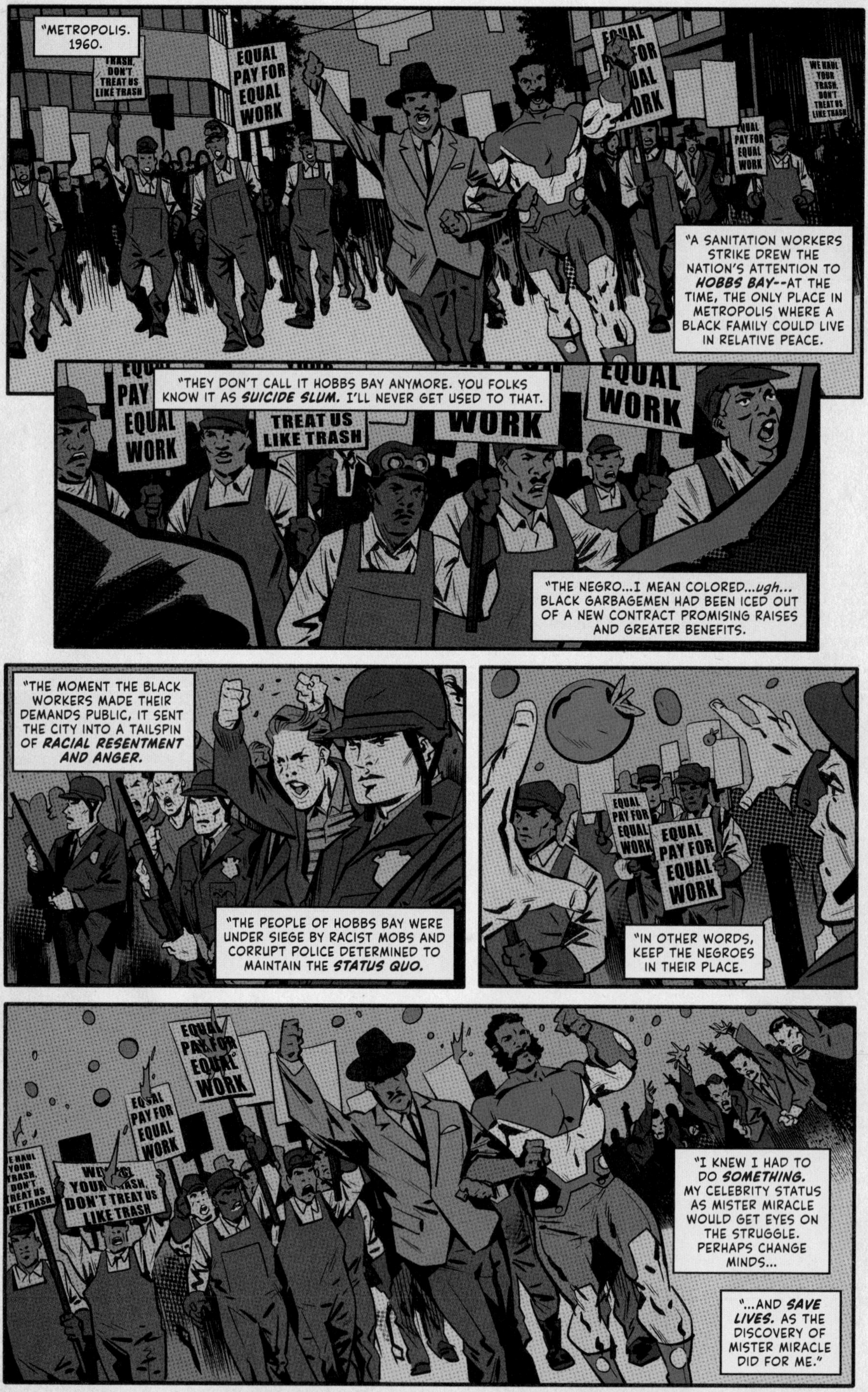
"METROPOLIS. 1960.
TRASH, DON'T TREAT US LIKE TRASH
EQUAL PAY FOR EQUAL WORK
EQUAL PAY FOR EQUAL WORK
WE HAUL YOUR TRASH, DON'T TREAT US LIKE TRASH
EQUAL PAY FOR EQUAL WORK
"A SANITATION WORKERS STRIKE DREW THE NATION'S ATTENTION TO HOBBS BAY--AT THE TIME, THE ONLY PLACE IN METROPOLIS WHERE A BLACK FAMILY COULD LIVE IN RELATIVE PEACE.
"THEY DON'T CALL IT HOBBS BAY ANYMORE. YOU FOLKS KNOW IT AS SUICIDE SLUM. I'LL NEVER GET USED TO THAT.
PAY FOR EQUAL WORK
TREAT US LIKE TRASH
WORK
EQUAL WORK
"THE NEGRO...I MEAN COLORED...ugh... BLACK GARBAGEMEN HAD BEEN ICED OUT OF A NEW CONTRACT PROMISING RAISES AND GREATER BENEFITS.
"THE MOMENT THE BLACK WORKERS MADE THEIR DEMANDS PUBLIC, IT SENT THE CITY INTO A TAILSPIN OF RACIAL RESENTMENT AND ANGER.
"THE PEOPLE OF HOBBS BAY WERE UNDER SIEGE BY RACIST MOBS AND CORRUPT POLICE DETERMINED TO MAINTAIN THE STATUS QUO.
EQUAL PAY FOR EQUAL WORK
EQUAL PAY FOR EQUAL WORK
"IN OTHER WORDS, KEEP THE NEGROES IN THEIR PLACE.
EQUAL PAY FOR EQUAL WORK
EQUAL PAY FOR EQUAL WORK
YOUR TRASH, DON'T TREAT US LIKE TRASH
DON'T TREAT US LIKE TRASH
"I KNEW I HAD TO DO SOMETHING. MY CELEBRITY STATUS AS MISTER MIRACLE WOULD GET EYES ON THE STRUGGLE. PERHAPS CHANGE MINDS...
"...AND SAVE LIVES. AS THE DISCOVERY OF MISTER MIRACLE DID FOR ME."

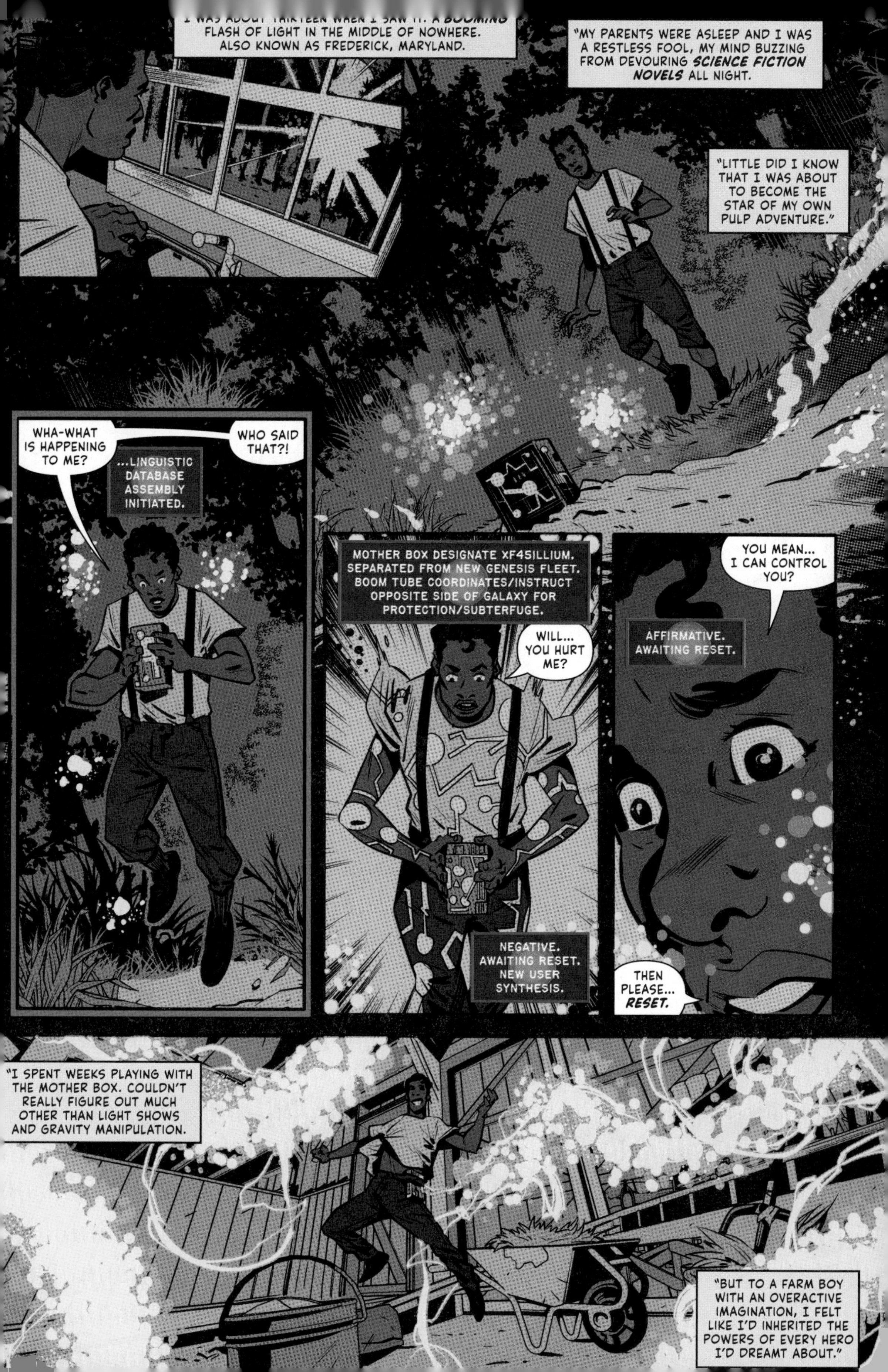

I WAS ABOUT THIRTEEN WHEN I SAW IT. A *BOOMING*
FLASH OF LIGHT IN THE MIDDLE OF NOWHERE. ALSO KNOWN AS FREDERICK, MARYLAND.
"MY PARENTS WERE ASLEEP AND I WAS A RESTLESS FOOL, MY MIND BUZZING FROM DEVOURING ***SCIENCE FICTION NOVELS*** ALL NIGHT.
"LITTLE DID I KNOW THAT I WAS ABOUT TO BECOME THE STAR OF MY OWN PULP ADVENTURE."
WHA-WHAT IS HAPPENING TO ME?
...LINGUISTIC DATABASE ASSEMBLY INITIATED.
WHO SAID THAT?!
MOTHER BOX DESIGNATE XF45ILLIUM. SEPARATED FROM NEW GENESIS FLEET. BOOM TUBE COORDINATES/INSTRUCT OPPOSITE SIDE OF GALAXY FOR PROTECTION/SUBTERFUGE.
WILL... YOU HURT ME?
NEGATIVE. AWAITING RESET. NEW USER SYNTHESIS.
YOU MEAN... I CAN CONTROL YOU?
AFFIRMATIVE. AWAITING RESET.
THEN PLEASE... ***RESET.***
"I SPENT WEEKS PLAYING WITH THE MOTHER BOX. COULDN'T REALLY FIGURE OUT MUCH OTHER THAN LIGHT SHOWS AND GRAVITY MANIPULATION.
"BUT TO A FARM BOY WITH AN OVERACTIVE IMAGINATION, I FELT LIKE I'D INHERITED THE POWERS OF EVERY HERO I'D DREAMT ABOUT."

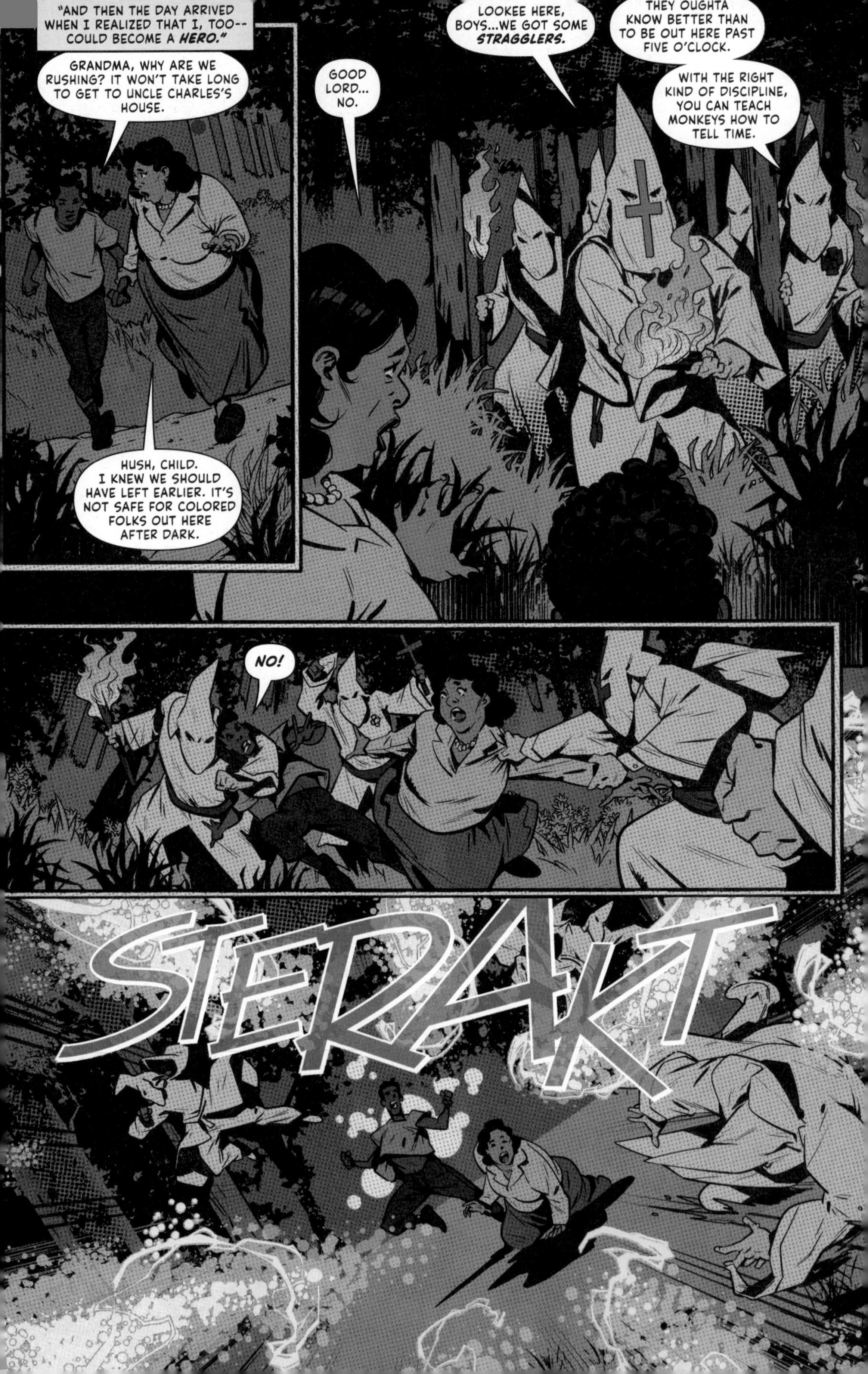
"AND THEN THE DAY ARRIVED WHEN I REALIZED THAT I, TOO-- COULD BECOME A *HERO.*"
GRANDMA, WHY ARE WE RUSHING? IT WON'T TAKE LONG TO GET TO UNCLE CHARLES'S HOUSE.
HUSH, CHILD. I KNEW WE SHOULD HAVE LEFT EARLIER. IT'S NOT SAFE FOR COLORED FOLKS OUT HERE AFTER DARK.
GOOD LORD... NO.
LOOKEE HERE, BOYS...WE GOT SOME *STRAGGLERS.*
THEY OUGHTA KNOW BETTER THAN TO BE OUT HERE PAST FIVE O'CLOCK.
WITH THE RIGHT KIND OF DISCIPLINE, YOU CAN TEACH MONKEYS HOW TO TELL TIME.
NO!
SFERAKT

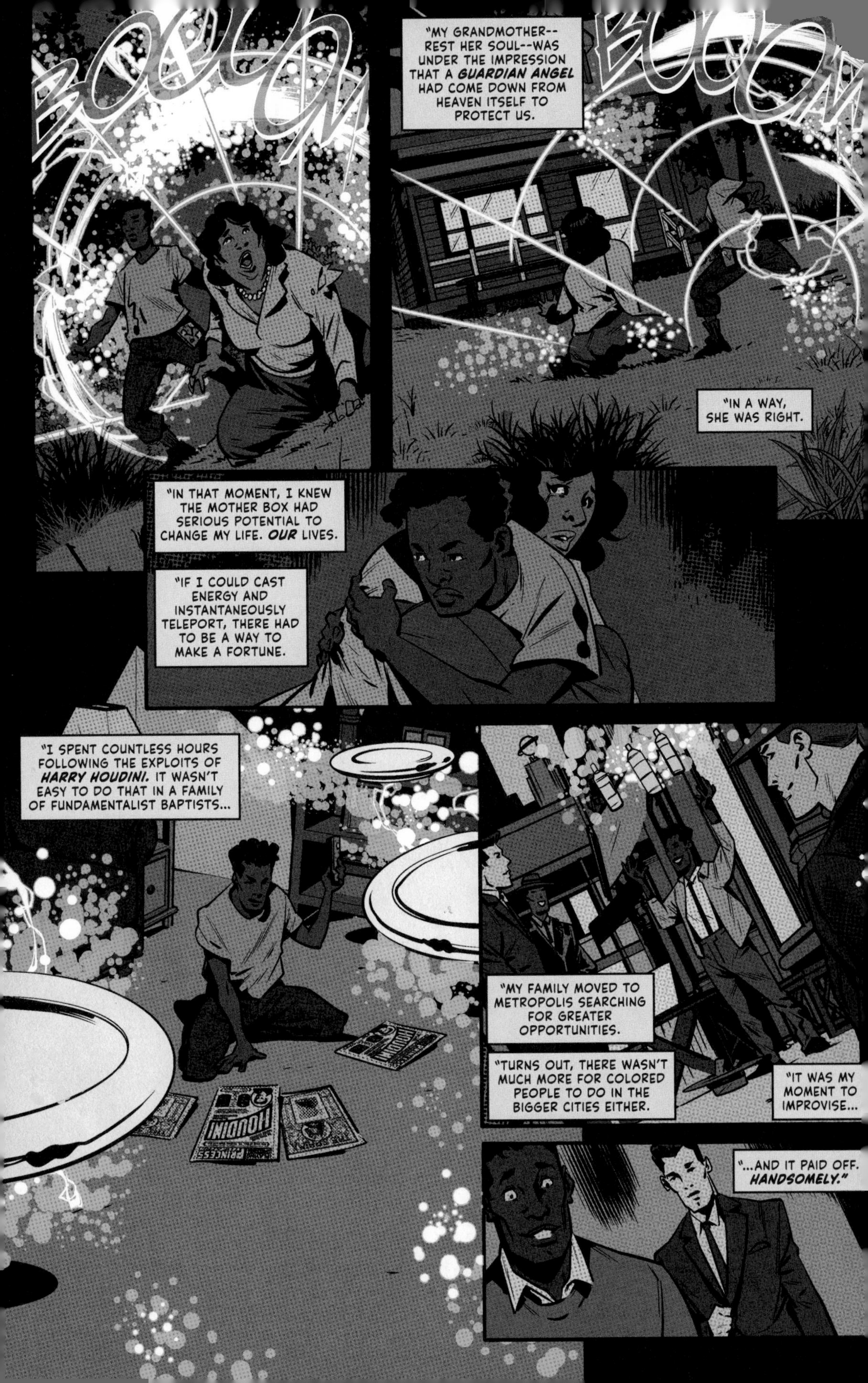
BOOOOM
"MY GRANDMOTHER--
REST HER SOUL--WAS UNDER THE IMPRESSION THAT A GUARDIAN ANGEL HAD COME DOWN FROM HEAVEN ITSELF TO PROTECT US.
BOOOM
"IN A WAY, SHE WAS RIGHT.
"IN THAT MOMENT, I KNEW THE MOTHER BOX HAD SERIOUS POTENTIAL TO CHANGE MY LIFE. OUR LIVES.
"IF I COULD CAST ENERGY AND INSTANTANEOUSLY TELEPORT, THERE HAD TO BE A WAY TO MAKE A FORTUNE.
"I SPENT COUNTLESS HOURS FOLLOWING THE EXPLOITS OF HARRY HOUDINI. IT WASN'T EASY TO DO THAT IN A FAMILY OF FUNDAMENTALIST BAPTISTS...
HOUDINI
HOUDINI
PRINCESS
"MY FAMILY MOVED TO METROPOLIS SEARCHING FOR GREATER OPPORTUNITIES.
"TURNS OUT, THERE WASN'T MUCH MORE FOR COLORED PEOPLE TO DO IN THE BIGGER CITIES EITHER.
"IT WAS MY MOMENT TO IMPROVISE...
"...AND IT PAID OFF. HANDSOMELY."

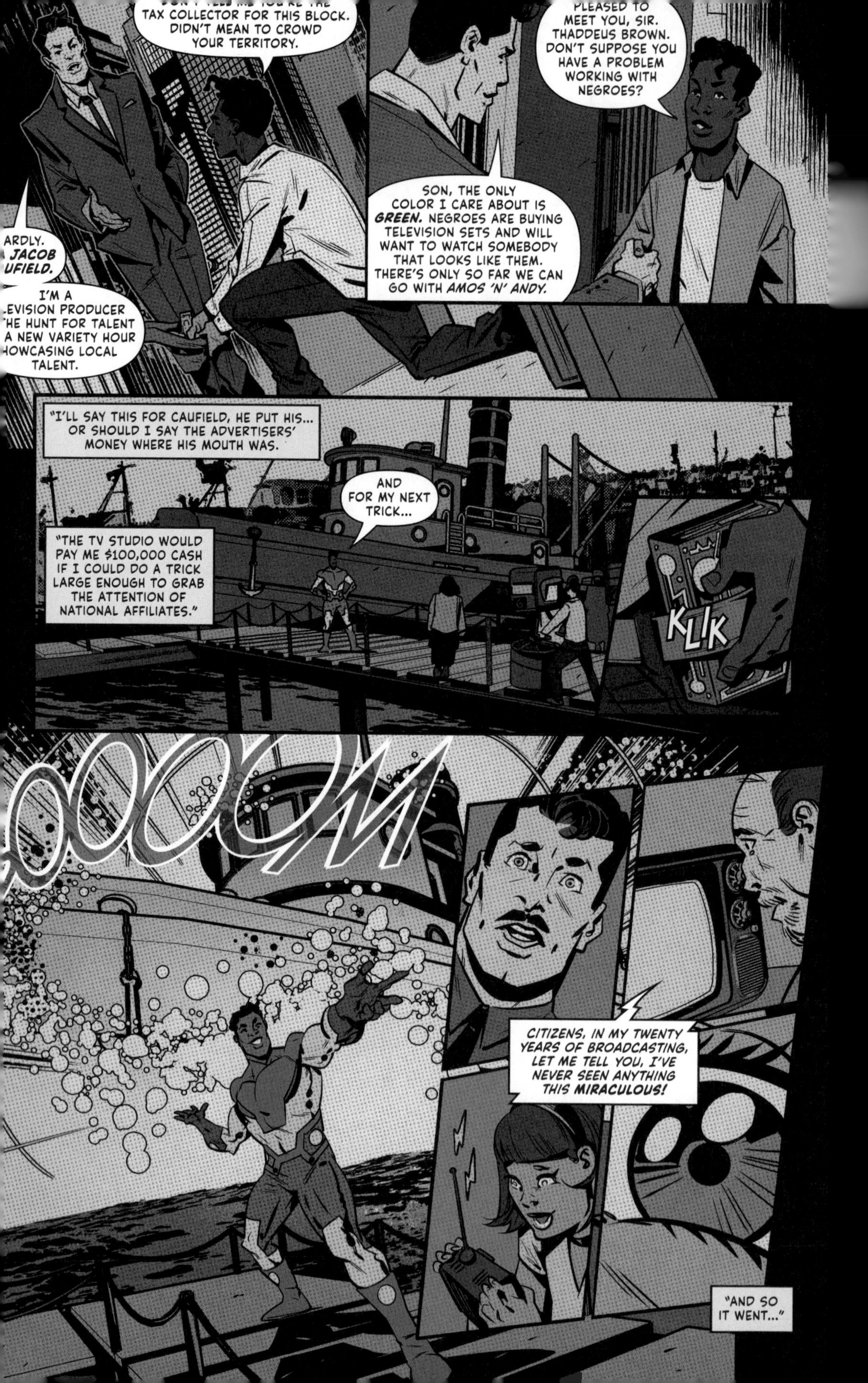

TAX COLLECTOR FOR THIS BLOCK. DIDN'T MEAN TO CROWD YOUR TERRITORY.
ARDLY. JACOB UFIELD.
I'M A EVISION PRODUCER HE HUNT FOR TALENT A NEW VARIETY HOUR HOWCASING LOCAL TALENT.
PLEASED TO MEET YOU, SIR. THADDEUS BROWN. DON'T SUPPOSE YOU HAVE A PROBLEM WORKING WITH NEGROES?
SON, THE ONLY COLOR I CARE ABOUT IS GREEN. NEGROES ARE BUYING TELEVISION SETS AND WILL WANT TO WATCH SOMEBODY THAT LOOKS LIKE THEM. THERE'S ONLY SO FAR WE CAN GO WITH AMOS 'N' ANDY.
"I'LL SAY THIS FOR CAUFIELD, HE PUT HIS... OR SHOULD I SAY THE ADVERTISERS' MONEY WHERE HIS MOUTH WAS.
AND FOR MY NEXT TRICK...
"THE TV STUDIO WOULD PAY ME $100,000 CASH IF I COULD DO A TRICK LARGE ENOUGH TO GRAB THE ATTENTION OF NATIONAL AFFILIATES."
KLIK
OOOOM
CITIZENS, IN MY TWENTY YEARS OF BROADCASTING, LET ME TELL YOU, I'VE NEVER SEEN ANYTHING THIS MIRACULOUS!
"AND SO IT WENT..."

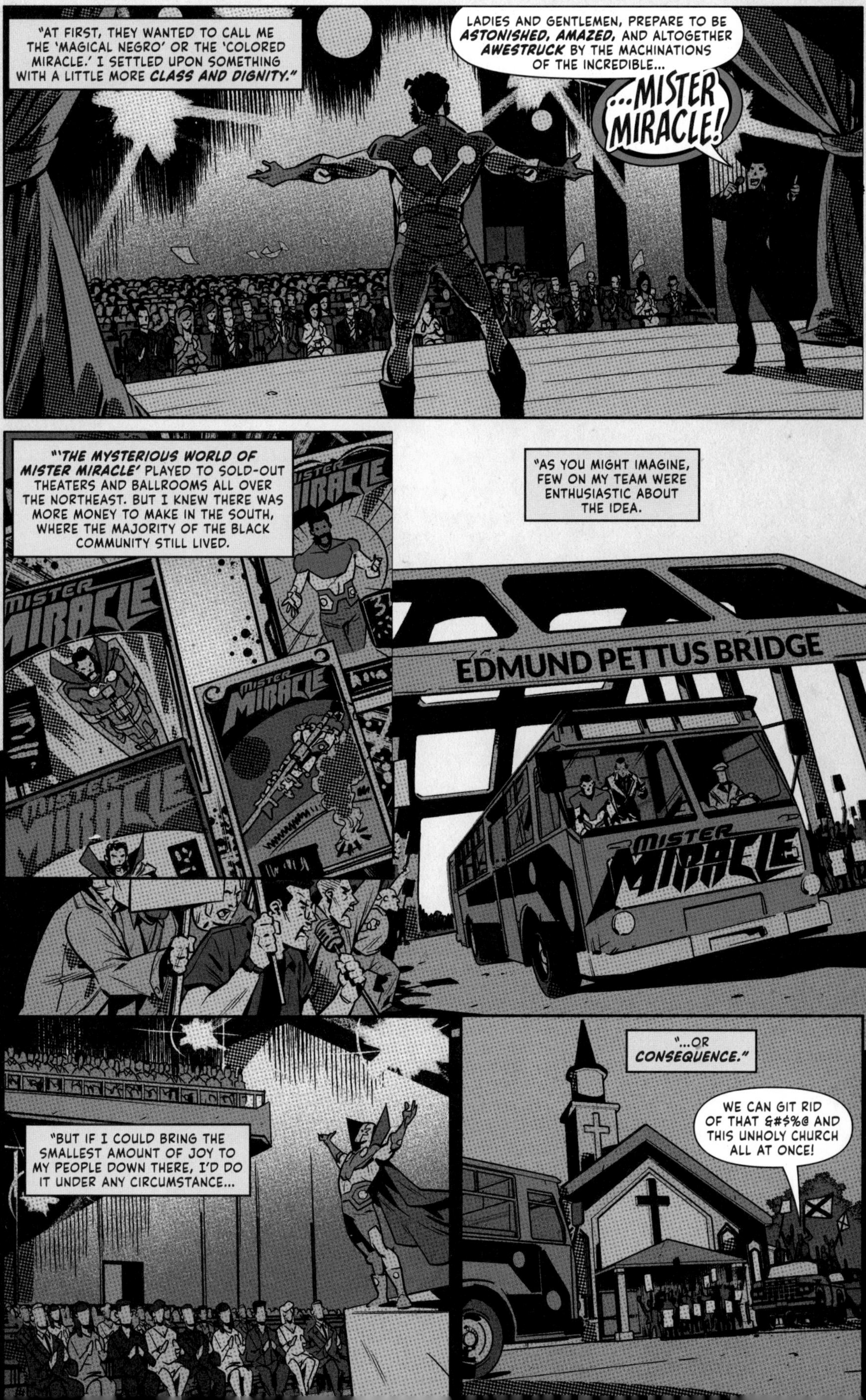
"AT FIRST, THEY WANTED TO CALL ME THE 'MAGICAL NEGRO' OR THE 'COLORED MIRACLE.' I SETTLED UPON SOMETHING WITH A LITTLE MORE CLASS AND DIGNITY."
LADIES AND GENTLEMEN, PREPARE TO BE ASTONISHED, AMAZED, AND ALTOGETHER AWESTRUCK BY THE MACHINATIONS OF THE INCREDIBLE...
...MISTER MIRACLE!
"'THE MYSTERIOUS WORLD OF MISTER MIRACLE' PLAYED TO SOLD-OUT THEATERS AND BALLROOMS ALL OVER THE NORTHEAST. BUT I KNEW THERE WAS MORE MONEY TO MAKE IN THE SOUTH, WHERE THE MAJORITY OF THE BLACK COMMUNITY STILL LIVED.
MISTER MIRACLE
"AS YOU MIGHT IMAGINE, FEW ON MY TEAM WERE ENTHUSIASTIC ABOUT THE IDEA.
EDMUND PETTUS BRIDGE
MISTER MIRACLE
"BUT IF I COULD BRING THE SMALLEST AMOUNT OF JOY TO MY PEOPLE DOWN THERE, I'D DO IT UNDER ANY CIRCUMSTANCE...
"...OR CONSEQUENCE."
WE CAN GIT RID OF THAT &#$%@ AND THIS UNHOLY CHURCH ALL AT ONCE!

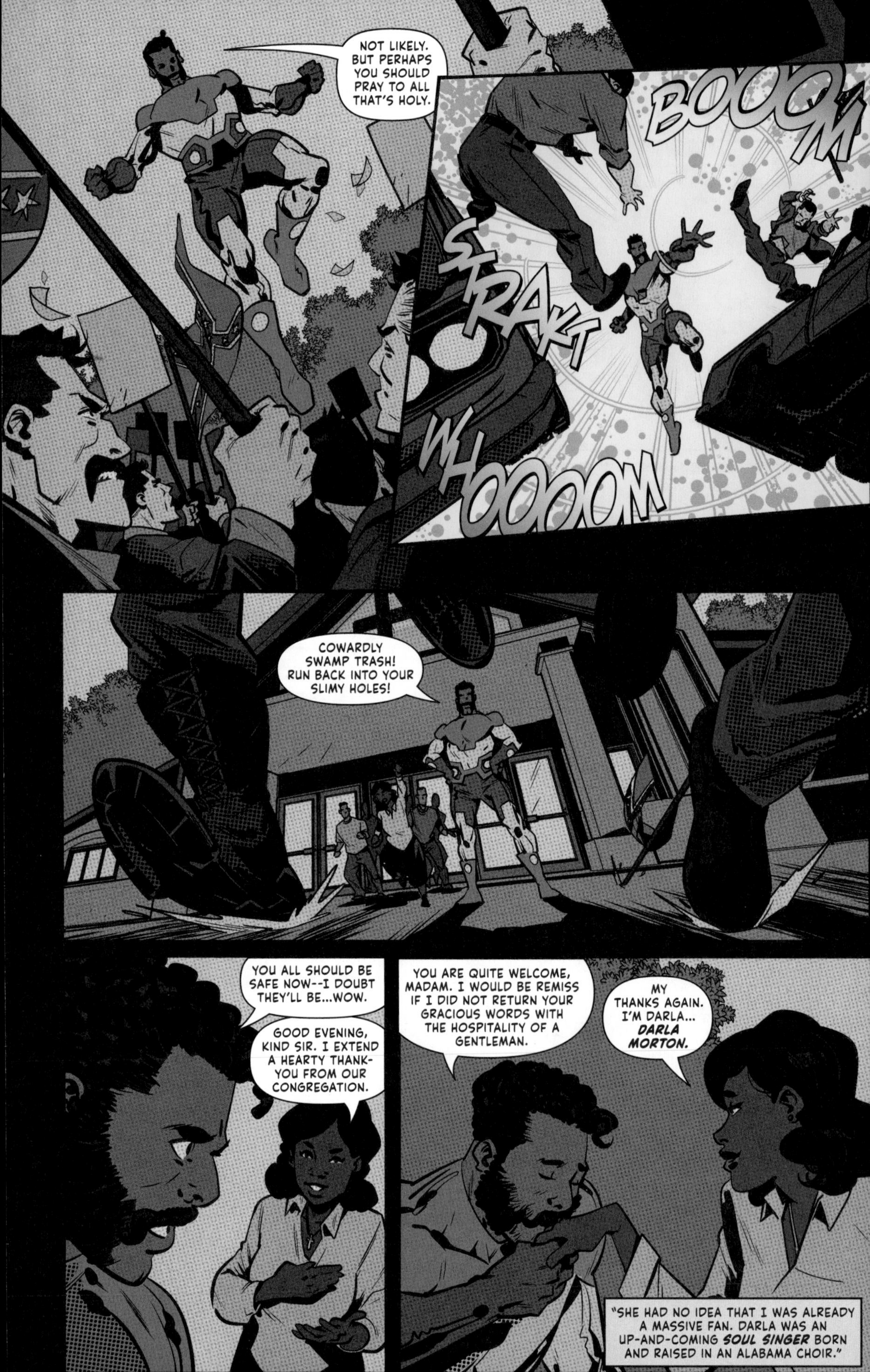
NOT LIKELY. BUT PERHAPS YOU SHOULD PRAY TO ALL THAT'S HOLY.
BOOOM
SHRAKT
WHOOOOM
COWARDLY SWAMP TRASH! RUN BACK INTO YOUR SLIMY HOLES!
YOU ALL SHOULD BE SAFE NOW--I DOUBT THEY'LL BE...WOW.
GOOD EVENING, KIND SIR. I EXTEND A HEARTY THANK-YOU FROM OUR CONGREGATION.
YOU ARE QUITE WELCOME, MADAM. I WOULD BE REMISS IF I DID NOT RETURN YOUR GRACIOUS WORDS WITH THE HOSPITALITY OF A GENTLEMAN.
MY THANKS AGAIN. I'M DARLA... **DARLA MORTON.**
"SHE HAD NO IDEA THAT I WAS ALREADY A MASSIVE FAN. DARLA WAS AN UP-AND-COMING **SOUL SINGER** BORN AND RAISED IN AN ALABAMA CHOIR."

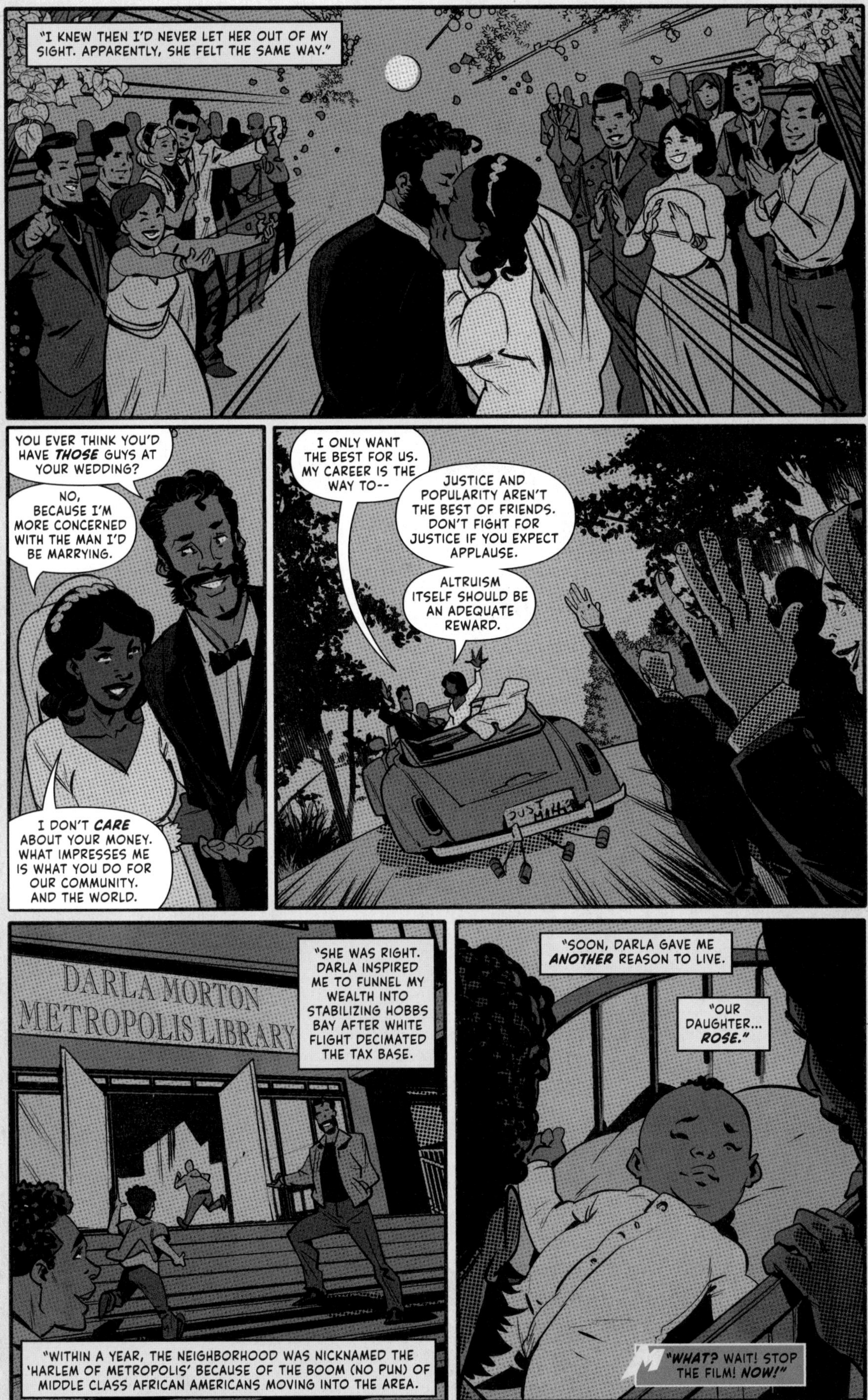
"I KNEW THEN I'D NEVER LET HER OUT OF MY SIGHT. APPARENTLY, SHE FELT THE SAME WAY."
YOU EVER THINK YOU'D HAVE ***THOSE*** GUYS AT YOUR WEDDING?
NO, BECAUSE I'M MORE CONCERNED WITH THE MAN I'D BE MARRYING.
I DON'T ***CARE*** ABOUT YOUR MONEY. WHAT IMPRESSES ME IS WHAT YOU DO FOR OUR COMMUNITY. AND THE WORLD.
I ONLY WANT THE BEST FOR US. MY CAREER IS THE WAY TO--
JUSTICE AND POPULARITY AREN'T THE BEST OF FRIENDS. DON'T FIGHT FOR JUSTICE IF YOU EXPECT APPLAUSE.
ALTRUISM ITSELF SHOULD BE AN ADEQUATE REWARD.
DARLA MORTON METROPOLIS LIBRARY
"SHE WAS RIGHT. DARLA INSPIRED ME TO FUNNEL MY WEALTH INTO STABILIZING HOBBS BAY AFTER WHITE FLIGHT DECIMATED THE TAX BASE.
"WITHIN A YEAR, THE NEIGHBORHOOD WAS NICKNAMED THE 'HARLEM OF METROPOLIS' BECAUSE OF THE BOOM (NO PUN) OF MIDDLE CLASS AFRICAN AMERICANS MOVING INTO THE AREA.
"SOON, DARLA GAVE ME ***ANOTHER*** REASON TO LIVE.
"OUR DAUGHTER... ***ROSE."***
"***WHAT?*** WAIT! STOP THE FILM! ***NOW!"***

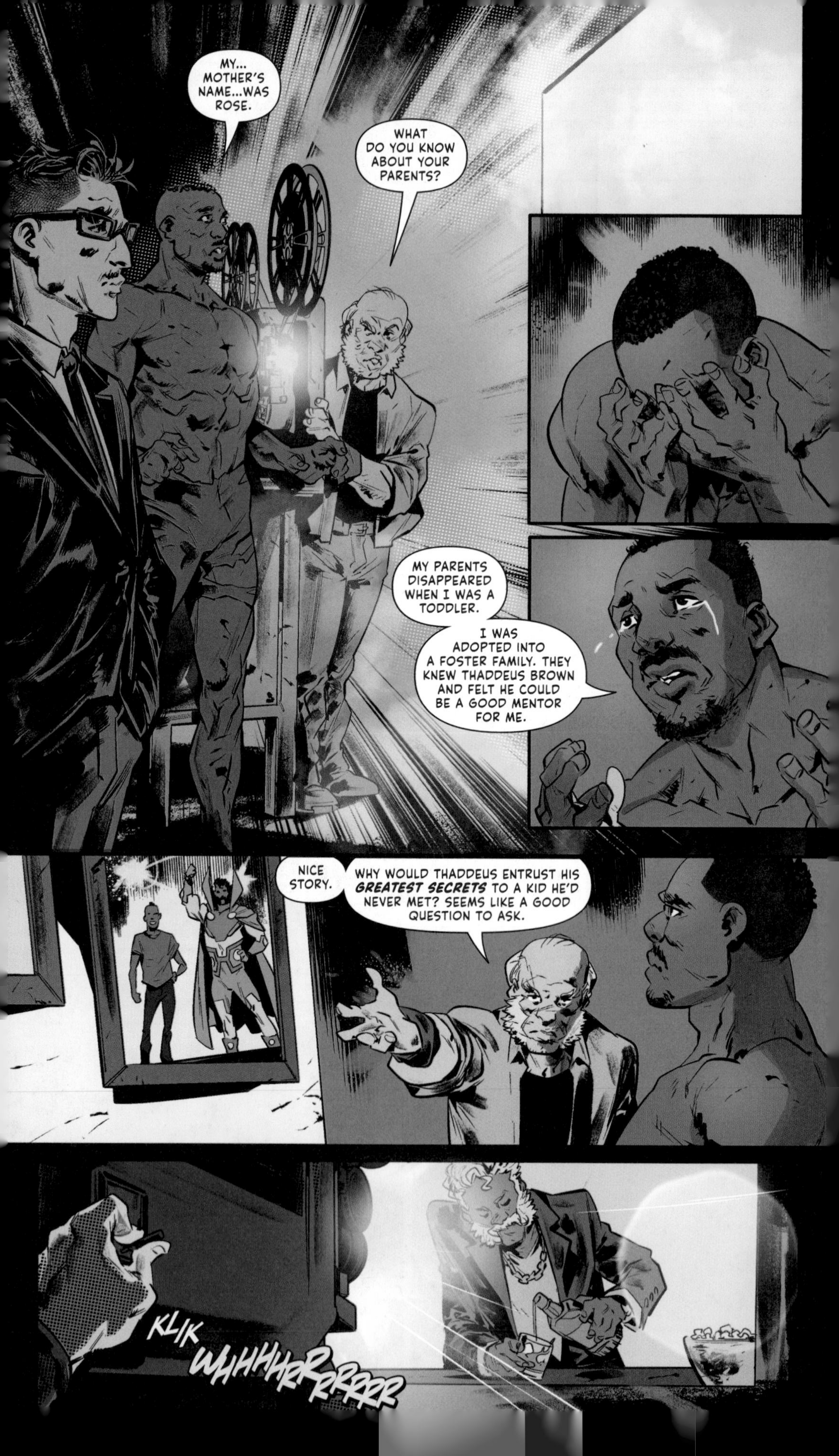
MY... MOTHER'S NAME...WAS ROSE.
WHAT DO YOU KNOW ABOUT YOUR PARENTS?
MY PARENTS DISAPPEARED WHEN I WAS A TODDLER.
I WAS ADOPTED INTO A FOSTER FAMILY. THEY KNEW THADDEUS BROWN AND FELT HE COULD BE A GOOD MENTOR FOR ME.
NICE STORY.
WHY WOULD THADDEUS ENTRUST HIS GREATEST SECRETS TO A KID HE'D NEVER MET? SEEMS LIKE A GOOD QUESTION TO ASK.
KLIK
WHHHHRRRRRRR

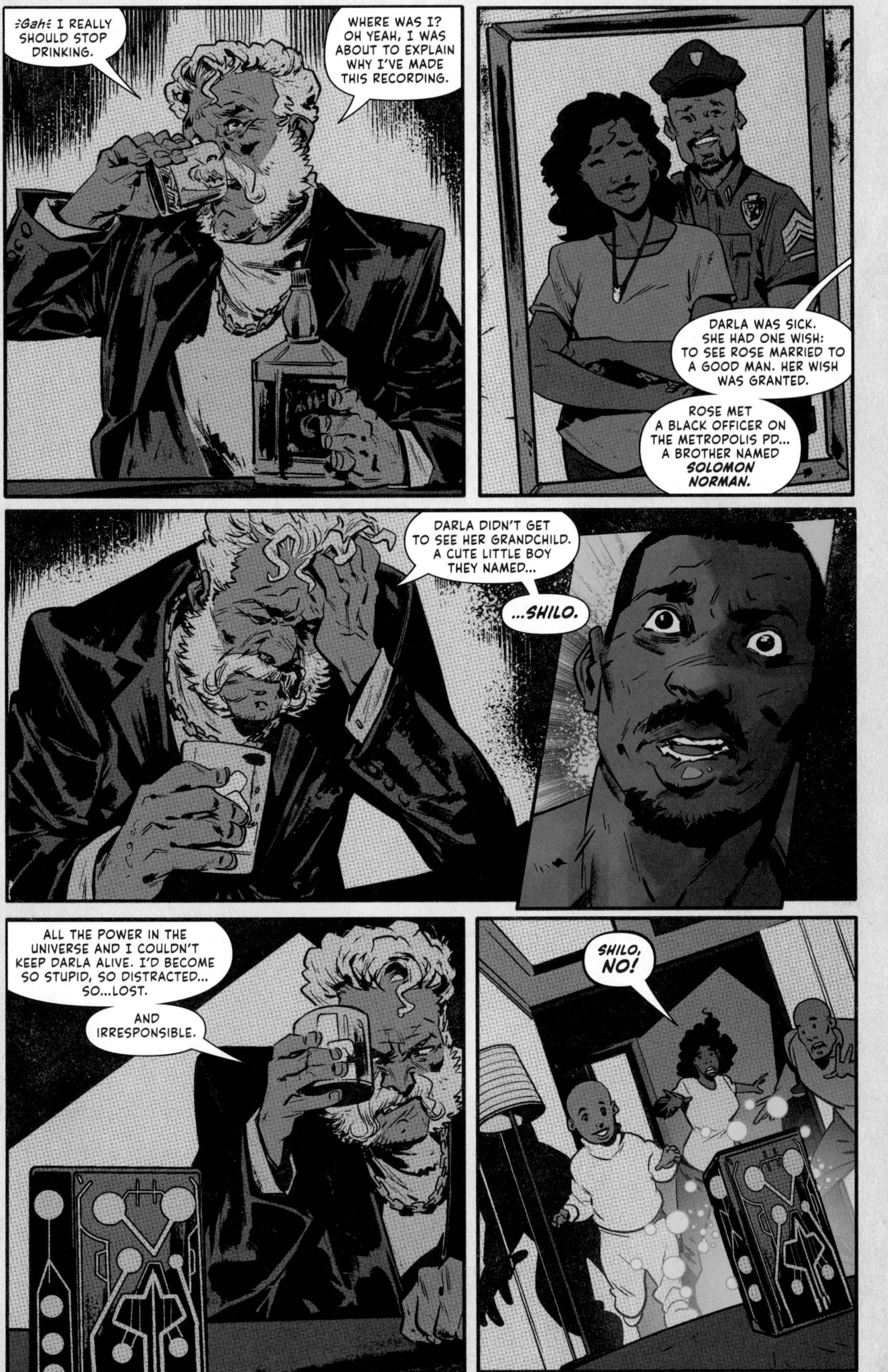
Gah I REALLY SHOULD STOP DRINKING.
WHERE WAS I? OH YEAH, I WAS ABOUT TO EXPLAIN WHY I'VE MADE THIS RECORDING.
DARLA WAS SICK. SHE HAD ONE WISH: TO SEE ROSE MARRIED TO A GOOD MAN. HER WISH WAS GRANTED.
ROSE MET A BLACK OFFICER ON THE METROPOLIS PD... A BROTHER NAMED **SOLOMON NORMAN.**
DARLA DIDN'T GET TO SEE HER GRANDCHILD. A CUTE LITTLE BOY THEY NAMED...
...SHILO.
ALL THE POWER IN THE UNIVERSE AND I COULDN'T KEEP DARLA ALIVE. I'D BECOME SO STUPID, SO DISTRACTED... SO...LOST.
AND IRRESPONSIBLE.
SHILO, NO!

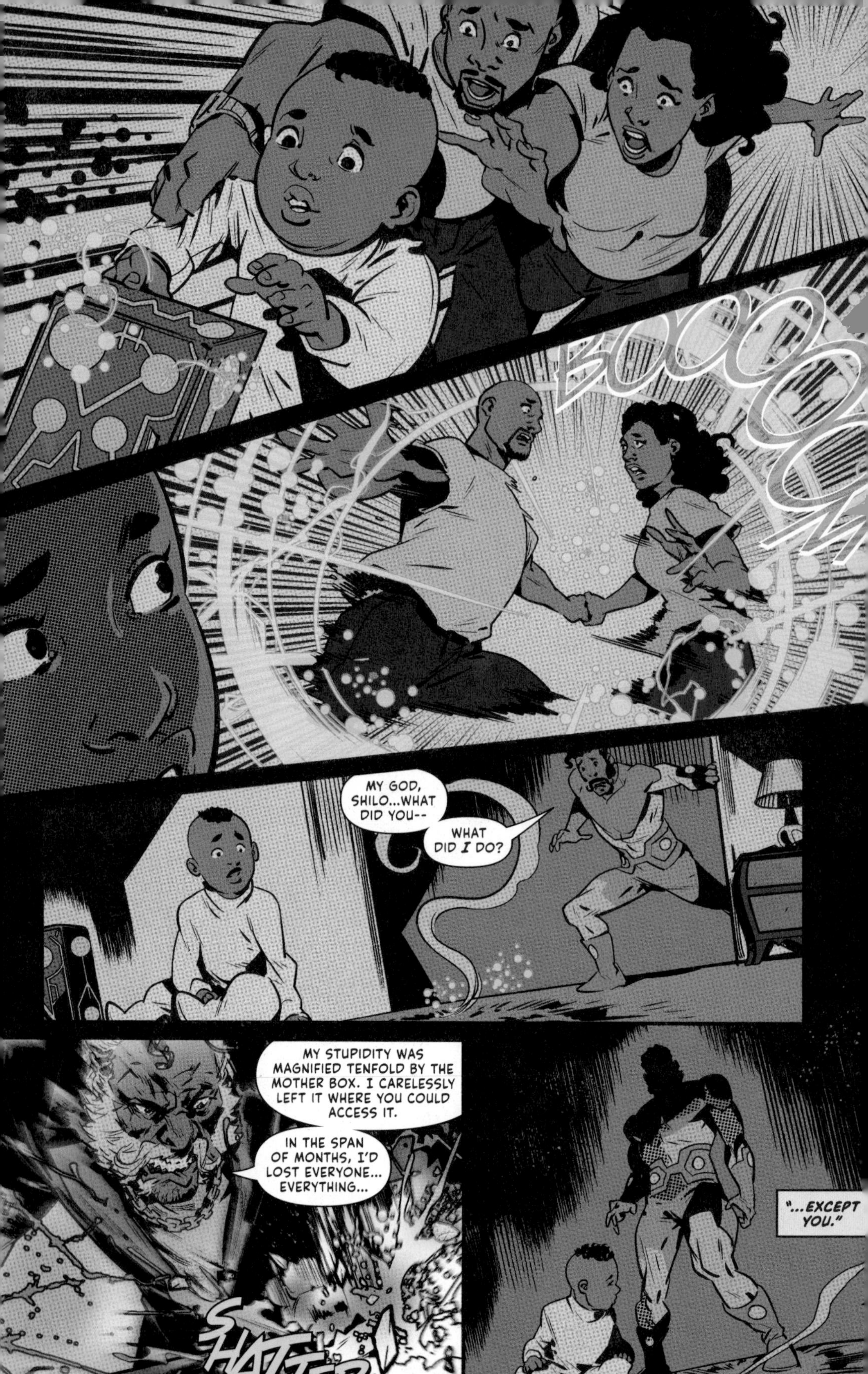
BOOOOOM
MY GOD, SHILO...WHAT DID YOU--
WHAT DID I DO?
MY STUPIDITY WAS MAGNIFIED TENFOLD BY THE MOTHER BOX. I CARELESSLY LEFT IT WHERE YOU COULD ACCESS IT.
IN THE SPAN OF MONTHS, I'D LOST EVERYONE... EVERYTHING...
SHATTER
"...EXCEPT YOU."

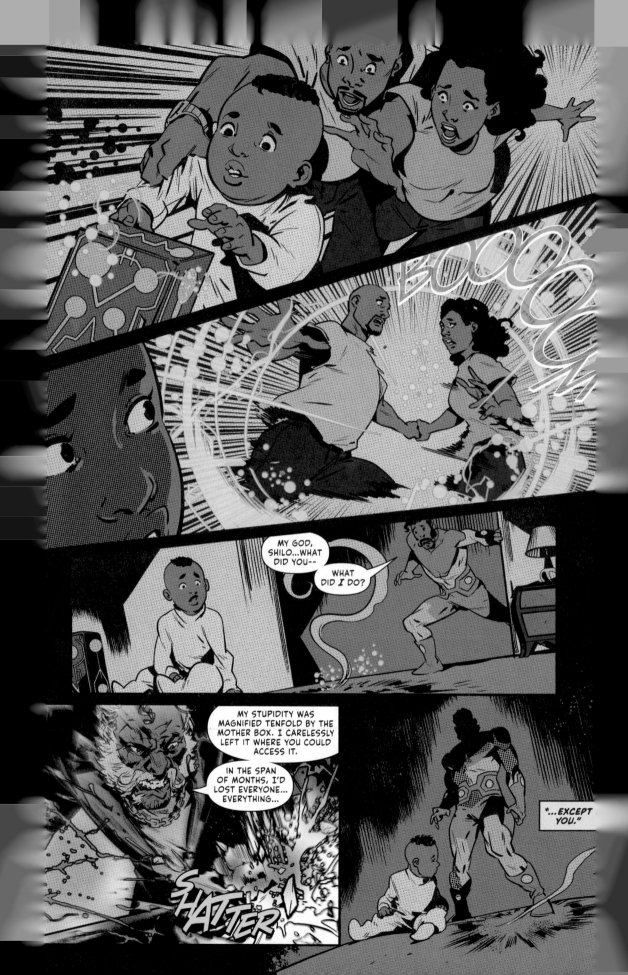

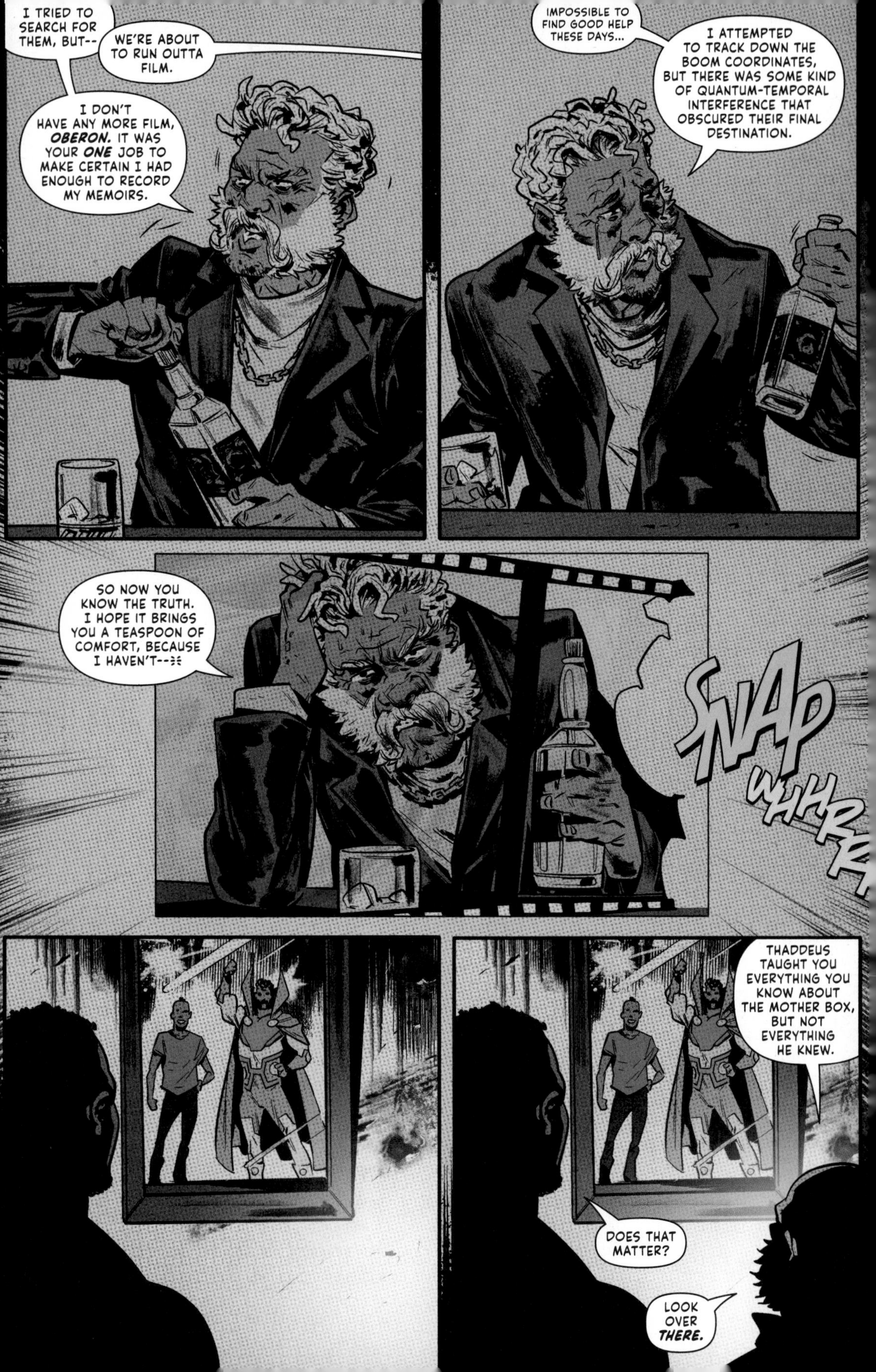
I TRIED TO SEARCH FOR THEM, BUT--
WE'RE ABOUT TO RUN OUTTA FILM.
I DON'T HAVE ANY MORE FILM, **OBERON.** IT WAS YOUR ***ONE*** JOB TO MAKE CERTAIN I HAD ENOUGH TO RECORD MY MEMOIRS.
IMPOSSIBLE TO FIND GOOD HELP THESE DAYS...
I ATTEMPTED TO TRACK DOWN THE BOOM COORDINATES, BUT THERE WAS SOME KIND OF QUANTUM-TEMPORAL INTERFERENCE THAT OBSCURED THEIR FINAL DESTINATION.
SO NOW YOU KNOW THE TRUTH. I HOPE IT BRINGS YOU A TEASPOON OF COMFORT, BECAUSE I HAVEN'T--
SNAP
WHRR
THADDEUS TAUGHT YOU EVERYTHING YOU KNOW ABOUT THE MOTHER BOX, BUT NOT EVERYTHING HE KNEW.
DOES THAT MATTER?
LOOK OVER ***THERE.***

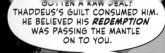GOTTEN A RAW DEAL? THADDEUS'S GUILT CONSUMED HIM. HE BELIEVED HIS *REDEMPTION* WAS PASSING THE MANTLE ON TO YOU.

THERE'S A MULTITUDE OF SECRETS YET TO BE UNCOVERED, SHILO.

THADDEUS TOLD ME A BIG ONE BEFORE THE END:

"THE TRUE POWER OF A MOTHER BOX CAN ONLY BE UNLOCKED WHEN THERE'S A PSYCHOMOLECULAR BOND WITH THE USER."

THE BOX IS ONLY A CONDUIT TO THE SOURCE ENERGY OF THE UNIVERSE. AS ALL LIFE IS MADE OF STARDUST AND STARDUST IS THE REMNANT OF THE SOURCE, A PERSON MUST ACCEPT THEIR PLACE IN THE *LIFESTREAM* BEFORE THEY'RE ALLOWED TRUE ACCESS.

WHAT DOES IT MEAN TO "ACCEPT THEIR PLACE IN THE LIFESTREAM"?

IF I HAD TO VENTURE A GUESS, I'D SAY IT MEANS YOU HAVE TO LEARN HOW TO *LOVE YOURSELF.*

THADDEUS UNDERSTOOD THAT FAR TOO LATE IN LIFE. LIKELY AT THE MOMENT OF DEATH. THEREFORE, THE TRUTH IS IMBUED IN HIS ASHES.

IS THAT POSSIBLE FOR YOU?

LOVING YOURSELF?

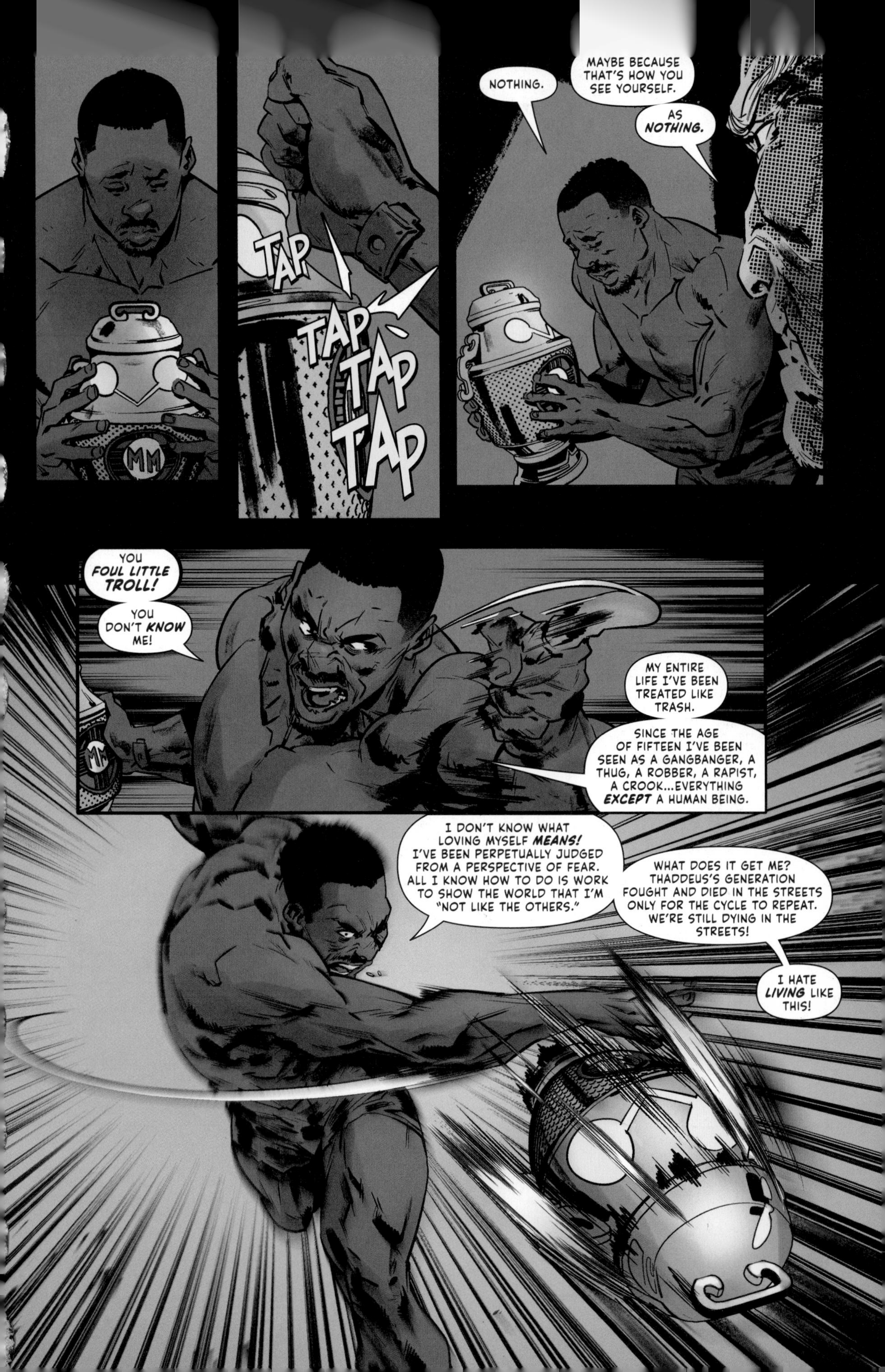
TAP
TAP
TAP
TAP
NOTHING.
MAYBE BECAUSE THAT'S HOW YOU SEE YOURSELF.
AS *NOTHING.*
YOU *FOUL LITTLE TROLL!*
YOU DON'T *KNOW* ME!
MY ENTIRE LIFE I'VE BEEN TREATED LIKE TRASH.
SINCE THE AGE OF FIFTEEN I'VE BEEN SEEN AS A GANGBANGER, A THUG, A ROBBER, A RAPIST, A CROOK...EVERYTHING *EXCEPT* A HUMAN BEING.
I DON'T KNOW WHAT LOVING MYSELF *MEANS!* I'VE BEEN PERPETUALLY JUDGED FROM A PERSPECTIVE OF FEAR. ALL I KNOW HOW TO DO IS WORK TO SHOW THE WORLD THAT I'M "NOT LIKE THE OTHERS."
WHAT DOES IT GET ME? THADDEUS'S GENERATION FOUGHT AND DIED IN THE STREETS ONLY FOR THE CYCLE TO REPEAT. WE'RE STILL DYING IN THE STREETS!
I HATE *LIVING* LIKE THIS!

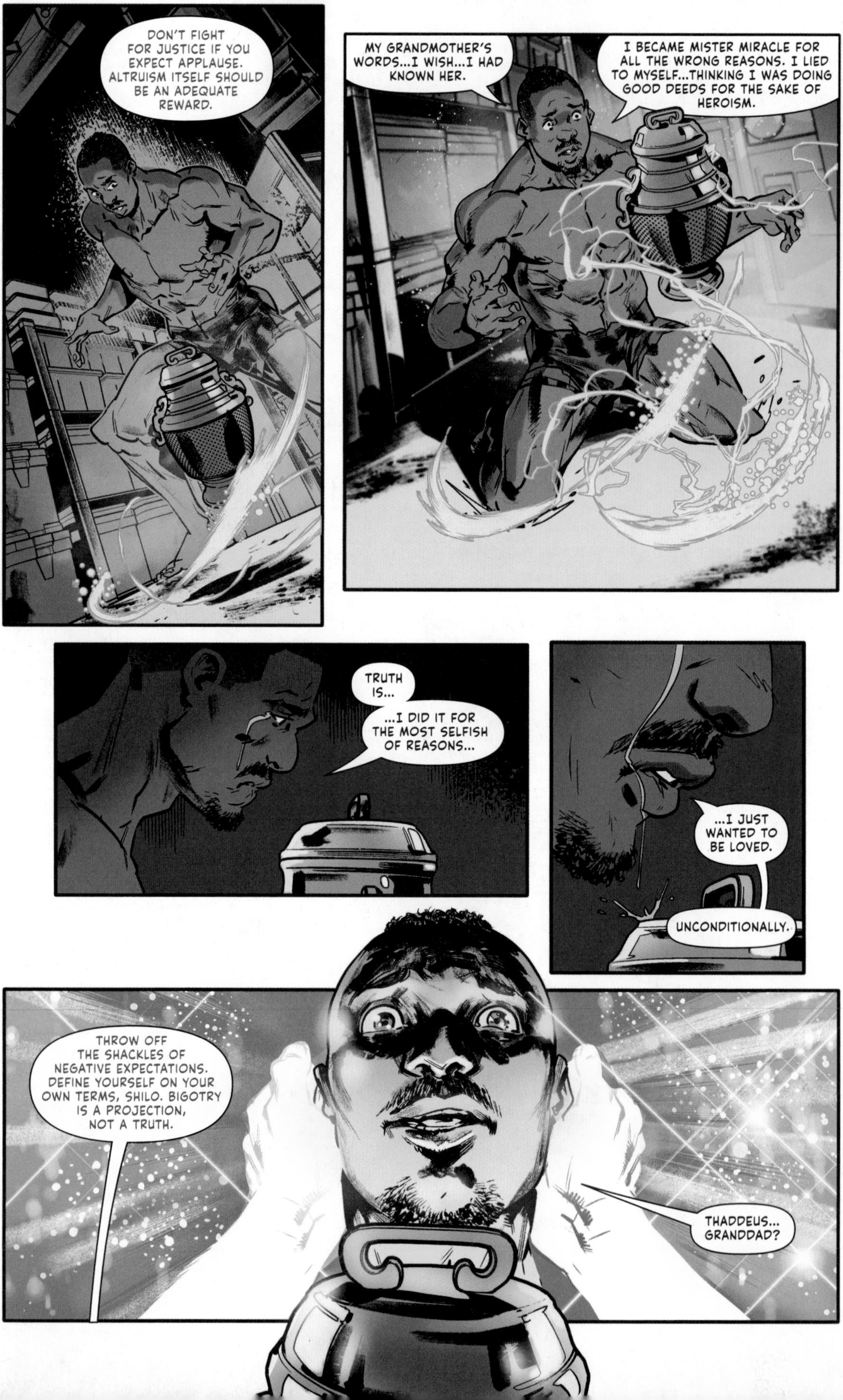
DON'T FIGHT FOR JUSTICE IF YOU EXPECT APPLAUSE. ALTRUISM ITSELF SHOULD BE AN ADEQUATE REWARD.
MY GRANDMOTHER'S WORDS...I WISH...I HAD KNOWN HER.
I BECAME MISTER MIRACLE FOR ALL THE WRONG REASONS. I LIED TO MYSELF...THINKING I WAS DOING GOOD DEEDS FOR THE SAKE OF HEROISM.
TRUTH IS...
...I DID IT FOR THE MOST SELFISH OF REASONS...
...I JUST WANTED TO BE LOVED.
UNCONDITIONALLY.
THROW OFF THE SHACKLES OF NEGATIVE EXPECTATIONS. DEFINE YOURSELF ON YOUR OWN TERMS, SHILO. BIGOTRY IS A PROJECTION, NOT A TRUTH.
THADDEUS... GRANDDAD?

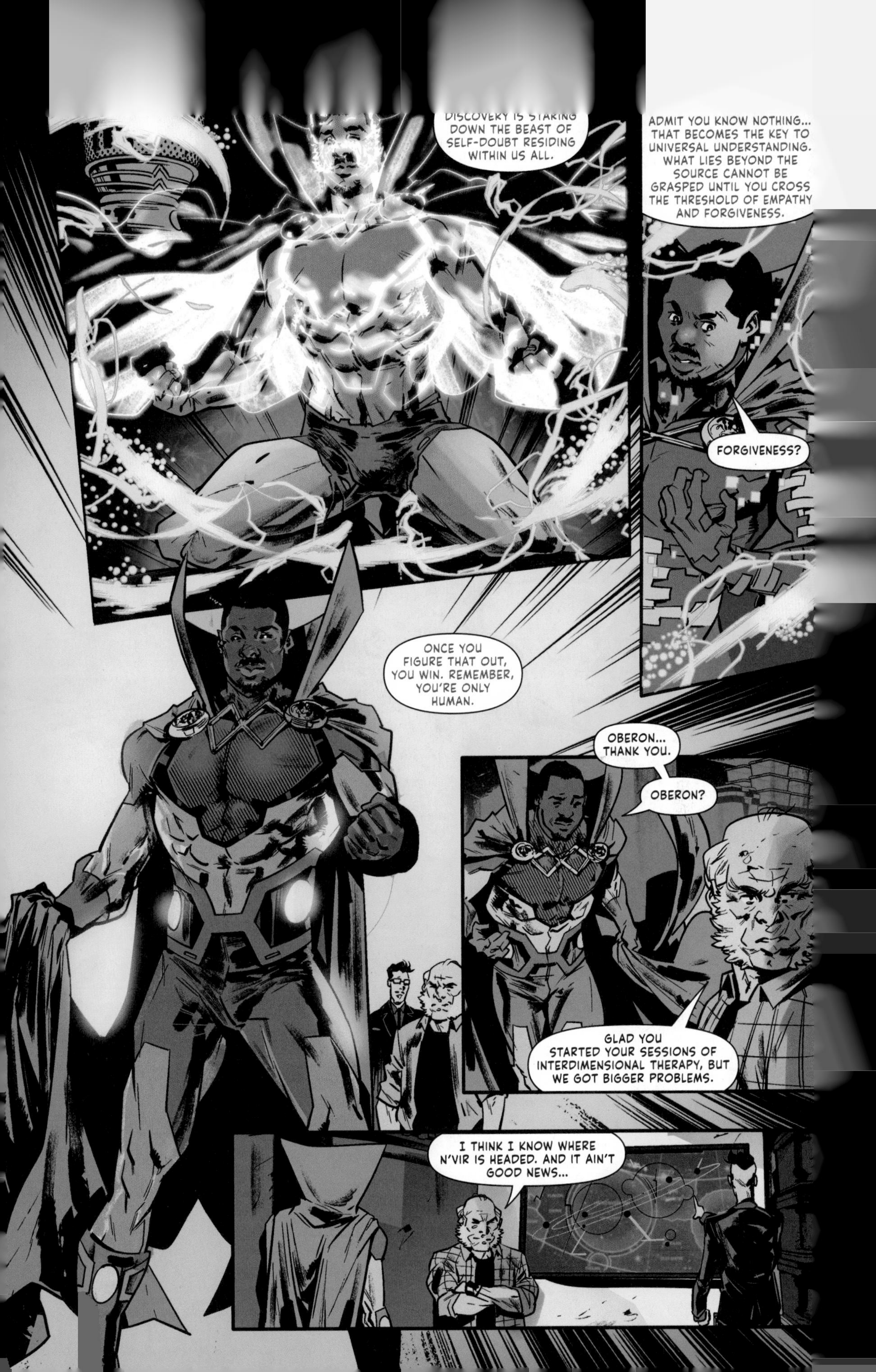
DISCOVERY IS STARING DOWN THE BEAST OF SELF-DOUBT RESIDING WITHIN US ALL.
ADMIT YOU KNOW NOTHING... THAT BECOMES THE KEY TO UNIVERSAL UNDERSTANDING. WHAT LIES BEYOND THE SOURCE CANNOT BE GRASPED UNTIL YOU CROSS THE THRESHOLD OF EMPATHY AND FORGIVENESS.
FORGIVENESS?
ONCE YOU FIGURE THAT OUT, YOU WIN. REMEMBER, YOU'RE ONLY HUMAN.
OBERON... THANK YOU.
OBERON?
GLAD YOU STARTED YOUR SESSIONS OF INTERDIMENSIONAL THERAPY, BUT WE GOT BIGGER PROBLEMS.
I THINK I KNOW WHERE N'VIR IS HEADED. AND IT AIN'T GOOD NEWS...

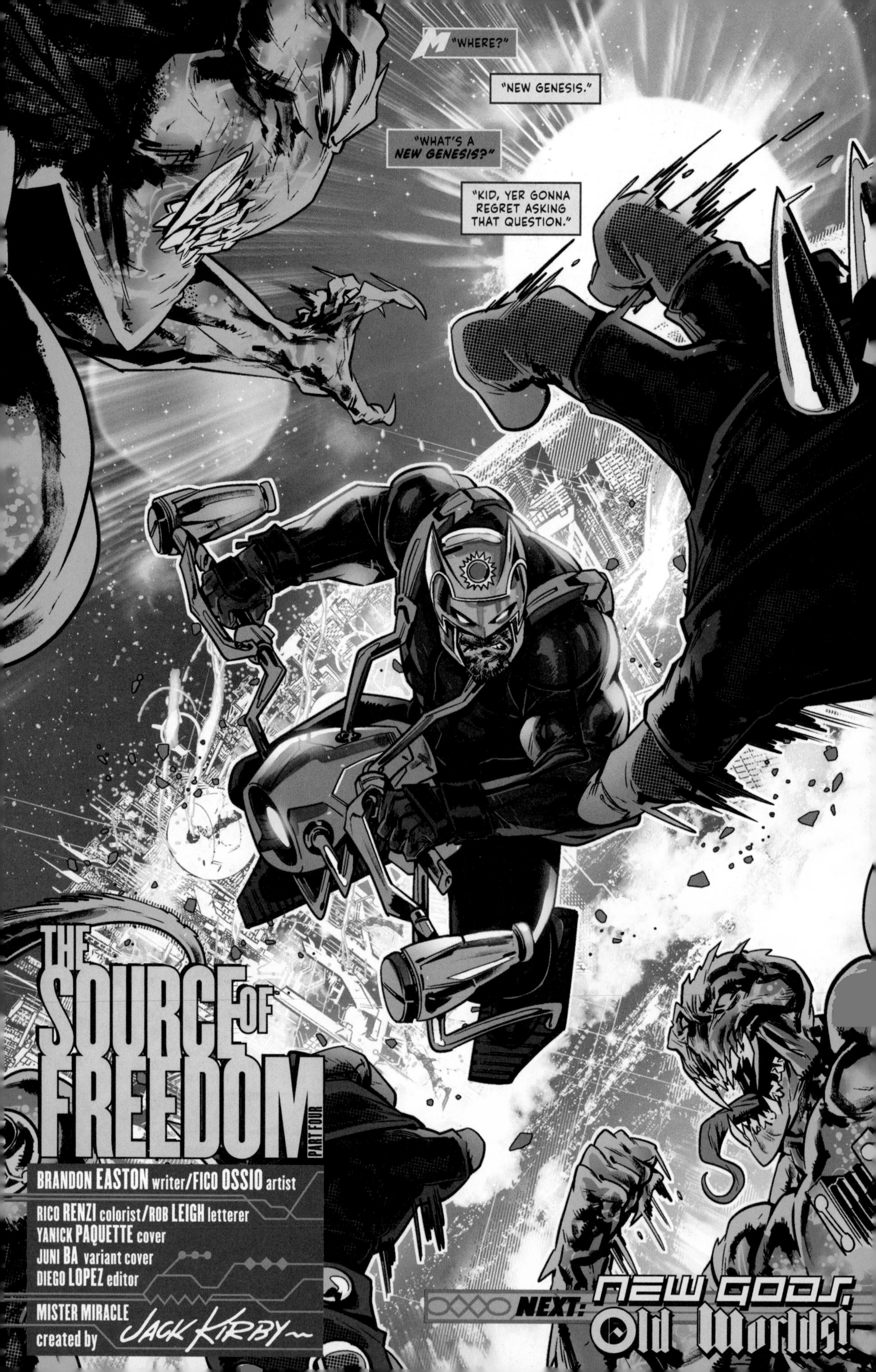
"WHERE?"
"NEW GENESIS."
"WHAT'S A *NEW GENESIS?*"
"KID, YER GONNA REGRET ASKING THAT QUESTION."
THE SOURCE OF FREEDOM PART FOUR
BRANDON EASTON writer/FICO OSSIO artist
RICO RENZI colorist/ROB LEIGH letterer
YANICK PAQUETTE cover
JUNI BA variant cover
DIEGO LOPEZ editor
MISTER MIRACLE created by JACK KIRBY
NEXT: NEW GODS, OLD WORLDS!

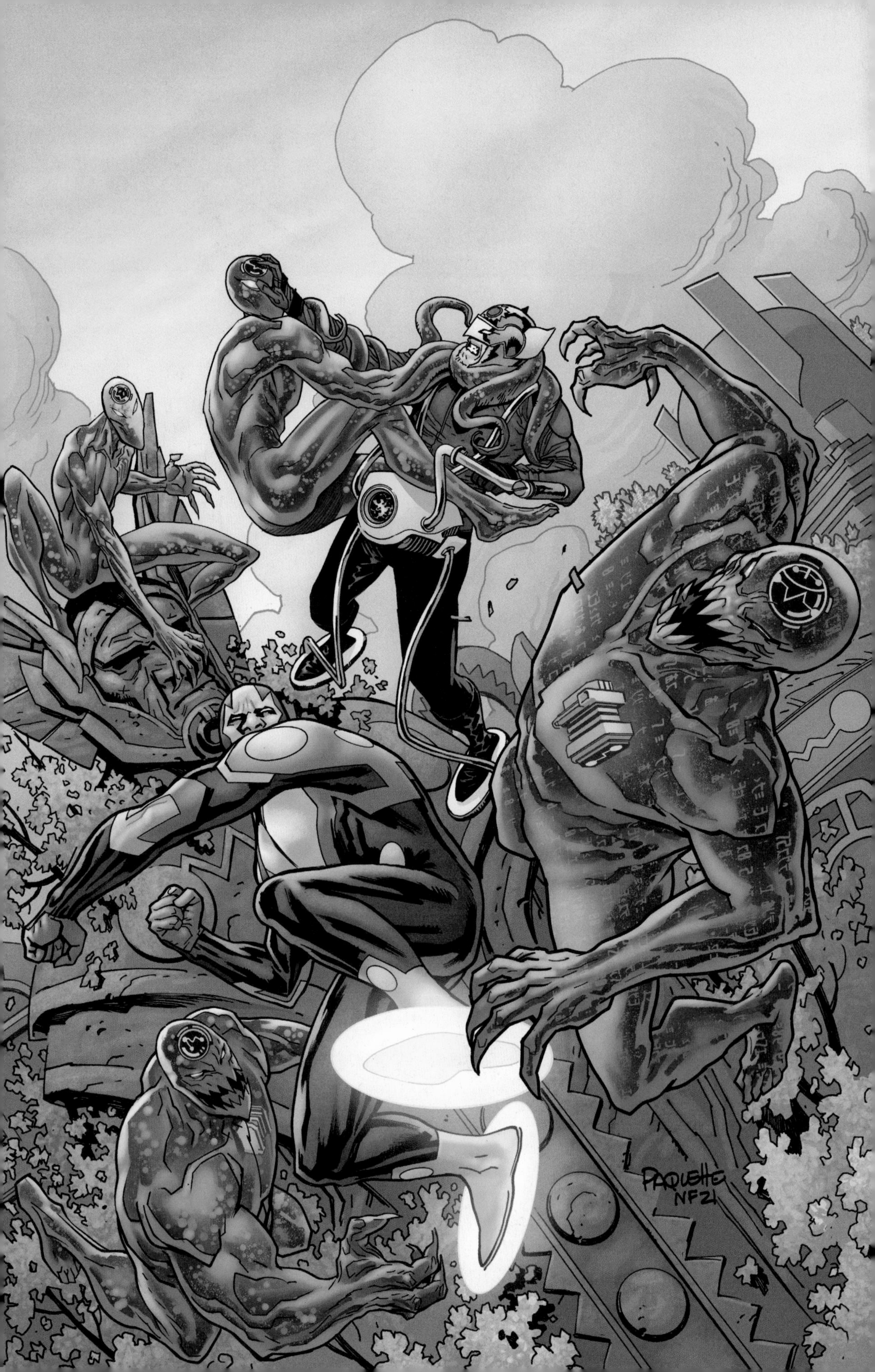
PAQUETTE
NF21

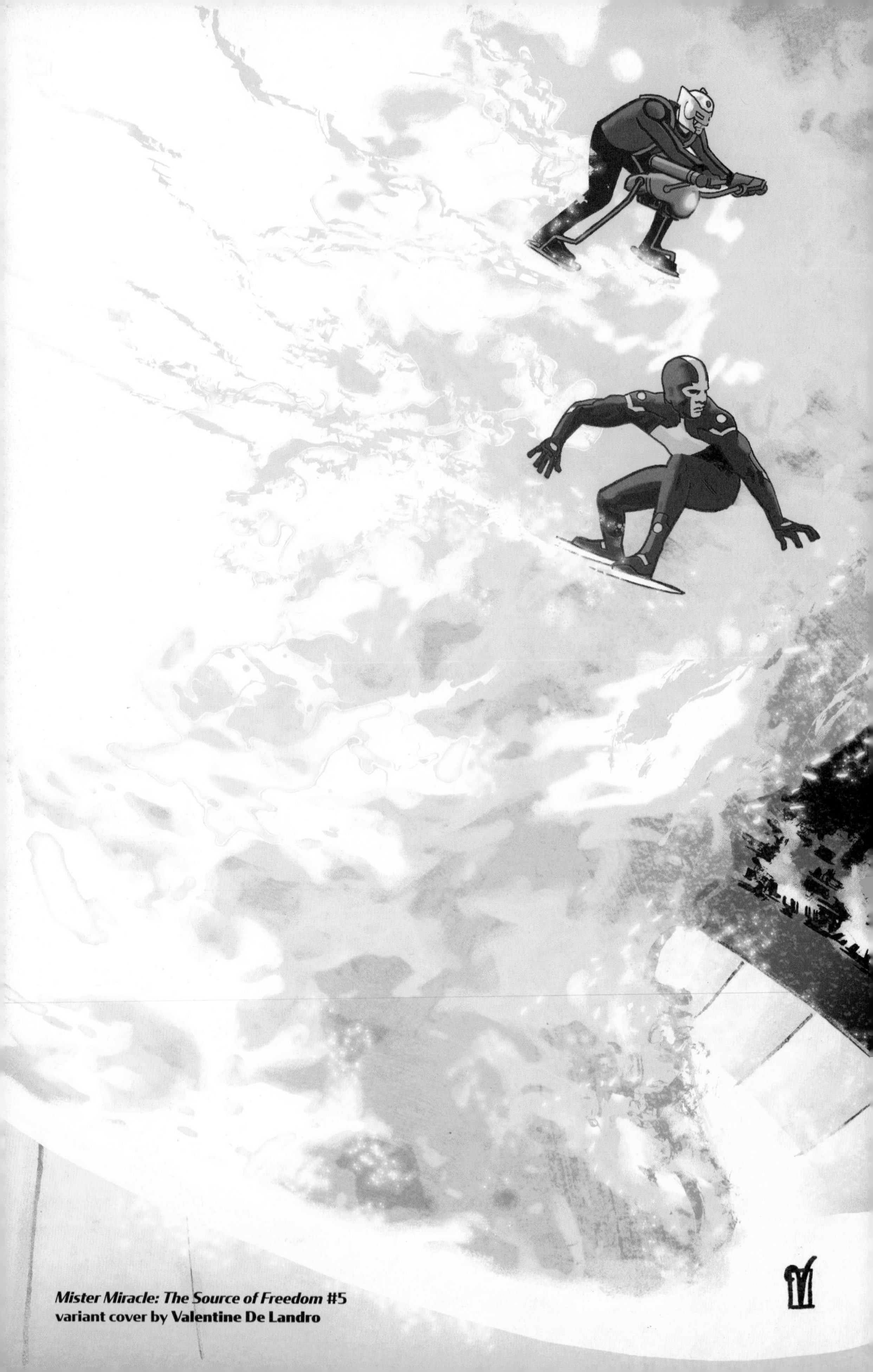

Mister Miracle: The Source of Freedom **#5**
variant cover by Valentine De Landro

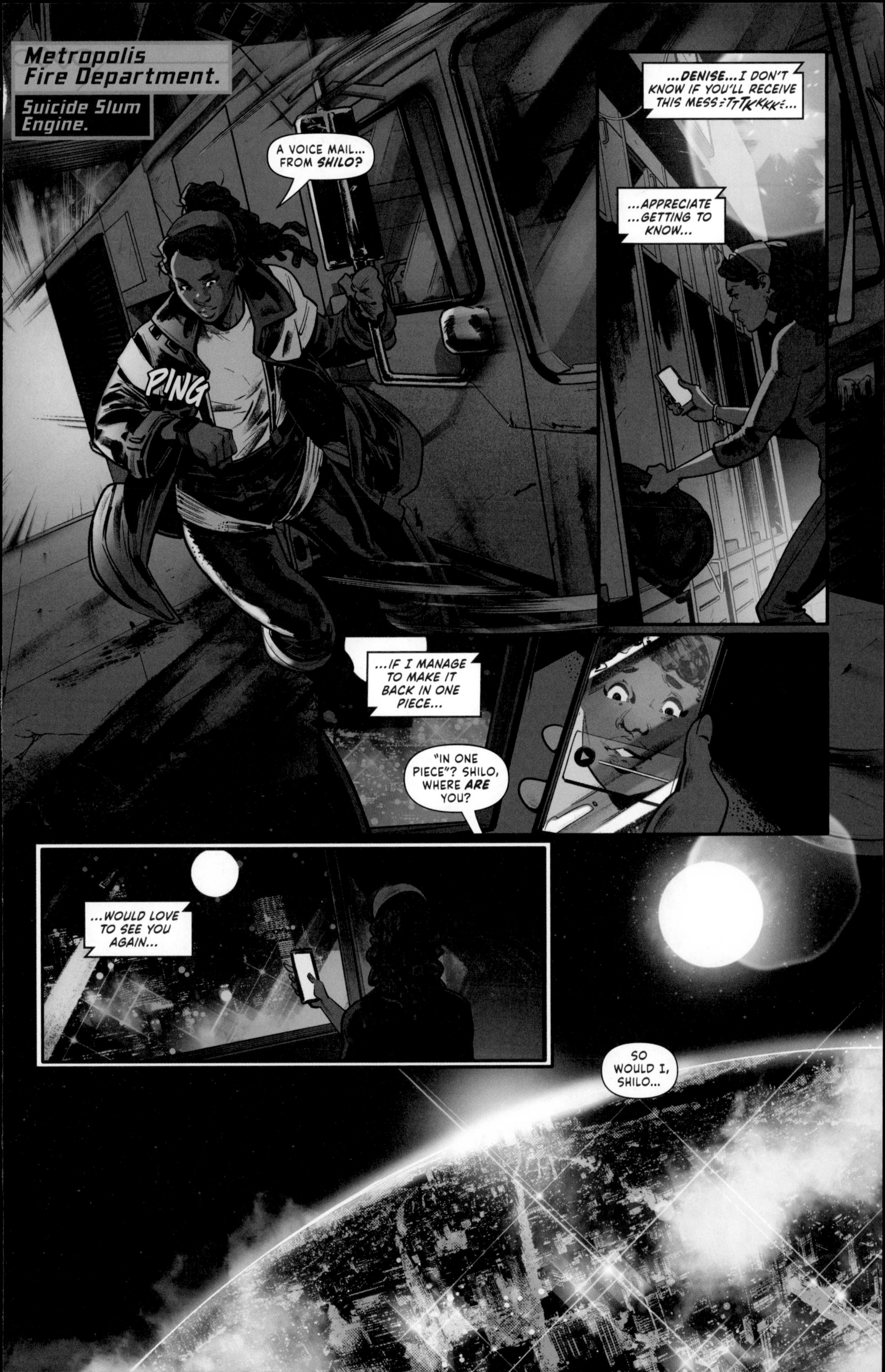

Metropolis Fire Department.
Suicide Slum Engine.
A VOICE MAIL... FROM SHILO?
PING
...DENISE...I DON'T KNOW IF YOU'LL RECEIVE THIS MESS=TTTKKKK=...
...APPRECIATE ...GETTING TO KNOW...
...IF I MANAGE TO MAKE IT BACK IN ONE PIECE...
"IN ONE PIECE"? SHILO, WHERE ARE YOU?
...WOULD LOVE TO SEE YOU AGAIN...
SO WOULD I, SHILO...

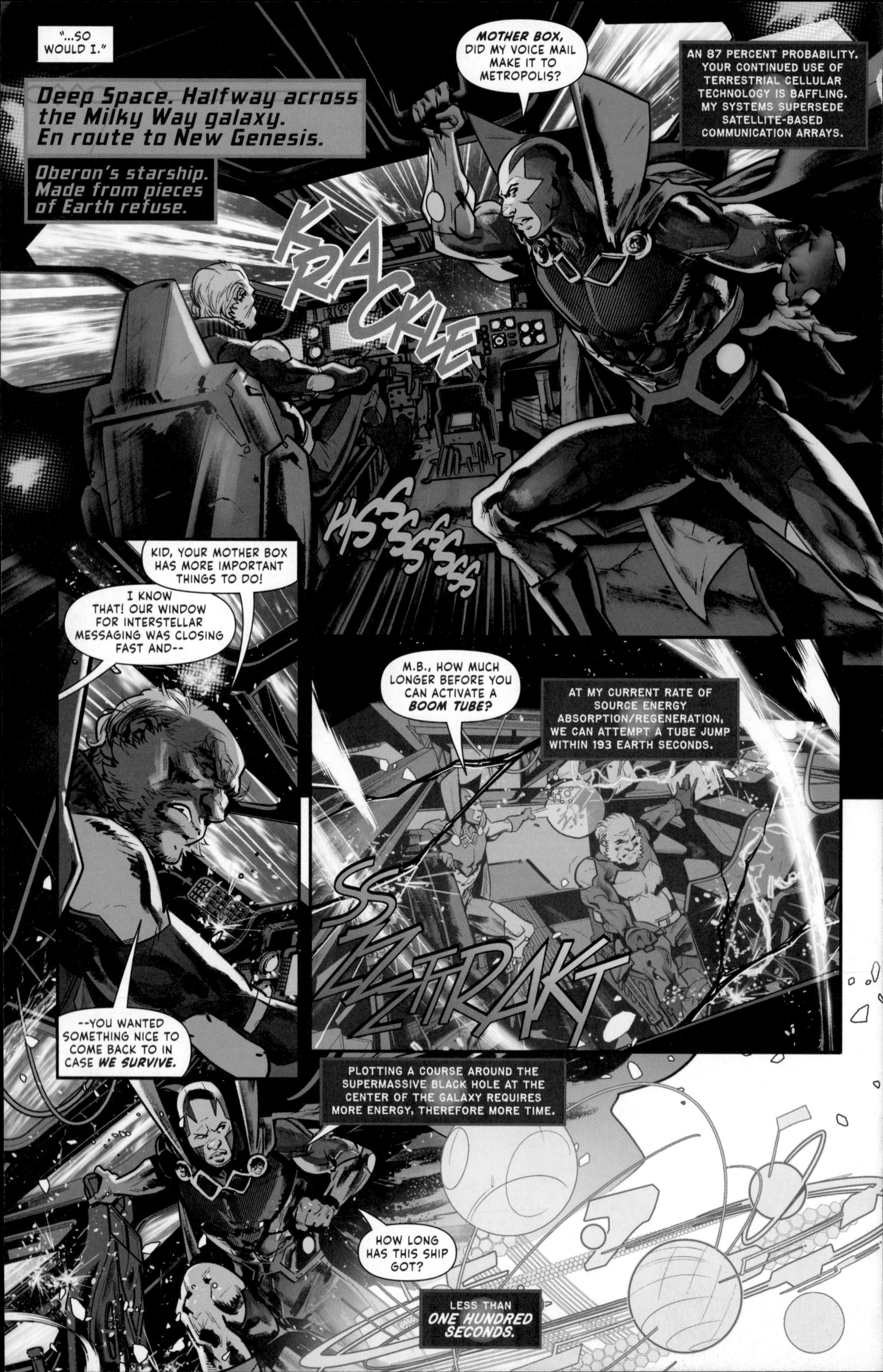

"...SO WOULD I."
Deep Space. Halfway across the Milky Way galaxy. En route to New Genesis.
Oberon's starship. Made from pieces of Earth refuse.
MOTHER BOX, DID MY VOICE MAIL MAKE IT TO METROPOLIS?
AN 87 PERCENT PROBABILITY. YOUR CONTINUED USE OF TERRESTRIAL CELLULAR TECHNOLOGY IS BAFFLING. MY SYSTEMS SUPERSEDE SATELLITE-BASED COMMUNICATION ARRAYS.
KRACKLE
HISSSSSSSSS
KID, YOUR MOTHER BOX HAS MORE IMPORTANT THINGS TO DO!
I KNOW THAT! OUR WINDOW FOR INTERSTELLAR MESSAGING WAS CLOSING FAST AND--
--YOU WANTED SOMETHING NICE TO COME BACK TO IN CASE WE SURVIVE.
M.B., HOW MUCH LONGER BEFORE YOU CAN ACTIVATE A BOOM TUBE?
AT MY CURRENT RATE OF SOURCE ENERGY ABSORPTION/REGENERATION, WE CAN ATTEMPT A TUBE JUMP WITHIN 193 EARTH SECONDS.
SSZZTRAKT
PLOTTING A COURSE AROUND THE SUPERMASSIVE BLACK HOLE AT THE CENTER OF THE GALAXY REQUIRES MORE ENERGY, THEREFORE MORE TIME.
HOW LONG HAS THIS SHIP GOT?
LESS THAN ONE HUNDRED SECONDS.

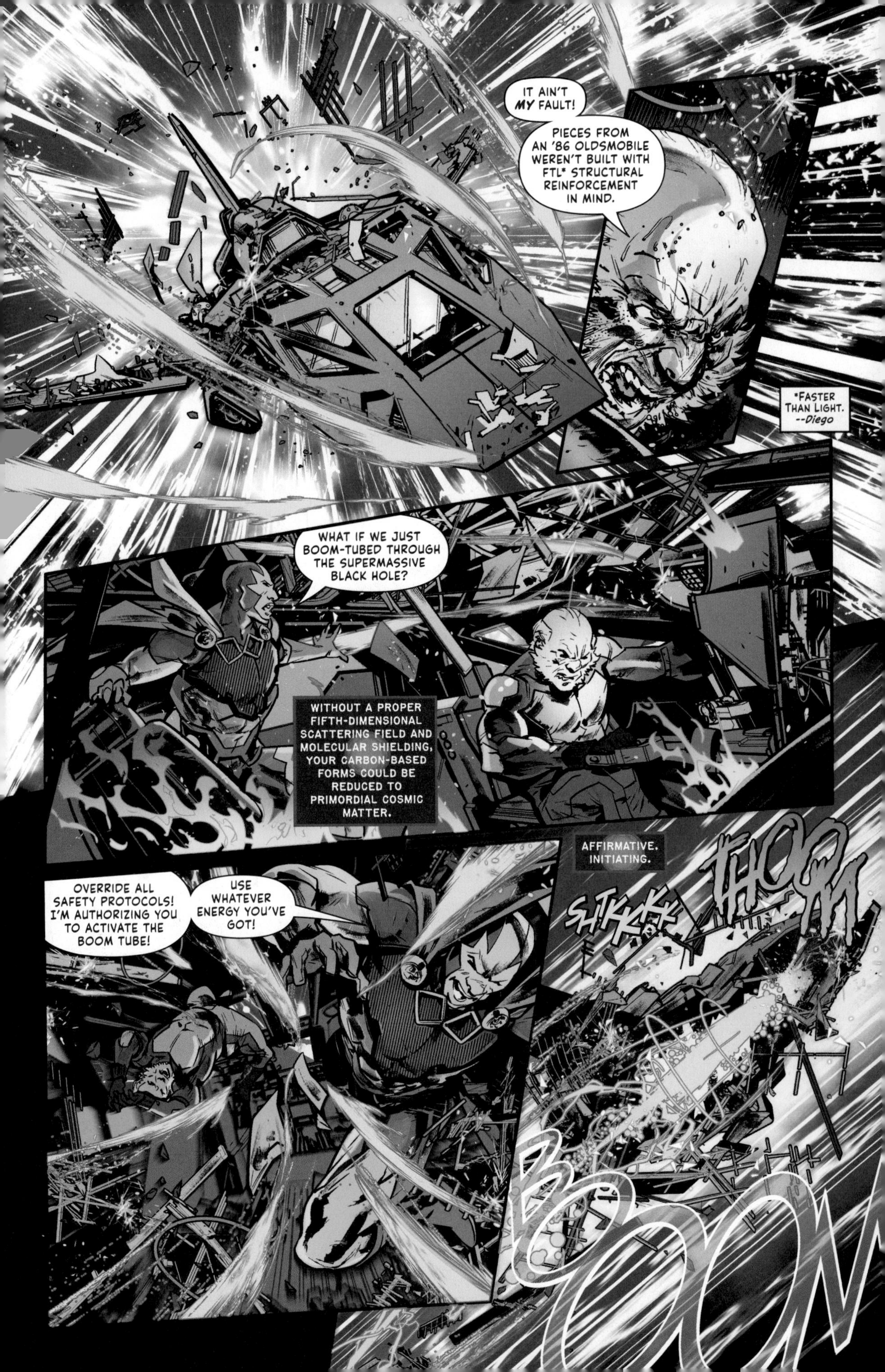
IT AIN'T MY FAULT!
PIECES FROM AN '86 OLDSMOBILE WEREN'T BUILT WITH FTL* STRUCTURAL REINFORCEMENT IN MIND.
*FASTER THAN LIGHT. --Diego
WHAT IF WE JUST BOOM-TUBED THROUGH THE SUPERMASSIVE BLACK HOLE?
WITHOUT A PROPER FIFTH-DIMENSIONAL SCATTERING FIELD AND MOLECULAR SHIELDING, YOUR CARBON-BASED FORMS COULD BE REDUCED TO PRIMORDIAL COSMIC MATTER.
OVERRIDE ALL SAFETY PROTOCOLS! I'M AUTHORIZING YOU TO ACTIVATE THE BOOM TUBE!
USE WHATEVER ENERGY YOU'VE GOT!
AFFIRMATIVE. INITIATING.
SHTKKKK
THOOM
BOOOM

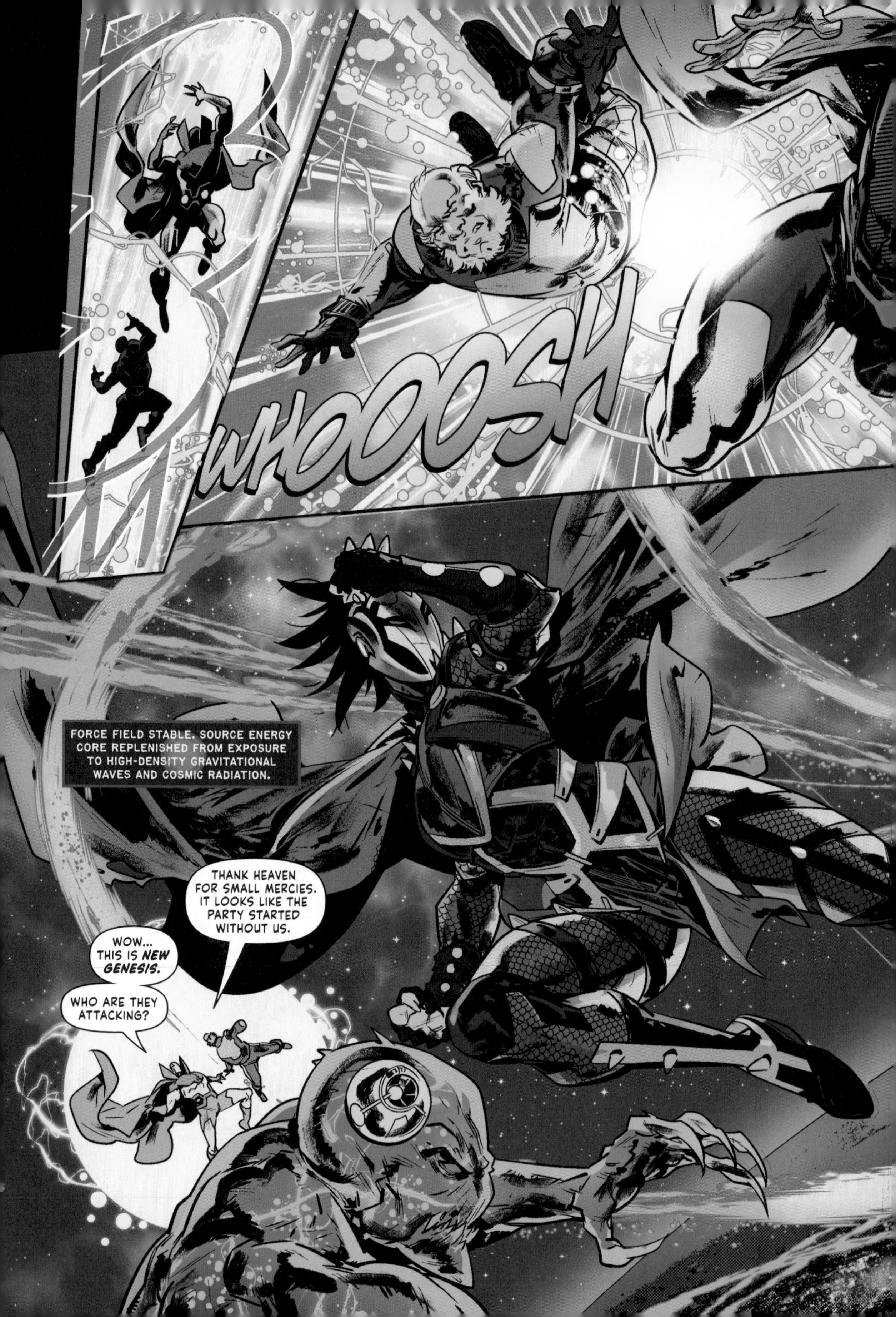
WHOOOOSH
FORCE FIELD STABLE. SOURCE ENERGY CORE REPLENISHED FROM EXPOSURE TO HIGH-DENSITY GRAVITATIONAL WAVES AND COSMIC RADIATION.
THANK HEAVEN FOR SMALL MERCIES. IT LOOKS LIKE THE PARTY STARTED WITHOUT US.
WOW... THIS IS NEW GENESIS.
WHO ARE THEY ATTACKING?

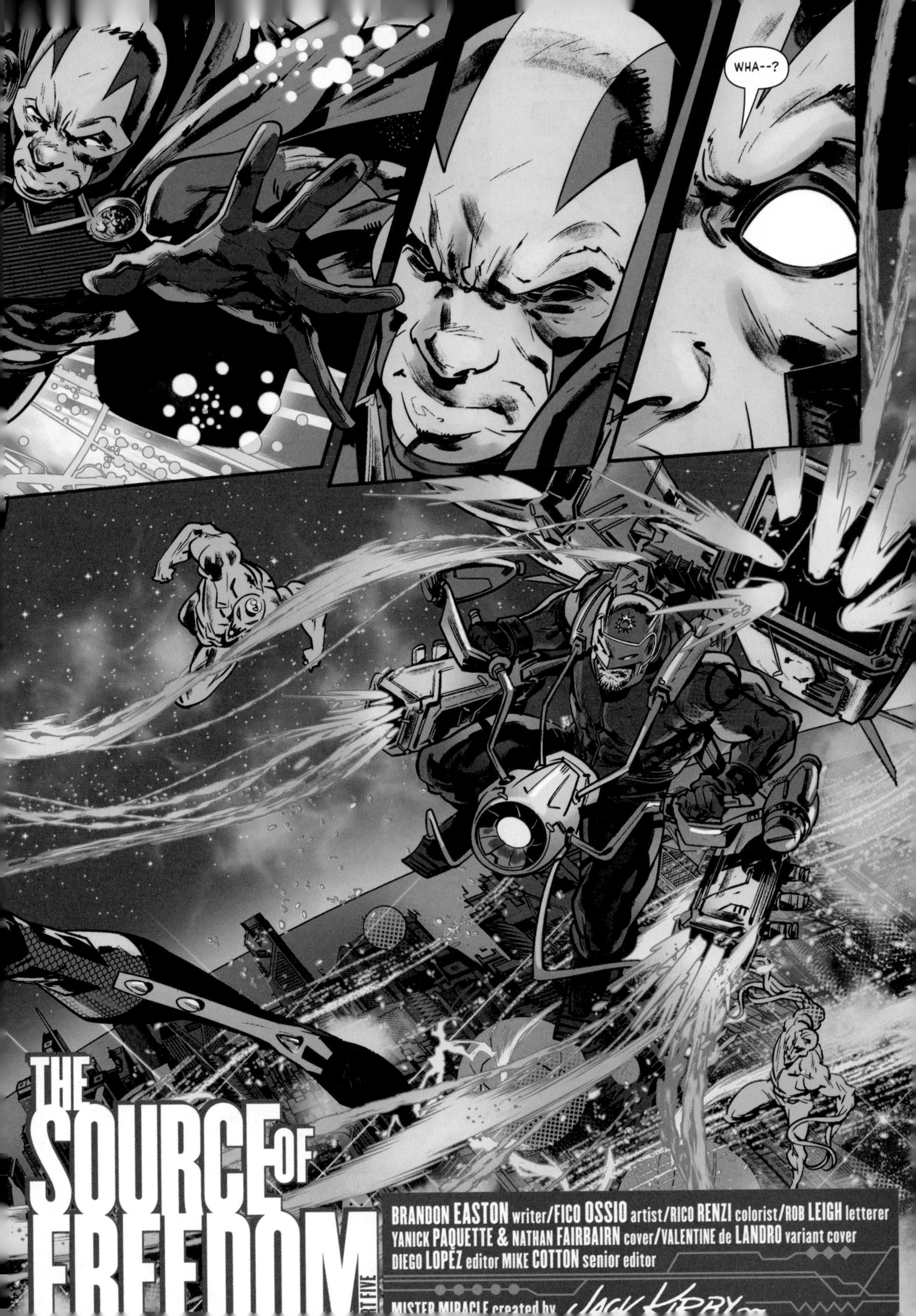
WHA--?
THE SOURCE OF FREEDOM
BRANDON EASTON writer/FICO OSSIO artist/RICO RENZI colorist/ROB LEIGH letterer
YANICK PAQUETTE & NATHAN FAIRBAIRN cover/VALENTINE de LANDRO variant cover
DIEGO LOPEZ editor MIKE COTTON senior editor
MISTER MIRACLE created by JACK KIRBY

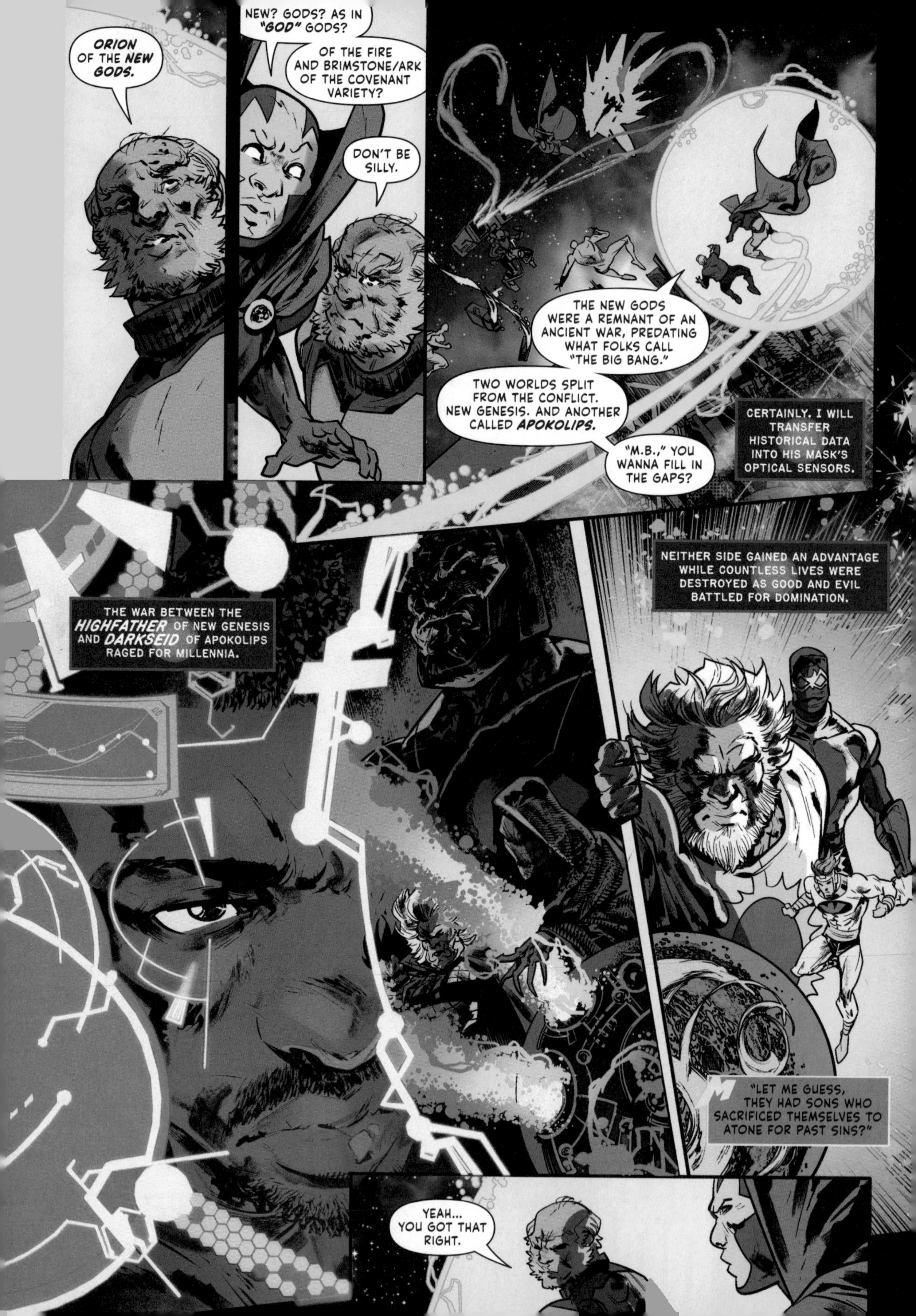
ORION OF THE NEW GODS.
NEW? GODS? AS IN "GOD" GODS?
OF THE FIRE AND BRIMSTONE/ARK OF THE COVENANT VARIETY?
DON'T BE SILLY.
THE NEW GODS WERE A REMNANT OF AN ANCIENT WAR, PREDATING WHAT FOLKS CALL "THE BIG BANG."
TWO WORLDS SPLIT FROM THE CONFLICT. NEW GENESIS. AND ANOTHER CALLED APOKOLIPS.
"M.B.," YOU WANNA FILL IN THE GAPS?
CERTAINLY. I WILL TRANSFER HISTORICAL DATA INTO HIS MASK'S OPTICAL SENSORS.
THE WAR BETWEEN THE HIGHFATHER OF NEW GENESIS AND DARKSEID OF APOKOLIPS RAGED FOR MILLENNIA.
NEITHER SIDE GAINED AN ADVANTAGE WHILE COUNTLESS LIVES WERE DESTROYED AS GOOD AND EVIL BATTLED FOR DOMINATION.
"LET ME GUESS, THEY HAD SONS WHO SACRIFICED THEMSELVES TO ATONE FOR PAST SINS?"
YEAH... YOU GOT THAT RIGHT.

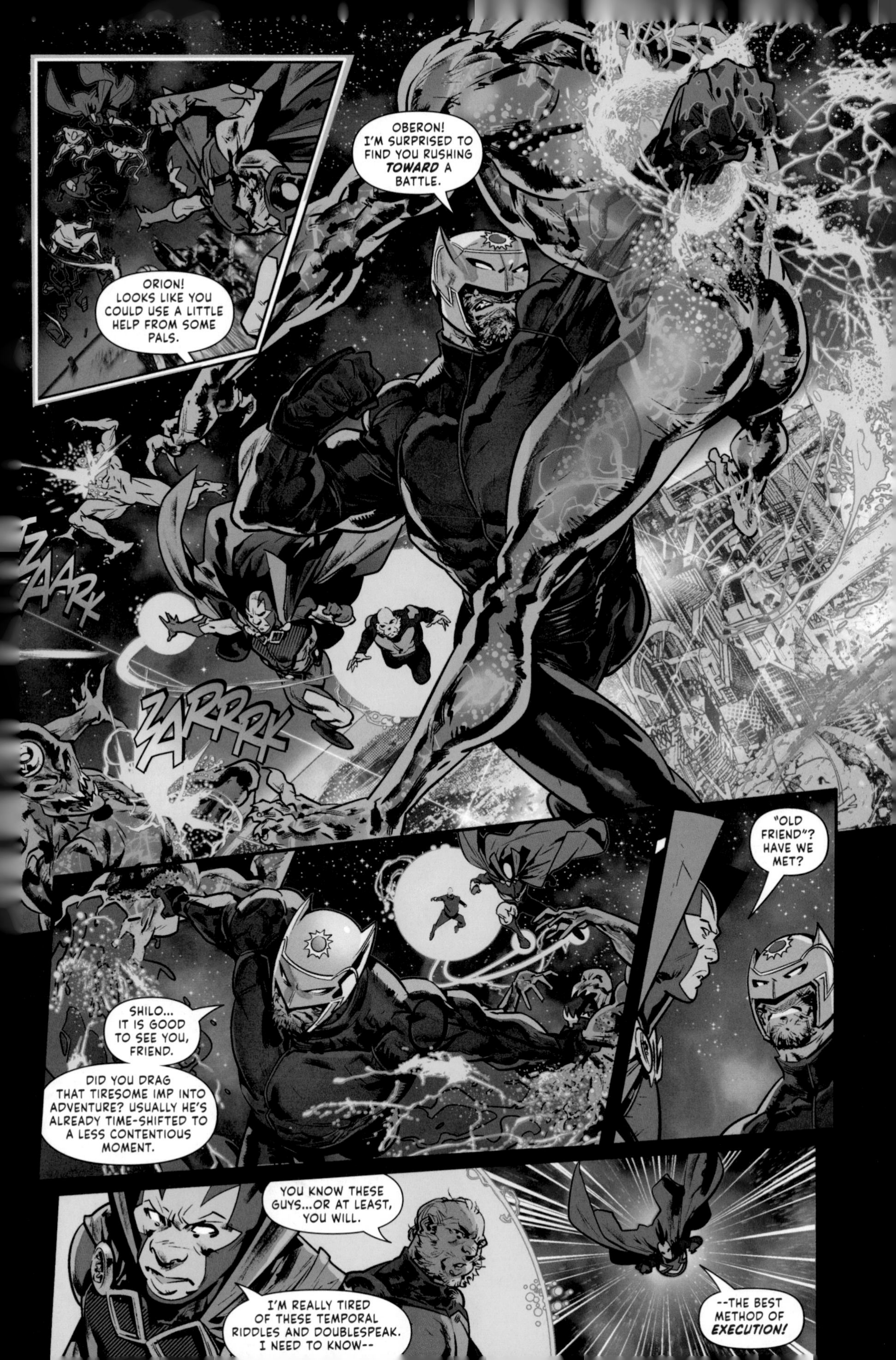
OBERON! I'M SURPRISED TO FIND YOU RUSHING TOWARD A BATTLE.
ORION! LOOKS LIKE YOU COULD USE A LITTLE HELP FROM SOME PALS.
ZZAARK
ZARRRK
SHILO... IT IS GOOD TO SEE YOU, FRIEND.
DID YOU DRAG THAT TIRESOME IMP INTO ADVENTURE? USUALLY HE'S ALREADY TIME-SHIFTED TO A LESS CONTENTIOUS MOMENT.
"OLD FRIEND"? HAVE WE MET?
YOU KNOW THESE GUYS...OR AT LEAST, YOU WILL.
I'M REALLY TIRED OF THESE TEMPORAL RIDDLES AND DOUBLESPEAK. I NEED TO KNOW--
--THE BEST METHOD OF EXECUTION!

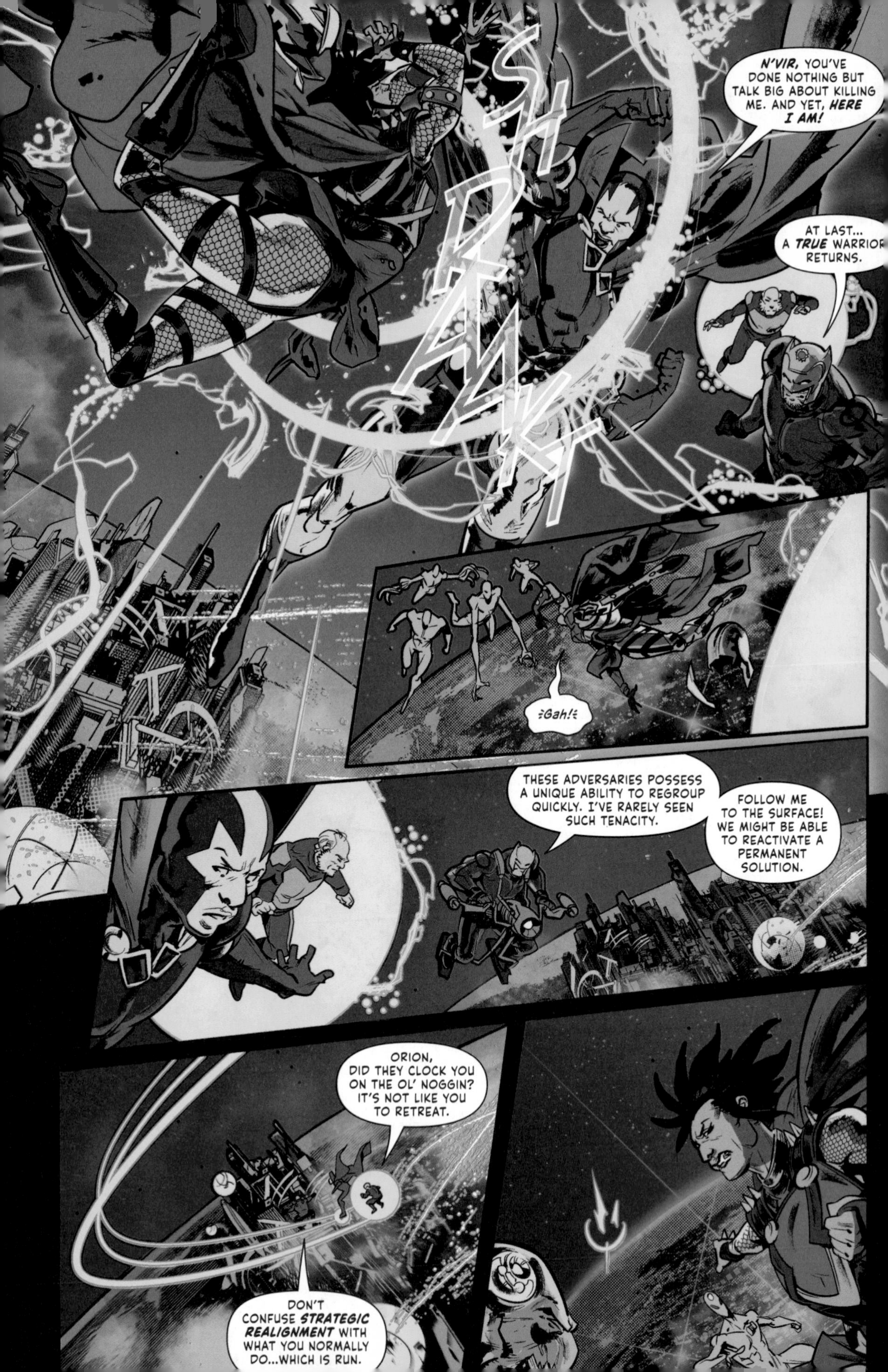

N'VIR, YOU'VE DONE NOTHING BUT TALK BIG ABOUT KILLING ME. AND YET, HERE I AM!
SHRAKK
AT LAST... A TRUE WARRIOR RETURNS.
Gah!
THESE ADVERSARIES POSSESS A UNIQUE ABILITY TO REGROUP QUICKLY. I'VE RARELY SEEN SUCH TENACITY.
FOLLOW ME TO THE SURFACE! WE MIGHT BE ABLE TO REACTIVATE A PERMANENT SOLUTION.
ORION, DID THEY CLOCK YOU ON THE OL' NOGGIN? IT'S NOT LIKE YOU TO RETREAT.
DON'T CONFUSE STRATEGIC REALIGNMENT WITH WHAT YOU NORMALLY DO...WHICH IS RUN.

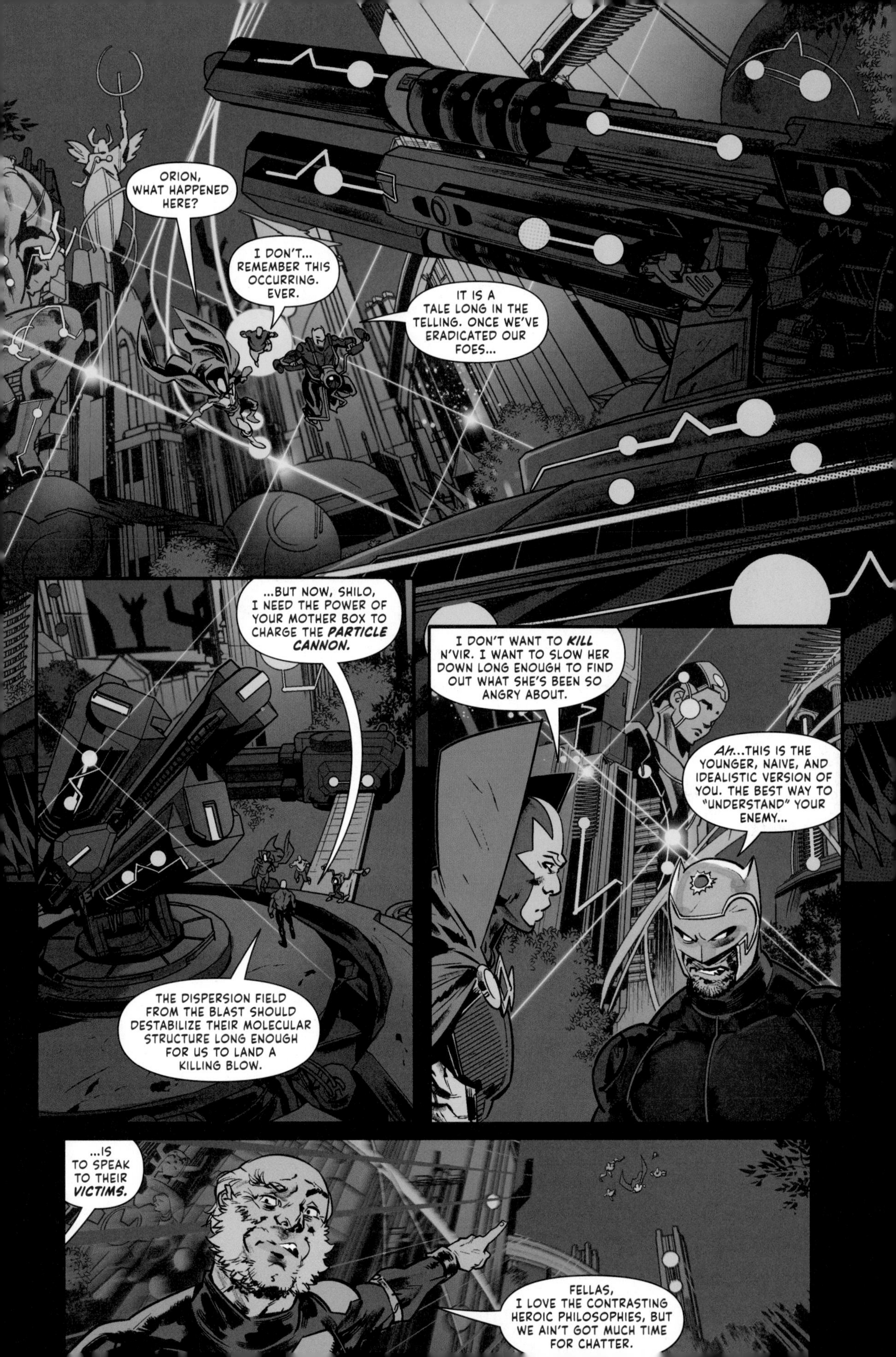
ORION, WHAT HAPPENED HERE?
I DON'T... REMEMBER THIS OCCURRING. EVER.
IT IS A TALE LONG IN THE TELLING. ONCE WE'VE ERADICATED OUR FOES...
...BUT NOW, SHILO, I NEED THE POWER OF YOUR MOTHER BOX TO CHARGE THE PARTICLE CANNON.
THE DISPERSION FIELD FROM THE BLAST SHOULD DESTABILIZE THEIR MOLECULAR STRUCTURE LONG ENOUGH FOR US TO LAND A KILLING BLOW.
I DON'T WANT TO KILL N'VIR. I WANT TO SLOW HER DOWN LONG ENOUGH TO FIND OUT WHAT SHE'S BEEN SO ANGRY ABOUT.
AH...THIS IS THE YOUNGER, NAIVE, AND IDEALISTIC VERSION OF YOU. THE BEST WAY TO "UNDERSTAND" YOUR ENEMY...
...IS TO SPEAK TO THEIR VICTIMS.
FELLAS, I LOVE THE CONTRASTING HEROIC PHILOSOPHIES, BUT WE AIN'T GOT MUCH TIME FOR CHATTER.

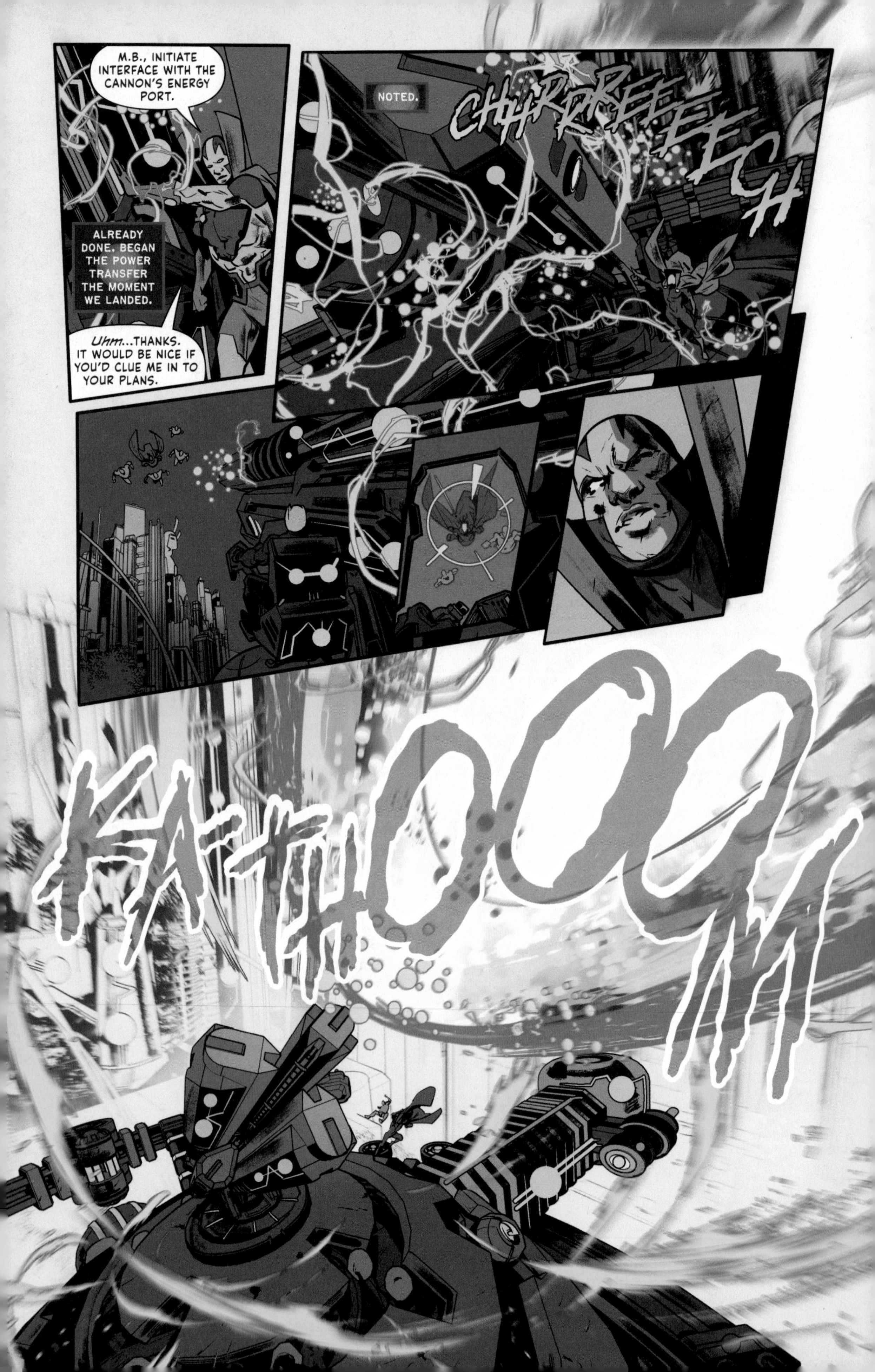

M.B., INITIATE INTERFACE WITH THE CANNON'S ENERGY PORT.
ALREADY DONE. BEGAN THE POWER TRANSFER THE MOMENT WE LANDED.
Uhm...THANKS. IT WOULD BE NICE IF YOU'D CLUE ME IN TO YOUR PLANS.
NOTED.
CHHRREEEECH
KA-THOOOM

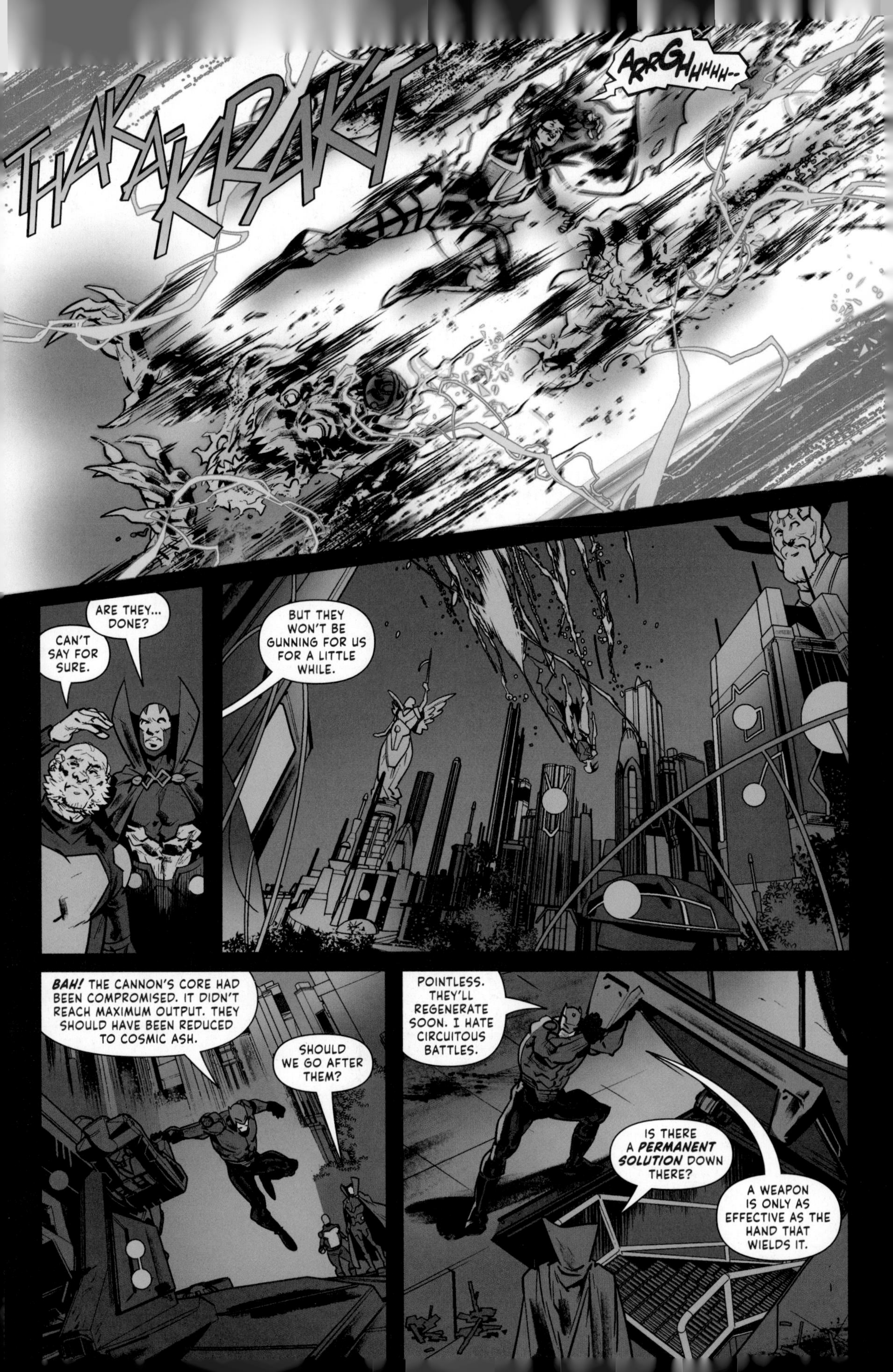
THAK-A-KRAKT
ARRGHHHHH--
ARE THEY... DONE?
CAN'T SAY FOR SURE.
BUT THEY WON'T BE GUNNING FOR US FOR A LITTLE WHILE.
BAH! THE CANNON'S CORE HAD BEEN COMPROMISED. IT DIDN'T REACH MAXIMUM OUTPUT. THEY SHOULD HAVE BEEN REDUCED TO COSMIC ASH.
SHOULD WE GO AFTER THEM?
POINTLESS. THEY'LL REGENERATE SOON. I HATE CIRCUITOUS BATTLES.
IS THERE A PERMANENT SOLUTION DOWN THERE?
A WEAPON IS ONLY AS EFFECTIVE AS THE HAND THAT WIELDS IT.

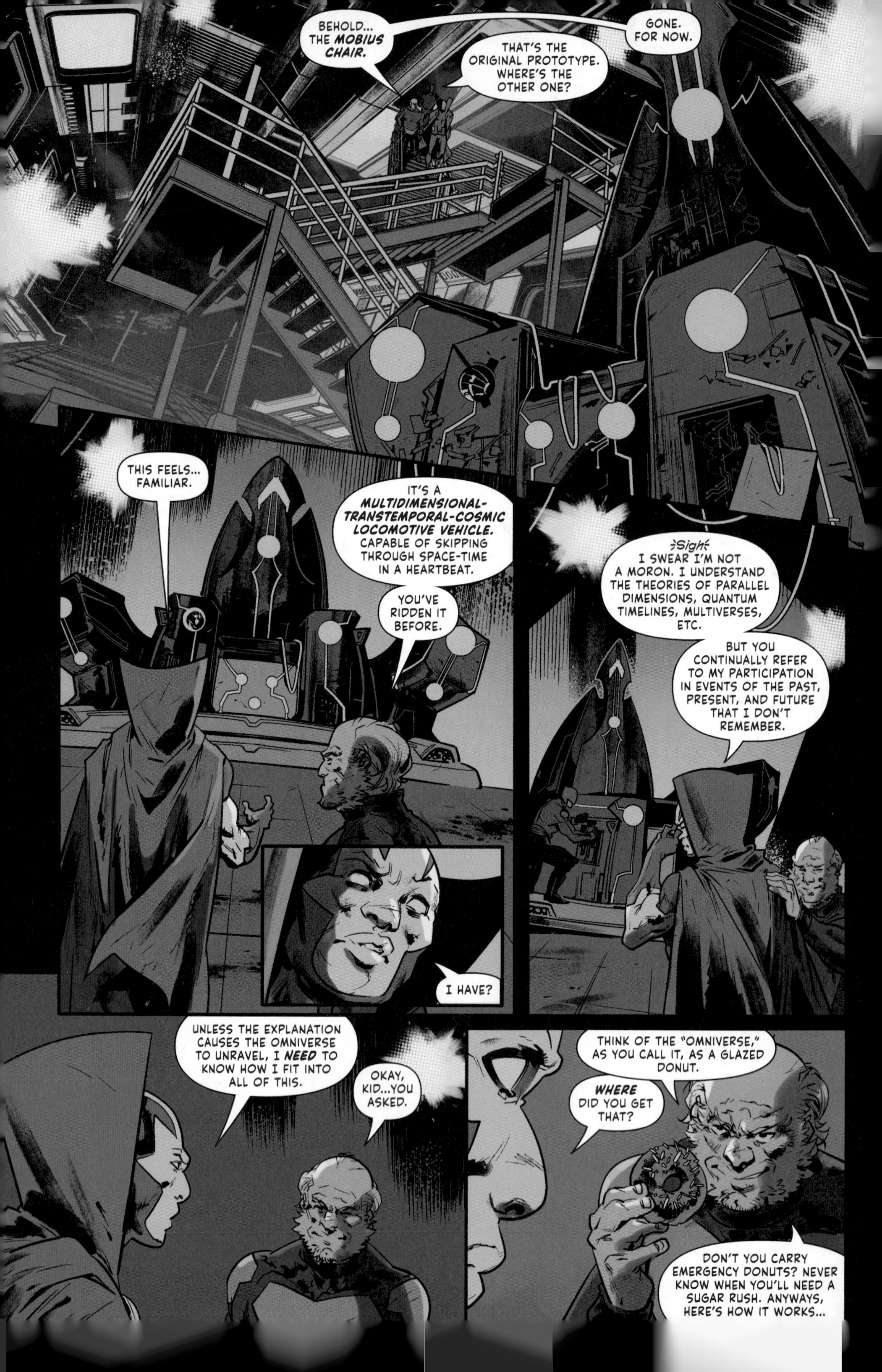

BEHOLD... THE *MOBIUS CHAIR.*
THAT'S THE ORIGINAL PROTOTYPE. WHERE'S THE OTHER ONE?
GONE. FOR NOW.
THIS FEELS... FAMILIAR.
IT'S A ***MULTIDIMENSIONAL-TRANSTEMPORAL-COSMIC LOCOMOTIVE VEHICLE.*** CAPABLE OF SKIPPING THROUGH SPACE-TIME IN A HEARTBEAT.
YOU'VE RIDDEN IT BEFORE.
I HAVE?
Sigh
I SWEAR I'M NOT A MORON. I UNDERSTAND THE THEORIES OF PARALLEL DIMENSIONS, QUANTUM TIMELINES, MULTIVERSES, ETC.
BUT YOU CONTINUALLY REFER TO MY PARTICIPATION IN EVENTS OF THE PAST, PRESENT, AND FUTURE THAT I DON'T REMEMBER.
UNLESS THE EXPLANATION CAUSES THE OMNIVERSE TO UNRAVEL, I ***NEED*** TO KNOW HOW I FIT INTO ALL OF THIS.
OKAY, KID...YOU ASKED.
THINK OF THE "OMNIVERSE," AS YOU CALL IT, AS A GLAZED DONUT.
WHERE DID YOU GET THAT?
DON'T YOU CARRY EMERGENCY DONUTS? NEVER KNOW WHEN YOU'LL NEED A SUGAR RUSH. ANYWAYS, HERE'S HOW IT WORKS...

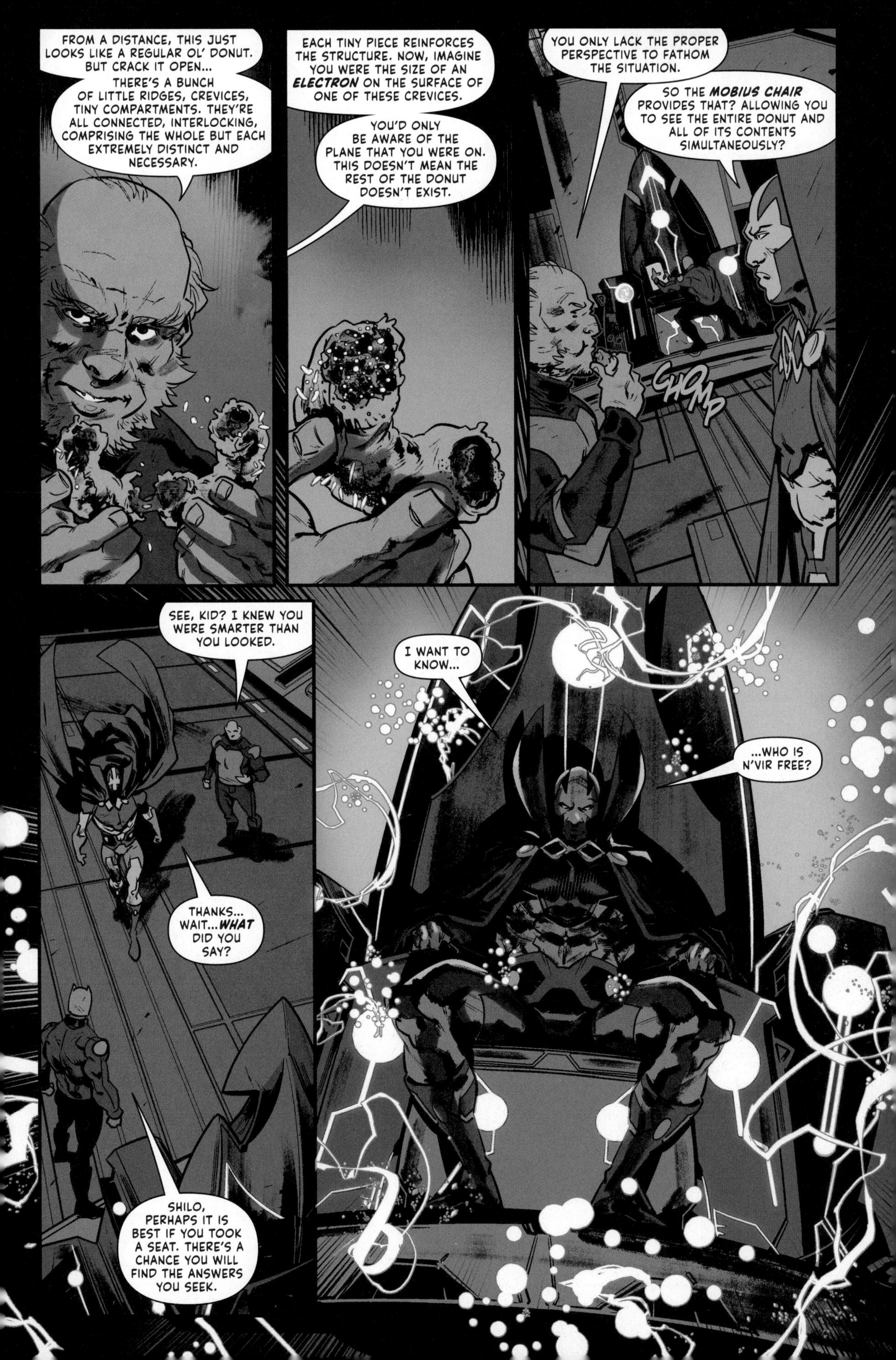
FROM A DISTANCE, THIS JUST LOOKS LIKE A REGULAR OL' DONUT. BUT CRACK IT OPEN...
THERE'S A BUNCH OF LITTLE RIDGES, CREVICES, TINY COMPARTMENTS. THEY'RE ALL CONNECTED, INTERLOCKING, COMPRISING THE WHOLE BUT EACH EXTREMELY DISTINCT AND NECESSARY.
EACH TINY PIECE REINFORCES THE STRUCTURE. NOW, IMAGINE YOU WERE THE SIZE OF AN ELECTRON ON THE SURFACE OF ONE OF THESE CREVICES.
YOU'D ONLY BE AWARE OF THE PLANE THAT YOU WERE ON. THIS DOESN'T MEAN THE REST OF THE DONUT DOESN'T EXIST.
YOU ONLY LACK THE PROPER PERSPECTIVE TO FATHOM THE SITUATION.
SO THE MOBIUS CHAIR PROVIDES THAT? ALLOWING YOU TO SEE THE ENTIRE DONUT AND ALL OF ITS CONTENTS SIMULTANEOUSLY?
CHOMP
SEE, KID? I KNEW YOU WERE SMARTER THAN YOU LOOKED.
THANKS... WAIT...WHAT DID YOU SAY?
SHILO, PERHAPS IT IS BEST IF YOU TOOK A SEAT. THERE'S A CHANCE YOU WILL FIND THE ANSWERS YOU SEEK.
I WANT TO KNOW...
...WHO IS N'VIR FREE?

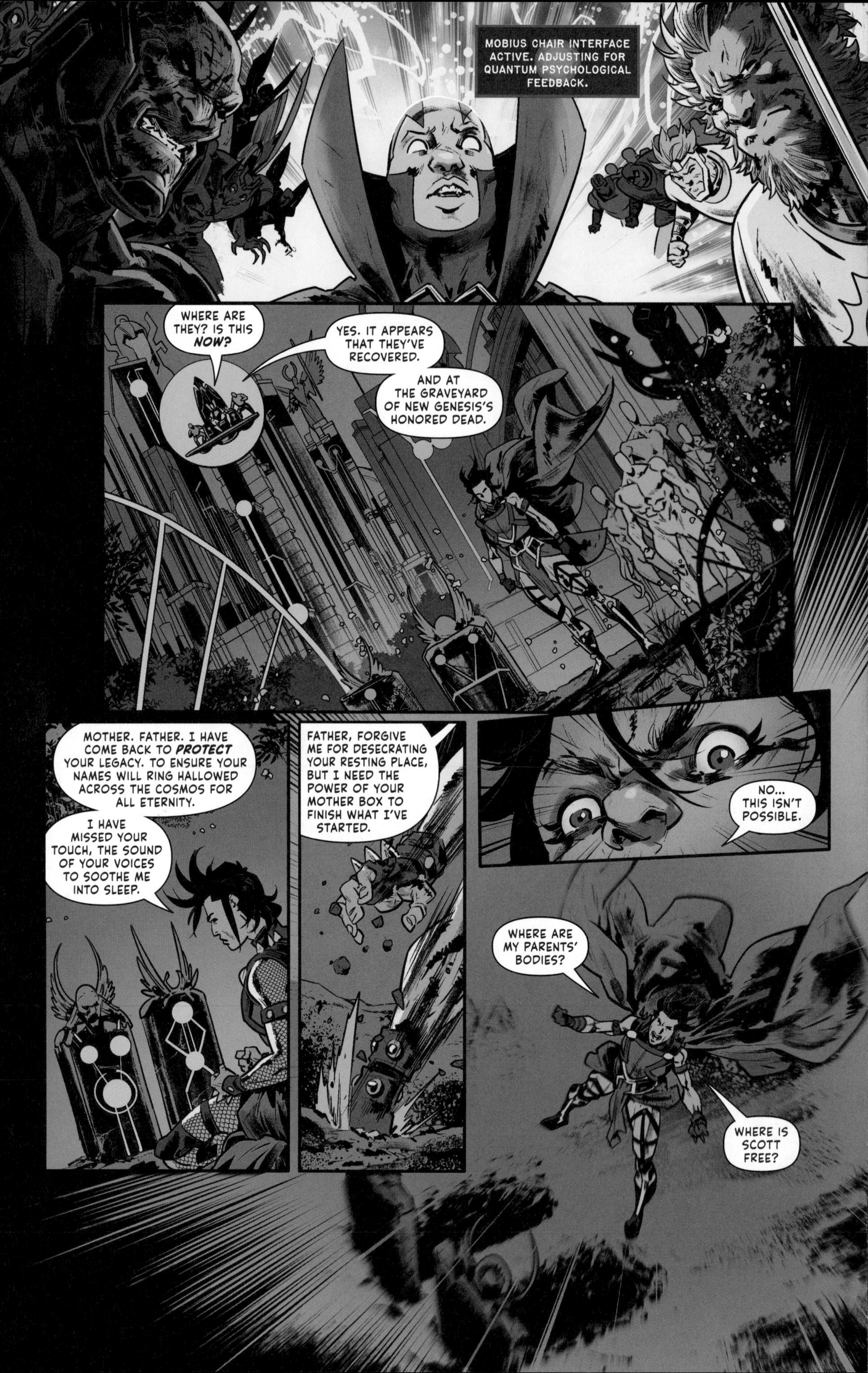
MOBIUS CHAIR INTERFACE ACTIVE. ADJUSTING FOR QUANTUM PSYCHOLOGICAL FEEDBACK.
WHERE ARE THEY? IS THIS ***NOW?***
YES. IT APPEARS THAT THEY'VE RECOVERED.
AND AT THE GRAVEYARD OF NEW GENESIS'S HONORED DEAD.
MOTHER. FATHER. I HAVE COME BACK TO ***PROTECT*** YOUR LEGACY. TO ENSURE YOUR NAMES WILL RING HALLOWED ACROSS THE COSMOS FOR ALL ETERNITY.
I HAVE MISSED YOUR TOUCH, THE SOUND OF YOUR VOICES TO SOOTHE ME INTO SLEEP.
FATHER, FORGIVE ME FOR DESECRATING YOUR RESTING PLACE, BUT I NEED THE POWER OF YOUR MOTHER BOX TO FINISH WHAT I'VE STARTED.
NO... THIS ISN'T POSSIBLE.
WHERE ARE MY PARENTS' BODIES?
WHERE IS SCOTT FREE?

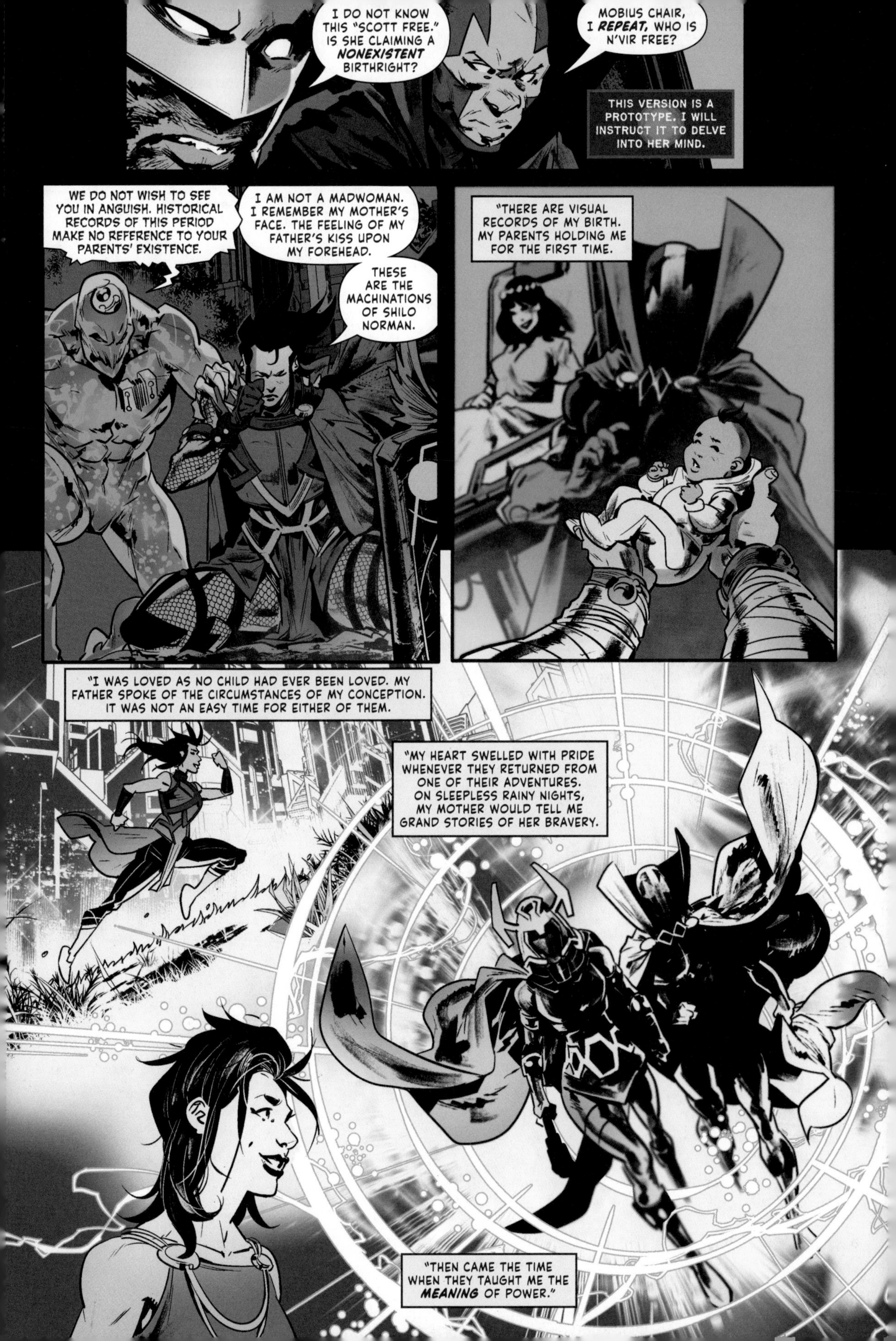

I DO NOT KNOW THIS "SCOTT FREE." IS SHE CLAIMING A NONEXISTENT BIRTHRIGHT?
MOBIUS CHAIR, I REPEAT, WHO IS N'VIR FREE?
THIS VERSION IS A PROTOTYPE. I WILL INSTRUCT IT TO DELVE INTO HER MIND.
WE DO NOT WISH TO SEE YOU IN ANGUISH. HISTORICAL RECORDS OF THIS PERIOD MAKE NO REFERENCE TO YOUR PARENTS' EXISTENCE.
I AM NOT A MADWOMAN. I REMEMBER MY MOTHER'S FACE. THE FEELING OF MY FATHER'S KISS UPON MY FOREHEAD.
THESE ARE THE MACHINATIONS OF SHILO NORMAN.
"THERE ARE VISUAL RECORDS OF MY BIRTH. MY PARENTS HOLDING ME FOR THE FIRST TIME.
"I WAS LOVED AS NO CHILD HAD EVER BEEN LOVED. MY FATHER SPOKE OF THE CIRCUMSTANCES OF MY CONCEPTION. IT WAS NOT AN EASY TIME FOR EITHER OF THEM.
"MY HEART SWELLED WITH PRIDE WHENEVER THEY RETURNED FROM ONE OF THEIR ADVENTURES. ON SLEEPLESS RAINY NIGHTS, MY MOTHER WOULD TELL ME GRAND STORIES OF HER BRAVERY.
"THEN CAME THE TIME WHEN THEY TAUGHT ME THE MEANING OF POWER."

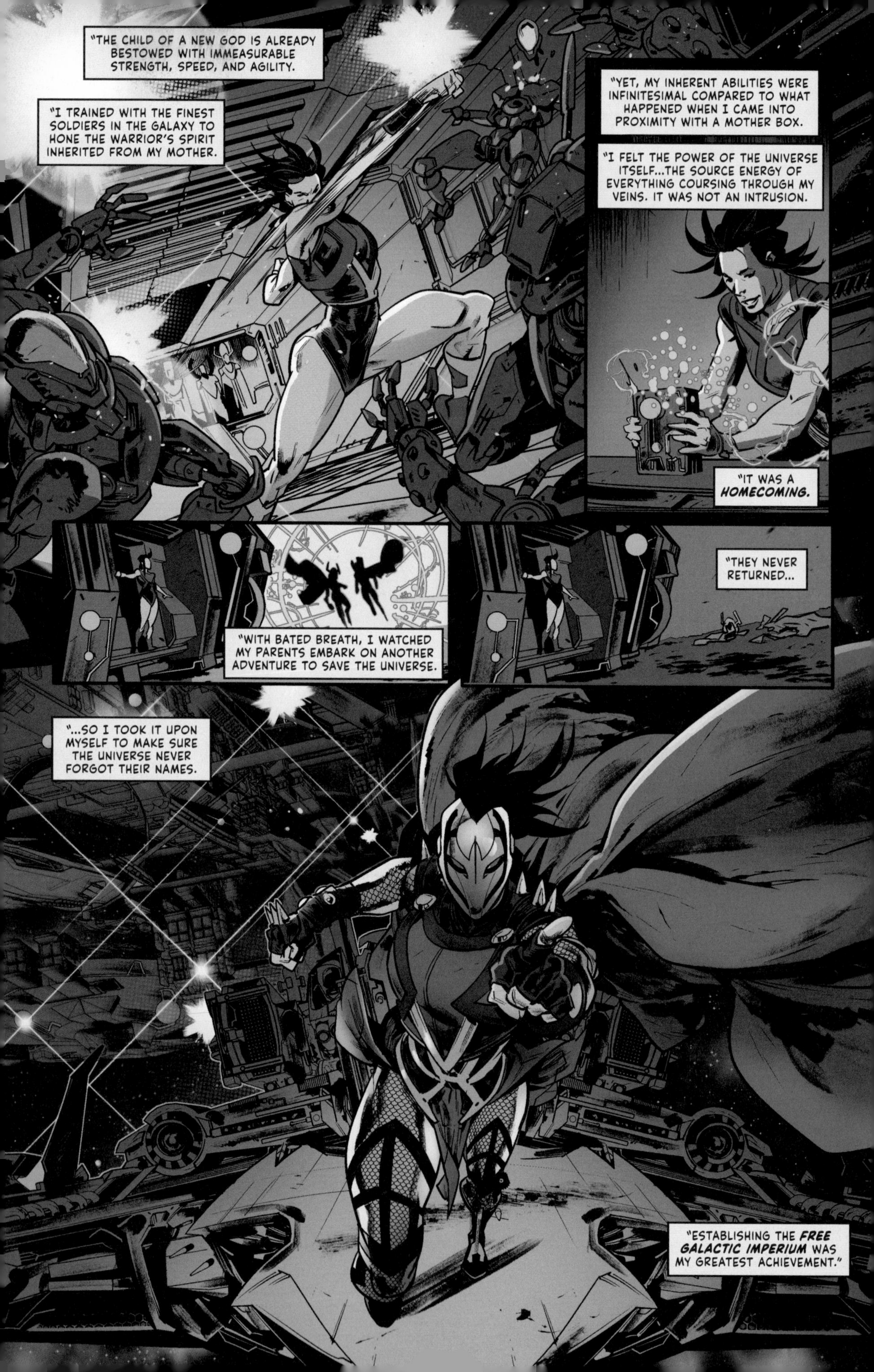
"THE CHILD OF A NEW GOD IS ALREADY BESTOWED WITH IMMEASURABLE STRENGTH, SPEED, AND AGILITY.
"I TRAINED WITH THE FINEST SOLDIERS IN THE GALAXY TO HONE THE WARRIOR'S SPIRIT INHERITED FROM MY MOTHER.
"YET, MY INHERENT ABILITIES WERE INFINITESIMAL COMPARED TO WHAT HAPPENED WHEN I CAME INTO PROXIMITY WITH A MOTHER BOX.
"I FELT THE POWER OF THE UNIVERSE ITSELF...THE SOURCE ENERGY OF EVERYTHING COURSING THROUGH MY VEINS. IT WAS NOT AN INTRUSION.
"IT WAS A *HOMECOMING.*
"WITH BATED BREATH, I WATCHED MY PARENTS EMBARK ON ANOTHER ADVENTURE TO SAVE THE UNIVERSE.
"THEY NEVER RETURNED...
"...SO I TOOK IT UPON MYSELF TO MAKE SURE THE UNIVERSE NEVER FORGOT THEIR NAMES.
"ESTABLISHING THE *FREE GALACTIC IMPERIUM* WAS MY GREATEST ACHIEVEMENT."

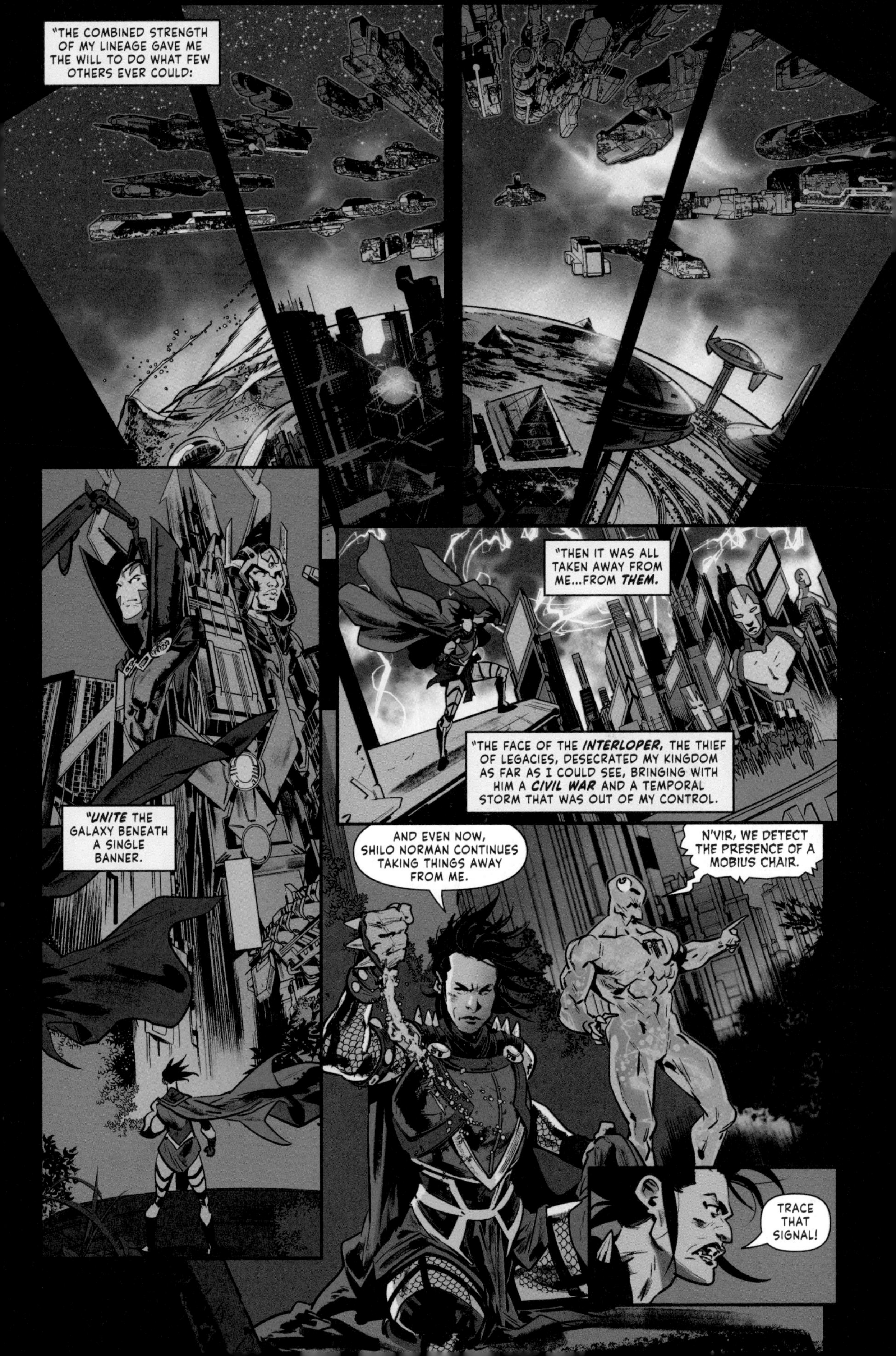
"THE COMBINED STRENGTH OF MY LINEAGE GAVE ME THE WILL TO DO WHAT FEW OTHERS EVER COULD:
"UNITE THE GALAXY BENEATH A SINGLE BANNER.
"THEN IT WAS ALL TAKEN AWAY FROM ME...FROM THEM.
"THE FACE OF THE INTERLOPER, THE THIEF OF LEGACIES, DESECRATED MY KINGDOM AS FAR AS I COULD SEE, BRINGING WITH HIM A CIVIL WAR AND A TEMPORAL STORM THAT WAS OUT OF MY CONTROL.
AND EVEN NOW, SHILO NORMAN CONTINUES TAKING THINGS AWAY FROM ME.
N'VIR, WE DETECT THE PRESENCE OF A MOBIUS CHAIR.
TRACE THAT SIGNAL!

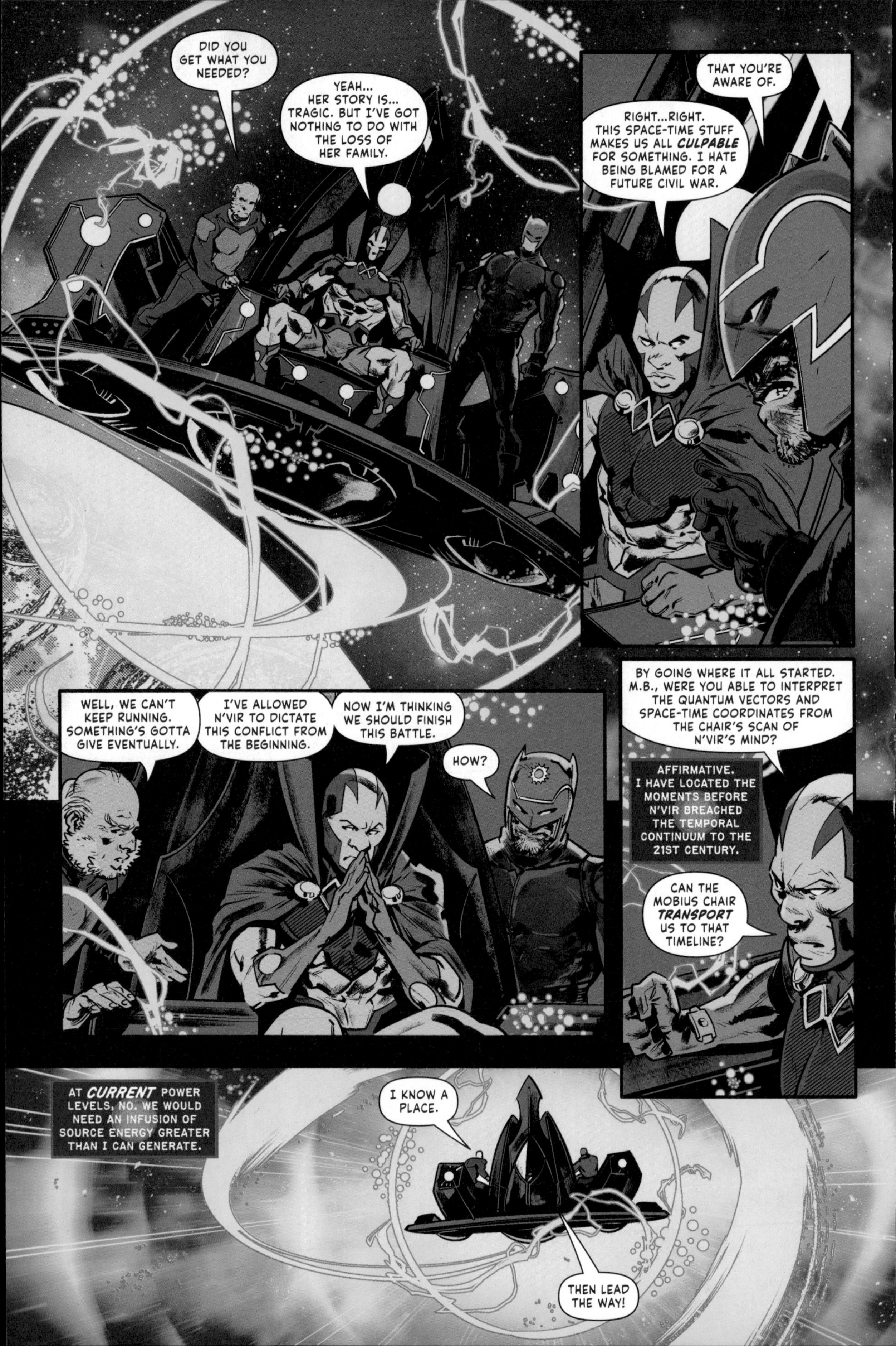
DID YOU GET WHAT YOU NEEDED?
YEAH... HER STORY IS... TRAGIC. BUT I'VE GOT NOTHING TO DO WITH THE LOSS OF HER FAMILY.
THAT YOU'RE AWARE OF.
RIGHT...RIGHT. THIS SPACE-TIME STUFF MAKES US ALL CULPABLE FOR SOMETHING. I HATE BEING BLAMED FOR A FUTURE CIVIL WAR.
WELL, WE CAN'T KEEP RUNNING. SOMETHING'S GOTTA GIVE EVENTUALLY.
I'VE ALLOWED N'VIR TO DICTATE THIS CONFLICT FROM THE BEGINNING.
NOW I'M THINKING WE SHOULD FINISH THIS BATTLE.
HOW?
BY GOING WHERE IT ALL STARTED. M.B., WERE YOU ABLE TO INTERPRET THE QUANTUM VECTORS AND SPACE-TIME COORDINATES FROM THE CHAIR'S SCAN OF N'VIR'S MIND?
AFFIRMATIVE. I HAVE LOCATED THE MOMENTS BEFORE N'VIR BREACHED THE TEMPORAL CONTINUUM TO THE 21ST CENTURY.
CAN THE MOBIUS CHAIR TRANSPORT US TO THAT TIMELINE?
AT CURRENT POWER LEVELS, NO. WE WOULD NEED AN INFUSION OF SOURCE ENERGY GREATER THAN I CAN GENERATE.
I KNOW A PLACE.
THEN LEAD THE WAY!

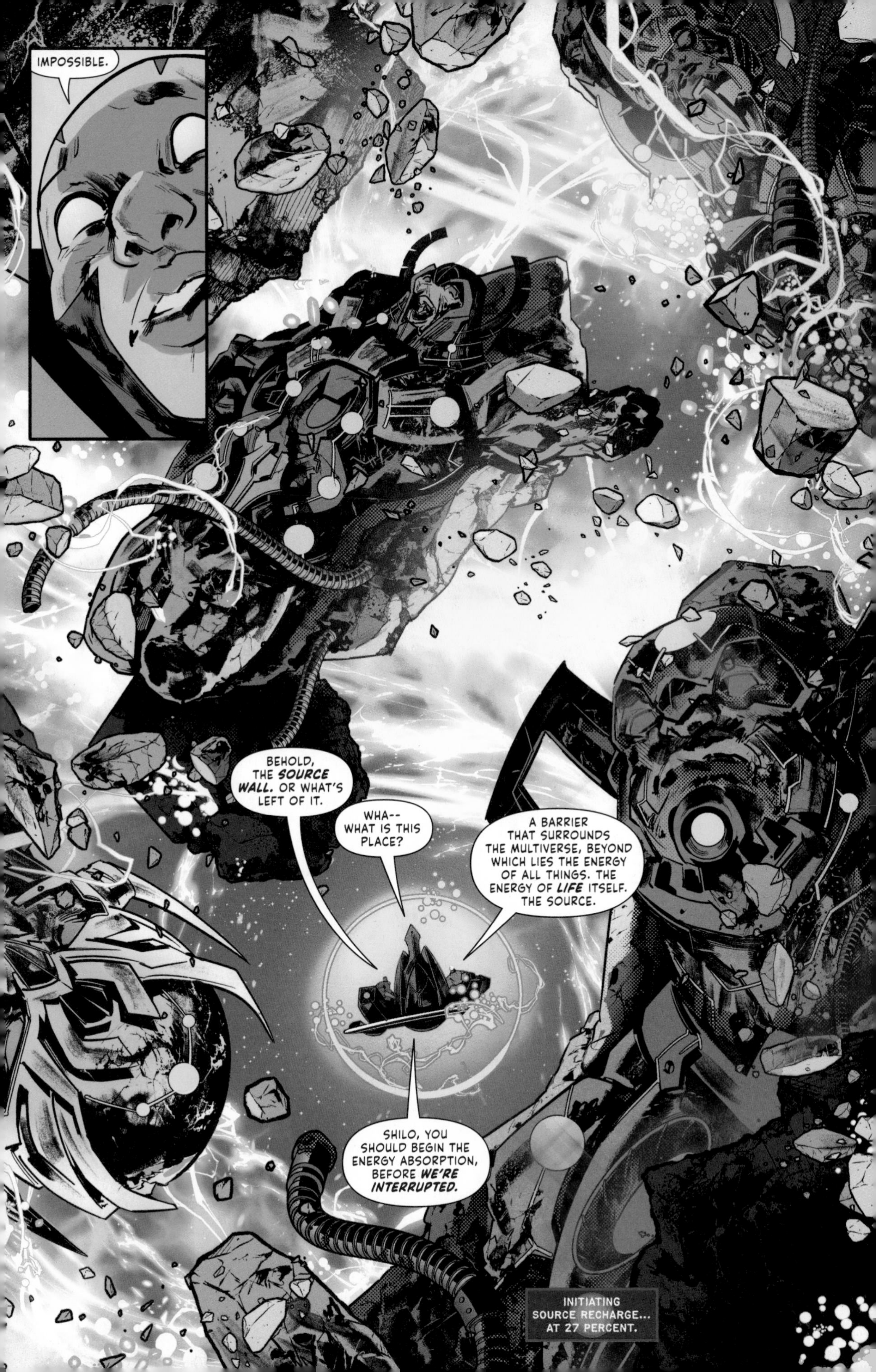
IMPOSSIBLE.
BEHOLD, THE SOURCE WALL. OR WHAT'S LEFT OF IT.
WHA-- WHAT IS THIS PLACE?
A BARRIER THAT SURROUNDS THE MULTIVERSE, BEYOND WHICH LIES THE ENERGY OF ALL THINGS. THE ENERGY OF LIFE ITSELF. THE SOURCE.
SHILO, YOU SHOULD BEGIN THE ENERGY ABSORPTION, BEFORE WE'RE INTERRUPTED.
INITIATING SOURCE RECHARGE... AT 27 PERCENT.

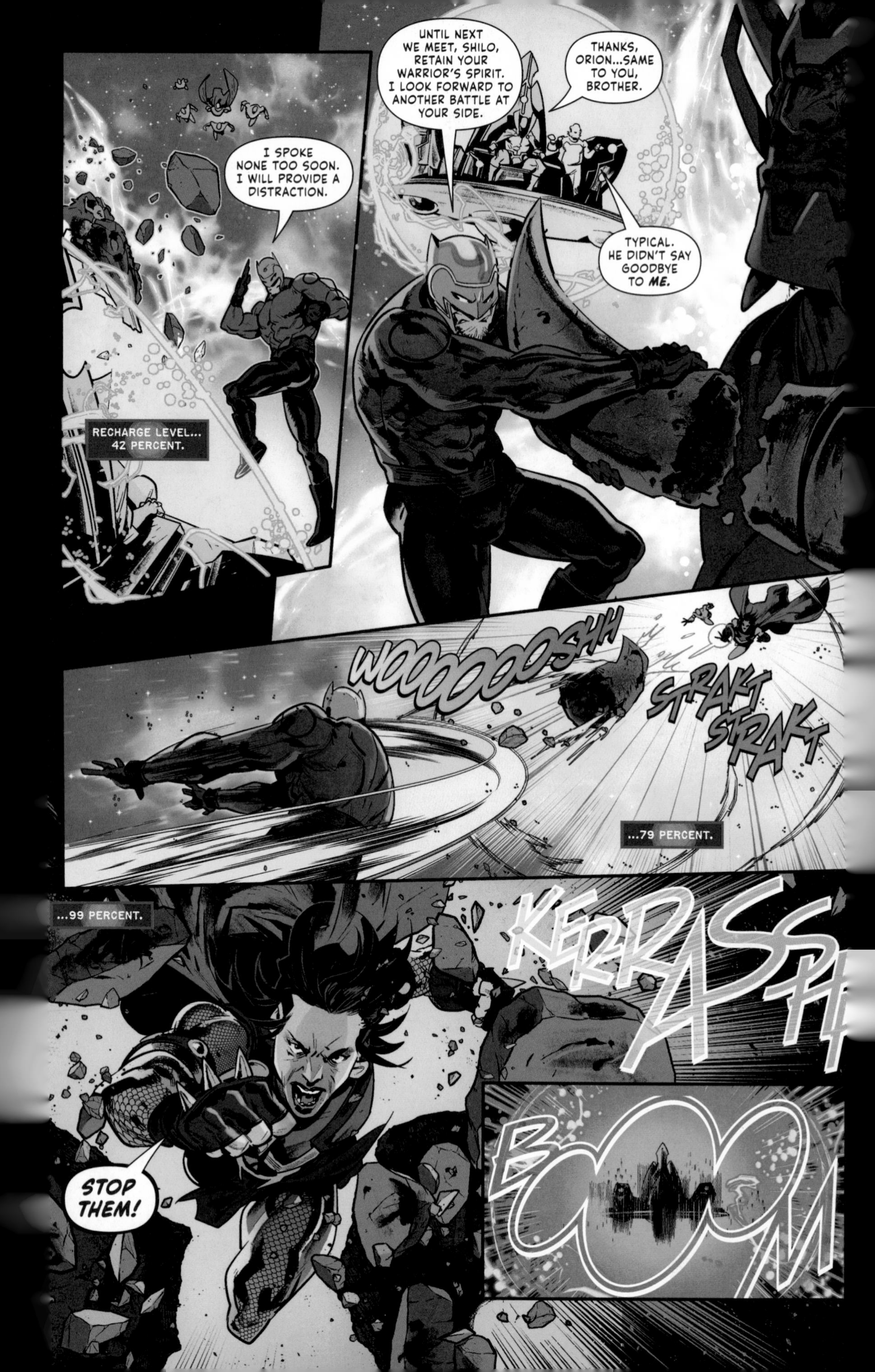
I SPOKE NONE TOO SOON. I WILL PROVIDE A DISTRACTION.
RECHARGE LEVEL... 42 PERCENT.
UNTIL NEXT WE MEET, SHILO, RETAIN YOUR WARRIOR'S SPIRIT. I LOOK FORWARD TO ANOTHER BATTLE AT YOUR SIDE.
THANKS, ORION...SAME TO YOU, BROTHER.
TYPICAL. HE DIDN'T SAY GOODBYE TO ME.
WOOOOOOOSHH
STRAKT STRAKT
...79 PERCENT.
...99 PERCENT.
KERRASSHH
STOP THEM!
BOOOM

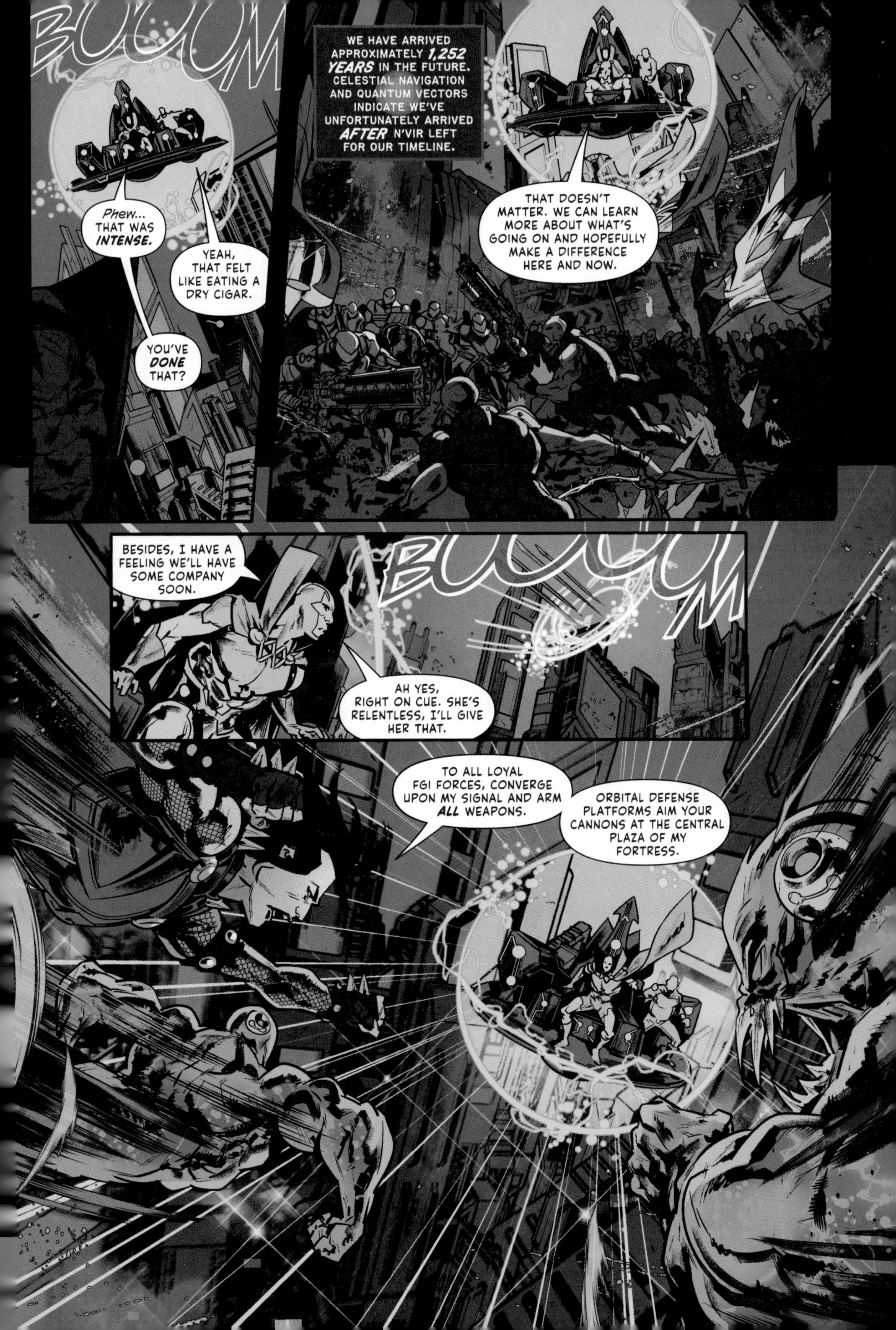
BOOOM
WE HAVE ARRIVED APPROXIMATELY 1,252 YEARS IN THE FUTURE. CELESTIAL NAVIGATION AND QUANTUM VECTORS INDICATE WE'VE UNFORTUNATELY ARRIVED AFTER N'VIR LEFT FOR OUR TIMELINE.
Phew... THAT WAS INTENSE.
YEAH, THAT FELT LIKE EATING A DRY CIGAR.
YOU'VE DONE THAT?
THAT DOESN'T MATTER. WE CAN LEARN MORE ABOUT WHAT'S GOING ON AND HOPEFULLY MAKE A DIFFERENCE HERE AND NOW.
BESIDES, I HAVE A FEELING WE'LL HAVE SOME COMPANY SOON.
BOOOOM
AH YES, RIGHT ON CUE. SHE'S RELENTLESS, I'LL GIVE HER THAT.
TO ALL LOYAL FGI FORCES, CONVERGE UPON MY SIGNAL AND ARM ALL WEAPONS.
ORBITAL DEFENSE PLATFORMS AIM YOUR CANNONS AT THE CENTRAL PLAZA OF MY FORTRESS.

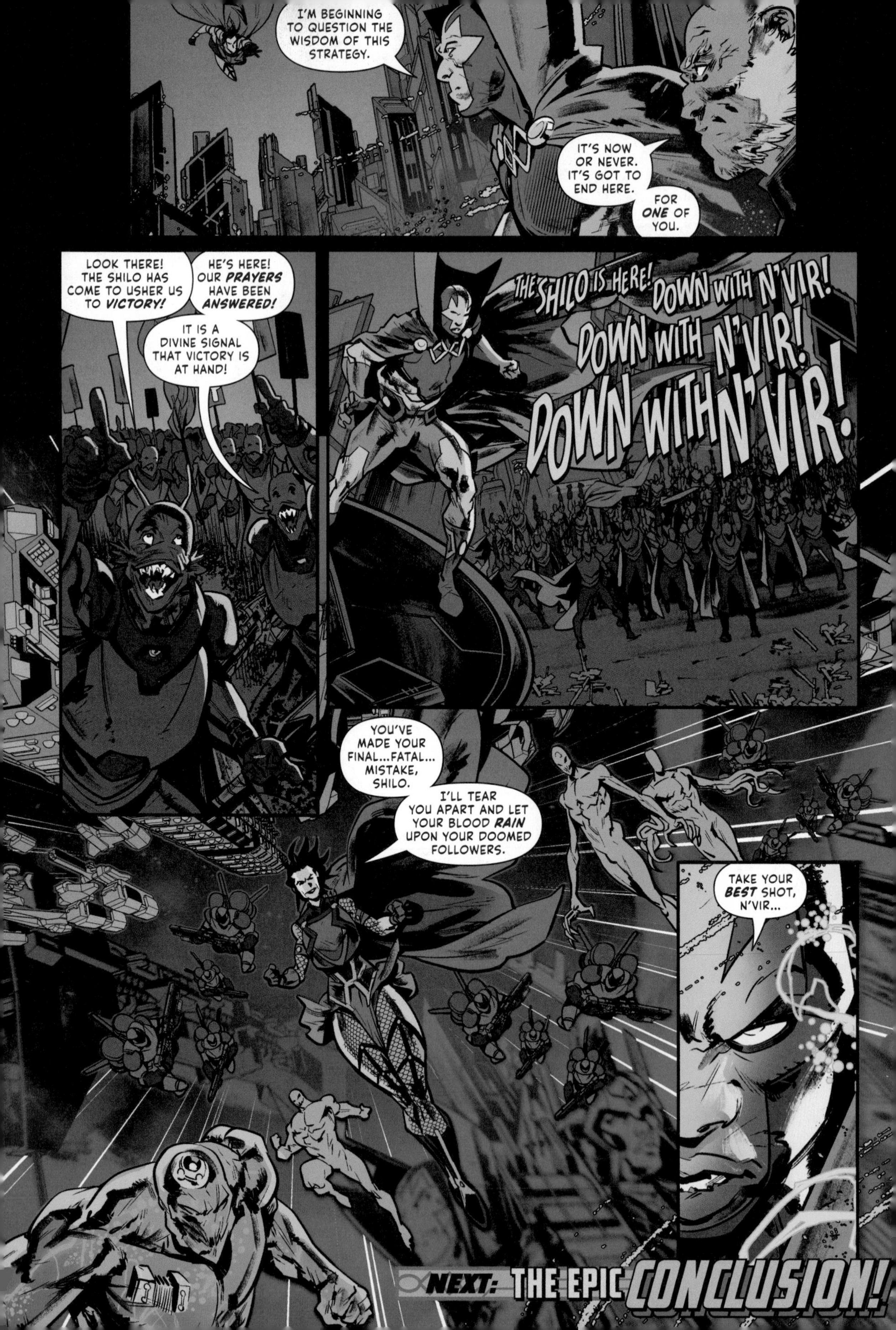
I'M BEGINNING TO QUESTION THE WISDOM OF THIS STRATEGY.
IT'S NOW OR NEVER. IT'S GOT TO END HERE.
FOR ONE OF YOU.
LOOK THERE! THE SHILO HAS COME TO USHER US TO VICTORY!
HE'S HERE! OUR PRAYERS HAVE BEEN ANSWERED!
IT IS A DIVINE SIGNAL THAT VICTORY IS AT HAND!
THE SHILO IS HERE! DOWN WITH N'VIR!
DOWN WITH N'VIR!
DOWN WITH N'VIR!
YOU'VE MADE YOUR FINAL...FATAL... MISTAKE, SHILO.
I'LL TEAR YOU APART AND LET YOUR BLOOD RAIN UPON YOUR DOOMED FOLLOWERS.
TAKE YOUR BEST SHOT, N'VIR...
NEXT: THE EPIC CONCLUSION!

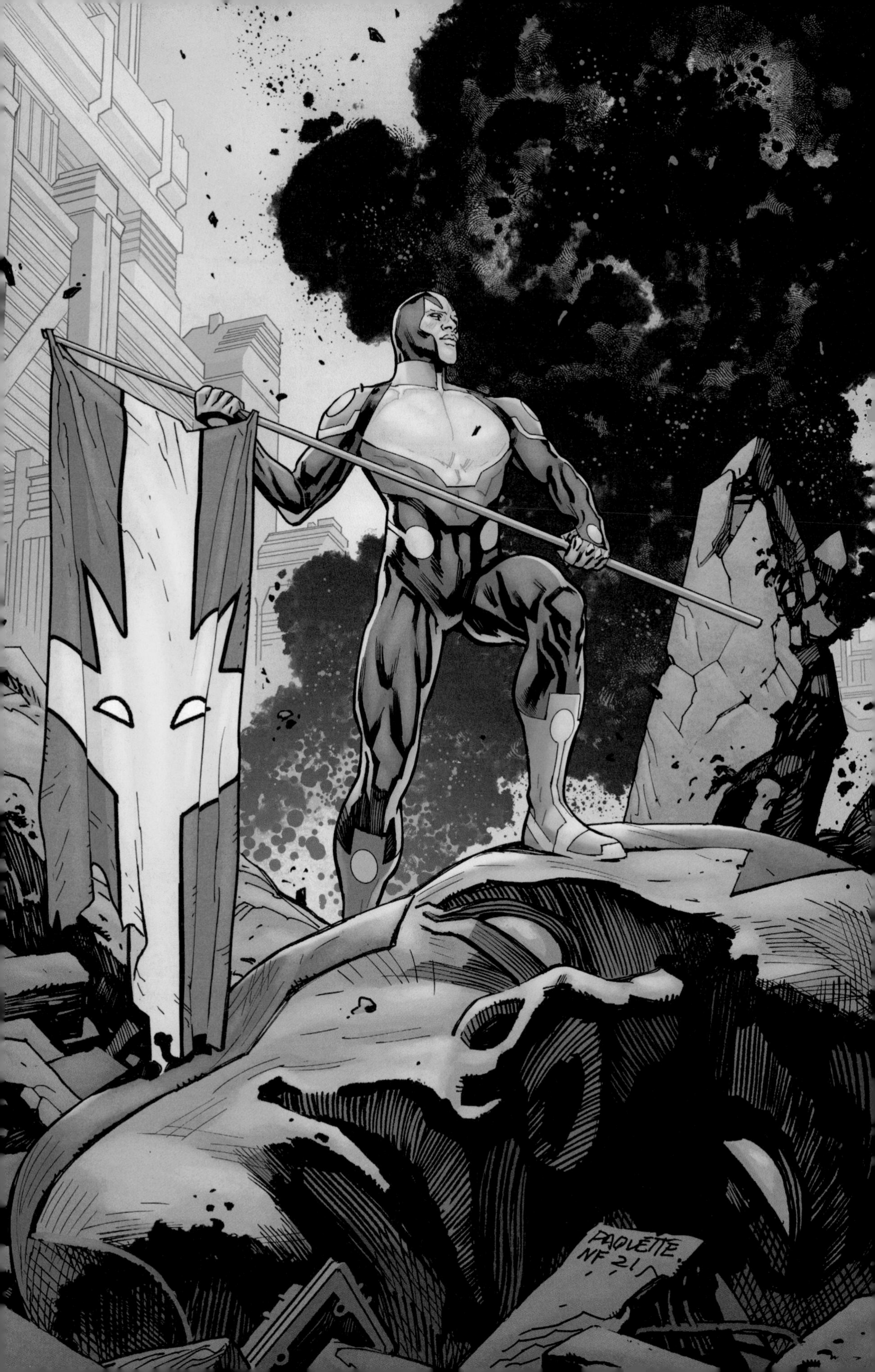
PAQUETTE
NF 21

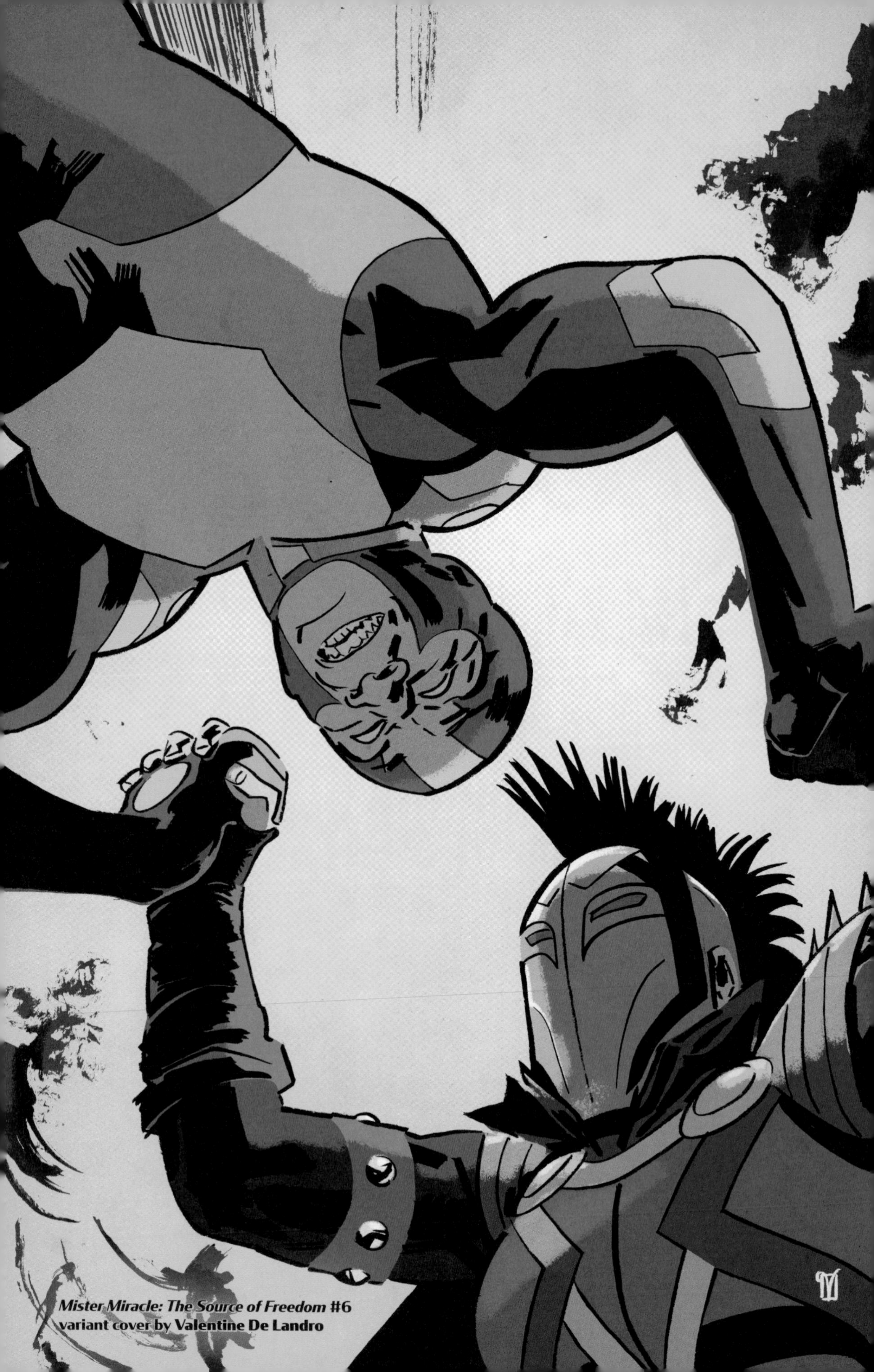

Mister Miracle: The Source of Freedom #6
variant cover by Valentine De Landro

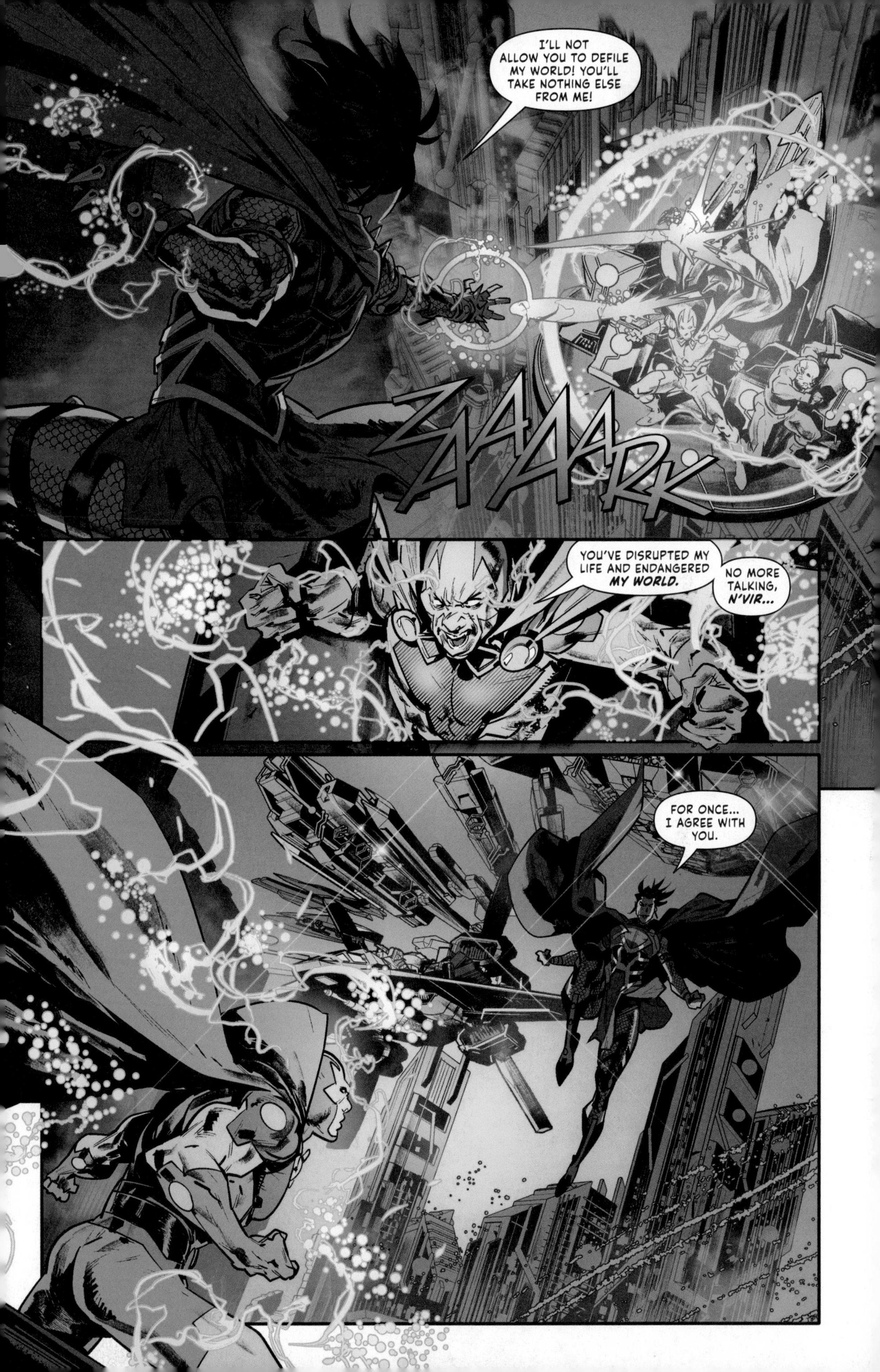
I'LL NOT ALLOW YOU TO DEFILE MY WORLD! YOU'LL TAKE NOTHING ELSE FROM ME!
ZAAAARK
YOU'VE DISRUPTED MY LIFE AND ENDANGERED **MY WORLD.**
NO MORE TALKING, ***N'VIR...***
FOR ONCE... I AGREE WITH YOU.

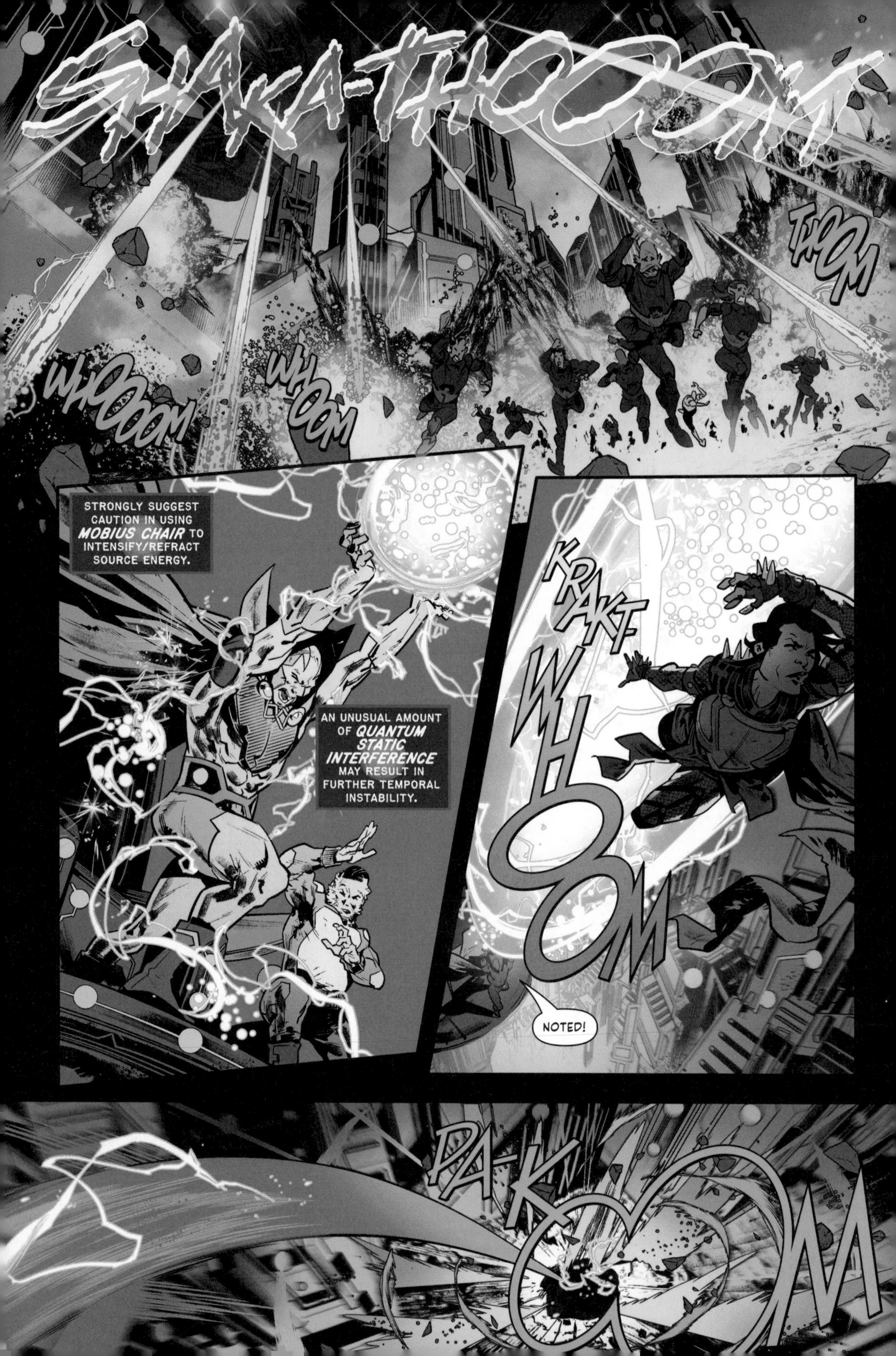
SHAKA-THOOOM
THOOM
WHOOOOOM
WHOOM
STRONGLY SUGGEST CAUTION IN USING *MOBIUS CHAIR* TO INTENSIFY/REFRACT SOURCE ENERGY.
AN UNUSUAL AMOUNT OF *QUANTUM STATIC INTERFERENCE* MAY RESULT IN FURTHER TEMPORAL INSTABILITY.
KRAKT
WHOOOM
NOTED!
PAKOOM

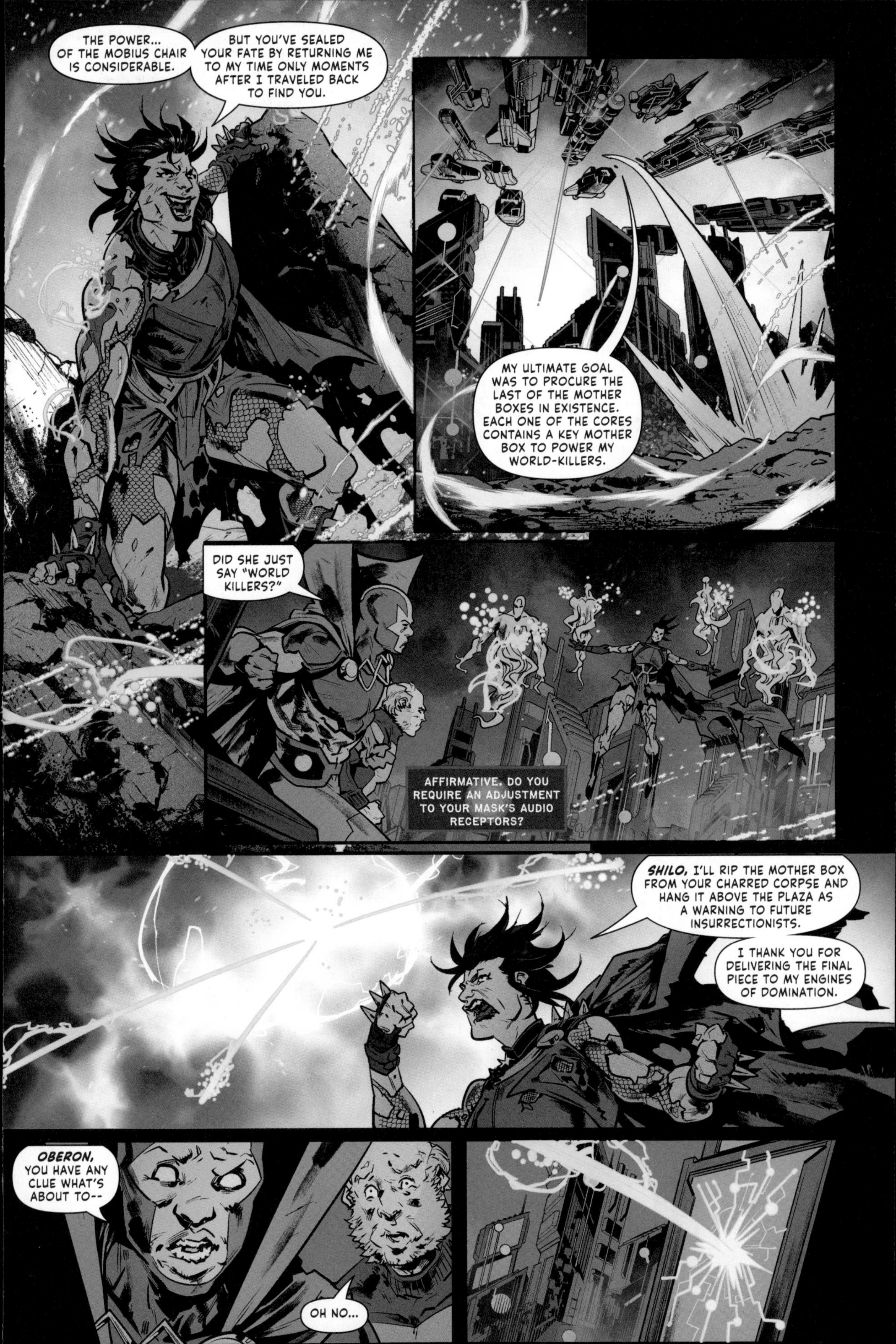
THE POWER... OF THE MOBIUS CHAIR IS CONSIDERABLE.
BUT YOU'VE SEALED YOUR FATE BY RETURNING ME TO MY TIME ONLY MOMENTS AFTER I TRAVELED BACK TO FIND YOU.
MY ULTIMATE GOAL WAS TO PROCURE THE LAST OF THE MOTHER BOXES IN EXISTENCE. EACH ONE OF THE CORES CONTAINS A KEY MOTHER BOX TO POWER MY WORLD-KILLERS.
DID SHE JUST SAY "WORLD KILLERS?"
AFFIRMATIVE. DO YOU REQUIRE AN ADJUSTMENT TO YOUR MASK'S AUDIO RECEPTORS?
SHILO, I'LL RIP THE MOTHER BOX FROM YOUR CHARRED CORPSE AND HANG IT ABOVE THE PLAZA AS A WARNING TO FUTURE INSURRECTIONISTS.
I THANK YOU FOR DELIVERING THE FINAL PIECE TO MY ENGINES OF DOMINATION.
OBERON, YOU HAVE ANY CLUE WHAT'S ABOUT TO--
OH NO...

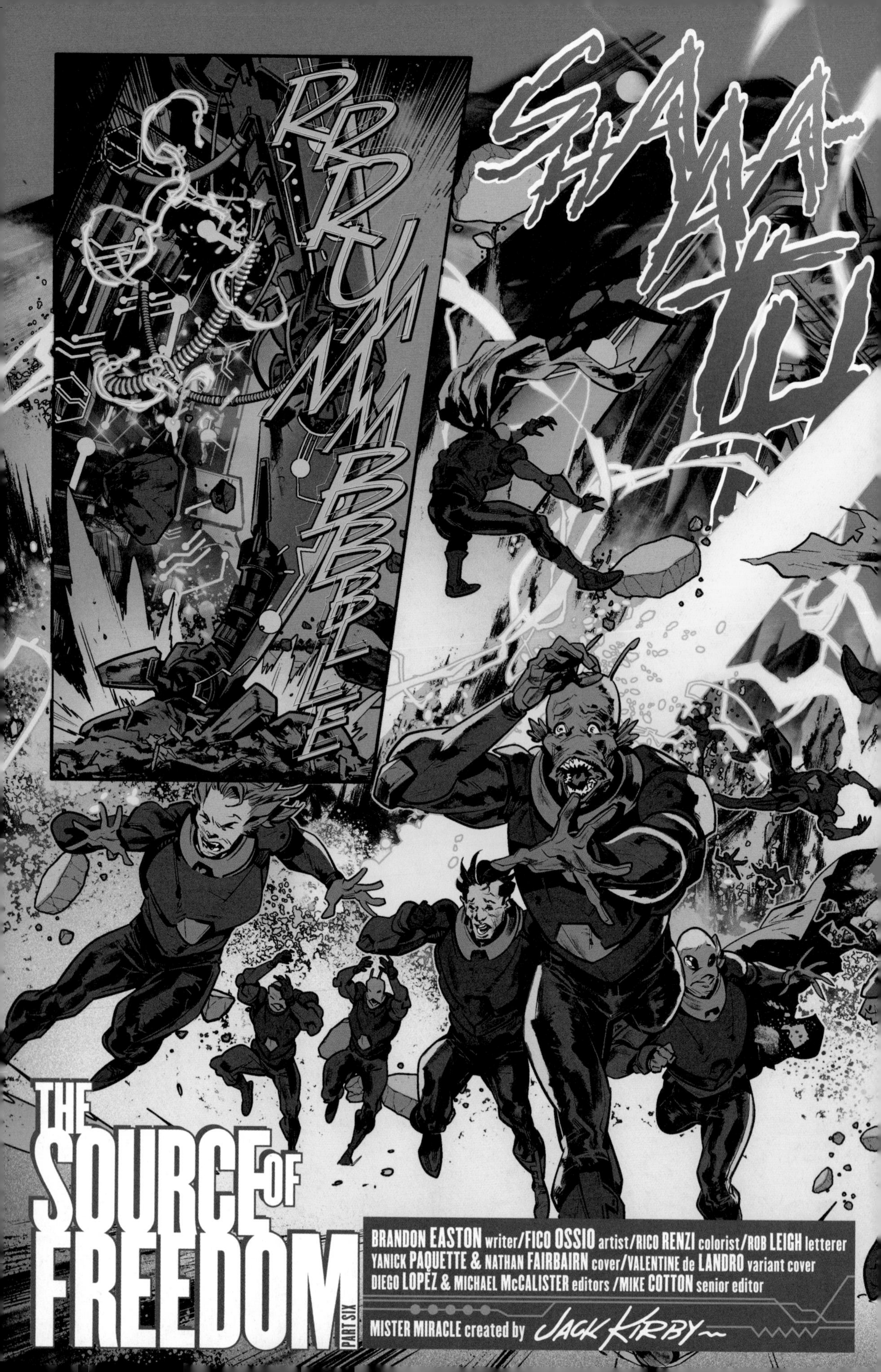
RRRUMMMBBBLE
SHAAA-TU
THE SOURCE OF FREEDOM
PART SIX
BRANDON EASTON writer/FICO OSSIO artist/RICO RENZI colorist/ROB LEIGH letterer
YANICK PAQUETTE & NATHAN FAIRBAIRN cover/VALENTINE de LANDRO variant cover
DIEGO LOPEZ & MICHAEL McCALISTER editors /MIKE COTTON senior editor
MISTER MIRACLE created by JACK KIRBY

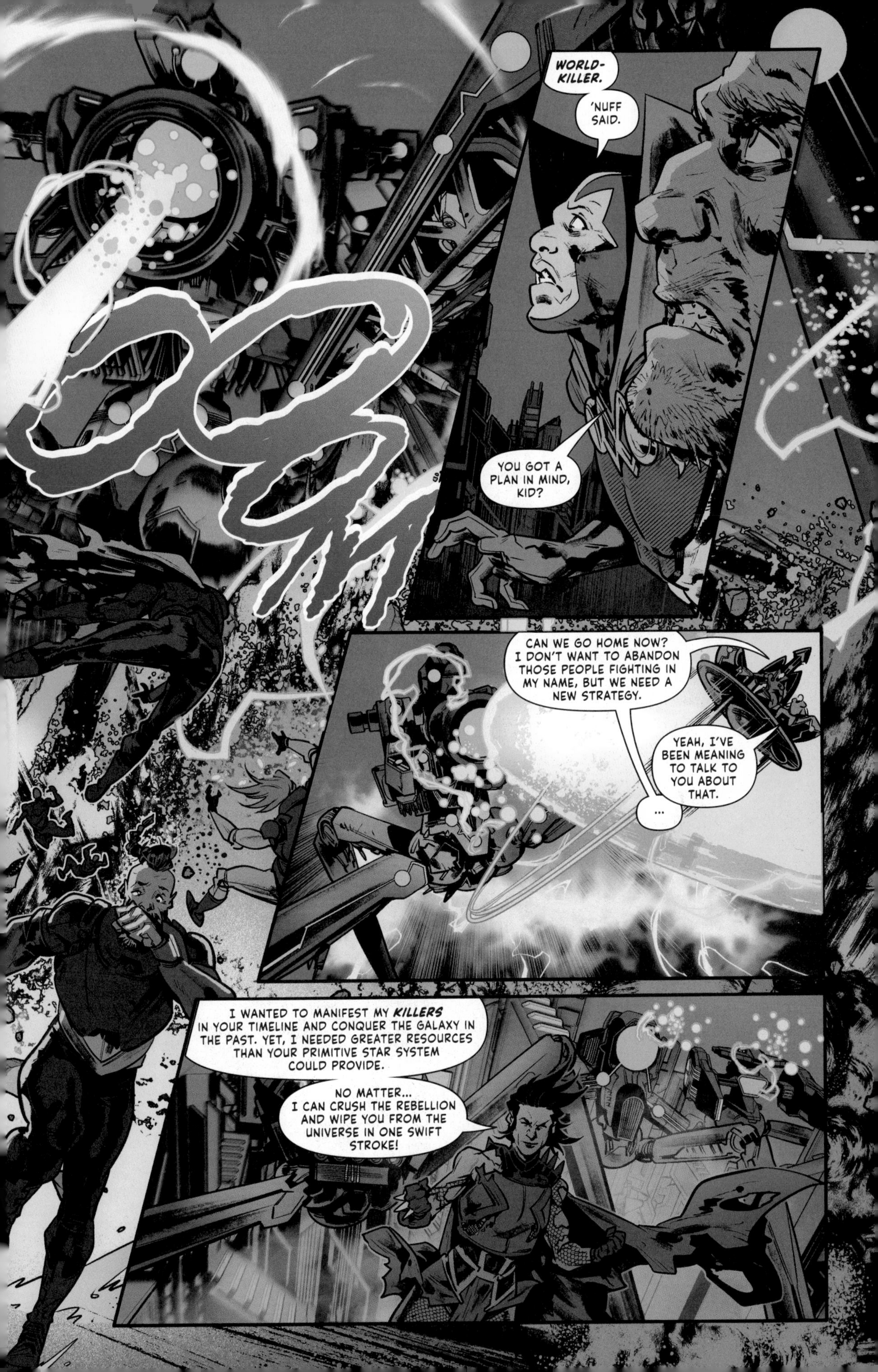
WORLD-KILLER.
'NUFF SAID.
YOU GOT A PLAN IN MIND, KID?
CAN WE GO HOME NOW? I DON'T WANT TO ABANDON THOSE PEOPLE FIGHTING IN MY NAME, BUT WE NEED A NEW STRATEGY.
YEAH, I'VE BEEN MEANING TO TALK TO YOU ABOUT THAT.
...
I WANTED TO MANIFEST MY KILLERS IN YOUR TIMELINE AND CONQUER THE GALAXY IN THE PAST. YET, I NEEDED GREATER RESOURCES THAN YOUR PRIMITIVE STAR SYSTEM COULD PROVIDE.
NO MATTER... I CAN CRUSH THE REBELLION AND WIPE YOU FROM THE UNIVERSE IN ONE SWIFT STROKE!

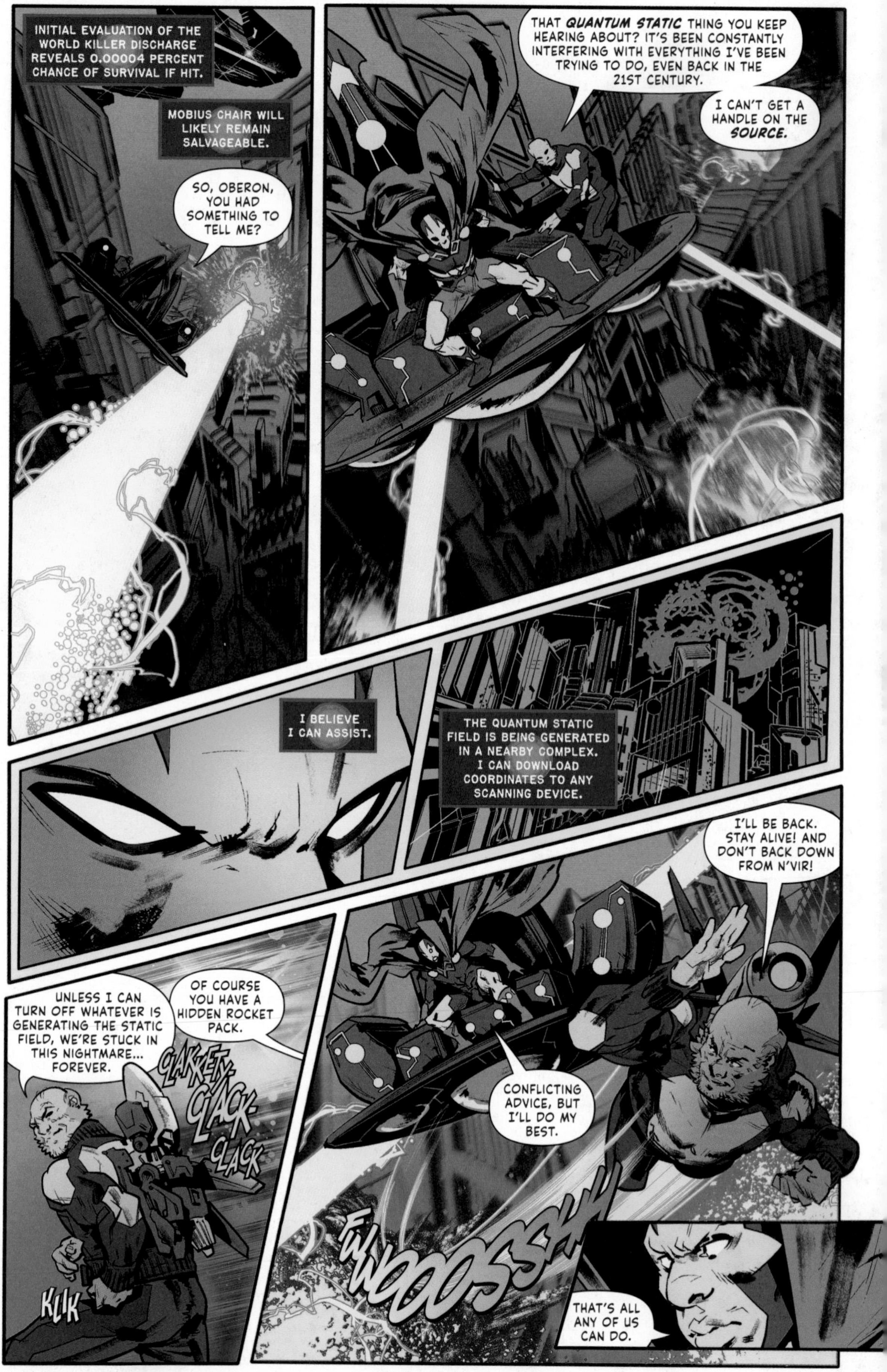
INITIAL EVALUATION OF THE WORLD KILLER DISCHARGE REVEALS 0.00004 PERCENT CHANCE OF SURVIVAL IF HIT.
MOBIUS CHAIR WILL LIKELY REMAIN SALVAGEABLE.
SO, OBERON, YOU HAD SOMETHING TO TELL ME?
THAT QUANTUM STATIC THING YOU KEEP HEARING ABOUT? IT'S BEEN CONSTANTLY INTERFERING WITH EVERYTHING I'VE BEEN TRYING TO DO, EVEN BACK IN THE 21ST CENTURY.
I CAN'T GET A HANDLE ON THE SOURCE.
I BELIEVE I CAN ASSIST.
THE QUANTUM STATIC FIELD IS BEING GENERATED IN A NEARBY COMPLEX. I CAN DOWNLOAD COORDINATES TO ANY SCANNING DEVICE.
UNLESS I CAN TURN OFF WHATEVER IS GENERATING THE STATIC FIELD, WE'RE STUCK IN THIS NIGHTMARE... FOREVER.
OF COURSE YOU HAVE A HIDDEN ROCKET PACK.
CLAKKETY-CLACK-CLACK
KLIK
I'LL BE BACK. STAY ALIVE! AND DON'T BACK DOWN FROM N'VIR!
CONFLICTING ADVICE, BUT I'LL DO MY BEST.
FWOOOSSHH
THAT'S ALL ANY OF US CAN DO.

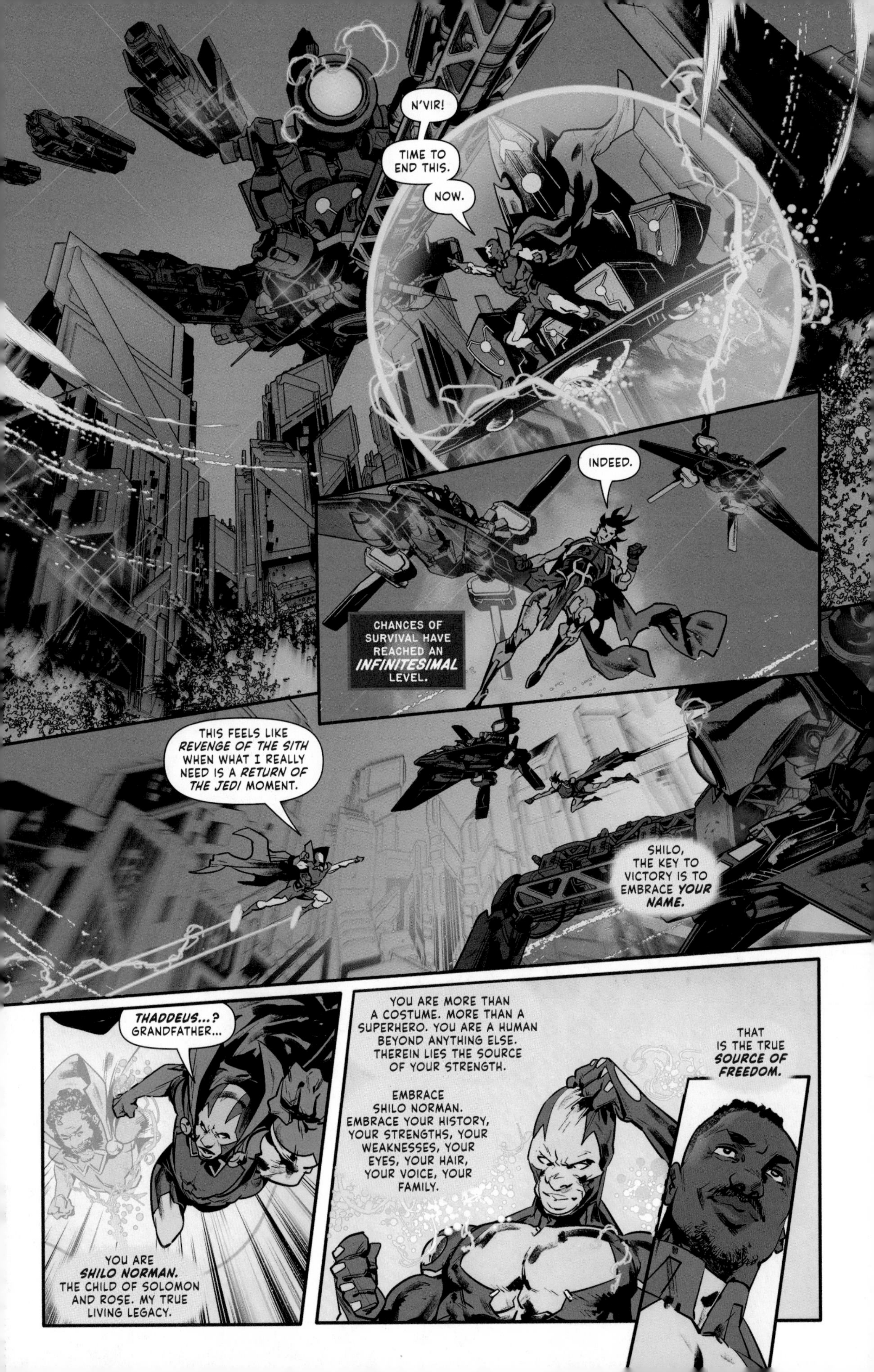
N'VIR!
TIME TO END THIS.
NOW.
INDEED.
CHANCES OF SURVIVAL HAVE REACHED AN *INFINITESIMAL* LEVEL.
THIS FEELS LIKE *REVENGE OF THE SITH* WHEN WHAT I REALLY NEED IS A *RETURN OF THE JEDI* MOMENT.
SHILO, THE KEY TO VICTORY IS TO EMBRACE *YOUR NAME.*
THADDEUS...? GRANDFATHER...
YOU ARE *SHILO NORMAN.* THE CHILD OF SOLOMON AND ROSE. MY TRUE LIVING LEGACY.
YOU ARE MORE THAN A COSTUME. MORE THAN A SUPERHERO. YOU ARE A HUMAN BEYOND ANYTHING ELSE. THEREIN LIES THE SOURCE OF YOUR STRENGTH.
EMBRACE SHILO NORMAN. EMBRACE YOUR HISTORY, YOUR STRENGTHS, YOUR WEAKNESSES, YOUR EYES, YOUR HAIR, YOUR VOICE, YOUR FAMILY.
THAT IS THE TRUE *SOURCE OF FREEDOM.*

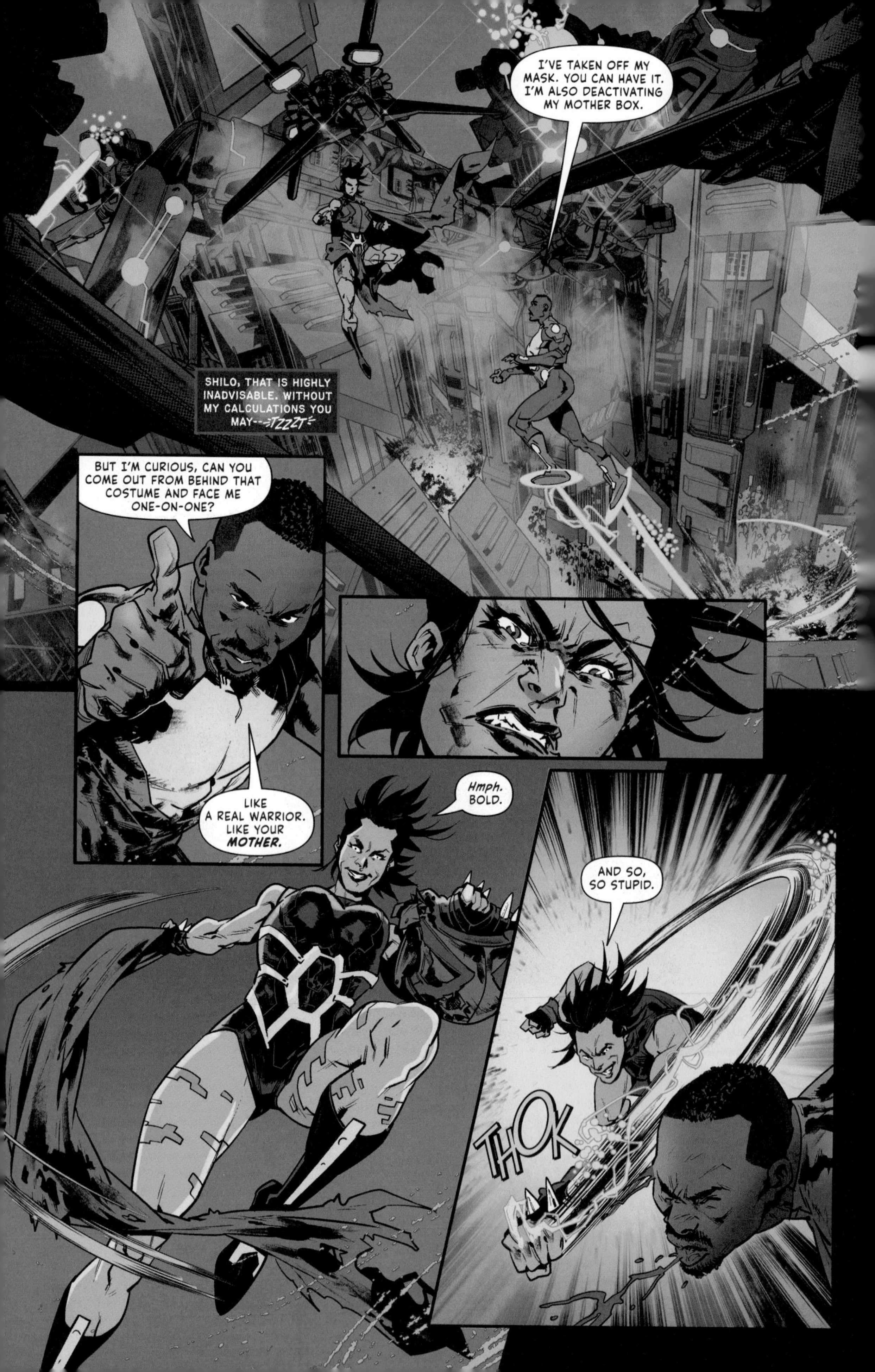
I'VE TAKEN OFF MY MASK. YOU CAN HAVE IT. I'M ALSO DEACTIVATING MY MOTHER BOX.
SHILO, THAT IS HIGHLY INADVISABLE. WITHOUT MY CALCULATIONS YOU MAY-- TZZZT
BUT I'M CURIOUS, CAN YOU COME OUT FROM BEHIND THAT COSTUME AND FACE ME ONE-ON-ONE?
LIKE A REAL WARRIOR. LIKE YOUR MOTHER.
Hmph. BOLD.
AND SO, SO STUPID.
THOK

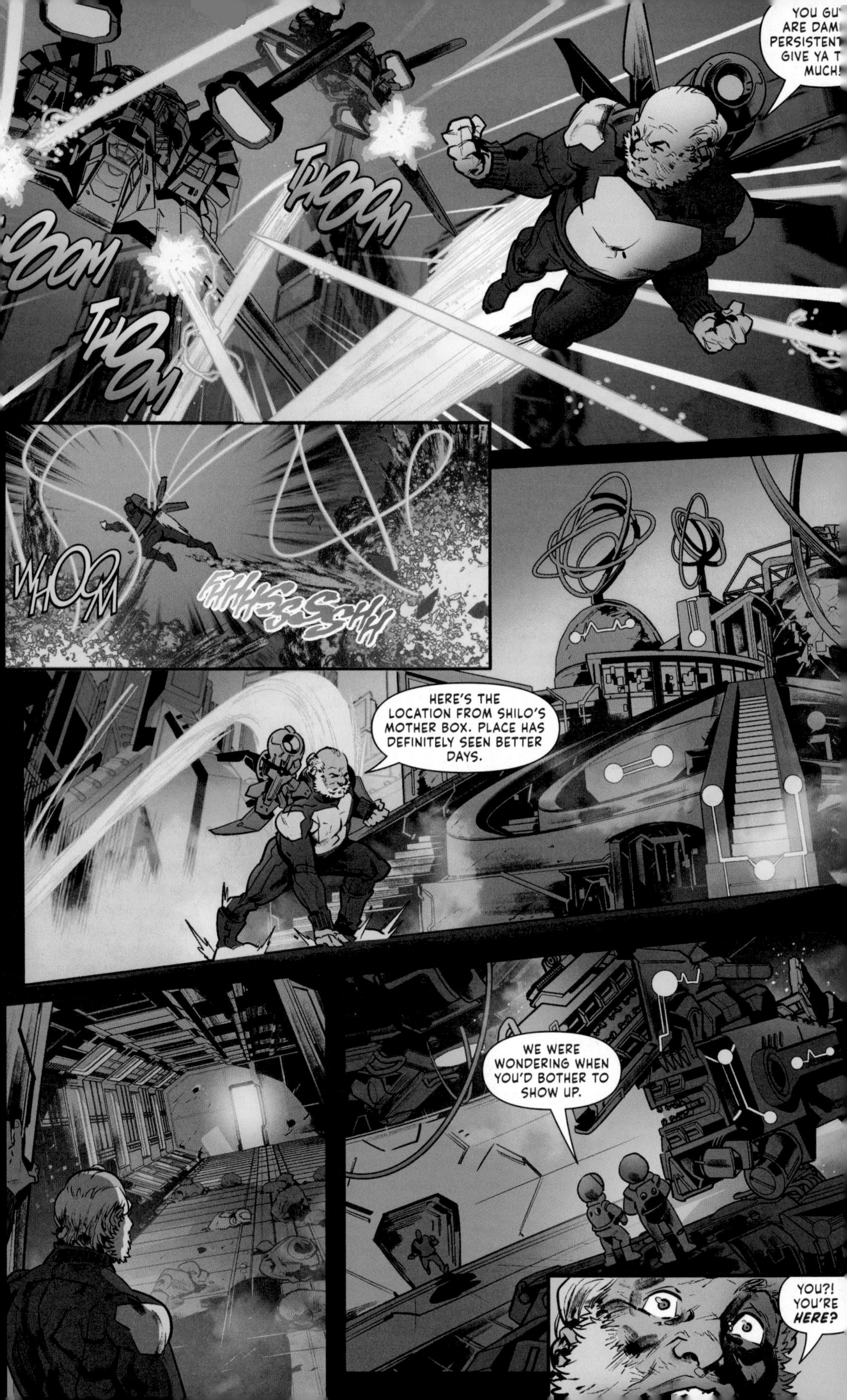
YOU GU
ARE DAM
PERSISTENT
GIVE YA T
MUCH!
OOOM
THOOOM
THOOM
WHOOM
FHHKSSSSHH
HERE'S THE LOCATION FROM SHILO'S MOTHER BOX. PLACE HAS DEFINITELY SEEN BETTER DAYS.
WE WERE WONDERING WHEN YOU'D BOTHER TO SHOW UP.
YOU?! YOU'RE *HERE?*

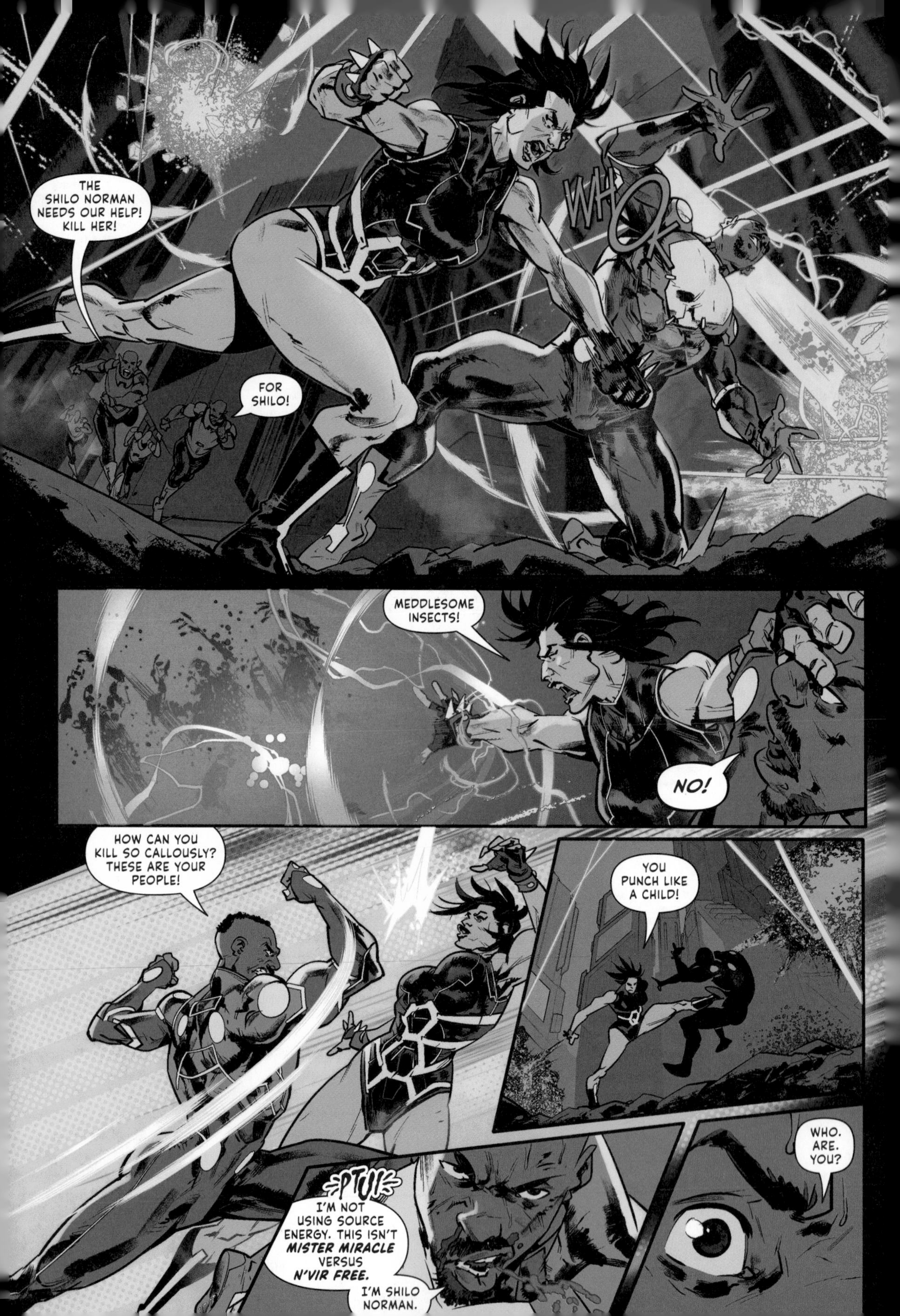
THE SHILO NORMAN NEEDS OUR HELP! KILL HER!
WHOOK
FOR SHILO!
MEDDLESOME INSECTS!
NO!
HOW CAN YOU KILL SO CALLOUSLY? THESE ARE YOUR PEOPLE!
YOU PUNCH LIKE A CHILD!
WHO. ARE. YOU?
PTUI
I'M NOT USING SOURCE ENERGY. THIS ISN'T *MISTER MIRACLE* VERSUS *N'VIR FREE.*
I'M SHILO NORMAN.

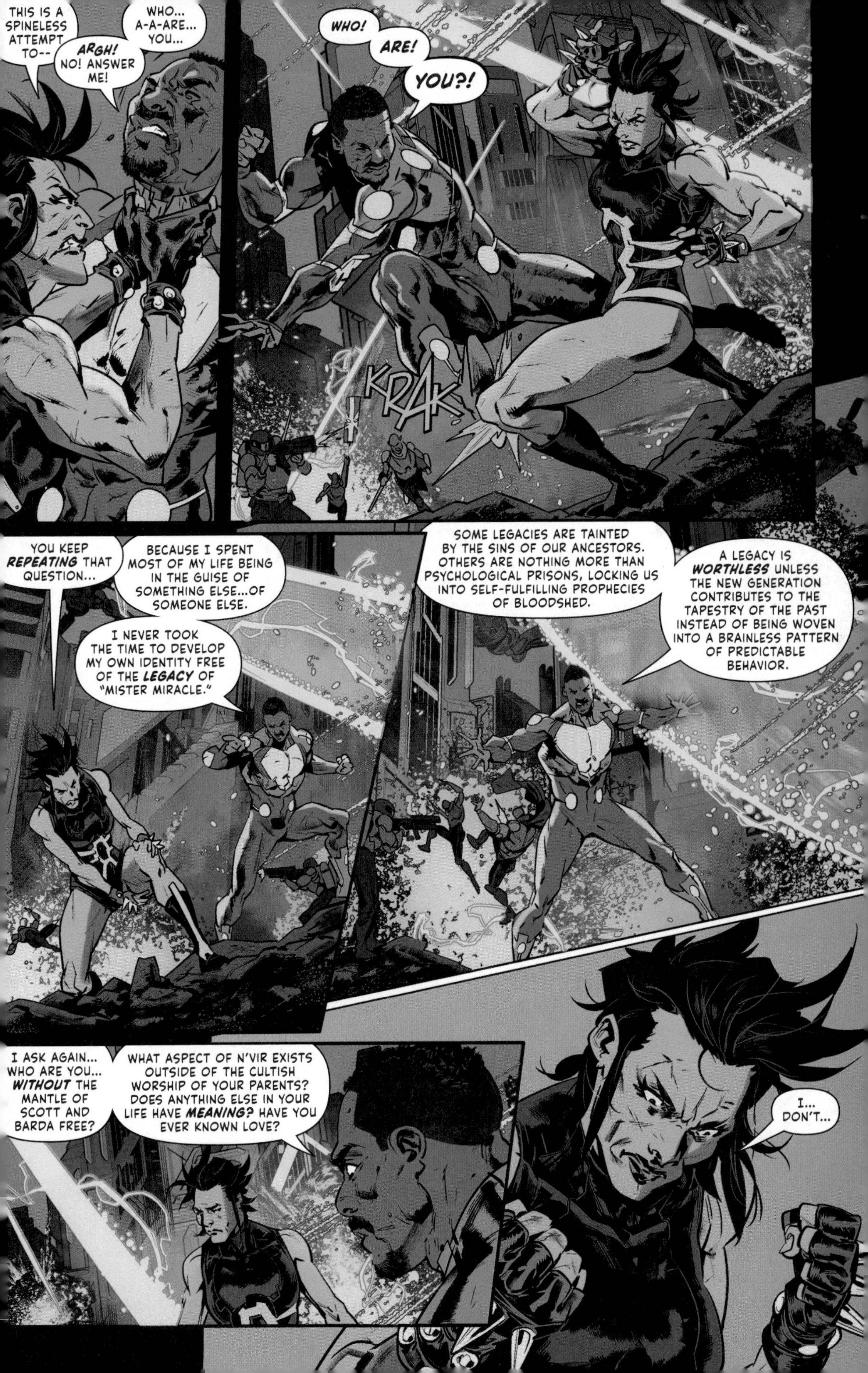

THIS IS A SPINELESS ATTEMPT TO--
ARGH! NO! ANSWER ME!
WHO... A-A-ARE... YOU...
WHO! ARE! YOU?!
KRAK
YOU KEEP REPEATING THAT QUESTION...
BECAUSE I SPENT MOST OF MY LIFE BEING IN THE GUISE OF SOMETHING ELSE...OF SOMEONE ELSE.
I NEVER TOOK THE TIME TO DEVELOP MY OWN IDENTITY FREE OF THE LEGACY OF "MISTER MIRACLE."
SOME LEGACIES ARE TAINTED BY THE SINS OF OUR ANCESTORS. OTHERS ARE NOTHING MORE THAN PSYCHOLOGICAL PRISONS, LOCKING US INTO SELF-FULFILLING PROPHECIES OF BLOODSHED.
A LEGACY IS WORTHLESS UNLESS THE NEW GENERATION CONTRIBUTES TO THE TAPESTRY OF THE PAST INSTEAD OF BEING WOVEN INTO A BRAINLESS PATTERN OF PREDICTABLE BEHAVIOR.
I ASK AGAIN... WHO ARE YOU... WITHOUT THE MANTLE OF SCOTT AND BARDA FREE?
WHAT ASPECT OF N'VIR EXISTS OUTSIDE OF THE CULTISH WORSHIP OF YOUR PARENTS? DOES ANYTHING ELSE IN YOUR LIFE HAVE MEANING? HAVE YOU EVER KNOWN LOVE?
I... DON'T...

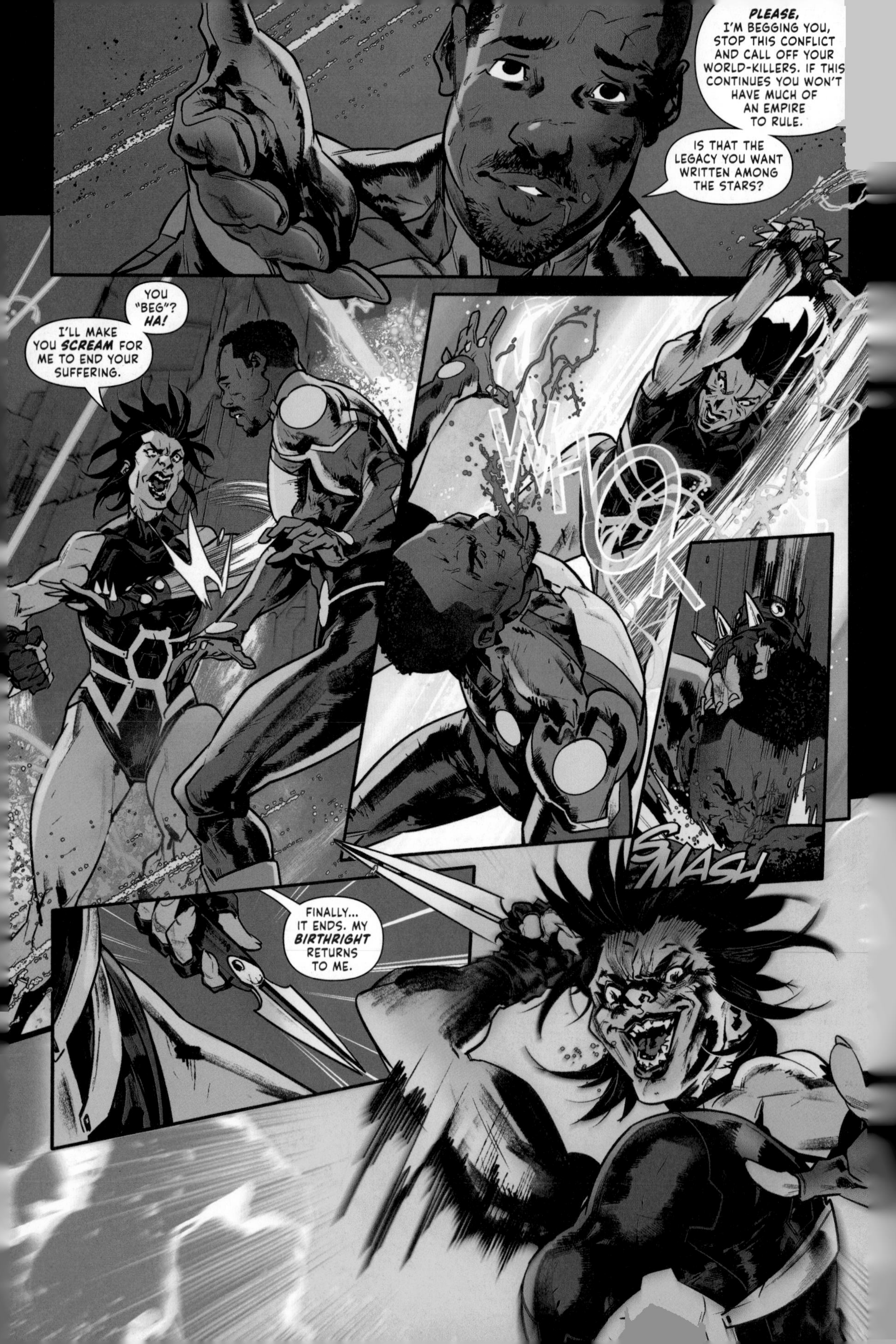
PLEASE, I'M BEGGING YOU, STOP THIS CONFLICT AND CALL OFF YOUR WORLD-KILLERS. IF THIS CONTINUES YOU WON'T HAVE MUCH OF AN EMPIRE TO RULE.
IS THAT THE LEGACY YOU WANT WRITTEN AMONG THE STARS?
YOU "BEG"? HA!
I'LL MAKE YOU SCREAM FOR ME TO END YOUR SUFFERING.
WHOK
SMASH
FINALLY... IT ENDS. MY BIRTHRIGHT RETURNS TO ME.

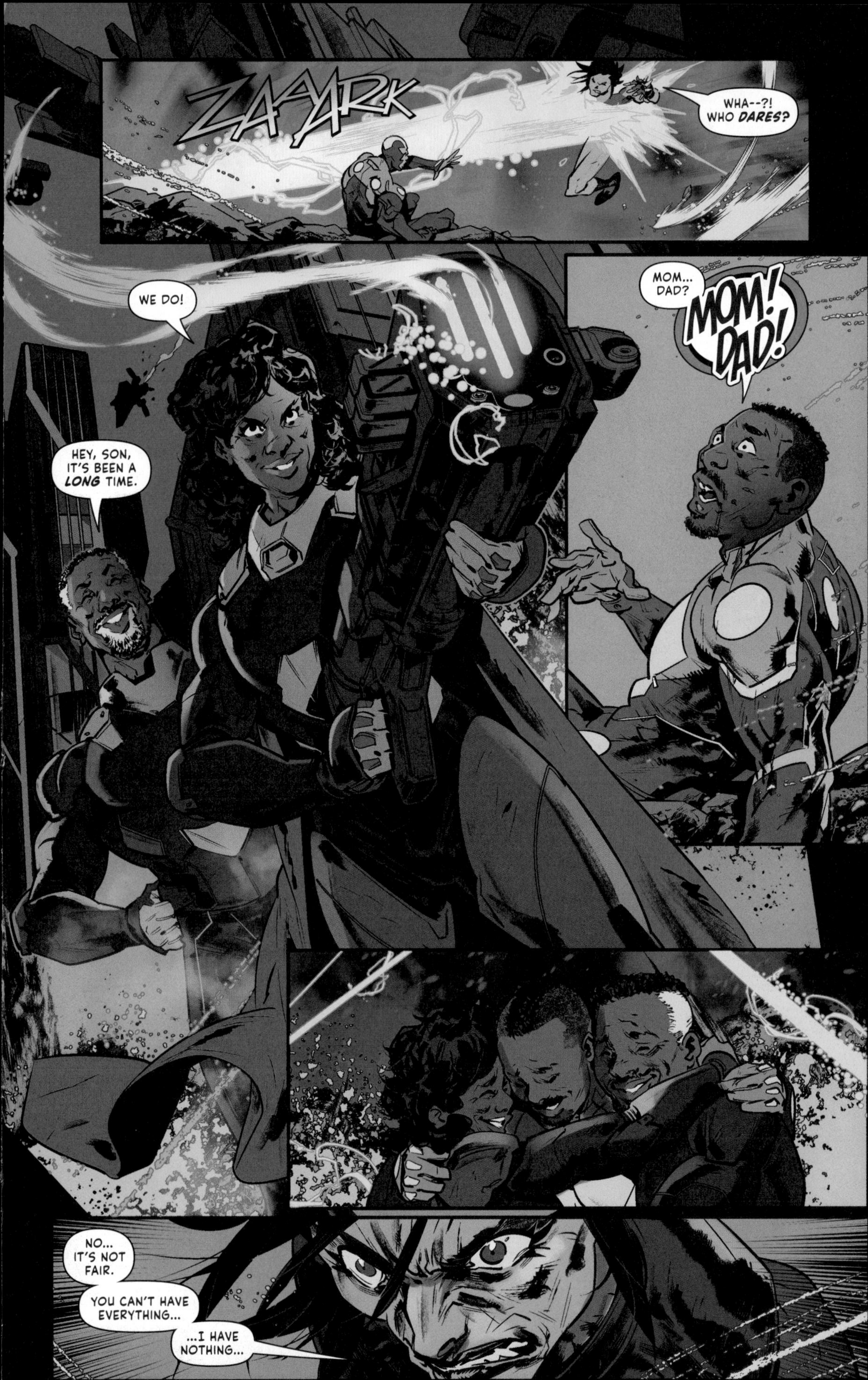
ZAAARK
WHA--?! WHO DARES?
WE DO!
MOM... DAD?
MOM! DAD!
HEY, SON, IT'S BEEN A LONG TIME.
NO... IT'S NOT FAIR.
YOU CAN'T HAVE EVERYTHING...
...I HAVE NOTHING...

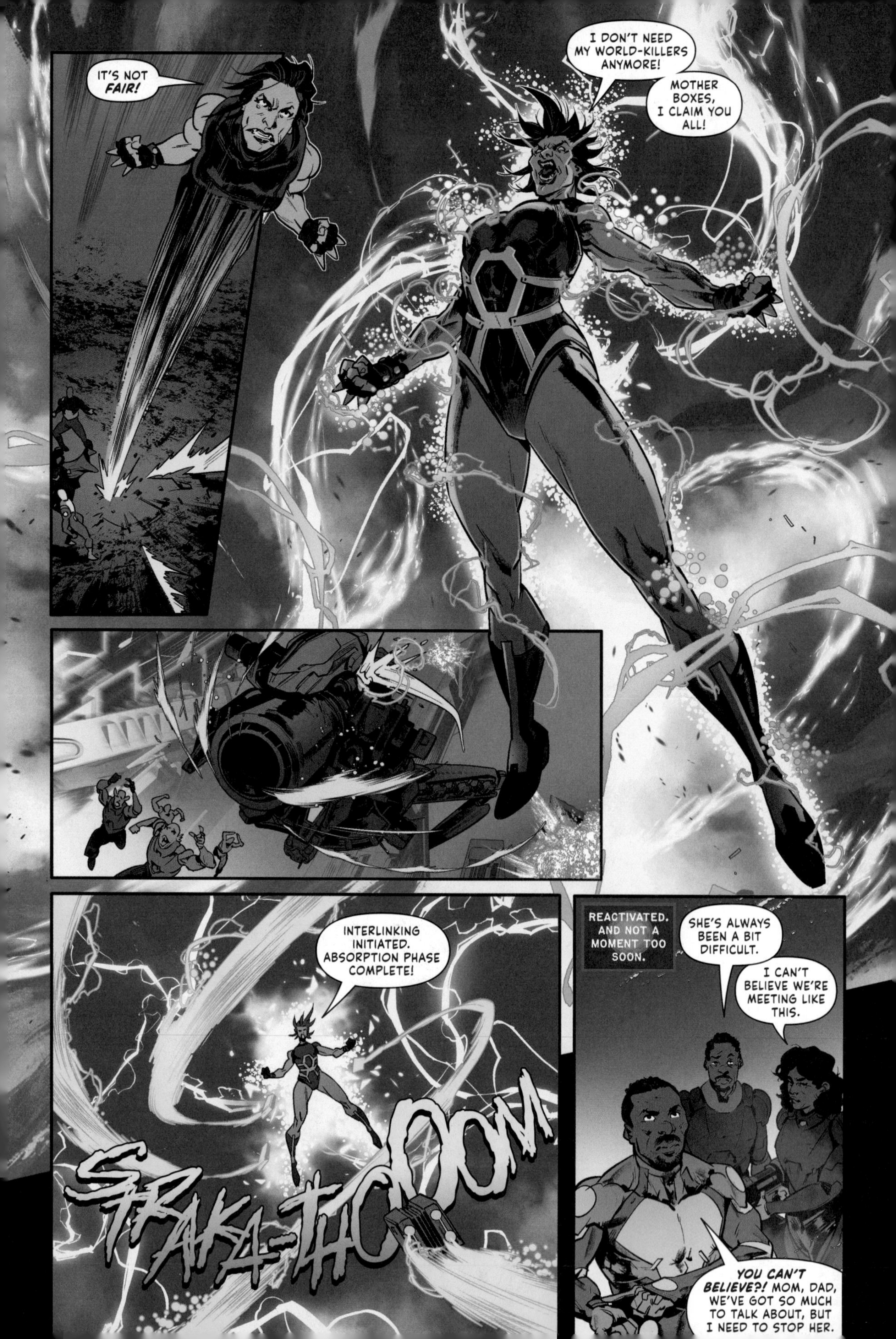
IT'S NOT *FAIR!*
I DON'T NEED MY WORLD-KILLERS ANYMORE!
MOTHER BOXES, I CLAIM YOU ALL!
INTERLINKING INITIATED. ABSORPTION PHASE COMPLETE!
STRAKA-THOOOM
REACTIVATED. AND NOT A MOMENT TOO SOON.
SHE'S ALWAYS BEEN A BIT DIFFICULT.
I CAN'T BELIEVE WE'RE MEETING LIKE THIS.
YOU CAN'T BELIEVE?! MOM, DAD, WE'VE GOT SO MUCH TO TALK ABOUT, BUT I NEED TO STOP HER.

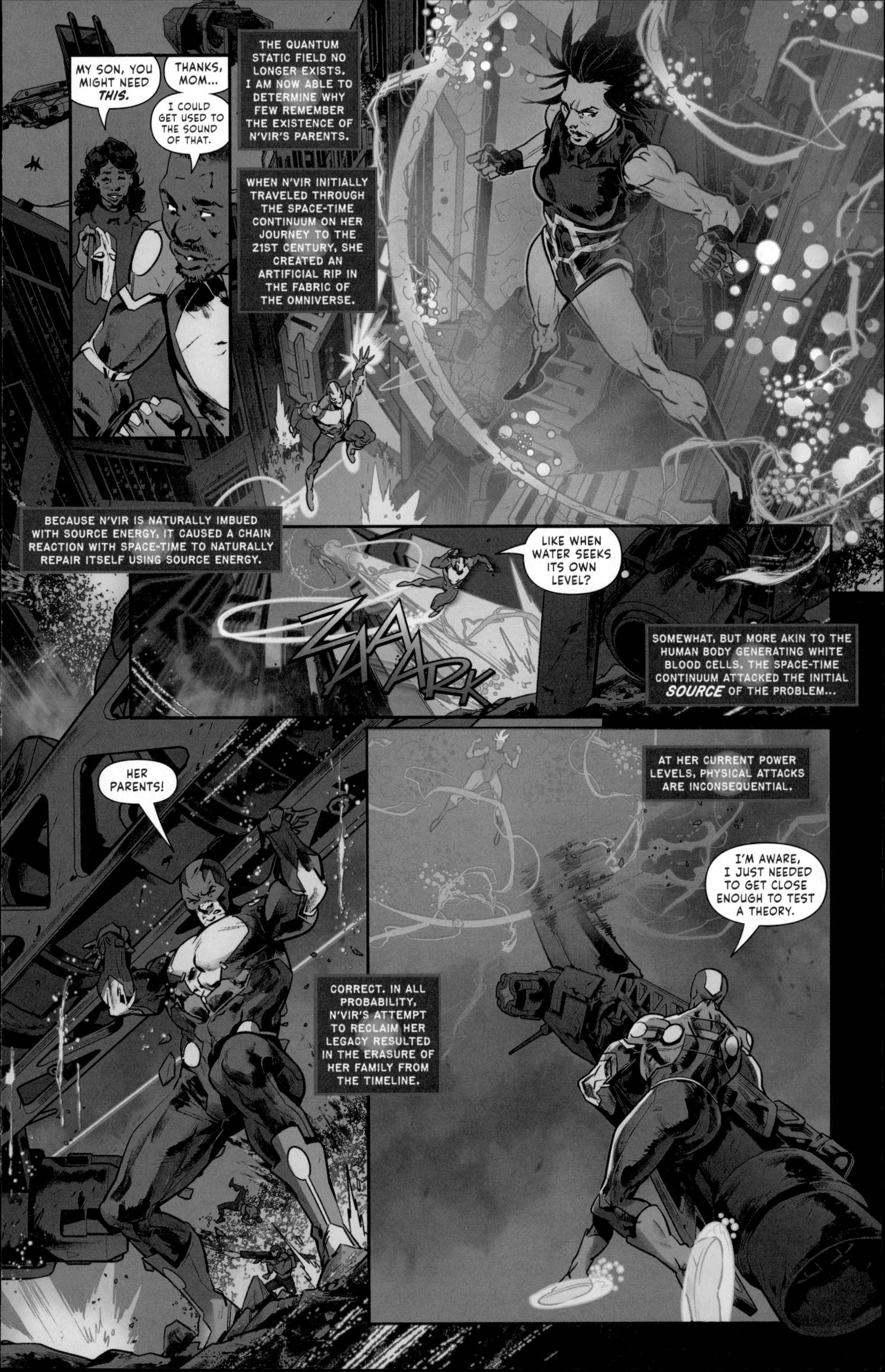

MY SON, YOU MIGHT NEED *THIS.*
THANKS, MOM...
I COULD GET USED TO THE SOUND OF THAT.
THE QUANTUM STATIC FIELD NO LONGER EXISTS. I AM NOW ABLE TO DETERMINE WHY FEW REMEMBER THE EXISTENCE OF N'VIR'S PARENTS.
WHEN N'VIR INITIALLY TRAVELED THROUGH THE SPACE-TIME CONTINUUM ON HER JOURNEY TO THE 21ST CENTURY, SHE CREATED AN ARTIFICIAL RIP IN THE FABRIC OF THE OMNIVERSE.
BECAUSE N'VIR IS NATURALLY IMBUED WITH SOURCE ENERGY, IT CAUSED A CHAIN REACTION WITH SPACE-TIME TO NATURALLY REPAIR ITSELF USING SOURCE ENERGY.
LIKE WHEN WATER SEEKS ITS OWN LEVEL?
ZZAAARK
SOMEWHAT, BUT MORE AKIN TO THE HUMAN BODY GENERATING WHITE BLOOD CELLS. THE SPACE-TIME CONTINUUM ATTACKED THE INITIAL *SOURCE* OF THE PROBLEM...
HER PARENTS!
CORRECT. IN ALL PROBABILITY, N'VIR'S ATTEMPT TO RECLAIM HER LEGACY RESULTED IN THE ERASURE OF HER FAMILY FROM THE TIMELINE.
AT HER CURRENT POWER LEVELS, PHYSICAL ATTACKS ARE INCONSEQUENTIAL.
I'M AWARE, I JUST NEEDED TO GET CLOSE ENOUGH TO TEST A THEORY.

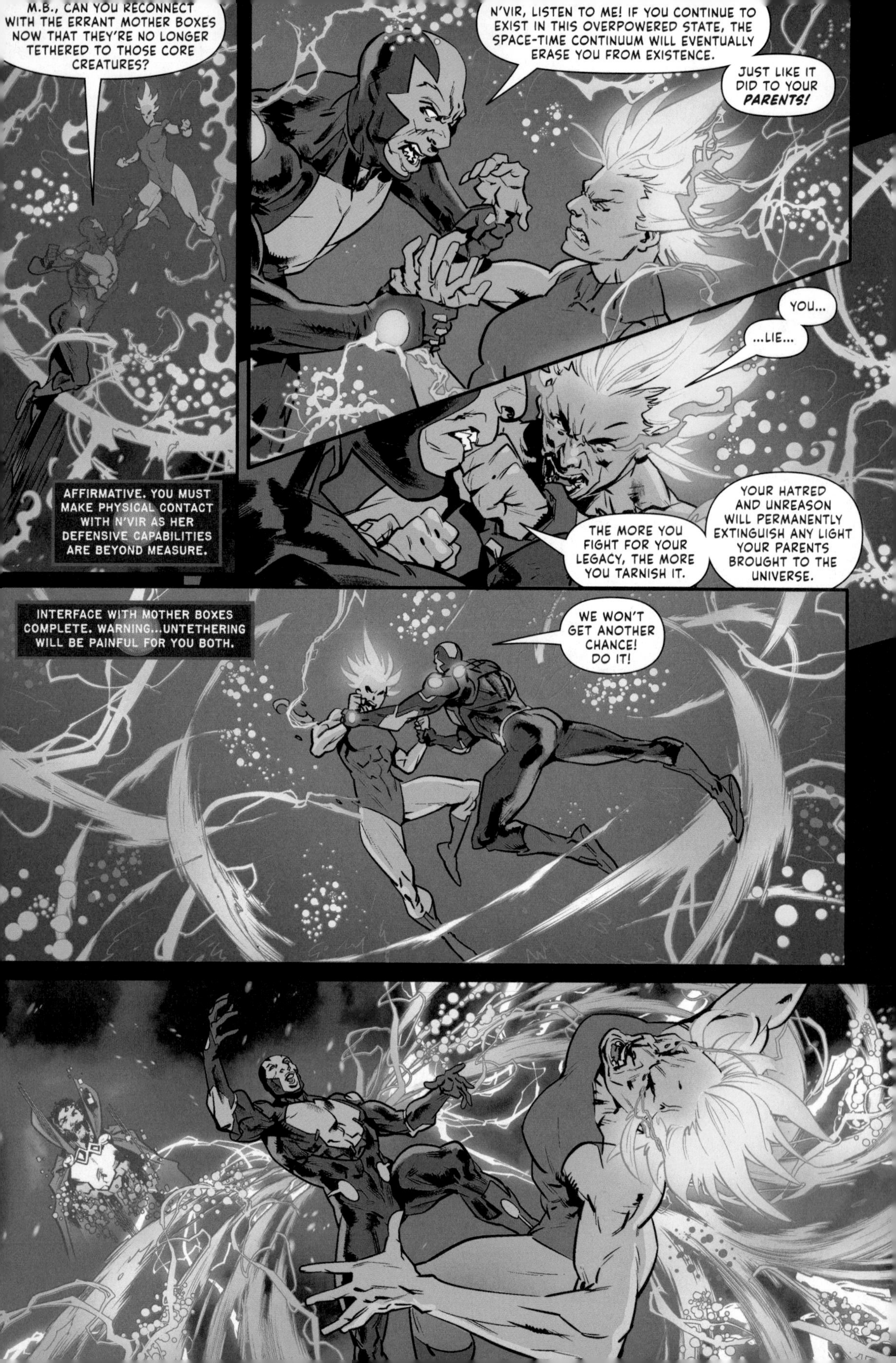
M.B., CAN YOU RECONNECT WITH THE ERRANT MOTHER BOXES NOW THAT THEY'RE NO LONGER TETHERED TO THOSE CORE CREATURES?
N'VIR, LISTEN TO ME! IF YOU CONTINUE TO EXIST IN THIS OVERPOWERED STATE, THE SPACE-TIME CONTINUUM WILL EVENTUALLY ERASE YOU FROM EXISTENCE.
JUST LIKE IT DID TO YOUR ***PARENTS!***
YOU...
...LIE...
AFFIRMATIVE. YOU MUST MAKE PHYSICAL CONTACT WITH N'VIR AS HER DEFENSIVE CAPABILITIES ARE BEYOND MEASURE.
THE MORE YOU FIGHT FOR YOUR LEGACY, THE MORE YOU TARNISH IT.
YOUR HATRED AND UNREASON WILL PERMANENTLY EXTINGUISH ANY LIGHT YOUR PARENTS BROUGHT TO THE UNIVERSE.
INTERFACE WITH MOTHER BOXES COMPLETE. WARNING...UNTETHERING WILL BE PAINFUL FOR YOU BOTH.
WE WON'T GET ANOTHER CHANCE! DO IT!

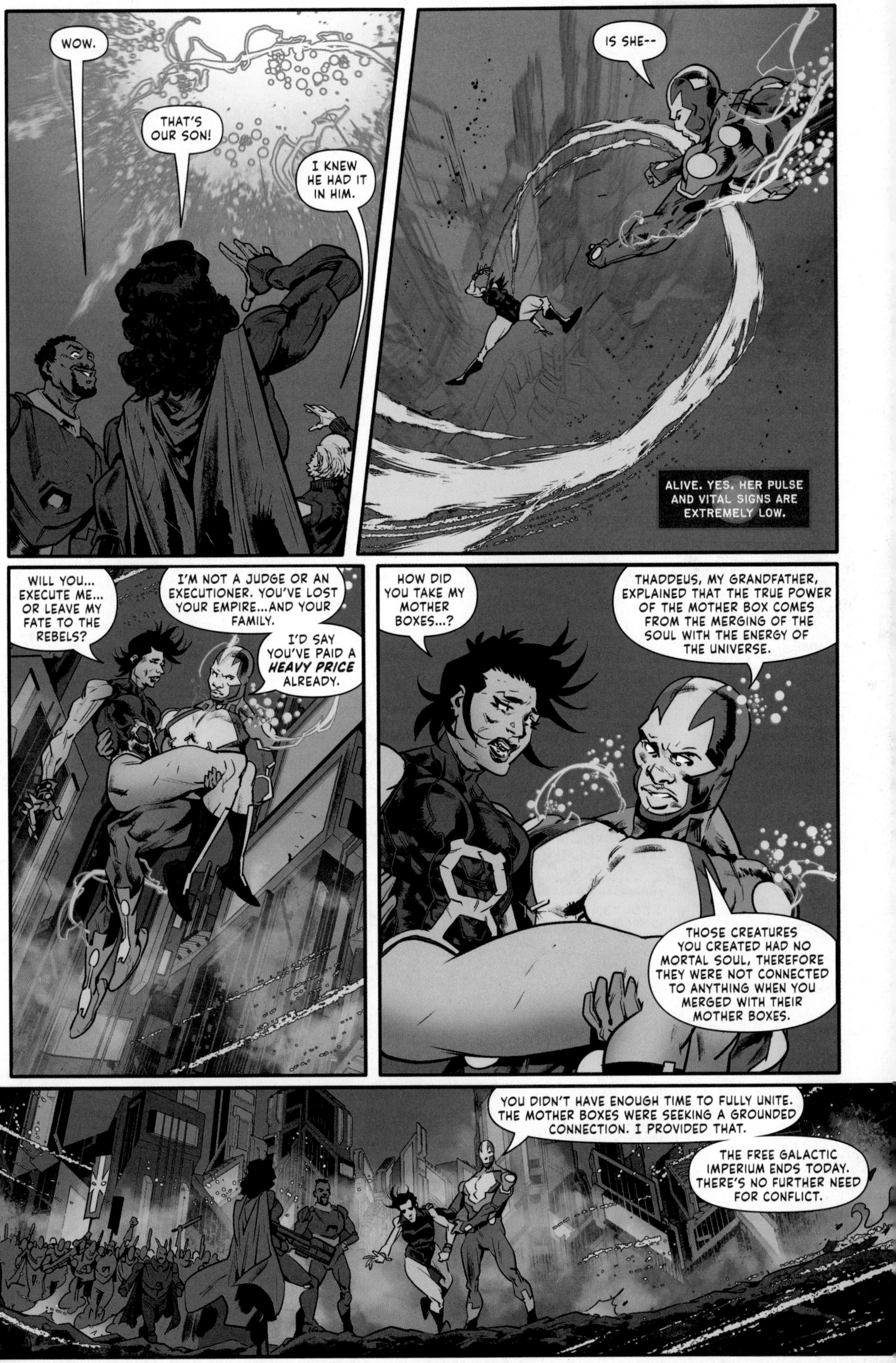
WOW.
THAT'S OUR SON!
I KNEW HE HAD IT IN HIM.
IS SHE--
ALIVE. YES. HER PULSE AND VITAL SIGNS ARE EXTREMELY LOW.
WILL YOU... EXECUTE ME... OR LEAVE MY FATE TO THE REBELS?
I'M NOT A JUDGE OR AN EXECUTIONER. YOU'VE LOST YOUR EMPIRE...AND YOUR FAMILY.
I'D SAY YOU'VE PAID A HEAVY PRICE ALREADY.
HOW DID YOU TAKE MY MOTHER BOXES...?
THADDEUS, MY GRANDFATHER, EXPLAINED THAT THE TRUE POWER OF THE MOTHER BOX COMES FROM THE MERGING OF THE SOUL WITH THE ENERGY OF THE UNIVERSE.
THOSE CREATURES YOU CREATED HAD NO MORTAL SOUL, THEREFORE THEY WERE NOT CONNECTED TO ANYTHING WHEN YOU MERGED WITH THEIR MOTHER BOXES.
YOU DIDN'T HAVE ENOUGH TIME TO FULLY UNITE. THE MOTHER BOXES WERE SEEKING A GROUNDED CONNECTION. I PROVIDED THAT.
THE FREE GALACTIC IMPERIUM ENDS TODAY. THERE'S NO FURTHER NEED FOR CONFLICT.

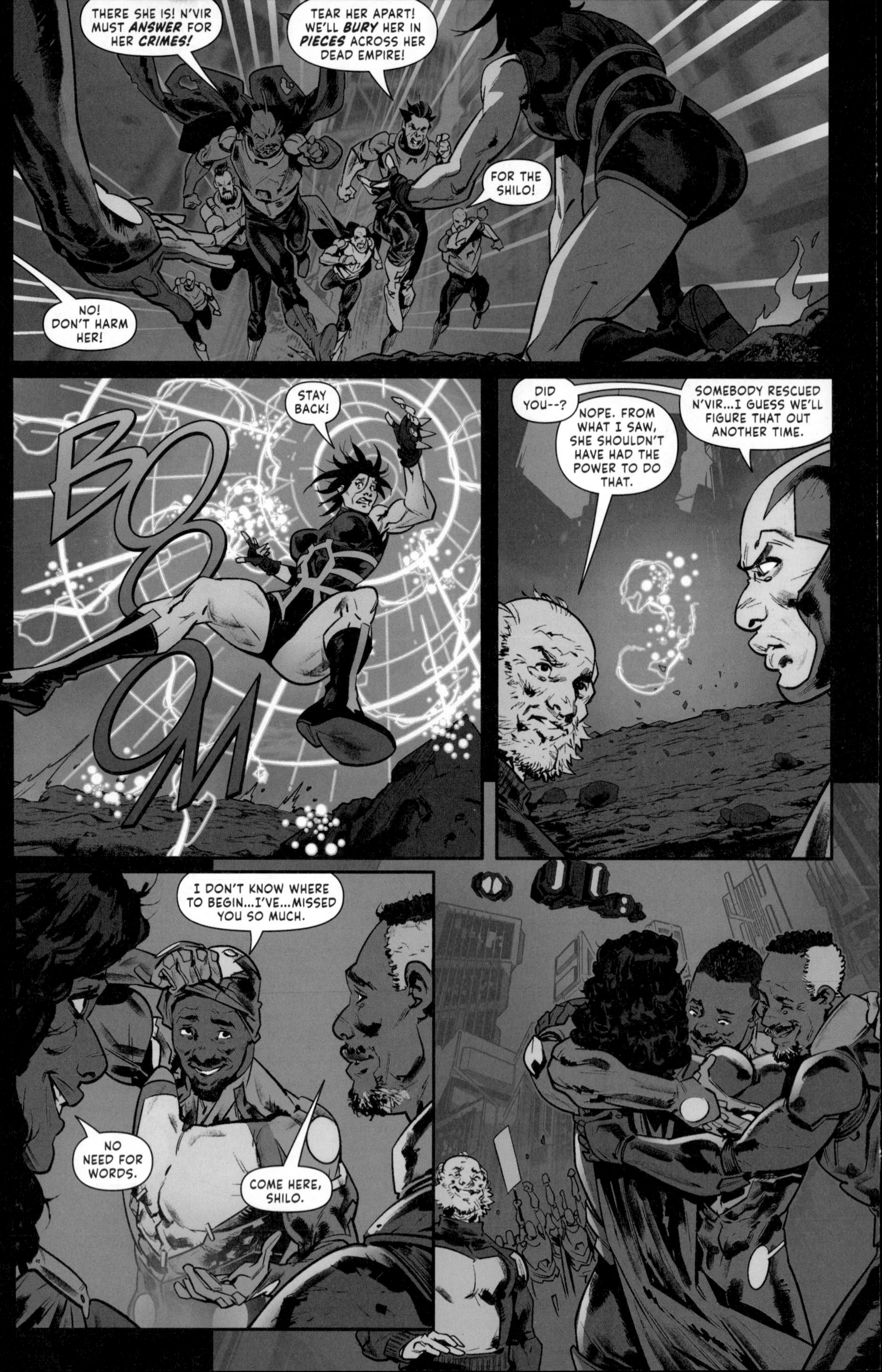
THERE SHE IS! N'VIR MUST ANSWER FOR HER CRIMES!
TEAR HER APART! WE'LL BURY HER IN PIECES ACROSS HER DEAD EMPIRE!
FOR THE SHILO!
NO! DON'T HARM HER!
BOOM
STAY BACK!
DID YOU--?
NOPE. FROM WHAT I SAW, SHE SHOULDN'T HAVE HAD THE POWER TO DO THAT.
SOMEBODY RESCUED N'VIR...I GUESS WE'LL FIGURE THAT OUT ANOTHER TIME.
I DON'T KNOW WHERE TO BEGIN...I'VE...MISSED YOU SO MUCH.
NO NEED FOR WORDS.
COME HERE, SHILO.

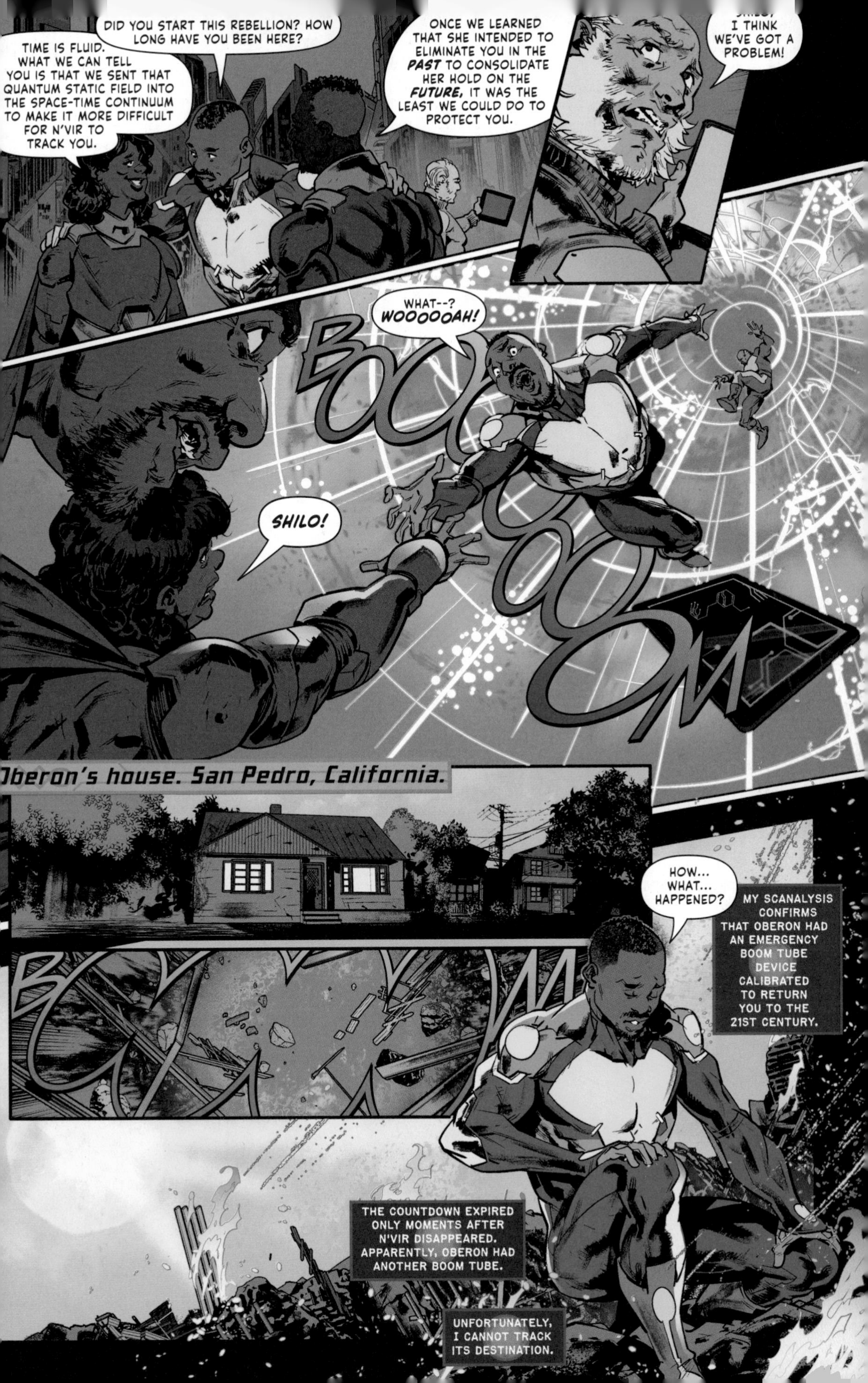

DID YOU START THIS REBELLION? HOW LONG HAVE YOU BEEN HERE?
TIME IS FLUID. WHAT WE CAN TELL YOU IS THAT WE SENT THAT QUANTUM STATIC FIELD INTO THE SPACE-TIME CONTINUUM TO MAKE IT MORE DIFFICULT FOR N'VIR TO TRACK YOU.
ONCE WE LEARNED THAT SHE INTENDED TO ELIMINATE YOU IN THE *PAST* TO CONSOLIDATE HER HOLD ON THE *FUTURE,* IT WAS THE LEAST WE COULD DO TO PROTECT YOU.
I THINK WE'VE GOT A PROBLEM!
WHAT--? WOOOOOAH!
SHILO!
Oberon's house. San Pedro, California.
HOW... WHAT... HAPPENED?
MY SCANALYSIS CONFIRMS THAT OBERON HAD AN EMERGENCY BOOM TUBE DEVICE CALIBRATED TO RETURN YOU TO THE 21ST CENTURY.
THE COUNTDOWN EXPIRED ONLY MOMENTS AFTER N'VIR DISAPPEARED. APPARENTLY, OBERON HAD ANOTHER BOOM TUBE.
UNFORTUNATELY, I CANNOT TRACK ITS DESTINATION.

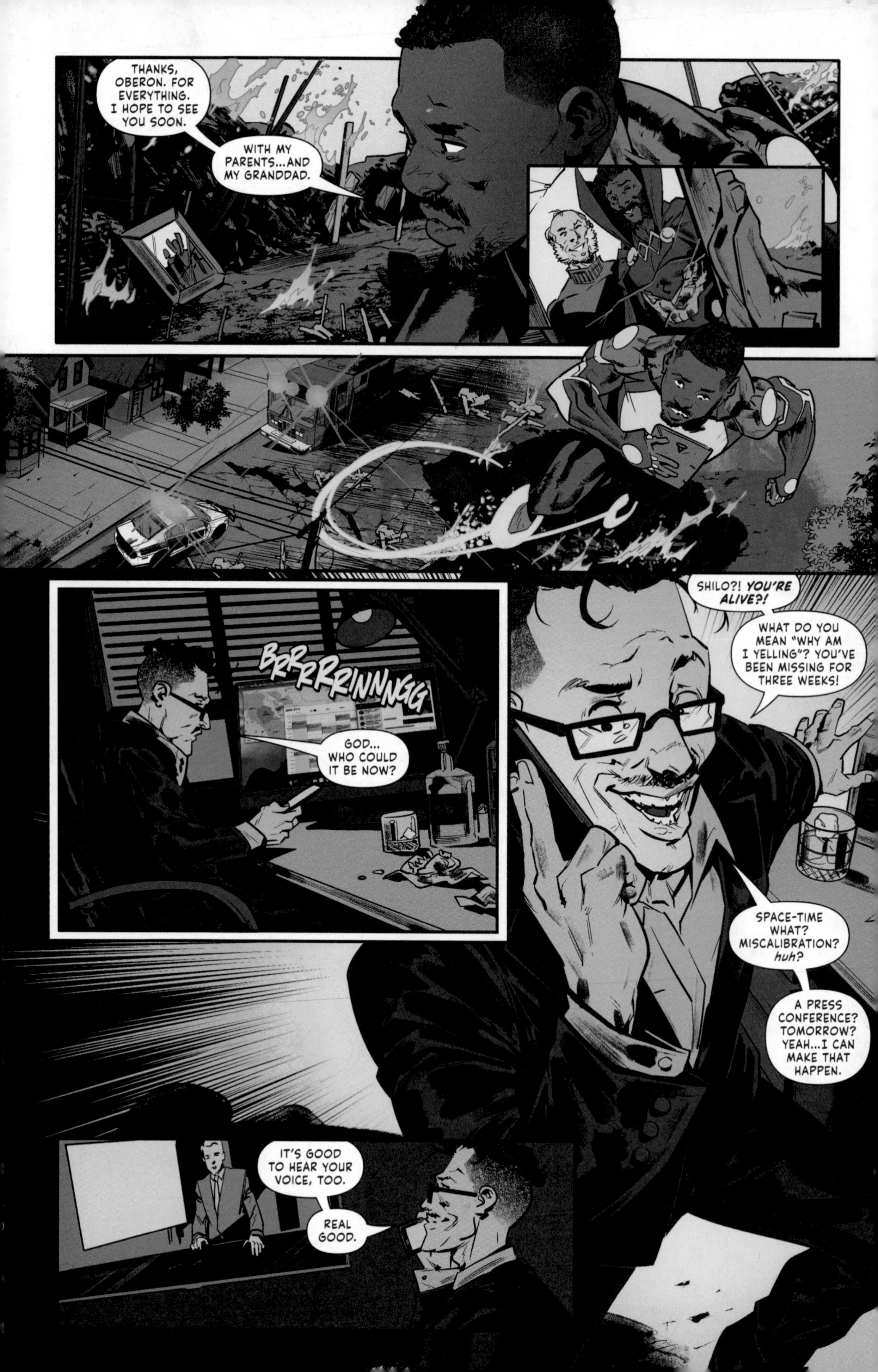
THANKS, OBERON. FOR EVERYTHING. I HOPE TO SEE YOU SOON.
WITH MY PARENTS...AND MY GRANDDAD.
BRRRRRINNNGG
GOD... WHO COULD IT BE NOW?
SHILO?! *YOU'RE ALIVE?!*
WHAT DO YOU MEAN "WHY AM I YELLING"? YOU'VE BEEN MISSING FOR THREE WEEKS!
SPACE-TIME WHAT? MISCALIBRATION? *huh?*
A PRESS CONFERENCE? TOMORROW? YEAH...I CAN MAKE THAT HAPPEN.
IT'S GOOD TO HEAR YOUR VOICE, TOO.
REAL GOOD.

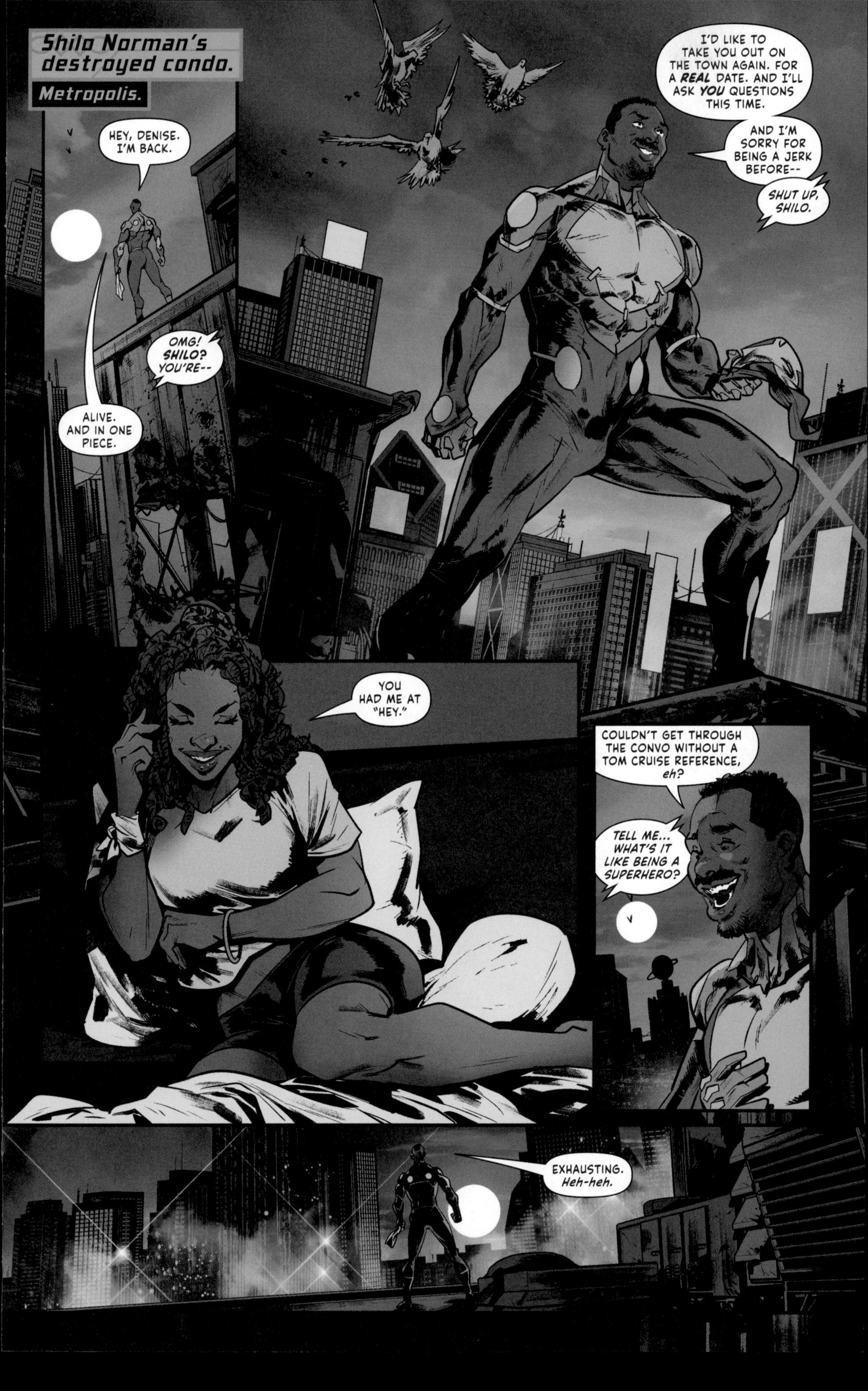
Shilo Norman's destroyed condo.
Metropolis.
HEY, DENISE. I'M BACK.
OMG! SHILO? YOU'RE--
ALIVE. AND IN ONE PIECE.
I'D LIKE TO TAKE YOU OUT ON THE TOWN AGAIN. FOR A REAL DATE. AND I'LL ASK YOU QUESTIONS THIS TIME.
AND I'M SORRY FOR BEING A JERK BEFORE--
SHUT UP, SHILO.
YOU HAD ME AT "HEY."
COULDN'T GET THROUGH THE CONVO WITHOUT A TOM CRUISE REFERENCE, eh?
TELL ME... WHAT'S IT LIKE BEING A SUPERHERO?
EXHAUSTING. Heh-heh.

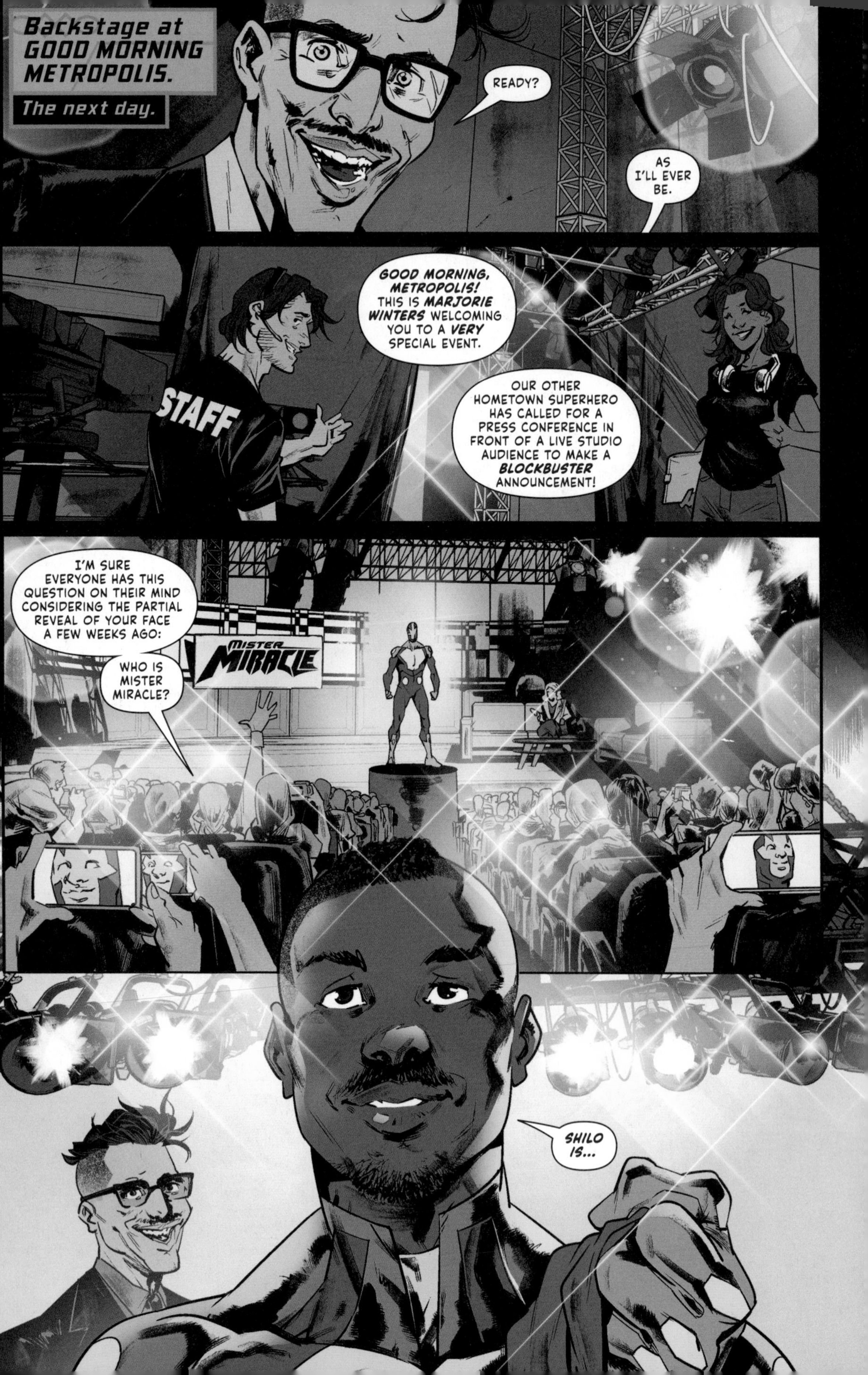
Backstage at GOOD MORNING METROPOLIS.
The next day.
READY?
AS I'LL EVER BE.
GOOD MORNING, METROPOLIS! THIS IS MARJORIE WINTERS WELCOMING YOU TO A VERY SPECIAL EVENT.
OUR OTHER HOMETOWN SUPERHERO HAS CALLED FOR A PRESS CONFERENCE IN FRONT OF A LIVE STUDIO AUDIENCE TO MAKE A BLOCKBUSTER ANNOUNCEMENT!
STAFF
I'M SURE EVERYONE HAS THIS QUESTION ON THEIR MIND CONSIDERING THE PARTIAL REVEAL OF YOUR FACE A FEW WEEKS AGO:
WHO IS MISTER MIRACLE?
MISTER MIRACLE
SHILO IS...

Character designs by FICO OSSIO

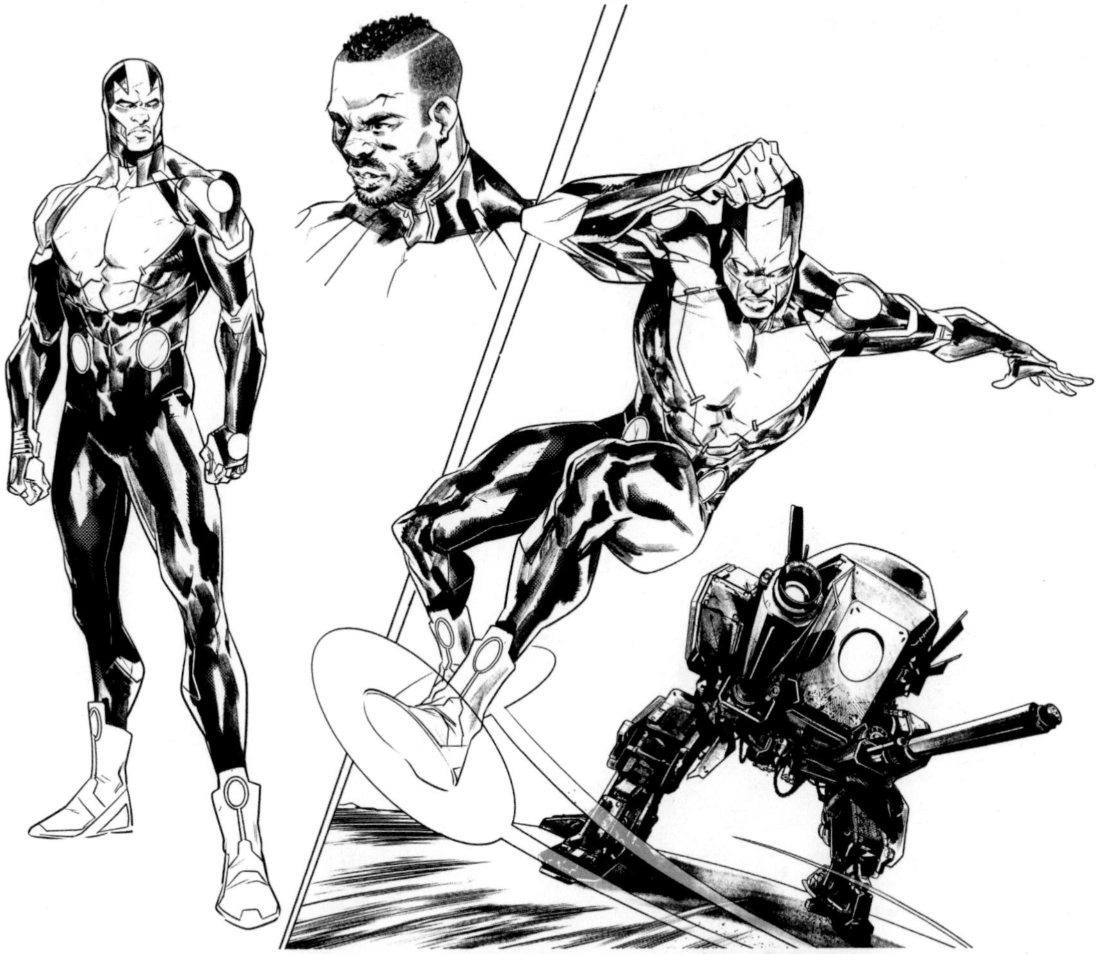

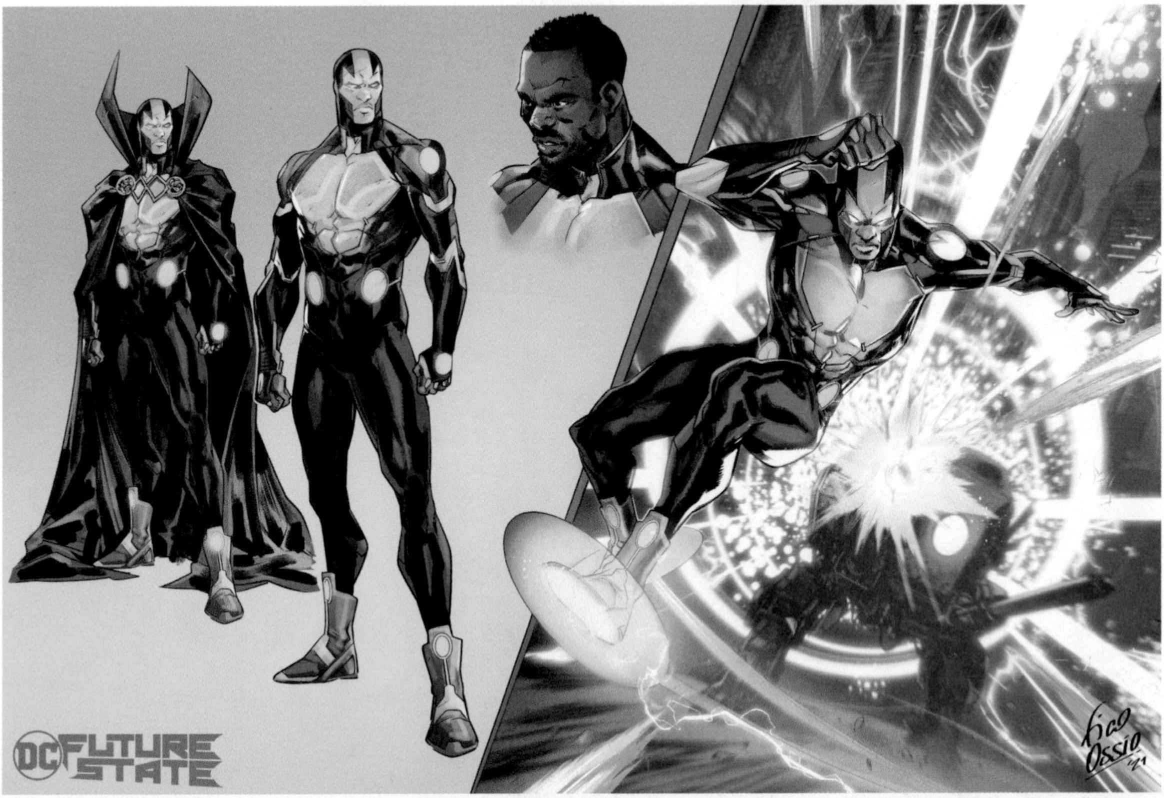
DC FUTURE STATE
Fico Ossio '21

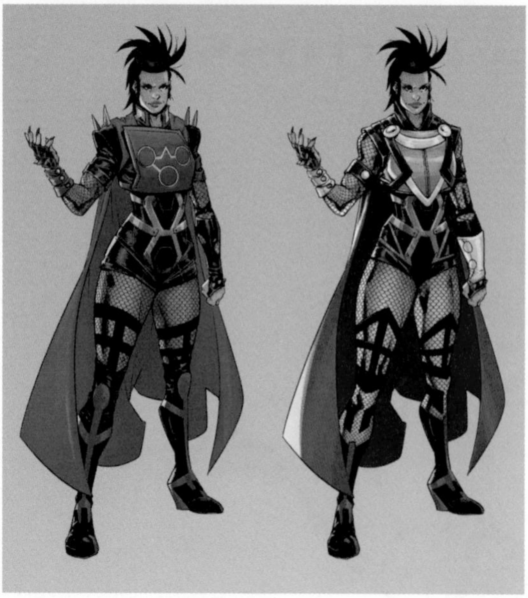

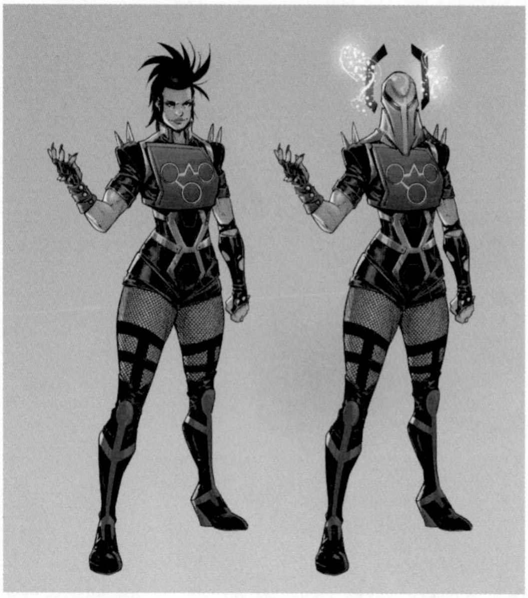

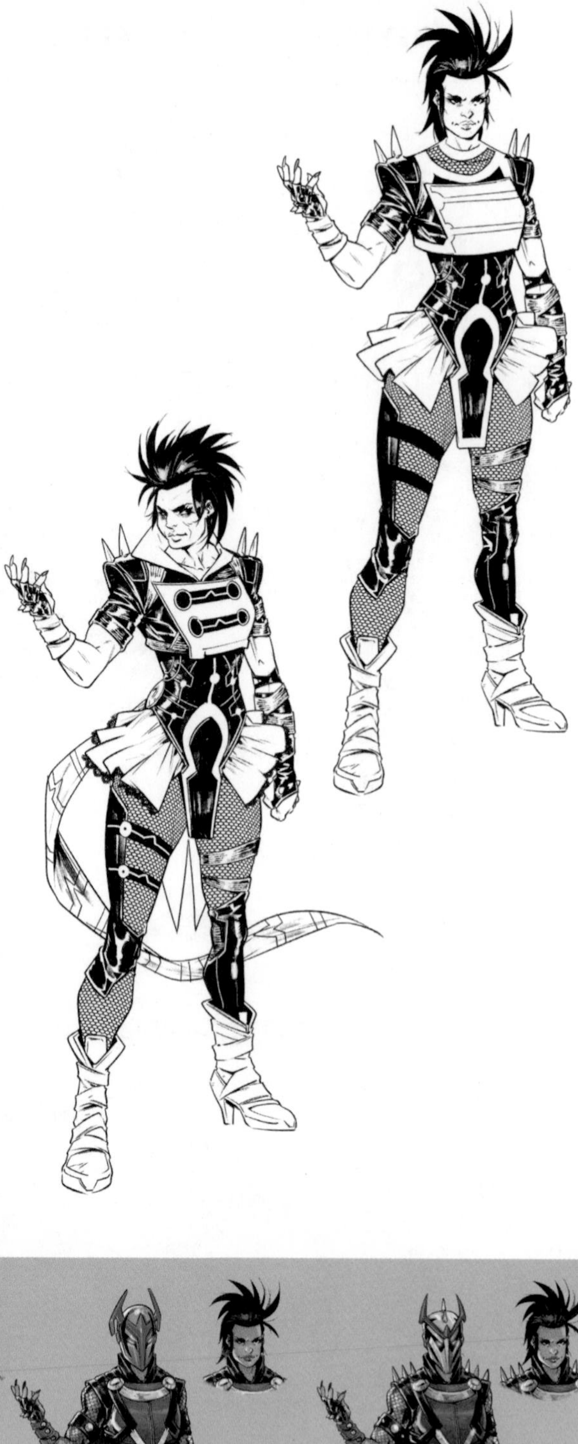

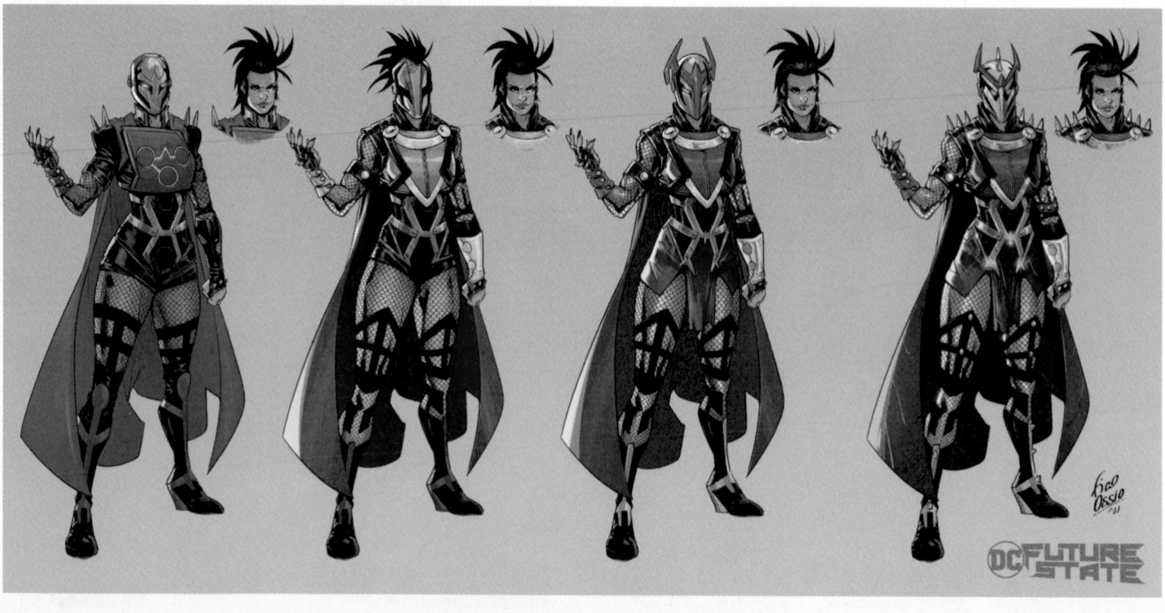
DC FUTURE STATE

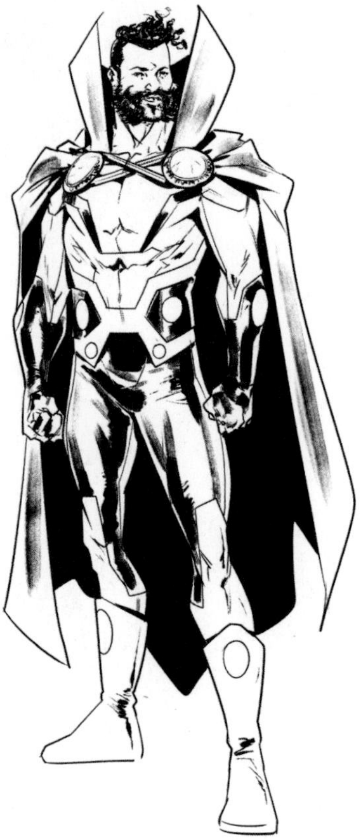

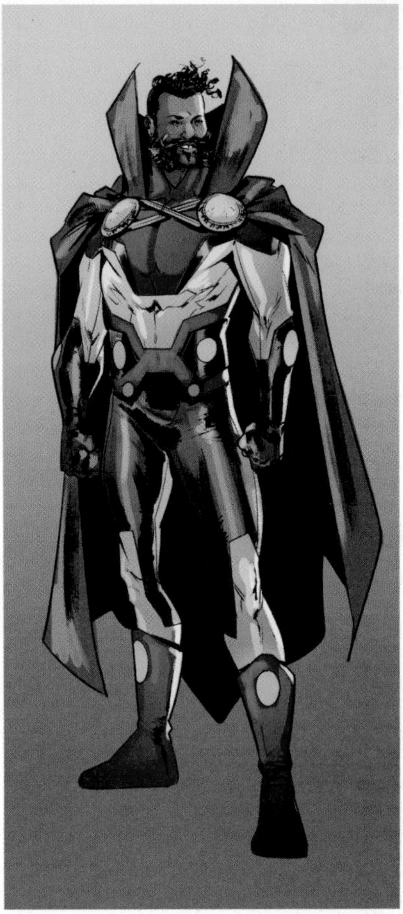

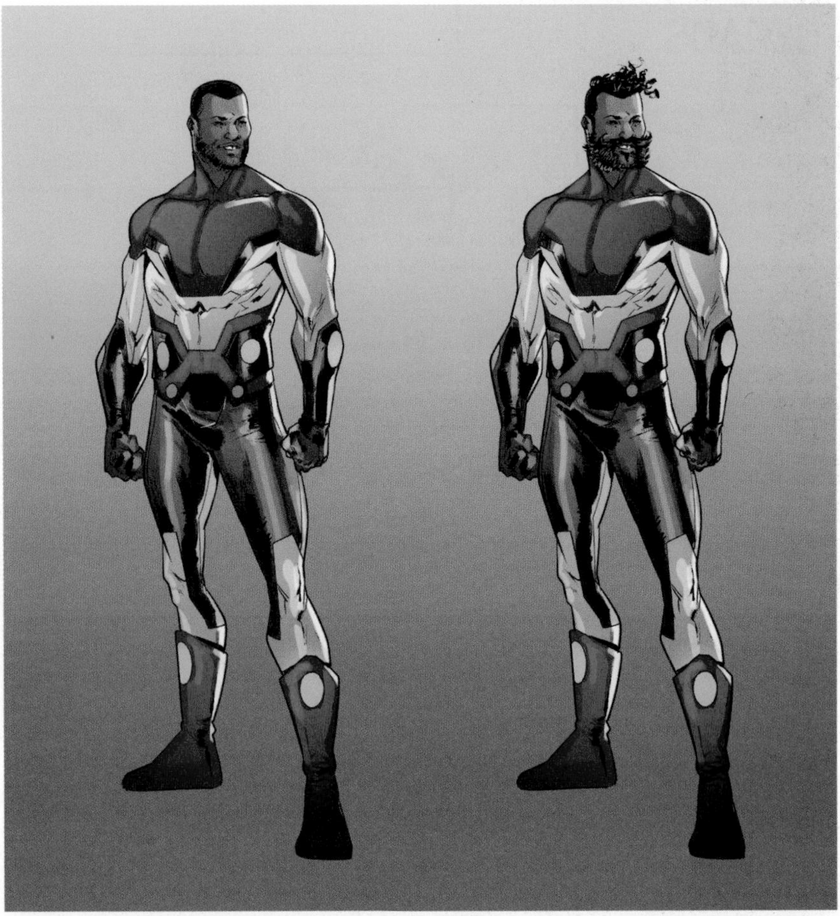

EISNER
AWARD WINNER
BEST WRITER
BEST ARTIST

TOM
KING

MITCH
GERADS

MISTER MIRACLE

TOM KING &
MITCH GERADS

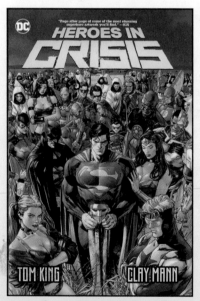

HEROES IN CRISIS

THE OMEGA MEN

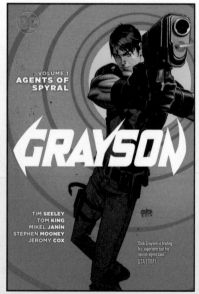

**GRAYSON: VOL. 1
AGENTS OF SPYRAL**